AFLAME WITH DEVOTION

AFLAME WITH DEVOTION

The Hannen and Knobloch Families and the Early Days of the Bahá'í Faith in America

JUDY HANNEN MOE

BAHÁ'Í PUBLISHING
WILMETTE, ILLINOIS

Bahá'í Publishing Trust

401 Greenleaf Avenue, Wilmette, Illinois 60091

 Published 2019

Printed in the United States of America on acid-free paper ∞

22 21 20 19 4 3 2

ISBN 978-0-87743-395-8

Cover design by Carlos Esparza

Book design by Patrick Falso

Contents

Note to the Reader

Much of the source material for this biography is comprised of historical documents such as correspondence, unpublished manuscripts, and personal papers—selections of which have been reproduced in the book. In an effort to maintain the integrity of the historical documents, spelling has been left untouched even when it is inconsistent with modern spelling or with the transliteration system later established by Shoghi Effendi for the rendering of Persian and Arabic words and names. Imperfect grammar and syntax have also been left uncorrected in historical documents in order to maintain the integrity of the documents.

The correspondence reproduced in the book also includes early translations of Tablets of 'Abdu'l-Bahá as well as accounts of encounters and interactions with Him. Such accounts are to be considered the recollections of those who recorded them, as "pilgrims' notes," and not as authenticated renderings of 'Abdu'l-Bahá's words and actions. The early translations of the Tablets, which were prepared at the time the Tablets were revealed and sent to the recipients together with the original Tablets, should be regarded as historical documents rather than as authoritative Bahá'í scripture.

Foreword and Acknowledgments

For many years, growing up near the Mother Temple of the West, I was acutely aware that I was the descendant of some very wonderful Bahá'ís. The fact that I was a fifth generation Bahá'í of American heritage (not Persian) had been a point of curiosity to many Bahá'ís I met over the years. I was often called upon to explain how this was so. I knew that my grandparents, Carl and Mineola Hannen, had grown up in the Washington D.C. Bahá'í community. I heard stories from family members that 'Abdu'l-Bahá had spoken at Carl's home when He came to America in 1912 and that he and Grandma had both actually met 'Abdu'l-Bahá. I was told that my great-grandmother Pauline and her two sisters, Fanny and Alma Knobloch, had been great teachers of the Faith and had lived off and on with my grandparents when they were not travel teaching for the Faith. I also heard that my great-grandfather, Joseph Hannen, was a stenographer and had taken notes of many of 'Abdu'l-Bahá's talks and had articles published in *Star of the West Magazine.* At some point along the way I learned that he was the person who received the Tablets of the Divine Plan from 'Abdu'l-Bahá and was entrusted to distribute copies to the rest of the Bahá'í community in the United States. All of these details of their lives had been very interesting to me and a source of great pride. However, they were also a source of mystery because my own father, Sohayl Carl Hannen, the link to this illustrious past, was strangely silent about the details of his famous grandparents and aunts. It was actually a bit awkward when I was questioned about them to admit how little I knew. He talked about his grandmother Pauline in terms of family events and pet names for her sisters, Tanta Ana and Dona. But he really shied away from extolling their virtues and great contributions to the Faith. The reasons for this are very complex, and have only partially and gradually been disclosed to me over my sixty years of life as his daughter.

Some of the truly significant events of the lives of the Hannens and Knoblochs can be found in a few published works that chronicle the events of Bahá'í history from 1900 to the 1930s. As a matter of fact, it was by reading these books as they came out over the last few decades that my knowledge of my family really began to grow. There are small mentions of the Hannens in several biographies of the time, but it was Gayle Morrison's book, *To Move the World,* about the life of Louis Gregory, that really piqued my interest and got me excited about who and what my ancestors were all about. After that book was published they were mentioned in several other books. One in particular that was of great help to me was Robert Stockman's *History of the Bahá'í Faith in America, Volume II.* Though no one yet had attempted to put together a more complete story of the Hannens' and Knoblochs' lives, it became obvious to me that they had contributed much to the history of the Bahá'í Faith in America and that their stories needed to be told. In this case, the Bahá'í part of this story really began with Pauline, but soon spread to her two sisters, her mother, her husband and his mother, and then to her sons and grandchildren and so on to many generations beyond. It also grew to include her friends and their children, one of whom married her son, and to even more nieces and nephews. Thus this is a story of a Bahá'í family that has now extended for seven generations.

Sometime in the 90s, I had made a feeble attempt to gather information about my family history by visiting the National Bahá'í Archives in Wilmette, IL. But at that time, the many boxes of papers and correspondence that had been donated by Pauline were not organized in a way that was easily accessible. In addition, modern tools such as cut and paste, scanning, and emailing were not available to me. Thus it was a very daunting project and one that my busy schedule did not allow me to continue. However, when a good friend, Tim Moore, former managing director of the Bahá'í Publishing Trust, approached me in 2008 with the idea of writing a book about the Hannens in anticipation of the events marking the centenary of 'Abdu'l-Bahá's visit, it peaked my interest again. At that point, I was a fulltime ESL teacher in a middle school in Rockford, IL and was very active in the Bahá'í community, serving as secretary of the Local Spiritual Assembly. I couldn't imagine how I would find time to do such a thing. However, when I was not elected secretary of the LSA that year after thirty years of being such, I took it as a sign I should attempt this project.

My first thought when I started to work on the project was to collect all the already published material I could find and organize it to tell their story, since I knew very little of it firsthand. I started with *Star of the West,* but soon realized that there was much more to this than I could have ever known. I thank my friend Randy Ballard for loaning me the Sifter program, which helps locate articles by subject or name. It was there that I learned what a huge role Joseph played in organizing events, recording and reporting on various activities around the country, and participating in various teaching opportunities. His name is everywhere in those magazines.

Soon I was led to make another visit to the National Bahá'í Archives. This time I was pleasantly surprised to find all the papers my ancestors had donated to the archives had been meticulously organized and placed in folders, making it relatively easy to locate materials. Many thanks go to Roger Dahl the archivist and his assistant Lewis Walker for all the many years of work they have put into making research easier for all historians. With their help and the help of my sister Linda Hawkins and her granddaughters, Chris Barnes and Desiree Steele, who came and helped sometimes, I learned that the Hannen-Knobloch collection was by far the biggest they had with twenty-three boxes, each with as many as thirty folders filled with hundreds of letters and papers. This project suddenly became rather daunting again as I realized there was much more material available than I could ever have time to read. Additionally, much of it was handwritten and not that easy to decipher. It soon became apparent that after my ancestors had become Bahá'ís they kept every piece of correspondence they received, including their own personal letters, because they realized the historical significance they contained. It will take historians many years to comb through the letters and tease out the thousands of details they contain about their many services and teaching endeavors. There is still plenty of material for several more books about the early teaching efforts in the southern, central, and eastern states as well as South Africa and Germany. What I actually was able to fit into this book is, I would guess, less than five percent of what is available.

As I read and studied these letters, the project became much like putting together a jigsaw puzzle and I found myself searching for missing pieces. I tried to fill in missing information by asking the grandchildren of Pauline and Joseph questions, but they were all getting up into their eighties and nineties, and the information was somewhat vague. I spent a week in Florida with the youngest of Carl's children, my aunt Barbara Griffin, who was helpful, but she admitted that being the youngest meant she hadn't been with Pauline that much. She did tell me at one point though that when Fanny lived in their home she shared a room with her, and Fanny would lull her to sleep telling her stories about Africa and other teaching trips while she brushed her (Fanny's) very long hair a hundred times. I even had a chance to talk with cousins I had not had the opportunity to know very well and learned of their great love and admiration for our mutual great-grandparents, even though no one on their side of the family had become Bahá'ís. These many revelations and chats were so worth the time and effort; I will always be grateful for that. Unfortunately, before this project could be completed, five of the six of Pauline and Joseph's grandchildren passed away. Also, while working on the book my mother suffered from dementia, and I, along with my four siblings, had to help my father (age ninety) to care for her. It was a source of great pride to them both that eventually a book would be published about their ancestors.

One of the perks I received in working on this project was making the acquaintance of Lex Musta, a self-taught historian of the Bahá'í Faith in Washington D.C. The more I got to know Lex, the more I realized he knew much more about my family than I did. When I learned the archives at the Bahá'í center in D.C. had eight more file boxes full of Hannen-Knobloch correspondence and other papers, I knew I had to investigate. Lex not only hosted my brother Jim Hannen, his wife Nancy, and me in his home when we came to search the archives, he also drove us around and gave us a tour of all the places where the historical events had taken place. It was an absolutely wonderful experience to explore the same neighborhoods I was writing about, and to have a running account of what happened. We are also indebted to Lex for arranging the special treatment thirteen members of our family received when we attended the Washington D.C. centenary events in 2012. He was generous with sharing the information he had collected and an invaluable asset whenever I had questions about historical events. I can't thank him enough.

I also want to give a special thanks to my sister-in-law Nancy Hannen and my nephew Dan Hannen, who had been doing their own research about our ancestors. In 2001, our family gathered together in Washington D.C. to rededicate the gravesite of the Hannens and Knoblochs. That is when I first met Lex Musta due to his acquaintance with Dan Hannen. Lex was instrumental in helping us gather information about the family for this event. Nancy wrote beautiful accounts of the lives of each of the people who were buried at this site. These materials formed a starting point for me when I began this project. Nancy graciously took on the task of collecting all the letters about Alma and highlighting them for me. I often shared chapters with her and my brother Jim to get their insights, and I can't thank them enough for all their loving support.

As the project moved along and more trips to Washington D.C., Wilmette, and Florida uncovered more and more information, the manuscript grew and grew. In my cousin Tom Hannen's home (Joe's son), tucked away in an old basket, I found a group of original letters Pauline had written to Alma about her visit with 'Abdu'l-Bahá in Dublin, New Hampshire. On a subsequent trip to the Washington D.C. archives I found a notebook in which Pauline had copied her letters to Alma about all her experiences with 'Abdu'l-Bahá during His visit in 1912. It became clear to me that the sisters had intentionally recorded the events of their lives knowing that these experiences would someday be historically significant. As I worked to uncover these materials, I often felt their assistance and presence. It appeared that Fanny, in particular, attempted to write a book about her experiences. Some of the recollections in this book are their intentionally written memoirs, but many are gleaned from combing through hundreds of their letters. The three sisters have a lifetime of correspondences between each other, as well as their many friends and acquaintances, containing thousands of stories of teaching experiences and other projects. Joseph, in his position as secretary of various institutions of the Faith, had a phenomenal amount of correspondence detailing all kinds of activities and transactions. It will take many years for interested historians to put together the pieces of this huge puzzle of information.

Among the vast materials that were located are Tablets written by 'Abdu'l-Bahá to various family members and friends. Some of these I've had for a while as I had been given a small leather-bound notebook, prepared by Alma Knobloch, containing typed copies of almost every Tablet sent to my family members over the years. These were translated by various people, sometimes before they arrived in America and often by Persian Bahá'ís living in the United States. In many cases those Tablets were later sent to the World Center to be kept in the International Archives. The English translations, which were prepared and sent to the recipients along with the original Tablets, and which are now preserved at the World Center, are considered historical documents. Unless otherwise noted, many of the translated Tablets in this book are the original translations of Tablets for which there are no new authorized translations. For Tablets that have been authorized and translations have been updated, I have used the newest translations. Information regarding where the Tablets are now published is included in the endnotes; this may also include parts of letters or other writings of 'Abdu'l-Bahá the sisters sometimes quoted in their manuscripts. The Research Department at the Bahá'í World Center have helped me to make clear what are authorized and what are historical documents, and anything previously published is presented in its most updated form.

The many Tablets and stories about 'Abdu'l-Bahá in this book made it necessary for the Publishing Trust to write to the World Center for guidance on the best way to handle quotes attributed to 'Abdu'l-Bahá and pilgrims' notes. For this and other reasons there were a few years of waiting after I submitted my initial manuscript. However, during that time I continued to find material that I felt was important to include in this book, resulting in a richer account of my ancestors' lives.

This time also provided me the opportunity to meet Jennifer Weibers, a wonderful lady who added to the depth of this book in many ways. She is the descendant of Bahá'ís who were friends with my grandparents in the Wilmette area. She had also started writing about the Knoblochs and Hannens and considered writing a book about the three sisters. As she had been living in Germany for several years, she decided she would concentrate her efforts on researching Alma Knobloch, who is often referred to as the Mother of the Bahá'í Faith in Germany. Jennifer's time in Germany afforded her the unique perspective to write about the history of the Faith in that country, and the influence Alma had on its growth. In contrast, this book is mostly centered on Pauline and Joseph, but does include Alma and Fanny as well.

Over the next few years, I had the chance to consult with Jennifer several times. Her expertise in historical writing helped me immensely with various issues. Specifically, she directed me to a story found in Ahmad Sohrab's files that gave firsthand accounts by Pauline and Joseph detailing how they became Bahá'ís, clarifying some of the confusion I had about that issue. She also put me in touch with several other Bahá'í historians and their works; helping to broaden my knowledge of the historical period about which I was writing. We had an opportunity to meet in person at the National Archives when she came to America to do her research, and this encounter really cemented our connection with each other. It was strengthened in 2015 when I had the pleasure of meeting her again under very unusual circumstances. I was in D.C. for the graduation of my granddaughter from Howard University, and she had come to the United States with a group of students to show them our capitol city. By chance we had a conversation on the phone and discovered we would both be in D.C. on the same weekend! We both had Sunday morning free and made plans to meet at the gravesite of the Hannens and Knoblochs at Prospect Hills Cemetery. What a special moment that was!

Another wonderful person whom I met while working on this puzzle, and who has been a huge help to me, is a young man named Baher Seioshansian—a volunteer archivist and historian—helping with the archives in Washington D.C. His dream is to have much of the material there typed up and made available online. He was wonderful about sending me manuscripts I was interested in, which I typed and sent back. Working with this material has given me the ability to read Fanny's and Alma's and several other people's handwriting pretty easily.

Another curious happening during that time period had to do directly with the National Archives. In 2015 I got a call from Lewis Walker that there was a box of papers from the Hannen Family he was tasked with organizing. We figured that in all likelihood this was a box of papers that had been in the Hannen Family for years and had been passed on to Barbara Griffin, and eventually to Sohayl Hannen.

Lewis was very, very helpful to me. He offered to mail me copies of anything he thought might be useful for this book, and this addition was truly amazing. Included were several letters Joseph had written to Pauline before and during the first years of their marriage, and before they became Bahá'ís. It also contained letters written by Joseph's father, who had abandoned the family when Joseph was a baby. Both of those time periods were mysteries to me before receiving the new materials. Additionally in that box were over one hundred letters of condolence written to Pauline after Joseph's death. However, the best treasures of all were the typed accounts by Pauline about 'Abdu'l-Bahá's visits with them in Washington D.C., as well as a series of letters written by Joseph about their pilgrimage travels. With these additional materials I was able to fill in many gaps, which would not have been filled if the manuscript had been published as originally submitted.

I admit it was thrilling for me to discover the many letters that passed between my ancestors and the many early believers whom I had grown up hearing and reading about. It was certainly amazing to discover the depth of the relationship my relatives had with 'Abdu'l-Bahá and Shoghi Effendi. I was extremely delighted to learn about the role they played in introducing the Faith to the African American community, and to Louis Gregory in particular. I have been immensely inspired by their enormous dedication to the Faith and their extreme loyalty to 'Abdu'l-Bahá. I feel exceedingly blessed that I was asked, and was offered the opportunity to accomplish this long-awaited task.

Finally, I want to thank my many friends in the Rockford Bahá'í community for their support during the years I've given to this project. Thank you to fellow writer Phyllis Peterson for providing information and moral support, and to Karen Johnson for help with editing issues. Thanks also go to Earle Rowe who helped me prepare photos for publishing. I also want to thank the editors Bahhaj and Marie Taherzadeh for all the work they put into editing this book. Especially, I want to thank my husband Bruce and daughter Shelly for helping with all the things around the house that I neglected while spending hours making a mess with all these papers. Thank you for your patience and support. I love you all.

- 1 -

Setting the Stage

It was a time of great expectations and searching. William Miller (1782–1849) of the Millerite Movement (later changed to Seventh Day Adventists Church) had preached, along with hundreds of other Bible scholars, that it was time for Christ to return. In the United States alone Miller gained as many as 200,000 followers. The predicted date of 1844, which he had calculated from prophecies in the Book of Daniel, had come and gone without any noticeable change in America. That, however, didn't stop the spiritually hungry from searching far and wide for some news of the Redeemer who would come and change the world's fortunes. When Christ didn't seem to return in 1844, in the manner expected by some, scholars and hopefuls revised their predictions and searched again in 1853. Many subsequent predictions have been made by various groups of Christians, Muslims, and Jews who have continued to seek and are awaiting the Coming of the Lord.[1]

At the time in which this story begins, at the start of the twentieth century, the spirit of expectation was still alive and many continued to anticipate and hope for the return of Christ's spirit. My ancestors, about whom this book is written, were among those of this mindset. They lived during the pivotal turn of the 1800s to 1900s. They experienced the expansion of new inventions such as the telephone, which allowed for people to be in closer contact with each other. Improvements in transportation, such as the automobile, meant their generation would soon be traveling farther and farther in record time. Improvements in ocean travel, which soon produced the likes of the Titanic, made travel across the ocean faster and more accessible to the middle class. Those with the means were taking voyages to new places and learning about what were, to them, exotic new cultures. These new inventions were beginning to touch people's lives and change the landscape forever. It is during those rapidly changing times that this story unfolds—the story of how my ancestors, the

Hannens, Knoblochs, and Barnitzes—found and dedicated themselves to the Bahá'í Faith.

Before we can understand their story though, it is important to understand how the Bahá'í Faith was first established in America. We must also learn the story of Mírzá Abu'l-Faḍl Gulpáygání (1844–1914), one of the foremost teachers of the Bahá'í Faith in his era, and one of the first teachers of my ancestors.

The Bahá'í Faith began in 1844 in Shiraz, Persia (present-day Iran), but had not made its way to America until 1893, when first mention of it was made at the World Parliament of Religions held in Chicago, Illinois. After that brief introduction, several people in that vicinity and a few other cities of the United States began to explore its teachings, and a small following of adherents began to grow and spread to other cities. One of the first to spread its teachings was Ibrahim George Kheiralla, who taught the Faith to many of the first believers in America, including, Lua Getsinger.

Mírzá Abu'l-Faḍl became a follower of Bahá'u'lláh (Prophet-Founder of the Bahá'í Faith), in 1876, and openly began to talk about his new faith in his home country of Persia. From its inception in Persia, the Bahá'í Faith has been met with aggressive repression and its members met with horrendous persecution. In the 1800s, because of the intolerant treatment of Bahá'ís in Persia, the mere act of teaching about Bahá'u'lláh led to several years of imprisonment for Mírzá Abu'l-Faḍl. Harsh treatment did not, however, dissuade this stalwart soul from his passion of spreading the teachings of Bahá'u'lláh, which he continued to do throughout his life. In 1889, he went to 'I<u>sh</u>qábád, where he became a focal point in the developing Bahá'í community there. In 1894, he journeyed to 'Akká and after ten months proceeded to Egypt, gaining recognition as an Islamic scholar at al-Azhar University.[2]

When Mírzá Abu'l-Faḍl arrived in America, there was a budding community of Bahá'ís. In 1901, at 'Abdu'l-Bahá's instruction, Mírzá Abu'l-Faḍl went to the United States for the expressed purpose of deepening the knowledge of the Bahá'ís in this newly arising community, and to help them understand the station of 'Abdu'l-Bahá and the reason He alone was the Center of the Covenant, having been appointed to that role by His Father, Bahá'u'lláh. In His Book of the Covenant, Bahá'u'lláh directed the believers to turn only to 'Abdu'l-Bahá for instruction and interpretation of His message.[3]

Mírzá Abu'l-Faḍl spent his first year in America writing a book called *Bahá'í Proofs*, which, when published in 1902, helped the American Bahá'ís acquire "their first thorough and accurate account of the Bahá'í Faith." It included biographies of the Central Figures of the Faith, and a selection of the writings of the Báb and Bahá'u'lláh. This book became a valuable resource for the burgeoning American Bahá'í community.[4]

Mírzá Abu'l-Faḍl arrived in America in early August of 1901 and remained until 1904. After visits to Chicago and Cincinnati, he made his way to Washington D.C., to the city where my ancestors, the Hannens, Knoblochs, and Barnitzes resided. He remained there until 1904. According to Robert Stockman, in his very detailed book, *The History of the Bahá'í Faith in America, Volume II:*

> Abu'l-Faḍl's visit to the Occident entailed considerable personal sacrifice. When he arrived in America in 1901 he was 57 years old, had never visited a Western country, did not speak a Western language and had to leave behind in Cairo many students, academic contacts, access to his own library and Cairo's formidable scholarly resources. In Washington he was alone, for only a handful of Arabic and Persian-speaking people resided there. None of the Bahá'ís spoke Arabic or Persian and thus they could not talk to him, although the Bahá'í community was loving. His foreign ways struck Washingtonians as strange—Charles Mason Remey says that once school boys, excited by Abu'l-Faḍl's Oriental robes, followed him for blocks, throwing missiles at him. Abu'l-Faḍl had to move to a different boarding house as a result.[5]

Mírzá Abu'l-Faḍl was not the first Bahá'í to live in Washington D.C. That distinction belongs to Charlotte Brittingham Dixon, who became a Bahá'í in Chicago after learning about the Faith from a woman with whom she studied. After Ms. Dixon moved back to the Princess Ann area of Washington D.C., she taught her whole family about the Faith and they all became believers, including her brother James Brittingham, the first believer in New York City, and his wife Isabelle, one of the outstanding Bahá'í teachers in the United States. According to Anita Chapman, author and creator of the D.C. Bahá'í History website, "When in 1898 she [Charlotte Brittingham Dixon] moved to Washington, she started the first group of Bahá'ís there, presenting lessons she had attended in Chicago, sharing what she had understood and aflame with enthusiasm. . . . By 1899 there were seven Bahá'ís in Washington." It was a beginning.[6]

According to Stockman, before 1902 the Bahá'í community in Washington D.C. was not very strong, due to the lack of deepened Bahá'ís. "Presumably, 'Abdu'l-Bahá asked the Washington Bahá'ís not to teach their religion yet, because He was concerned that the Bahá'í Faith would acquire a bad reputation in the capital of the United States." However, "His prerequisites for teaching were soon filled. Phoebe Hearst, widow of a United States Senator, visited in 1900 and hosted some Bahá'í meetings in her Washington home. Alice and Laura Barney, prominent in Washington social life, had returned from Paris as Bahá'ís by 1901; Charles Mason Remey, scion of a prominent naval family, came home from Paris where he had also embraced the Faith by autumn of 1903. Because the Washington Bahá'í community now had prominent members, teaching of the Faith resumed."[7]

- 2 -

A Family Awakens

Within this budding Bahá'í community of Washington D.C., Mírzá Abu'l-Faḍl settled to awaken the waiting souls. He began by organizing a class about the message of God's most recent Messenger, Bahá'u'lláh. During this age of Biblical expectation, there were many living in Washington who were watching and waiting for some great happening to occur. There were often lectures to attend or visitors to investigate who presented their perspectives on Bible prophecy and the "Second Coming" of Christ. Mystics from the East, theosophists, preachers, and charlatans all had their audiences. People flocked to lectures and classes in search of knowledge about any possible fulfillment of these prophecies. It was common to have meetings on these topics with audiences of a hundred or more in attendance. Among those with shared interests in these topics were my ancestors, the Barnitz, Hannen, and Knobloch families. The husbands, Richard Barnitz and Joseph Hannen, worked for the same railroad company where they may have met and become acquaintances.

There are several accounts that have been uncovered explaining how the families first heard of the Faith. The first story I heard was from my aunt Barbara Hannen Griffin, the granddaughter of Joseph and Pauline Hannen on one side, and of Leona and Richard Barnitz on the other. She shared with me that her mother, Mineola Barnitz Hannen, had said "It was Mamma, Grandma Barnitz who really started the whole thing rolling in our family." Barbara explained, "Grandma Barnitz would go to all the lectures she would hear about—looking to learn about whatever was going to happen in the endtimes."[1] Mineola told Barbara, "If it wasn't for her mother, [Mrs. Leona Barnitz] no one in the family would have known or heard about Bahá'í." This was confirmed in a letter that Leona received from 'Abdu'l-Bahá telling her to be thankful to her father for teaching her to watch for the coming of the Lord.[2] Mineola's mother claimed that she told the Hannens about some classes she had heard about where a Persian man was lecturing about a new religion. In a note found on the back of a photograph, Mineola wrote that Grandma Phelps (not a relative) "found the Bahá'í Faith first and told Mamma (Leona Barnitz) about it. Ma came in right away and grandma (Phelps we presume) took 6 years before she accepted—but was very firm and her whole family accepted."[3] This seems to be the story from the Barnitz side of the family. After hearing this story I began to gradually uncover other accounts that differ slightly from this family lore, however, this may very well be how the Barnitz side of the family came into the Faith.

The first published account of how Pauline Hannen came to accept the Faith of Bahá'u'lláh is told by Mírzá Ali Kuli-Khan. Khan, an eminent Persian Bahá'í, served as 'Abdu'l-Bahá's English-language secretary from 1899–1901. He was sent to the United States in 1901, at the request of 'Abdu'l-Bahá, to help translate His letters and other Bahá'í materials. He also helped Mírzá Abu'l-Faḍl with his classes and other affairs in Washington. Pauline attended the classes given by Mírzá Abu'l-Faḍl, held in the upstairs of a building between Thirteenth Street and Massachusetts Avenue. According to Khan:

> "This little Mrs. Hannen would come upstairs to be taught the Bahá'í Faith leaving her baby [Paul] in its carriage downstairs, outside the front door. (Innocent days, those!) She visited a number of times, and sat quietly while Mirza explained the prophecies about the coming of the Lord. Just sat and listened, accepted a cup of tea from Mirza's hands, said goodbye, went downstairs and pushed the baby home" [to 1252 Eighth St., N.W.].
>
> One day Khan said to Abu'l-Fadl, "Does this little girl understand what we are talking about? Is she really interested?" They both decided that since she kept coming back, she must be interested, although she said nothing. Impatient, Khan made up his mind to find out for himself whether she was receiving the message or not. On her next visit he simply asked her, was she satisfied with his explanations, or did she need more answers to be convinced? She suddenly beamed at them. "How could there be anything more wonderful than this great Faith? After you receive this, what else in the world would you wish to possess?"[4]

For many years this was the published story known to Bahá'ís, but as I read accounts written by Alma and Fanny explaining their versions of how they became Bahá'ís, something was missing. It wasn't until I came across Pauline and Joseph's own accounts, hidden away for over 100 years, and written for Ahmad Sohrab in 1909, that I was able finally to put the pieces together. According to these newly uncovered accounts, it was Joseph who was the first in the family to meet a Bahá'í and to be invited to a prayer meeting. Below is his account of that fateful meeting:

Alla ho Abha!

Praise be to God, who hath most greatly blessed this generation and hallowed the present day as the time of His Perfect Manifestation. If our lives were eternal in this sphere of action, and every instant were to be devoted to serving Him, we could not then begin to adequately show our gratitude for His great Mercies!

My knowledge of the Truth dates from 1902. I had during the preceding summer entered into a new business relation; previous to that time it had seemed my life was being shaped anew, as following a considerable period in the service of a large corporation [Southern Railway Company] with offices at Washington, and where I had every prospect of a life-work, I had left Washington because of a better offer, had in a sense wearied of the new environment and under such conditions had entered upon a new work which brought me home again. These facts are significant as but for the changes involved I should not have heard of the Bahá'í Revelation, through the source whence it came to me, at least.

Early in this new business association [Viavi] I met Mrs. Sarah Etta Sargent, who arranged to enter the employ of my company. This involved several weeks' preparation and personal instructions. During the course of the training the subject of spiritual powers possessed by some persons, was mentioned. Mrs. Sargent said that she knew a Mrs. Jones, who could accomplish wonderful things through prayer, and who could also tell me about a most interesting religious movement; and I was invited with Mrs. Hannen, to see her.

We called one memorable night; about October 1901 [Perhaps 1902], and though the Message was not given then, Mrs. Hannen was directed to Mirza Abul Faz'l [Mírzá Abu'l-Faḍl] to be told of the new movement.

Going back into my earlier life, I can see preparation for the Message of Unity, for although not actively religious there was an undercurrent of liberal thought which first found satisfaction through the present Teachings. I was "raised" in a Methodist environment and recall vividly how as a mere boy my heart rebelled at the idea of millions of "Heathen" dying every year and going to Perdition, or at least being debarred from Heaven because they did not believe in One of whom they had never heard! In my childish way I felt that somehow they might be right as well as we, though there was no room for such belief in the orthodoxy with which I had been surrounded. Finding myself unable later to abide by the "Discipline" of that denomination, I withdrew and later joined the Congregational Church with which I am still connected.

It will be seen from the foregoing facts that I was ready to accept the Revelation of Baha'o'llah, when Mrs. Hannen, having been taught, told

> me of its basic principles. In fact, I may say that never since it came to me have I resisted its power, tho' it was long ere I could claim enough of its spiritual influx to call myself a follower.[5]

This letter confirms other memoirs that Fanny and Alma wrote of their experiences. It also corroborates the story that Pauline wrote to Ahmad Sohrab the same year. It likewise sheds light on the role Sarah Sargent played, as well as a Mrs. A. Jones (both of Washington D.C.), in awakening Pauline to this new truth. Here is part of Pauline's version:

> In the year 1902 this humble and unworthy servant was given the pearl of greatest price, the Glorious & Wonderful Message of Baha'o'llah the returned Christ. Through Mrs. S. E. Sargent, my sister Fanny Knobloch, my husband, and myself were invited to call upon a Mrs. A. Jones, who was and is well known for her gentleness and powerful prayers.
>
> This Saturday evening was a memorable one; it seemed to me it was an evening of symbols. We made our visit and were greatly attracted to these ladies because of their joy and sincerity, and although no word concerning this Mighty Truth was spoken, I felt rather than knew that a great change in my life was soon to take place. So strong was this feeling that on our way home I spoke of it in this way. In the first place when we left home the moon and stars were shining brightly, no cloud in the sky. During our visit, it thundered and lightened [sic] and the earth received a great down pour of rain; on leaving the moon & starts were again shining brightly. Walking home I was very quiet & thoughtful. At last I spoke to my sister and husband saying it seems to me we are on the eve of great changes. They both smiled and asked why, then I said: we left home in clear beautiful weather, while visiting there was a terrible storm & now it is clear & calm again. This is a symbol to my mind, we are now contented in our old way of living and thinking, there will soon be a great upheaval & tempest of thought perhaps & then peace & contentment. They laughed and so did I at the picture, but this really was prophetic of my own condition.
>
> The next morning instead of going to my church I went to Mrs. Jones's prayer Meeting she held every Sunday morning. Again I was contented and happy; still no word concerning the Truth of Baha'o'llah. At the close of the Meeting Mrs. Sargent said to me, would you not like to visit a wonderful Teacher from Persia? He is able to answer any questions you have concerning the Bible.
>
> I rather feared to meet this oriental but my love for the Truth was greater than my fear of man so I promised to meet her the next day Monday at the rooms of Mirza Abul Fazl, then living on Mass Ave. I asked my

dear mother to go with me. She said if it will make you happy of course I will go, but I don't think you need him.

At three o'clock, Monday, Nov. 24, I received a Message from this venerable Teacher, through his interpreter, Mirza Ali Kuli-Khan, that completely changed my whole life; from that hour on I was a new creature.

After giving me wonderful answers to my questions, I was told in a straightforward manner that Christ had returned, that the world at large rejected his claim just as the people always in times past had treated the Messengers of God. Although Mirza Ali Kuli-Khan went on with proof and argument I heard nothing, only the words ringing in my ears. "Christ has come again in the flesh." Mirza Khan has since told me he felt he had wasted time and breath on me, my face was a perfect blank, no sign of interest, denial, belief, opposition, surprise, nor the least sign of understanding, but dear Mirza Abul Fazl had said to him, she was overcome with the spirit, she will be an active Believer and her saint of a mother also.

Dear Mamma understood nothing of this wonderful news, being German and understanding but little English. How quickly was the prophecy of Saturday night coming true again great sheets of rain, and great tears rolling down my cheeks unheeded as I walked slowly, thoughtfully to my home after putting Mamma on the car. Truly, thunder & lightening & storms of thought raged through my being, my soul crying out in the greatest agony of prayer. Such a prayer as I had never known in my life, begging for sight. Believing that Hell itself could not compare to the agony of my soul, the rest of that Monday, Tuesday and part of Wednesday, losing sleep & flesh and appetite. Glory be to God in the Highest and Praise be unto Him for the unutterable joy that flooded me on that memorable afternoon, when my happy heart sang out. I know that my Redeemer liveth. Though I did not know it then, it was the Fete Day of Abdul-Baha, Nov. 26, 1902, celebrated for the first time at the home of Miss Barney. Here, through earnest pleading on my part the family went with me and we heard Mirza Abul Fazl lecture for the first time and Mrs. Fisk spoke to us all, refreshments were served, the people were good and kind to us strangers, telling us more of the wonderful Truth.[6]

So, it seems Mrs. Sargent should be given credit for introducing the Hannens to the Faith, as well as Mrs. Jones for contributing to their enlightenment. The stories about Mírzá Abu'l-Faḍl's classes and their influence appear to be verified in these two accounts. As will be seen later, the accounts given by Alma and Fanny will make more sense when combined with the above recollections.

Robert Stockman's research confirms that during the few years Mírzá Abu'l-Faḍl was in Washington, hundreds of people attended Bahá'í meetings and classes and the community grew rapidly. Among those to accept the new religion was Pauline Hannen. "The youngest daughter of German Lutheran immigrants, Pauline was born on 29 August 1874 in Washington and was raised in the South. She married Joseph Hannen on 8 November 1893 and bore two sons: Carl (born in 1895) and Paul (born in 1900). She became a Bahá'í on 26 November 1902 because she was convinced that it fulfilled the prophecies of the Bible."[7]

Although Pauline was born in America, her parents, Karl August Knobloch (1832–1887) and (Bertha) Amalie Knobloch (1837–1908) and four of their children, Fanny (1859), Ida (1861), Alma (1864), and Paul (1866), had emmigrated from Bautzen in the Kingdom of Saxony, Germany around 1866—right after the American Civil War ended—and eight years before Pauline was born. Karl August was an architect in Germany, and, according to his oldest daughter Fanny, was offered an exceptional opportunity to work in the United States. She recounts that she came to America with her father first and that they stayed in New York City for a while. The family followed shortly after and they eventually settled in Washington D.C.[8]

A look at websites about German architects in the late 1800s and early 1900s reveals that there was a large number of German immigrants building in the Washington D.C. neighborhood where the Knoblochs settled. The three-story row houses, like the one Pauline and Joseph lived in on 1252 8th St., NW, for their married life together, were built by German architects and craftsmen. Many German immigrants lived in that part of the city, and the Prospect Hills Cemetery where many of these German immigrants were later buried, is also found in this quadrant not far from where the Knobloch and Hannen families lived.[9]

Amalie and Karl August's second daughter, Ida Amalie (1861–1869), died as a young girl just a few years after immigrating to America. Another son, Karl William, was born in Washington the same year Ida died—five years before Pauline was born—however he passed away sometime before she found the Bahá'í Faith. The next to last of Amalie and Karl's children was baby Bruno Wilhelm Knobloch, who was born and died as an infant in 1872 before Pauline was born.[10] Pauline's beloved older brother Paul, although he survived infancy, died in 1894 when Pauline was twenty years old.

Pauline's older sisters had known the lifestyle of their parents back in their homeland. They had experienced living in a beautiful old home with big lawns and gardens and live-in servants and gardeners. They experienced German Christmases with large family gatherings of aunts and uncles and cousins.[11] Pauline, though, was born to the big city life of Washington D.C. For a while the family lived in Wilmington, North Carolina, but in 1887, when Pauline was fourteen, her father passed away and the family moved back to Washington. She had been through more than her share of loss by the time she was twenty-eight and learned of the Bahá'í Faith. Not only had she lost her father and her two brothers Paul and Karl William, but she had endured the loss of an infant daughter of her own. Her name was Gladys—she died in 1898, the year Pauline's oldest son Carl was three years old. Her son Paul was born in 1900.[12] In many of Pauline's letters to 'Abdu'l-Bahá and others, one finds her longing to have a daughter, and although the death of her daughter was no doubt very tragic for her, she does not mention the baby's death in any letters that I came across.

Pauline's mother and siblings were strong Christians, all baptized in either St. Peter's Church in Bautzen, or a Lutheran church in Washington D.C. Her father is thought to have had a part in building The Lutheran Memorial Church in Washington D.C. According to church records both her mother and sister were flower girls in the church, which was a position of some importance.[13] They had also taken part in teaching the Sunday school classes. By 1902, when Pauline was learning about this new Faith, only Amalie; her mother; and the three daughters, Fanny, Alma, and Pauline; were still living. Pauline tells in her own words of her efforts to interest her family in her new-found religion:

> During 1903–04 I alone of my family was rejoicing in the New-born Faith. Naturally my endeavors were directed to those nearest and dearest to me: my mother, Mrs. A. Knobloch, my sisters, Fanny and Alma, my husband, Joseph H. Hannen, and his mother, Mrs. M. V. Alexander. I embraced every opportunity of trying to center their thoughts on the new Revelation of God. They were devout Christians and needed many proofs. I became a nuisance to them all.
>
> The only time to reach my sister Fanny was on Sundays. Finally in desperation she would burst out, "Oh, can't you talk about anything else now but religion?"
>
> My mother was patient and marveled at my loquacity. "How strange," she would say, "You have always been so quiet and timid. Now you seem to have been aroused, as out of sleep, into a fluent speaker. When you talk, I can see. When you are absent, doubts assail me."
>
> My sister Alma was absorbed in her business during the week and in active church duties on Sundays, so I would enter her workroom where she was busy with her helpers. [She was a seamstress.] At such times, only a light-colored, intelligent seamstress, Pocahontas Pope, was present. I would talk, talk, talk, giving the Glad Tidings of Bahá'u'lláh as prophesied in the Holy Bible. At last in self-defense (for time and Money) she would say, "My cup is full. It can contain no more. Please stop now."
>
> My husband, Joseph, and his mother, their hearts full of tenderness, exercised the utmost love and tolerance toward my new-fangled Religion. Both knowing that unlike the Athenians I did not continually run after

a new thing, believed never-the-less that this enthusiasm if given time would pass, returning me to my normal life. This never occurred as they expected. Instead, each member of my family received the Light of Truth in his own way, even Pocohontas.[14]

Alma was on a trip back to their homeland of Germany when Pauline accepted the Bahá'í Faith. When she returned, Alma and her mother Amalie began to take an interest in Pauline's new-found faith, yet not without some obstacles to overcome, given their deep involvement with the Lutheran Church. According to several sources, they both became Bahá'ís in 1903, just a year after Pauline. In Alma's letter she mentions going to Germany because of her health. A letter from 'Abdu'l-Bahá mentions the death of Alma's betrothed and perhaps this loss may have contributed to her nervous condition. I have long wondered about whether Alma or Fanny ever had any love interests as there is no other mention of this kind of relationship in any of the letters I have found. Relatives have said that both she and Fanny had been engaged but their beloveds died before they had a chance to marry. Alma writes:

> It was in the year 1903—after returning from an extensive trip to Europe in hopes of my health—having over taxed my strength—my family seemed worried for the results were not as they had hoped for.
>
> Mrs. Sargent, a friend of my sister, when inquiring about my depression said: why not consult with Mrs. Jones who has such marvelous power in prayer—& has wonderful results. She spoke to my other sister & they both made an appointment with Mrs. Jones & called. At this first meeting they received the Great message, which my sister Mrs. Hannen accepted but my other sister Fanny it took two years before she embraced the Truth.
>
> Never will I forget the afternoon my dear sister, Mrs. Hannen asked me if we could go up to my room, that she had something of importance to tell me. Trembling & with emotion she told me that the "Lord was on Earth & in Prison and some more details. Petting her, thinking she had become over nervous from hearing such strange news, told her, we will see into this, & find out all about it. I really wanted to take her in my arms, for she looked so sweet & gentle, but we both went down & joined the other guests.
>
> A few days later this sister brought me a short prayer to be read 9 times for healing, & begged me to use it, which naturally I did.
>
> *O my God! Thy Name is my healing. Thy Remembrance is my remedy. Thy nearness is my hope. Thy Love is my joyous companion, & Thy*

*Mercy is my refuge in this world & in the worlds to come. Verily Thou art the Giver, the All-Knowing, the Wise!**

The way she passed this little prayer to me, & the pleading & beautiful look in her face made a deep impression upon me. Having been a Bible class teacher in the oldest Lutheran Church in Washington for years, & very active in a number of Welfare organizations, this experience was the strangest & my sister surprised me.

Imagine my surprise when using this prayer for the first time, such a strong spiritual vibration passing through my entire body. By the time I had repeated it the ninth time I fully realized that I had heretofore not prayed at all, in fact had only repeated words. Such was the effect of this healing prayer.

Thrilled with this new discovery, & fully feeling my nothingness & utter unworthiness of this great Gift of spiritual experience, I gladly accepted the invitation to attend the noon day prayer hour at the home of Mrs. Jones.

Feeling very weak when entering the living room where a small group had gathered around the open hearth. They seemed strange like detached souls. The words they read from Baha'o'llah seemed powerful & their prayers vibrating that Spirit for which we all crave. I attended these noon-day prayer hours several times. Living at the extreme other side of the city & being at noon, it was not very convenient; at least this is what I told myself. In reality it had been too powerful for me. I felt that one must investigate & find out what it is all about, & get to the Truth.

We attended their public meetings, had talks with their great Persian teacher Mirza Abdul Fazl [sic] who was in Washington at the time, studying their literature until the early morning hours of dawn. A few months later was asked if I would like to attend a study class to which a few had been invited to attend & only those who come regularly twice a week in the afternoon. Some of those who took part were Col. Fitzjerald, Charles Mason Remey, Miss Laura Barney, Mms de Astre, Mrs. Phelps, Mirza Ahmad Esphahane, Ali Kuli-Khan interpreted, my sister & I & a few others.

We were told to bring a notebook & pencil. Mirza Abdul Fazl [sic] explained with the greatest care & exactness the Prophecies of our

* This translation has since been replaced with an authorized translation beginning with the words "Thy Name is my healing . . ." and can be found in *Bahá'í Prayers,* p. 94 (Bahá'í Publishing Trust, 2002).

Bible—explaining the use of the different symbols which are current in the orient, & of which we in the Occident are unfamiliar & have little or no knowledge of, & gave us a college course as he termed it.

Mirza Abdul Fazl told us we would soon be scattered in different parts of the world, & that he expected much from me being the smallest of the class. He often inquired about my Bible Class which had increased so much that the class room was beginning to be too small. He advised me to refer to Baha'o'llah & Abdul-Baha to other great teachers of different religions & of our faith, using their explanations & using their names, & let it for the student to decide which appeals to them. The increase of the class & the interest by Pastor Menzel who had been a very good friend, but had been asked by the church Board to give up his Bible class to me. You can imagine the result the following year.

Having been advised to write to Abdul-Baha, who was then a prisoner at Acca Syria, received an answer within a very short time, Christmas 1903. This Tablet (or letter) was marvelous & took years to understand.

Alma S. Knobloch[15]

In a manuscript Alma titled "Experiences with 'Abdu'l-Bahá" she wrote about a dream she had soon after becoming a Bahá'í:

The first dream—vision in Oct. 1903 Mirza Abdul Fazl [sic] received a Tablet from Abdul-Baha in which He told of the difficulties in Acca, & if anything should happen to Him no matter how, or even through the bite of a dog—how that it was through His brother Mohammed Ali, who has been the cause of much difficulties.

Mirza Abdul Fazl told of this Message & asked of 6 of the believers in Washington, Ali Kuli-Khan & Ahmad to pray for the safety of Abdul-Baha. (9 including himself)

When kneeling & supplicating for Abdul-Baha's safety, the power of the Spirit was strong & powerful, that my entire body was greatly affected, feeling exhausted, I finally laid down. Being wide awake, I saw a most magnificent large sun in its most glorious splendor casting its rays on the water. Its waves gradually coming up closer & closer until they entirely covered me.

In my first letter to Abdul-Baha I asked Him for an explanation of this dream that made such an impression, & still see it clearly . . . . (His reply which is in the letter to follow.) My sister Pauline who had urged me to write said: make a wish & it will be granted. It was in November, & there were great troubles in Acca, & oft times letters were held in security for months at Port Said by Ahmad Yazdi. But my wish was to receive an answer for Christmas, & Christmas Eve was told that my Tablet had come, which was translated Dec. 26. The Tablet made a very deep impression & took over a year before I understood its contents. [16]

The letter she referred to from 'Abdu'l-Bahá arrived 26 December 1903. It contained an explanation of the dream Alma had soon after hearing about the Bahá'í Faith from her sister.

O thou maid-servant of God!
In these times thanksgiving for the bounty of the Merciful One consists in the illumination of the heart and the feeling of the soul. This is the reality of thanksgiving. But, although offering thanks through speech or writings is approvable, yet, in comparison with that, it is but unreal, for the foundation is spiritual feelings and merciful sentiments. I hope that you may be favored therewith. But the lack of capacity and merit in the Day of Judgement does not prevent one from bounty and generosity, for it is the day of grace and not justice, and to give everyone his due is justice. Consequently, do not look upon thy capacity, nay, rather, look upon the infinite grace of the Bounty of Abha whose grace is comprehending and whose bounty is perfect.

I beg God through the confirmation and assistance of the True One thou mayest show the utmost eloquence, fluency, ability and skill in teaching the real significances of the Bible. Turn toward the Kingdom of Abha and seek the bounty of the Holy Spirit. Loosen the tongue and the confirmation of the Spirit shall reach thee.

As to that great Sun which thou sawest in a dream: That is His Holiness the Promised One and the lights thereof are His bounties. The surface of the water is transparent body—that is, pure hearts. Its waves are the moving of the hearts, the cheering of the souls—that is, the spiritual feelings and merciful sentiments. Thank thou God for that thou hast had such a revelation in the world of dreams.

As to the fact that man must entirely forget himself, by this is meant that he should arise in the mystery of sacrifice and that is the disappearance of mortal sentiments and extinction of blamable morals which constitute the temporal gloom, and not that the physical health should change into weakness and debility.

I humbly supplicate to the Threshhold of Oneness that heavenly blessings and merciful forgiveness may overtake thy dear mother, sisters and loving relations, especially thy betrothed who suddenly departed from this world to the next one.[17]

In another account Alma shares an incident that occurred as she was transitioning from being very involved with her church, to taking on her identity as a Bahá'í. During this time, it was quite common for those who had heard of, and perhaps even accepted the Bahá'í message, to remain active in their former churches. As we learned from Joseph's account, this was also true in his case. In fact, he remained the superintendent of Sunday school for the congregational church he belonged to for many years after becoming a Bahá'í, feeling it was a good example of how Bahá'ís could be good churchmen as well.[18] Since the roots of their new Faith were based on the belief that Bahá'u'lláh was the Return of Christ's Spirit, they felt they were fulfilling His wishes by accepting His Return. Alma also accepted this new Faith, but continued teaching Sunday school at her Lutheran Church. Eventually though, this arrangement did not sit well with some clergy as we will see. She explained:

> Pastor Menzel had been asked by the Christian Endeavor of our Lutheran Church to attend as delegate the International Religious Congress at New York, and had begged me to take charge of his confirmation classes during his absence. These two classes received Religious instructions to fit them to join the Church on Easter. There were many extra duties during this time, having been asked by the Church elders to take over the Pastor's Bible class the year previous and which I had increased in number five fold and had attentive and active members who became greatly interested.
>
> On Pastor Menzel's return, he stopped over in Baltimore for a conference of his . . . [this remains blank]. On his return he acted different and distant, I took this as result of the Congress at N.Y. for they did not accept the Baha'i Cause as a true Religion and it was not recognized as a spiritual Christian movement. He asked me to remain after service; he had something to tell me. His sermon was on Luke, "The end of the world." After distributing the flowers at the alter to some of the members of my class for the sick, I was waiting. [I] at last went to him and reminded him. "Oh Yes" he replied and returned with me to the center before the alter and asked if I could come an hour earlier to the Garanage [sic] and tell the officers of the Sunday school and some of the Church Elders just what I believed before the regular teachers meeting. Naturally [I] was very glad to do so and said, why not ask some more to hear about it. "No," he said he would rather not. How impatient I was for that Tuesday evening to come, & at the appointed time arrived at the Parsonage and found all three—two of the Sunday School . . . the president of the Church . . . a trustee and two of the Elders. Pastor Menzel was very nervous, going in & out—closing doors & pulling down window blinds. All seemed very unnecessary—& unusual.
>
> At last he sat down—& opened with prayer. Then turning to me said, "Miss Knobloch, will you tell what you believe—your Faith?" I was glad to do so. By that time was realizing what it was about, for Rev. Menzel had asked me about the Baha'i teachings & what they taught—& how

they explained a number of Biblical questions that they could not give reasonable answers to the youth. We had had several long talks, & at the close he said, "I don't blame you for getting these informations [sic]."

I asked him for his Bible. He remained motionless & again asked. After the third time, [I] began to explain his text of the Sunday Sermon—& given [sic] forth the Baha'i Message. The room to me was illumined. All seemed breathless. It was wonderful.

When I was through, Rev. M- apologized not having much time during the week to work on his sermon & his face was crimson. Then he accused me of mentioning the name of Christ with Mohammed & made some other remarks, which brought displeasure.

Nervous & flushed he flout [sic] several questions about believing in Mohammed & asked what I had to say about that!—all of which I quietly answered.

They begged me to attend the teachers' meeting, which was held in the Chapel. I really had not thought of doing otherwise, having attended Concordia Lutheran Church since my fourth year, & having taught for 19 years. It seemed a natural part of my life. All had been kind and loving at all times.

There was a strange, tense atmosphere during this meeting. Pastor Menzel who conducted it was not at ease, & I was glad it was over to return home to tell my precious mother about this experience. It had been only a half year since she had taken charge of a class of eight little girls, wishing to do something for the Kingdom after she had accepted the Baha'i Cause. Mr. Fred Imhoff, the president of the Church Elders, asked to see me home. On the way he said, "Miss Knobloch, we all love you. God in Heaven will reward you for all you have done for the advancement of the Sunday school. We will always feel grateful." With tears he bade me good night at the door, and he was truly sincere.

My dear mother's face was a study of patience and love. In her gentle way she comforted me & said that Baha'o'llah was with me. What more could I ask for? We did not attend Sunday school the following Sunday & were told we were missed. My Bible class held a consultation after class, all expressing their determination to leave and not attend any more & appointed a committee to call on me to beg that I return. Mr. Houseman was very earnest in his pleas.

Later the S.S. [Sunday school] teacher sent a committee the Miss Kemp [sic] to ask me to return, & among other things she said was that whatever I had, what they had not, it certainly did not lessen my love & activities & had surely added to my strength as a successful teacher.

Did we return? No. For my part I felt like a bird free, & could fly—out of the cage that had held me for so long. I recall my brother Paul, who

> one day asked me if my conscience [sic] permitted me to keep on teaching those children. I answered, yes & will & felt that someday these problems that we cannot answer & explain will be made clear—and keep on praying and if not in this world, then in the next, it will be understood. He was not of my opinion & had given up his class of boys, and as an excuse, he was busy with his studies at the University. This was before we had heard of the Baha'i Teachings.
>
> When the Church elders held their meeting they told Pastor Menzel that he must see to it that Mrs. & Miss Knobloch return to the Church or his resignation would be accepted. He called, stayed several hours. We had a pleasant visit & when he left said *Auf Wiedersehen*.
>
> When some of the elders called, we begged that they would not make any change on our account. The pastor was only doing his duty on behalf of the Synod, & has a large family of small children.[19]

Many readers, who have had to make a life change like this one, can empathize with how difficult it can be to give up a way of life and a whole community of friends in order to live with their new convictions. It was a sacrifice in many ways but obviously one they were willing to make in order to follow this new Manifestation of God and return of their Lord.

The most difficult person in the family to convince was Pauline's eldest sister, Fanny, who, according to family accounts, was the most outspoken of the group. Pauline and her two young sons would visit with Fanny every Sunday afternoon to discuss the Bahá'í Faith. They concentrated on Bahá'í interpretation of Bible scriptures, which to a devout Christian is of utmost significance. In particular, Christian enthusiasts, who were filled with hope of the return of Christ's spirit, were attracted to the Faith. The message at that time concentrated on showing how the Bahá'í Faith fulfilled the prophecies of the Second Coming of Christ as found in the Old and New Testaments.

Before Pauline and Fanny started studying the Faith together, Fanny had been curious but wary of joining a new Faith. She had even warned Pauline not to have anything to do with the Bahá'ís. The following is the story Fanny tells about her first encounters with the Faith:

> Very often the most marvelous experiences either enter our lives in such an unobtrusive way that it is difficult to recognize their greatness. Thus, in November of 1902 [this year might be off as it conflicts with other accounts], in my official capacity, I was seated one morning at my desk when Mrs. Sargent, uninvited, entered the office and interrupted my work. I looked up questioningly and, to my surprise, was told of a Mrs. Wilt [the other accounts recall Mrs. Jones] whose prayer had a wonderful power. PRAYER! What a subject during business hours! However, hear-

ing that this prayer was being offered before dawn, I interrupted her with the remark, "Why, she isn't half awake then, in the dark!"

I was informed that Mrs. Wilt let the cold water run over her hands and bathed her face before praying. It was bitter cold winter weather and one's fingers would curl up if held under the cold water faucet. So her statement arrested my attention. I said, "Your friend must love the one she prays for dearly, to get up before dawn in this dreadfully cold weather to pray." Mrs. Sargent increased my amazement by adding, "Yes, she is doing this for nineteen mornings, and she does not even know the young wife and mother whose life she has despaired of but who is now, thanks to God, holding her own."

A few days later Mrs. Sargent was called in for further questioning because, during those intervening mornings, strange to say, I had awakened before dawn, pushed back the covers and, feeling the intense cold in the room, had asked myself, "Why, Oh why, is this lady out in the northeast section of the city getting up now and praying on her knees for someone whom she does not know personally? What a remarkable woman she must be!"

Although not in the least inclined to have an interest in forms of religion, I found myself seeking an interview with this Mrs. Wilt, which was graciously granted. My sisters and brother-in-law, Mr. Joseph Hannen accompanied me to her home during a raging blizzard. My mental picture of so spiritual a person was that of a frail, fair-complexioned, spiritual looking woman, but, to my surprise, when the door opened I was facing a dark, olive-complexioned lady possessing a sturdy figure. At the close of our visit, where we had been listeners, we were invited to come the following Sunday and meet her friends. When I was later asked by my brother-in-law Joseph, "What did you get out of this talk?" my reply was, "That lady's God is a living reality, not something ethereal or off at a great distance, but a <u>living reality</u>!"

Sunday morning the four of us were missing from our different church duties, having gone to Mrs. Wilt's home, where we met about twenty others. There was some reading of beautiful teachings from the Orient; then silent prayer was asked for. Following the example of the others and placing my hands over my eyes, I prayed for my loved ones. Peeking about and seeing everyone busily praying, I prayed for all my relatives far and near and, again peeking, now began to pray for my business associates. Then one lady offered a prayer aloud, and the meeting closed—another queer episode in my life history!

After we came out, I advised my sisters and Joseph never to go there again, saying, "We do not want to get mixed up in this Orientalism." None of us did go again except my younger sister Pauline, who not only went to Mrs. Wilt, but also attended a class conducted by Mirza Abu'l-Fazl, a great Persian teacher then visiting our city. After these visits, Pauline, who was married, would come out to our home with her two sons each Sunday afternoon to discuss the Baha'i interpretation of our Scriptures with our beloved mother, who was well versed in the Bible. The constant conversation dealing with religion became quite trying to me, so I asked Pauline not to discuss religion—anything but religion! The following Sunday when she visited us she said she, Joseph and the boys had been to the circus, and exclaimed about the great patience that must have been exercised to train these animals, especially the seals, clumsy creatures, flopping themselves on top of a small island, tossing a ball placed upon their nose, others permitting a small gun to be fired. Very excitedly she drew a mental picture of the scene and concluded with, "Just think of the patient persistent and tireless effort of the trainer! If we would but give such persistent and tireless effort to gaining a knowledge of God, heaven would soon be established upon the Earth." "Oh," I said, "can't you even go to the circus without thinking about religion?" Pauline's laughter was my only answer.

Not long afterward, while attending class at Sunday school, composed mainly of white-haired, retired chaplains of the army, ministers and retired missionaries, the subject of Christ's feeding of the multitude on the mount with the five loaves and fishes came under discussion. During the discussion Dr. Merril E. Gates, our leader, was asked, "Did the Savior really multiply the bread and the fishes?" Another member, not waiting for the leader's explanation, said, "Dr. Gates, might it not be that our Savior used a power which was not known to the people of the day, and they believed they had eaten, even though they had partaken of no food?" (He referred to hypnotism and mesmerism.) A full half hour was used in this discussion, but no satisfactory conclusion was reached by the time we adjourned. Although not a Bible student, this discussion jarred me, no doubt due to an innate reverence for Christ implanted by my deeply religious parents. This make-believe attributed to Jesus shocked me. While walking home from Church I became so engrossed in thought that unconsciously I came to a standstill. Upon noticing the curious looks of passersby I quickened my steps, only to find myself doing the same thing again. Today we understand it so much better, due to words such as follow:

> *The Manifestations of God are sources of miraculous deeds and marvellous signs. Any difficult or impossible matter is to them possible and permitted. For they show forth extraordinary feats through an extraor-*

> *dinary power, and they influence the world of nature through a power that transcends nature. From each one of them marvellous things have appeared.* [New authorized translation of Some Answered Questions, p. 74]

Several days later Pauline came home from her class, where Mirza Abu'l-Fazl had treated the same subject and explained that Jesus the Christ, being all-powerful, could have caused the very grain to grow before their eyes, to mature, and the flour to change into bread, had He WILLED it. After a pause, Mirza Abu'l-Fazl asked the Christians in the class, "Was it anything so wonderful to satisfy the material hunger of those multitudes for one short afternoon? How much more wonderful is it to know that He fed the multitudes with the Bread of Life for nineteen hundred years, and baskets of crumbs that were gathered, you Christians are living today! These are the books of your apostles!"

This explanation was startling to me. How different from the solutions given by the members of the Bible class which I had attended! They were learned men, many of them retired ministers, who had sincerely taught the Bible for many years. Yet here came one brought up in the Mohammedan Faith and revealed this jewel of wisdom concealed in the parable of our New Testament. This was the turning point which caused me to thereafter attend the Baha'i meetings, eager for more light, which desire, thank God, came to me after two years of struggle.

Eventually our entire family became ardent Baha'is.[20]

Fanny's account mentions they went to the home of Mrs. Wilt. This must be the same person as Mrs. Jones, but I cannot account for why she calls her by a different name. Otherwise the accounts seem to be in accordance with each other.

Leona Slydel West Barnitz, my other great-grandmother, who had attended Mírzá Abu'l-Faḍl's classes with Pauline and Alma, also became a Bahá'í around this time. She was already a mother of five children ranging in age from about four to twenty. The oldest was her son West, named after her maiden name of West, from her family which can be traced all the way back to the early Virginia Colony. Although West may have believed in Bahá'u'lláh, he was probably in his early twenties at that time and left the family to move to California. He was not known to be active in the Faith. The next three girls though, all became staunch believers. Leone St. Claire (1885–1953), called Aunt Lonie by family, was the oldest of the girls, seventeen years old in 1902, but very tiny in stature. She never married, although she was a very beautiful young lady. She became a personal secretary of Mrs. Agnes Parsons, and is mentioned often in articles about the Washington D.C. Bahá'í community, as "Miss" Leone St. Claire Barnitz, to distinguish her from her mother of the same name.*

Beulah, known as Aunt Billy to our family, came next, and also was quite tiny, never reaching five feet in height. She later married Ralph Brown and moved to the Milwaukee area where she served on assemblies and remained active in the Faith until her passing. Mineola (1893–1995) was the youngest daughter and was the means of connection between the Hannen and Barnitz families—when she married Carl Hannen in 1918—after WWI. Finally came David (1898–1980), also short enough to be a horse jockey for a period of his life, active in the Bahá'í communities in which he lived throughout his life. He and Lonie lived a long time with their parents in Washington. It was through him the family papers from the Barnitz side were passed down to Mineola, and finally to her son Joseph. (The chair known in our family as 'Abdu'l-Bahá's chair because He sat in it on several occasions when He visited Washington D.C., also was passed down through David Barnitz to Mineola, then to her daughter Barb and finally to the author.**

Leona's husband, Richard Harrison Barnitz, became a Bahá'í as well. Little information is mentioned about his activities in the Faith. However, we do know that he was an adventuresome man who loved the daring and dangerous life of the railroad. His job was to grab mailbags off the hooks as the trains moved through the stations. At one point he had a work related accident from which it took him a long time to recover. He developed a patent on an invention for a new kind of mailbag catcher that made the job safer. Richard was also known for telling stories about his life. One such story was written by his granddaughter Marjory Brown (Neddin) when she was young. It has him playing with Abraham Lincoln's son Tad in the White House.[21] When he was a boy the family lived in the same neighborhood as the White House, so it might possibly be true. In any case, he and Leona were known as Ma and Pa Barnitz to the family friends, and they were thought of as loving and caring grandparents. Their home at 2626 University Place, NW, was a center of Bahá'í activity from the time they became Bahá'ís until well beyond the time of their passing to the Abhá Kingdom. It was the home in which Edward Getsinger stayed at times when his wife Lua was in 'Akká with 'Abdu'l-Bahá and the Holy Family. When Leona died in 1933 and Richard in 1942, their daughter Leone and son

* Usually the mother's name is spelled "Leona" and the daughter's "Leone," and it is thus on their headstones; however, the mother addresses her daughter as "Leona" in letters.

** The chair is currently in the Rockford, IL Bahá'í center meditation room, on loan from the Hannen family.

David continued to live in the house for several more years. Ma and Pa Barnitz and all their children were part of this thriving and growing Washington D.C. community of Bahá'ís. They attended classes for adults and children, helped to organize Feasts and various other kinds of meetings, and attended numerous activities. Mrs. Barnitz was even an alternate delegate to the National Convention in 1916.

During that period of two or three years (1902–1904) when the families learned of Bahá'u'lláh and began to take His message into their hearts, there was a lot of personal teaching going on; yet we mustn't forget the important role Mírzá Abu'l-Faḍl's class and explanations played in those changes of hearts. Pauline's account of these days offers a glimpse of how the Faith progressed during those first few years:

> Through the great love and kindness of my Mother and Mother-in law, great opportunities were mine to hear and learn more concerning proofs and arguments. Therefore in the winter and spring of 1903 it became my great privilege & that of my sister Alma, to join a class taught by Mirza Abul-Fazl, on the Book of Daniel. These were wonderful lessons & a great opportunity to understand the Teaching of God in a broader & clearer light.
>
> We attended the weekly Meetings every Friday evening where Mirza Abul-Fazl taught. Often being able to take home only a little ray of truth but this rich spiritual food was enough to keep us busy until the next Meeting.
>
> Mirza Abul-Fazl's profound knowledge of the Bahá'í Revelation, of our Bible as well as his knowledge concerning the deepest scientific questions, was so profound that we could not appreciate it until the blessing was taken from us. Then only did we realize the wonderful opportunities lost and held very sacred those lessons we received and could remember.
>
> During this year, 1903, each member of my family openly declared themselves Believers in Baha'o'llah. The rest of the winter of 1902 & 3 & the spring of 1903, regular Prayer Meetings were held every morning at ten o'clock at the home of Mrs. Jones. These I attended regularly two or three times a week since this was the only place where the Holy Tablets & prayers were read and discussed that I knew of. These meetings were sometimes largely attended, sometimes not so . . . because Believers were few in number, but always a great spiritual blessing to us all.
>
> When dear Mirza left us to go to Green Acre in the summer of 1903 Madam de Astre kept us new ones together by having meetings on 11 st. and always found someone to teach us more of the truth.
>
> In the fall of 1903, Mr. Hannen arranged with the Business Men's Bible class, of the First Congregational Church, to have Mirza address

these men, to which the other adult classes were invited making an audience quite large, more than a hundred listeners. He spoke of Christ feeding the multitude, he won the respect and admiration of nearly all & to this day it is referred to as that wonderful talk by the Oriental.

A second time that season he was requested to address them, again winning their love & respect. In the winter of 1904, dear Mirza Abul-Fazl, Khan & Ahmad blessed the home of my mother and sisters, having been invited to give the Message to some of the Elders of the church invited by Mr. Hannen and some of our friends. This was a heavenly feast for us & for my dear mother and sisters.

In the spring or early summer of 1904, Mirza left us again for Green Acre. In his farewell address he mentioned several names, among them he mentioned us saying he hoped we would open our homes & hold Meetings during the summer. After he left the Believers agreed to attend the summer meetings, so the home of Mr. & Mrs. Phelps was opened for Monday evenings where prophecies & questions were discussed and answered. Friday evenings they met at our house, 1252 8 St. N.W. where the Message was given if strangers were present and the study of the Iqhan began.[22]

The following words of Alma Knobloch shed more light on the nature of the all-important classes held by Mírzá Abu'l-Faḍl. When Alma talks about his statements, she notes 'Abdu'l-Bahá's explanations are authentic or authoritative. We are reminded of 'Abdu'l-Bahá's reasons for sending him to America, to strengthen the friends in the Covenant:

An experience in the early part of my life, after becoming interested and active in the studies of Baha'i Teachings, attending Mirza Abul-Fazl's study class to which a few of the Washington Believers had been asked to attend, Mirza Abu'l-Fazl said several times that it was his hope that all attending this class would be scattered throughout the world. Miss Laura Barney was the first to be called by Abdul-Baha to come to Acca, and although very busy with her mother's financial affairs, her father had recently died, she went to Acca, and we knew that the conditions at that time was [sic] very serious and trying for Abdul-Baha & family. It was during these three years that Laura Barney received the many answers to her questions & had them published—*Some Answered Questions.* Mr. Remey, Col. Fritzjerel [sic, probably Fitzgerald], Pauline, Mrs. Barnitz, Mrs. Phelps, Mmd'l dAstre and a few others. We found Mirza Abul-Fazl most careful and precise in all his statements, and when we had finished the course, which was rather difficult, Mirza Ali Kuli-Khan translator, we were told not to give out our notes that we had taken. We were not to spread his interpretations—that only Abdul-Baha's explanations are to be used and are authentic.

I carefully put my notebook away and felt that another page of my life had been turned, and was starting a new, broad and beautiful life.[23]

\- 3 -

Joseph's Early Story

According to Pauline's sister Alma, Joseph H. Hannen accepted this new religion in 1904 and deeply appreciated his wife's patience in bringing him into the Bahá'í Cause. Joseph was born in 1872 to Frank and Mary Virginia (Anthony) Hannen in Richmond, Virginia. His parents were married in 1868 in Philadelphia, the hometown of Frank's parents. Letters that were found among family papers give congratulations to the couple for the birth of a baby girl in 1870. Unfortunately, letters were found giving condolences for the death of the same baby girl a short time later that year. The letters are very hard to decipher, but one letter of condolence from Joseph's grandfather Henry Hannen, who lived in Philadelphia, had exceptional spiritual insight about the passing of their beloved daughter. He spoke of the baby being in heaven and quoted from the Bible in his effort to console the grieving couple. This brings to mind the Methodist environment that Joseph described in his account to Ahmad Sohrab.

Joseph Henry Hannen was named after his paternal grandfather. Letters to Mary Virginia from Frank's father, written a few years after Joseph's birth, indicate he was concerned and even ashamed of the poor behavior of his son. The story told to the grandchildren was that Joseph's father left to get milk for him when he was a baby, and never returned home. Letters sent to Mary Virginia in 1873 indicate that Frank was not to be trusted and clearly had issues that were hard to live with; hinting of spousal abuse and neglect. A letter from a cousin uses even harsher words about his bad behavior toward her. The feeling one gets after reading the correspondences is that Mary Virginia was not sorry to see him go.[1]

The letters also hint of the loss of Mary's own parents around that time. It appears that Mary had support from different relatives and may have spent some time living with a sister or two. Family members were trying to get her to move to Philadelphia. Luckily another box of Hannen family letters was discovered in the Bahá'í National Archives containing several letters written by

Frank Hannen, as well as a few by a cousin, shedding a little more light on the situation. The cousin's letter confirmed what the family had understood which was that Frank was not behaving well when he was with Mary and she was right to have been rid of him. However, the letters from Frank were written to relatives of Mary trying to determine where she was living and how she and little Joey were doing. He wrote, "I wish that I could ascertain whether dear Mary has any affection remaining for me & if I could give indubitable proof that my dissipated and wayward habits are entirely overcome (which I could do) whether there would be any prospect of a final reconciliation. She was and is the one grand Love and passion of my life . . . "[2] The letter is dated in 1881 indicating that Joseph was nine years old when it was written, so Frank would have left sometime before that.

As early as 1877, though, there is a letter written by a cousin who mentions Mary leaving a man (presumably Frank) and that he (the cousin) would be happy to have her live with him and his wife and help with raising Joey along with his children. At that point Joey would have been five. It is unclear if she ever took him up on that offer; however, it seems she lived instead with a sister or aunt.

In 1882, Frank wrote again to a Mr. and Mrs. Jos Anthony asking for information about "Dear Mary & our little son Joey. God grant they are well & at least more happily & pleasantly situated than I have been! Can it be that I have passed out of their & your thoughts? Please do not ignore me! Tis the prompting of an affectionate heart (erring tho it was in the past) that leads me to beg information concerning those whom I never shall forget or cease to love & I hope you will not think I would take any undue advantage of, or annoy them. . . ."[3] He went on to say he had a proposal to make regarding Joey's support and schooling which he hoped Mary would not reject. Since we have no further letters from him it is my assumption that she did reject his offer.

We know that Mary and little Joseph eventually moved to Washington D.C. where Joey attended school and eventually met Pauline Knobloch sometime before December of 1890. Mary's granddaughter Eleanor Hannen Raley told me that Mary Virginia Anthony Hannen, after moving to Washington D.C. was married two more times. Eleanor spent a considerable amount of time with Mary Virginia while growing up, and shares that her grandmother was a beautiful and vivacious woman. She reports that Mary's second husband's last name was Covington, but she felt that he just wanted her as a housekeeper and after a while she had enough of that. Perhaps when she divorced him she stopped using that name. Her third husband's last name was Alexander, but Eleanor never met him. Pauline mentioned in her report to Ahmad Sohrab that her mother-in-law, who had been living with her and Joseph, married someone and moved out of the house for a while. Presumably she is referring to Mr. Alexander, but no one seems to know what happened to him. There is a brief mention of him in one of Joseph's letters to Pauline, which gives some further measure of credence to his existence. In that letter Joseph wrote that his mother's divorce from her husband, Mr. Alexander, was finalized. It's curious that Mary Virginia still liked to use that name, but she was just as often called Mrs. Hannen. For the most part, she is referred to as *Mother,* while Pauline's mother is referred to as *Mamma* in the letters.[4]

Mary Virginia lived with Joseph and Pauline for much of their married life—except for a few years after she married her third husband—and then again until she passed. Mrs. Alexander also became a believer after she heard the Faith's message. 'Abdu'l-Bahá often sent His love and greetings to her and even wrote a special Tablet for her later on. He showed special kindness to her when they met in 1912. Some of her Christian grandchildren to this day believe that she was a Christian to the end of her life. This could easily be explained by the practice mentioned earlier where some early Bahá'ís maintained membership in their church even after accepting Bahá'u'lláh. However, the headstone on her grave in Richmond, Virginia, does have the Greatest Name engraved on it.

As mentioned previously, we know Joseph met Pauline Knobloch sometime before 1890. In fact, the earliest letter we have of Joseph's is a letter he wrote to himself in the form of a diary entry. It starts out with the musings of a teenage boy, age eighteen at the time, regarding the subject of women and the meaning of love. After a few pages he explains the reason for wanting to start this diary. He writes:

> I better commence this record of my life [with] a description of its motive power, my Love. She is dark with coal black hair, short and curly. Eyes from where portals the Light of Heaven verily shines out, a beautiful face the form of a Venus de Milo, and a disposition descriptive of which the word angelic would seem to be inadequate. Such is a feeble, alas too feeble, description of Pauline. Heaven only knows the extent—the depth, breadth and width—of my love for her. Tis pure, pure as she—and tis time and lasting as steel. When I meet her, my whole soul seems to go out to her in rapt adoration, and I spend my happiest hours of existence in her presence. Hers is a beneficent purifying effect on me, for I feel in the actions of my life, as though I must do the very best I can in order to be as worthy of her as in me lies. I pray to God to make me better, that I may be more worthy of her.[5]

Joseph was clearly smitten with Pauline and appears to have been as much attracted to her beautiful soul as to her physical beauty. In December of 1891, in the midst of their courtship, Joseph wrote to his friend Max regarding some kind of quarrel or distress he caused Pauline. He asked Max to tell Pauline how regretful he felt about what happened between them, and ask for her forgiveness from the bottom of his heart. His letter conveyed his sense of agony over this situation.[6] Apparently she forgave him, because they were married in 1893.

However, it appears from the glimpses offered in several letters, that Joseph and Pauline had periods of separation from each other even shortly after their marriage. Some of Joseph's letters to Pauline written in August of 1894 reveal how much he missed her while she was on a vacation in a cottage at Colonial Beach in Maryland. (This same beach later became the scene of a Bahá'í summer camp planned by the Barnitz family who became very significant to the Hannens. Perhaps it was here where the families first met each other.)

In his letter Joseph mentioned a special coin that was of interest and wrote "You used to say that I was as fond of my coins as I was of you, but such is not the case, because I don't care to look at them while you are away. It is the same way with the newspaper. When you are not there, it does not seem to be worth reading. But I must be patient and I am trying my best to be, for I know you need the trip."[7] He goes on to inquire about her appetite, which might indicate that she was in the early stages of pregnancy with her first child, Carl, who was born in 1895. In this and future letters there seems to be a concern when Pauline went away to the country, that she needed a healthier atmosphere than could be found in the city of Washington D.C.

His letters contain observations regarding various people he had seen as well as business deals he was arranging that would soon have them out of debt. He also indicated that he was with his parents, which I assume to be his mother and perhaps her newest husband, who were feeding him lots of fruits and vegetables and trying to keep him from getting too lonesome. Throughout his correspondences one feels his enthusiasm for a future when they would not need to be separated so much. Moreover, the letters indicated that he was able at times to meet Pauline at the beach for the weekends:

> Dearest, my love for you is growing stronger and stronger. I can hardly wait until the time when we shall be together, and it seems as if the time between now and then is just about wasted, for it is hardly what could really be called "living," without you by my side. My sweet guardian angel, I shall be so happy when we can again together tread Life's happy paths, and stop along the roadside ever and anon, we two twin souls, to renew our vows of love and to just be happy that we are together.[8]

In 1897, Joseph wrote another lengthy letter to Pauline on Southern Railway Company letterhead stationery, indicating he must have been working for the company by then. I found this to be an amusing and very interesting letter for several reasons. I gather from its contents that Pauline was again in need of a break from city life. She and Fanny decided to take an extended trip to the mountains of South Carolina and Tennessee to commune with nature and get back to the basics. It's just the kind of thing some folks might do today, and I find it remarkable they felt a need for that back in the 1800s as well. From the tone of Joseph's letter, one might guess he was not in complete understanding of the necessity of this trip, but was at least willing for her to take it. I include portions of the letter here, starting with Joseph in distress:

> The receipt of your first letter from East LaPorte filled me with great dismay & I wondered how in the world you were going to exist. While one could possibly dispense with the use of a water closet, it seemed as if one could not live without bread. I thought of all the savage countries I could, but all of them have something in the shape of bread. I came very near buying a barrel of flour and a chamber, and shipping them to you by express—again, I thought perhaps they have no oven to bake bread in. I was greatly relieved last night when I went home to learn that what you meant was they had nothing but hot biscuits. They would take the place of bread first rate with me & I should never complain of the difference, but I know you don't like hot bread, and am sorry you could not get it a day old. But this trouble I think can be remedied for in a day or so they could have bread as you want it.
>
> The lack of a water closet seems almost barbaric, don't it? I didn't have any idea that the place would be so crude and barren. It is fortunate you are well and in search of adventure and travel instead of health. Have you become more accustomed to the surroundings? While the general tone of your letters shout lack of many comforts, I am yet led to hope and pray that through it all there is some pleasure for you in the wild beauty of Nature—a pleasure not to be had except at the cost of leaving the city and the comforts of civilization behind you. That part of it must be grand, and I am sure you will always remember that part of the trip.
>
> Now dearie, if the discomforts are too much—particularly if you don't get enough to eat, or proper food—don't stay a day longer. Telegraph me at once, and I will arrange so you can go to Ashville or somewhere else for the balance of the time. My advice to you would be, if you think it healthy, to stick it out thinking that perhaps when you have accustomed yourself to the surroundings you may find instruction and learning in it. But of course I don't know the place as you do. Anyway, don't feel that you have to stay.
>
> The people in the region you are in must be a complete novelty to you. Not everyone has seen the Mountaineers of North Carolina and Tennessee, and it will be a feature to be able to say you have seen them in their own country.

Joseph goes on to describe activities he was doing while she was gone, trying to impress her with the fun times he was having in the city, and teasing her about her need for being in the country. He ends with these words:

> And now dear little Sweetheart, I must draw my letter to a close. I pray to God every night, and often during the day, that he may bless you and keep you well and happy. While I cannot come to you my love is with you always. I shall be so happy when you return with good health, happy with nothing left I hope but good recollections, all the rude imperfections forgotten and obliterated—like the mountains themselves which from a distance seem perfect, like a picture. Yet when you get to them and climb their summits, the sides are rough and craggy, and the beauty now seems all in the valley below. So, home now seems to you more beautiful, just as perhaps the Mountains did seem perfect to you in your recollection.[9]

As mentioned previously, Joseph worked for the Southern Railway Company where it is said he "made an enviable record in positions of steadily increased responsibility." This job must have taken on more responsibility after the birth of their two sons—Carl in 1895, and Paul in 1900—as there are a series of letters from1901, which Joseph wrote to Pauline while they were again separated, this time due to his work. It appears his job kept him traveling and he spent a good deal of time in Portsmouth, Virginia. They evidently had an arrangement for getting together on weekends. At that time Pauline would have been caring for her two young sons, Paul being an infant, and one presumes having Joseph's mother living with them must have helped in this situation. His letters during this period are imbued with a sense of loneliness in his longing to be with Pauline, and he also assures her often that he is behaving well, not smoking more than two cigars in the evening, and limiting his beers to just two a day. His letters were quite long and full of the details of his days so she could see how he spent his spare time away from her. When reading these letters, I am reminded of Joseph's father's struggles with alcohol addiction, and I get the impression Joseph may have struggled with his own temptations concerning alcohol before meeting Pauline and becoming a Bahá'í. Perhaps this is what he's referring to when writing about the purifying effect Pauline had on his soul. He often assured her that he was behaving according to her wishes, and his letters are filled with pages of how much he misses Pauline, how much he loves her, and how he longs for the day when his job will allow them to be together all the time.

In 1902, the year Joseph and Pauline were introduced to the Bahá'í Faith, he was connected to the Viavi business—a business that sold health products. Pauline's sister Fanny was also associated with Viavi, at least since 1901, and perhaps it was even Fanny who introduced him to the company. Given the content of the letters written during the frequent separations of 1901, he may have felt this was an opportunity to be home with the family more regularly. In 1902 he was building his business, which eventually became very successful. He was in active charge of the Correspondence Service Department of the Washington Division of the Eastern Viavi Company, a department of the business that he established and exclusively managed from its inception.[10]

Viavi products had to do with physical healing of all sorts, including some homeopathic remedies. They specialized in women's health issues, [11] but other correspondences indicate the products were sought after by friends ailing with influenza and various other maladies. One piece of correspondence included a list of the 146 cities that had Viavi offices. My Aunt Barbara claims that her aunts and grandma were always rubbing some Viavi product on her and her siblings and cousins, for any number of aches and pains. This type of business probably allowed him the luxury of setting his own schedule so as to make time for teaching and other Bahá'í service, as he became more involved with the administration and teaching work of the Faith. Joseph's grandson, Sohayl Hannen, recounted that Joseph and Fanny Knobloch were often able to combine their business travels with their Bahá'í service, thus making a living while at the same time teaching the Faith.

- 4 -

Guidance Pours Forth

During the first few years of their lives as Bahá'ís, information is scarce about the young families and their activities. *Star of the West* magazine, which so wonderfully described the many activities that took place in Washington and other early Bahá'í communities, did not begin publication until 1910. Only by gleaning small glimpses from letters here and there, and personal accounts of family members over several generations, can their lives be assembled. Fortunately for the world of historians and history buffs, Joseph Hannen was an organized and meticulous secretarial minded individual. Once he realized the importance of the great Faith he had embraced, he made carbon copies of every letter he wrote and kept them, along with all the correspondence he received (signed and dated with the date he replied) in files. These were eventually turned over to the National Archives Committee. However, during those first few years, there was little correspondence that was saved except for those mentioned in the previous chapter.[1]

The other, and perhaps most significant of these glimpses into the past, are the correspondences new believers often received from 'Abdu'l-Bahá's own hand. These Tablets were a source of great inspiration and undoubtedly laid a wonderful spiritual foundation for their recipients. Stockman explains, "In thousands of letters the North American Bahá'ís asked Him to give His advice, or name their children, or bless their husbands, or provide them with a prayer to say for a deceased relative. The majority of the letters that Americans wrote to 'Abdu'l-Bahá were personal, not doctrinal, but they did raise many theological and philosophical questions. His replies are considered infallible and immediately became part of Bahá'í scripture. The American Bahá'ís thus had an intimacy with part of their scriptures because they had personally called it into existence."[2] These letters, or Tablets, as they preferred to call them, were copied and often made into pamphlets and circulated among all the Bahá'ís. In the Hannen family archives, there are several much-worn leather notebooks filled with pages of hand-typed or written copies of letters and quotes from 'Abdu'l-Bahá and Bahá'u'lláh. Most likely the family carried these notebooks with them to refer to when they went on their many teaching trips.

Over the next two decades, before 'Abdu'l-Bahá's passing, the Hannens and Knoblochs received numerous Tablets from Him. They were especially blessed because Joseph's eventual role as special correspondent with 'Abdu'l-Bahá for the Southern States, enabled him to keep an ongoing line of communication with 'Abdu'l-Bahá. The first of these Tablets to be received by a family member was addressed to Pauline Hannen, dated 29 May 1903:

O thou who art attracted by the Fragrances of God!
Thou hast opened thine eyes to the morn of Oneness, obtained the light of Faith and Knowledge, sown a pure seed in the soil of the heart and planted flowers of significances in the garden of thy spirit. Now irrigate it with the spiritual outpourings and the severance from all else save God, so that thou mayest be favored with the attributes and manners of the Spiritual Ones and be confirmed by the assistance of the Holy Spirit.

I hope to God that those mentioned may all be strengthened by the guidance of the Holy Spirit. If the one God bestows the Eternal Bounty, He will submerge all of them in the Sea of Guidance.

But thank thou God for thou art looked upon by the eye of Favor and a recipient of grace and compassion. I beg of God that thou mayest become a fruitful tree and be filled like unto shells with the Pearls of the Knowledge of God.

Upon thee be greetings and praise!
'Abdu'l-Bahá Abbas
Translated by Ali Kuli-Khan, May 29, 1903[3]

Surely receiving this beautiful Tablet from her newfound Beloved must have been a treasure that would sustain her and bring assurance to her soul. Over the next few years many of Pauline's family and friends, such as the Barnitz family, were submerged in a sea of guidance and began their transformation through the revitalizing words of the Holy Spirit—shared gradually through the letters and teachings of 'Abdu'l-Bahá.

At this point in the development of the Bahá'í Faith in America, there was very little of the revealed words of Bahá'u'lláh available in English. The believers' main link to Bahá'u'lláh was the precious correspondence with 'Abdu'l-Bahá. When any of the friends were privileged to go to 'Akká and be in the presence of the Master, as they called Him, they would write accounts of such visits and publish them as well. It's interesting to note that the letters received from 'Abdu'l-Bahá, for which originals have been found, are considered authenticated, and the English translations of these letters, which were prepared at that time and sent to the recipients along with the originals, are considered historical documents. Many of the letters or Tablets in this book are such. Some, however, have been retranslated more recently and are thus considered authorized translations. We have endeavored to use the most recent translations whenever possible in this book. Notes taken by pilgrims are considered "pilgrim's notes" and, although informative and interesting, are not authoritative scripture and they should not be taken as representing 'Abdu'l-Bahá's exact words but rather, as only the recollections of the hearer. In some of Pauline's correspondences she speaks of sending her notes to 'Abdu'l-Bahá for His signature or approval. At that time in history, before these distinctions had been made, everything that came from the Master was treated like manna from heaven. In the forward to the book *Agnes Parsons' Diary*, Sandra Hutchison gives an account of how the early Bahá'ís regarded 'Abdu'l-Bahá:

> But the fealty of the American Bahá'ís to 'Abdu'l-Bahá was inspired by more than their recognition of His station. To them, He was "the Master"—a loving teacher who had nurtured them from afar through scores of letters, a Christ-like figure about whom they had heard numerous tales from returning pilgrims to the Holy Land. In fact, many of the early American Bahá'ís believed that it was He, not Bahá'u'lláh who represented the return of Jesus as prophesied in the New Testament, and it took repeated denials to disabuse them of this notion: His only station, He told them, was the station of servitude and the name He wished to be known by was 'Abdu'l-Bahá—the "Servant of Bahá."[4]

According to Stockman, the Washington D.C. community grew more quickly than some other early communities "because it had access to more reliable and accurate information on Bahá'í teachings. The Washington Bahá'í community, perhaps was more deepened than even that of Chicago, for Mírzá Abu'l-Faḍl had remained in Washington for three and a half years and had lectured and written extensively. As a result, Washington was perhaps the most successful community in North America after Chicago."[5] They also had the continuing assistance of Persian believers to help them communicate with 'Abdu'l-Bahá more accurately and frequently. After Abu'l-Faḍl and Ali Kuli-Khan, 'Abdu'l-Bahá sent another young Persian believer in 1903 to carry on their work. His name was Mirza Ahmad (Esphahani) Sohrab, often referred to as "Ahmad" in many of the translated Tablets. Although within the correspondences written to Joseph Hannen, there are letters complaining about the competency of Ahmad's translations, no one doubted his sincerity of Faith and strength in the Covenant at that time.[6] In any case, the believers were dependent on the English proficiency of the servants of God that 'Abdu'l-Bahá deemed fit to send to America for this purpose. They were highly esteemed individuals in the community because of their ability to convey the Master's wishes and their close connection to Him.

Of the Washington Bahá'í community, Stockman goes on to say, "They also published booklet-sized compilations of Tablets. Beginning in 1905, Charles Mason Remey published Bahá'í pamphlets of his own composition, which further enhanced the community's importance among the North American Bahá'ís."[7] This growing body of literature and available knowledge of the teachings of the Faith greatly enhanced the community's ability to grow. Certainly, because Joseph took advantage of the translators to correspond directly with 'Abdu'l-Bahá, the Hannens and Knoblochs benefited greatly. They received many Tablets addressed to one or more of them over the remaining years of 'Abdu'l-Bahá's life and were frequently mentioned in Tablets sent to other believers. The second such Tablet, which arrived from the Holy Land, was addressed to Joseph Hannen. It directly addressed an issue dear to his heart, that of teaching the Faith. It beseeched Joseph to "give the glad-tidings," which he did for the rest of his life. Here are the contents of this soul-stirring letter:

> *O thou who art advancing toward the Kingdom of God!*
> *What thou hast written became evident, and what thou hast heard from Mirza Ameen Ullag regarding the necessity of many teachers in America is true, I HAVE SAID SO. Indeed, there is need of a thousand teachers, each one severed from the world, attracted by the Holy Spirit in the Supreme Concourse, and joyful through the Kingdom of God, and in perfect sanctity, holiness and sufficiency.*
>
> *This matter of teachers requires the greatest condition—that is—they should never stain themselves with the world; they should not look for the least pecuniary reward from any soul, nay, rather, they should bear the utmost poverty and with perfect wealth of nature through the bounty of God may they associate with the people. They should seek no reward and recompense. Freely have they received, freely should they give them the Glad Tidings through the Bounty of Divine Providence and the Revelation of the Sun of Truth in this Age. . . .*
>
> *His Holiness Christ says: "When ye leave the city, clean off your shoes from the dust thereof." The holiness of the teachers must reach this degree. Thus may they utter with eloquence, while in ecstasy and great joy, and guide the people to the manifest light.*
>
> *If this be the endeavor, strive with your life and heart and guide the people to the Kingdom of God, lead them to the straight pathway, inform them of the greatness and magnitude of this Cause, and give them the Glad Tidings through the Bounty of Divine Providence and the Revelation of the Sun of Truth in this Age. . . .*
> *Thy name is Joseph. Let thy title be Baha.*
> *Upon thee be greetings and praise!*
> *(Signed)*

'Abdu'l-Bahá Abbas!
Received January 29, 1906[8]

As one can see, the grammar is sometimes not perfect in these early translations, but the meaning and intent are obvious: "TEACH THE FAITH." Soon more letters came, all encouraging the beloved new souls to "loosen their tongues" and teach a waiting humanity about this new message from God.

The next Tablet was addressed to Pauline's Mother (Amalie Knobloch) and sister Fanny:

O ye two dear maid servants of God!
The Lord of the Kingdom has invited, chosen and guided you through His pure Favor, Feeding you from the Heavenly Table of Divine Knowledge.

Know ye the value of this favor and bounty and loosen your tongues in praise showing forth the power of Knowledge and Assurance and breathing the Spirit of Guidance into the hearts of the seekers.

Ask from God that ye stand firm and steadfast in this Great Cause.

I pray in your behalf, asking assistance and favor for you.

I hope that you may become confirmed and helped.

Upon ye be greetings and praise. (signed) 'Abdu'l-Bahá Abbas
Trans. March 27, 1906 [9]

On this same date, Joseph received his second precious message from 'Abdu'l-Bahá:

O thou son of the Kingdom!
How noble is man, if he would walk in the path of the Almighty! And how beautiful is he if the Light of God illumines his face! How wise is he, if he becomes instructed in the World of the Kingdom! How mighty is he if he stand in the Divine Path, and how perceiving is he if he listen to the Call of the True One!

Therefore, thank thou God that the intelligence, and thy soul and heart were agitated and moved; consequently make thy feet steadfast and firm, in order that day by day thine favor may be increased and the world of existence be adorned.

Upon thee be greeting and praise!
(signed) 'Abdu'l-Bahá Abbas
Translated by Mirza Ahmad
March 27, 1906[10]

It was not too long before another letter was received; this time addressed to Mrs. Amalie Knobloch. It is evident from these letters that 'Abdu'l-Bahá was taking great care to water His tender new roses in His new garden in North America. He lovingly encouraged these saplings to spread their branches and teach new souls and plant new seeds. The next letter was much longer than the others, but it included directions to be passed on to other believers in the area, as well as encouragement for her own endeavors. Keep in mind that Amalie was already sixty-eight years old at the time she received this letter. Although living in distant lands, 'Abdu'l-Bahá had His hand on the pulse of this rapidly expanding community and continually nurtured them from afar.

O thou venerable maid servant of God!

Thy letter was duly received. Its contents signified true spirituality and steadfastness.

O thou maid servant of God! Consider not merit and aptitude! Thou shouldst rather consider the favors and benefits of the Blessed Perfection.

When we think of self, we find that merit and aptitude (ability) are lost. When we regard Truth, we discover that the Favors of God are infinite and not conditional upon merit and aptitude.

Observe how the small seed grows and thrives by means of vernal showers, the heat of the heavenly sun and the zephyrs until it grows to a fruitful tree. Now see where the former state of the seed is, and the present state of stem, leaves, blossoms and the wonderful fruits, consequently the Divine gifts make a sea out of one drop of water! And make out of one seed a heavenly tree.

I implore God to promote thee day after day in the stages of Eternal Glory and to make thee the instrument to spread the Word of God! Summon thou, the souls to the Law (Cause) of God, and bring them to the Divine Kingdom!

O thou maid servant of God, give my best compliments to Dr. A.S. Newman and say unto him: "The Book of vocables is folded while Truth and Sublime Realities are promulgated, the sayings are abrogated while acts are resurged. The bodies are grieved, while spirits are saved. The sound of the Trumpet is high and the hosts of angels are spread throughout all horizons (regions or universe)."

I hope that thou mayest be chosen and not of the pretenders. Be thou gifted with speech and not silent! Be thou active and not passive! Be thou full of joyful tidings and not hopeless! Be thou existing and not lost, so that the eyes may see and darkness may be changed into illuminations! Strew thou pure seeds over purified land (souls) that thou mayest witness the Divine Bounty!

It would be in vain, if for a thousand years, thou plant seeds into salsuginous [salty] *ground. In this case days simply pass and no result can be gained. Then spread the seeds over blessed ground and plant them until thou, in a very short time, viewest a very large harvest and the heavenly blessings will be inferred!*

Express my best compliments to the maid servant of God Alma, and say unto her, "Be thou not sad at the antipathy of others, and let not the accu-

sations and rebukes of the clergy grieve thee! But be joyful, certainly thou shalt experience the hatred of enemies and rebuke of opponents! And shall be the target of the arrows of oppression, just as thou didst hear concerning the adversaries of the Beloved Ones in the Cycle of Christ and how they preferred the rebukes and the antipathies of others."

(signed) 'Abdu'l-Bahá Abbas
Cairo
Translated by Hussein Rouhy
Received July 25, 1906[11]

'Abdu'l-Bahá even sent special Tablets to the sons of Pauline and Joseph:

O ye two tender plants in the Abhá Paradise!
Render thanks unto God that ye have sprouted in this heavenly garden. God willing ye will become firmly rooted, will develop and grow through the outpourings of the heavenly clouds and will attain perfection and bring forth fruit through the radiance of the Sun of Reality. Avail ye yourselves of the opportunity in these days, and appreciate the value of this glorious century. Strive ye earnestly to become fruitful trees, brilliant lamps and as two stars shining above the horizons of East and West.
And upon ye be the glory of the Most Glorious.
'Abdu'l-Bahá
Dec. 9, 1906[12] (New translation)

In 1909 The Bahá'í Publishing Society, which had been in existence since 1902, published a compilation titled *Tablets of 'Abdu'l-Bahá Abbas,* which contained many of the Tablets that had been sent to the Bahá'í friends throughout the United States. As per 'Abdu'l-Bahá's instructions, the names of those to whom the Tablets were written and any names contained within the Tablets were removed. The Publishing Society also removed the greetings and salutations at the end of the Tablets. The introduction to the book explains that all the original Tablets were to be gathered for preservation in the Publishing Society's archives, and the friends were encouraged to maintain this practice for all future Tablets.

The following Tablets, which appear in *Tablets of 'Abdu'l-Bahá Abbas,* were addressed to the Barnitz family. Unfortunately, they are not dated. The first is to Mrs. Leona Barnitz:

O thou who art commemorating the praises of God!
Verily, I read thy letter of elegant expression, for which I supplicate God to make thee meek, humble and fit for the effulgence of the light of His love among the maid-servants; and (I beg God) to make all mankind the chil-

dren of His Mercy! This is the utmost mercy of 'Abdu'l-Bahá for which he is endeavoring night and day and is summoning all to this fountain which is flowing with the pure water of the gift of God. Verily, I pray God to assemble all mankind in the shadow of the standard of peace and under the tents of love in the Paradise of El-ABHA; so that all of them may become the children of God and His beloved ones. Verily thy Lord is compassionate to the servants who are rightly guided.

As to thee: Appreciate the value of thy father, for he taught thee to await the manifestation of the Light of Lights. Verily he hath inhaled the fragrance of the Paradise of El-ABHA and his nostrils are therewith perfumed. Therefore, he bade thee anticipate and prepare thyself for the appearance of the Kingdom of God.[13]

Mrs. Barnitz, as mentioned in a previous chapter, had been waiting all her life for something to happen. Not surprisingly, and yet still fascinating, 'Abdu'l-Bahá, as revealed in the above Tablet, knew it was her father who had taught her to be ready.

The next two Tablets are addressed to Beulah and Mineola Barnitz respectively. These Tablets also were undated, but presumably revealed while they were still young. To Beulah Barnitz He wrote:

O thou young in age and great in mind! (There is) many a young child who is mature and grown up, and many an aged [one] who is ignorant and stupid. Growth and maturity are in intellect and understanding and not in age and duration of life. Verily thou has known thy Lord while thou art young in age; but there are thousands of women who are heedless of the commemoration of God, veiled from the Kingdom of God and deprived of the Bounty of the gift of God. As to thee, thank thy Lord for this great gift. I beg of God to heal thy mother, who is revered in the Kingdom of God.[14]

To Mineola, my grandmother, He wrote:

O thou dear one!
Blessed art thou, for thou hast entered into the bosom of the training of God and drunk the cup of knowledge while thou art young in age among girls. Thank thou God for that He hath caused thee to taste the sweetness of His love at thy earliest childhood. I beg of God to protect thee from wavering in the cause of God, to make thee firm in the Covenant of God, to guard thy mother in the stronghold of His great Kingdom and to make thee a girl successful and nurtured from the breast of the love of God, refreshed from the milk of His knowledge in this great day.[15]

Besides the wonderful Tablets that appeared gradually from 'Abdu'l-Bahá, guidance also came from other sources. With the help of Howard MacNutt, Ali Kuli-Khan published *The Book of Ighan* (the Kitáb-i-Íqán, in English, the Book of Certitude), one of Bahá'u'lláh's most important works. This book revealed how the Bahá'í Faith related to other major religions, offering the Bahá'ís a broader view of their religion that transcended the perception that it was simply the fulfillment of Christian prophecies. They could now see how religion had been progressively revealed to humanity throughout history. This access to the writings of Bahá'u'lláh no doubt had an uplifting effect on the believers.

In 1904 Fareed translated the Hidden Words, in which Bahá'u'lláh revealed the universal spiritual teachings found in all religious scriptures and, as He wrote, "clothed it in the garment of brevity." By 1906 the Bahá'í Publishing Society published in one volume several Tablets of Bahá'u'lláh titled Tablet of Ṭarázát, Tablet of the World, Words of Paradise, Tablet of Tajallíyát, and the Glad Tidings. Additionally, the Tablet of Ishráqát was published in1908.[16] Having access to these precious words naturally influenced the kinds of activities the Bahá'í community members involved themselves in. Teachings such as the establishment of a universal auxiliary language inspired many Bahá'ís, including Joseph and Pauline, to take an interest in learning Esperanto. I have found, among their Bahá'í literature collection, pamphlets printed in Esperanto, which many at the time thought had the potential to evolve into a universal language. The writings on the importance of educating children likely inspired Pauline's great interest in teaching children's classes, while the exhortation to consort with all peoples and religions no doubt inspired Joseph to become very involved with the Persian American Educational Society. As more and more guidance poured forth, the family became increasingly involved in spreading the Word.

- 5 -

The Real Work Begins

As early as 1904, 'Abdu'l-Bahá was addressing the Washington community as a whole in such Tablets as the one below, found copied in one of Alma's many notebooks:

> To the believers of Washington D.C. by 'Abdu'l-Bahá
> Through Miss L. Barney, received 7 December 1904.
> *O God grant Washington happiness & peace. Illumine that land with the light of the faces of the friends. Make it a paradise of glory. Let it become the envy of the green gardens of the earth.*
> *Help the friends increase their numbers. Make their hearts sources of inspiration & their souls dawnings of light.*
> *Thus may that city become a beautiful paradise & fragrant with the fragrance of musk.*
> *'Abdu'l-Bahá Abbas*[1]

Stockman asserts that, "Because of its talent and organization, by 1907 Washington was probably the most important Bahá'í community in the United States after Chicago and New York."[2] The Washington Bahá'í community's talents and resources included the ability to send out circulars and announcements throughout the country, to organize large events, and promote the building of the Bahá'í House of Worship in Chicago. Several members contacted government officials and people of prominence in order to share the Bahá'í message.[3] Although it is difficult to verify exactly who did what in the community at that time, we can presume that Joseph Hannen most likely took part in many of these activities by the sheer immensity of his correspondences, and through articles about Bahá'í life in Washington. He had a reputation for always being cheerful and happy and whenever something needed to be done, he did it quickly, without complaint.[4]

The following article titled, "Who's Who in Viavi?" published by the company Joseph worked for, gives an excellent description of the kind of man Joseph was, both within the Bahá'í community, as well as in his work outside the Faith:

> There is a man in Washington D.C. who has made good in the Viavi Business; "made good" in the full sense of all that term implies. He has charge of one of the departments of the Washington headquarters through which he manages a large territory contiguous to the Washington office. The volume of business done through that department speaks in no uncertain tones of the capabilities of the man at its head—speaks in the mute but undisputable language of figures; and the five figures that stand as the result of just one year's work speak more voluminously of the achievements of this manager than all the adjectives of praise we might corral from the latest unabridged.
>
> The man to who we refer is Mr. Joseph H. Hannen. It has not taken Mr. Hannen a lifetime to accomplish what he has done in Viavidom, for it was but a short decade ago that he joined the Viavi ranks. His earlier business experiences were, first, as stenographer with law firms; then later he was for ten years connected with passenger departments of the Southern Railway and Seaboard Air Line Railway, from which position he came into the Viavi business. . . . Mr. Hannen has the personal qualifications, either inherent or acquired, that not only start him after the things he wants but also insure that he will get it. He is a polished and affable gentleman; sincere, earnest, kind. His principles and practices are based upon religious convictions which emphasize the brotherhood of man, and these convictions, without any ostentation, however, are shadowed forth in all his business transactions, and they tint and illumine his everyday associations with those about him. Mr. Hannen is an able writer, and also a fluent talker; he puts himself unreservedly into his work and reaps big returns.
>
> Not only is Mr. Hannen a success as far as the figures of the business go, but one of the largest elements of his success is his ability steadfastly to hold to his organization those whom he secures as workers. Once enlisted under his banner the recruit is apt to become a veteran; there are few deserters from his army of workers.
>
> Mr. Hannen's home is in Washington, D.C. and his wife is sister of Miss Fanny Knobloch, the well-known and much admired Viavi traveling organizer in the Washington Division.
>
> We could have no better New Year's wish for Mr. Hannen than that

the success that has attended his work in the past may go with him in the years to come.[5]

The Viavi Company saw these qualities in him, which appear to be the same qualities 'Abdu'l-Bahá saw and nurtured within him as well.

In 1906, several communities in the United States were organizing themselves into various sorts of consultative bodies to do the work of the Faith. Mason Remey made an effort to organize a consultative body for the D.C. Bahá'ís. By 1907 this body became known as the Working Committee, and Joseph was one of its members. This group of dedicated believers took on many tasks related to organizing the Bahá'í activities for this growing community.[6]

It would seem 'Abdu'l-Bahá was pleased with the decision to organize the Washington Bahá'ís given His response in this Tablet dated 30 April1907:

> *What a fine group ye have assembled! . . . If that committee be firm, it shall grow; if it show forth steadfastness, it shall receive heavenly bounty; if it pursue its work with perseverance, it shall achieve remarkable results.*[7]

As usual, His approval was sought, and received, and included the ever-present instruction in encouraging phrases that inspired the souls to more service. To Mason Remey, He added in a Tablet dated 4 June 1907:

> *The founding of such a body will redound to the distinction of the Faith of God, and provide a means whereby the divine message may be diffused throughout those parts. My fervent hope is that this body will so develop from day to day that it will become an assemblage of the All-Merciful.*[8]

During this time, another previously mentioned ancestor, and new believer, was becoming more involved with organizing the community in another way. Stockman tells us that Leona Barnitz, "was the prime mover behind the creation of a Bahá'í summer program, what today would be called a summer school, at Camp Mineola in Colonial Beach, Virginia. For Bahá'ís and their friends, it offered classes only on the Bahá'í Faith, not on other religions and philosophies. It was the first of a score of Bahá'í summer schools in North America and of hundreds around the world to be patterned after Green Acre."[9] A photo of Camp Mineola was found among the Barnitz papers and seemed to consist of many tents set up in a large campsite. Her daughter Leone states that she served at this camp between the years 1903–08. Mention of the camp is found in several family correspondences, as well as photos of family members enjoying camp activities.[10] On 26 March 1906, 'Abdu'l-Bahá sent this letter to those who had previously attended the camp in 1905 and had sent a supplication to Him. The complete list of all those who attended is written in Pauline's handwriting on the back of the copy found in the archives. It includes the Hannen family members, Mr. and Mrs. Barnitz and their three daughters, several Phelpses, Knoblochs, and many others.

He is God!
O ye Friends of 'Abdu'l-Bahá!
From the gathering of those illuminated faces and flowers of the rose-garden (of God) in Camp Mineola, utmost joy and fragrance (to me) was the result.

I hope that Assembly, like sparkling stars, may shed the lights of love and unison upon the human world, and become the cause of happiness and joy of the inhabitants of the earth, that they may become like unto clear mirrors reflecting (the rays) of the Sun of Truth, and give, the Glad-tidings of the Manifestation of the Lord of the Kingdom.

I ask the blessings of God that year by year He may add souls to that Assembly, and in future it may become doubled and a hundred-fold.

How blessed it is that this Assembly may become firmly established, and it is sure that the heavenly confirmations will pour down!

Signed 'Abdu'l-Bahá Abbas[11]
Trans. By Mirza Ahmad

During this time, one of the most significant developments in the Bahá'í community was the work being done to build the first Mashriqu'l-Adhkár, or House of Worship, in the Western Hemisphere. The Chicago House of Spirituality had been petitioning 'Abdu'l-Bahá for several years for permission to build an edifice in the United States similar to the first Bahá'í House of Worship in 'Ishqábád, Russia. In 1903 'Abdu'l-Bahá gave His consent for the Chicago House of Spirituality to begin working toward their goal. Robert Stockman gives a detailed account of their efforts and explains how this endeavor helped unify the American Bahá'í community. He reveals that initially some of the other communities, and Washington in particular, wanted to build their own House of Worship, but 'Abdu'l-Bahá urged them instead to help Chicago. "As a result," Stockman says, "Washington Bahá'ís became a major force in the Temple work."[12] One way they were able to achieve this was to utilize the skills and available resources of the Hannens—who helped circulate letters to encourage support for the "Temple." This is but one example of how Joseph's skills and equipment used in his business enabled him to serve the community in unique ways.

Stockman explains, "The Washington Working Committee's first idea, in April 1907, was only indirectly related to the Temple and national organization: it believed that the American Bahá'ís needed a periodical. Such a publication could create a consciousness that did not yet exist—and could disseminate news about the Temple."[13] Although the idea of a publication was temporarily shelved, it did open a broader debate concerning the idea of a national Bahá'í organization. After a second circular was sent out, several of the smaller Bahá'í communities and groups created a "Temple" committee, or branch, in support of the Chicago Temple. The circular letter that was sent out by the Washington Bahá'ís had, as its purpose, "to bring to the mind of each and every Bahá'í in this land the necessity for united service in this work [building the Temple] and to exhort them to make haste to raise this standard of unity."[14] As documented in Stockman's book, the Washington Working Committee, involving Joseph Hannen, was instrumental in these issues relating to the promotion of the Temple work and the gradual evolution of several active centers into a national Bahá'í community. By the time the second National Convention of the Temple Unity was held in 1910, Joseph was elected to be a member of that national organization.[15] This marked the beginning of many years of activity and service by him at the national level.

These efforts eventually led to the formation of the first national Bahá'í periodical—entitled *Bahá'í News*—producing monthly newsletters, and evolving ultimately into *Star of the West.* Joseph Hannen's name appears in almost every issue. He gave monthly reports on the activities of the Washington community, wrote detailed reports about National Conventions, and as secretary of the Persian American Educational Society, he gave reports on the activities of that organization as well. During 'Abdu'l-Bahá's visits in 1912, he took the stenographic notes for many of His talks in Washington and Chicago, later printed in *Star of the West.* When 'Abdu'l-Bahá's teaching plans (Tablets of the Divine Plan) were introduced to America, Joseph took on even more secretarial tasks with great efficiency and skill. Joseph, with Pauline as his constant helpmate, jumped into the work of the Cause without reservation. Their sole aim was to be of service in any way 'Abdu'l-Bahá, and later Shoghi Effendi, requested of them.

In 1906, Alma Knobloch had the chance to move away from Washington to Dunkirk, New York, and was looking forward to an increase in opportunities to teach more people about the Faith. In a letter to Alma, Pauline recounted a dream she had in which the Master told Alma to work where she was; she would be greatly tested but that it was a sign of God's favor. Pauline continued, "Don't you think that was strange, possibly that same night Mrs. Mills opened her home for you where you can dressmake just enough for your need, and keep right on in the work that has opened up so wonderfully for you." Her next words give a hint to the dynamics in the family. She writes, "I wish I could help you, but my place is here. Fanny needs but very little encouragement and she would leave all and teach in her way, who knows [sic] you have always made the start and the rest of us usually make a quick second, so she may be out in the field too." She goes on to share more information about teaching the Faith and some of the interested friends. She speaks of her mother giving the message to their doctor, who in turn spoke of wanting to go to the Holy Land. She also mentions she was looking forward to meeting Roy Wilhelm for the first time, calling him one of the "Big guns," as he was coming to Washington D.C. soon. Pauline ends the letter with a very telling paragraph about how she longs to be able to be out in the field, teaching about God's new Messenger: "Dear Alma, how I would love to be at work with you. I have what you once wished for, children and home. You have what I have always hoped for. So it goes, now I pray most earnestly that you may reach many, many souls, and that I may be patient and contented and may reach a few."[16]

The following account, which is part of Pauline's report to Ahmad Sohrab written in 1909, gives more wonderful details about those formative years and how the celebration of feasts and holy days developed in the beginning stages:

> On Nov. 12, 1904 for the first time in Washington, the Birthday of the Blessed Perfection was celebrated in our humble home, Tablets revealed by Baha'o'llah were read, music by Louise Shuman and Miss Helbig, poem composed by Mr. Hannen was read, and all were happy. Mr. Remey gave each guest a rose, as well as a few words concerning his trip to Acca & Mrs. Dixon also took us in spirit to that holy Spot.
>
> August 1904, Mr. Hannen, the two boys Carl & Paul and myself visited New York for the especial purpose of saying a last farewell to our Beloved Teacher Mirza Abul-Fazl. The first face we saw in the sea of faces on the Pier was the smiling face of Mirza. Madam de Astre had offered to serve us if we came & she was standing there bright and happy. We received further instructions from Mirza at his rooms as well as at the home of Mr. Dodge where we met many beautiful believers. A special Meeting was held at the home of Mrs. Jones, that we might meet more of the friends & have the great joy of hearing Mrs. Getsinger speak for the first time. Here for the first time we met our dear spiritual brother Dr. Ameen U. Fareed, also dear Mrs. Brittingham. Dear brother Ahmad we had met in Washington before & who was and is dearly beloved by all. His first appearance in our midst is well remembered because of the lesson of obedience he taught us. Though his knowledge of the English language was very limited, never the less when his great teacher Mirza Abul Fazl [sic] told him to read some of the Hidden Words, he obeyed.
>
> Since this visit to New York, our home has been wonderfully blessed by having as guests under its roof, such souls as Lua Getsinger, Mrs. Brittingham, Mr. Ober, Ahmad, Prof Barakatullah and many others. Have we not been wonderfully blest, our whole family since my dear mother's home was also a nest for the Birds of Abha. We are devoutly thankful to God for His great Mercy & Generosity, should our blood be spilled in

His path it would be nothing in return for His Great Bounties. May our lives be spent in Servitude in His Holy Cause.

On May 23, 1905 a Heavenly Spiritual feast was held at this home in memory of the Declaration of the Bab and the Birthday of Abdul-Baha. Although only twenty or so were expected more than forty guests assembled. Among them the beautiful soul Miss Sarah Farmer, who told of her trip to Acca, & Mrs. [Brittingham] Dixon, also Mr. Remey and Ahmad; so the house was truly filled with the spirit of the Lord. At Miss Farmer's request all present testified in one way or another of their joy & reason for believing in this Truth. Here for the first time I chanted the Commune, that had come to me during the Fast. Mr. Hannen had written a poem in honor of the Day, this was sung by all, to the tune of an old hymn.

But before this we had another wonderful Spiritual feast, it was the Narooz [sic] feast. A table extending the whole length of the two rooms, around which the guests were assembled & personal Tablets were read, prayers were read of praise & glorification and supplications, there was also music.

This was the beginning of the establishment of the nineteen-day Feasts. Up to this time Mr. Remey & Mrs. Moss, Mrs. Phelps & others had given wonderful Feasts, but not at regular times.

Since 1905 these nineteen day feasts have been kept up regularly. Until two years ago most of them were given in this home because our rooms were larger & we were more centrally located. Our house was open at a moment's notice. The past two years the Assembly has outgrown our house. Now other homes or the Hall is used, and this Meeting is the greatest means of unity and love.

The Narooz of 1906 was another wonderful day in our life. We had as guests Mrs. Lua Getsinger & Miss Meadowcroft, who joined us in helping Ahmad to prepare for the Feast to be as nearly oriental as it could be done. Ahmad had been busy for weeks coming nearly every day to prepare one or another kind of Persian china, spoons . . . etc. At last, all arranged, the guests arrived. First a flash-light picture was taken of all the friends, then small tables were scattered about the two rooms, the feast prepared by Ahmad was served by the Bahá'í young boys & girls. Mrs. Getsinger read and spoke, other Tablets and prayers. Again we felt we had been greatly blessed.[17]

I was pleased to find this piece about the photo taken at Naw-Rúz in 1906, because we have a large group photo with quite a bit of the family present and I always wondered when and where it was taken. Now the mystery is solved—it was in the Hannen home.

The historical accounts of these three Bahá'í families—the Hannens, Knoblochs, and Barnitzes—establishes that they were among the "doers" in the community. They worked hard to attend to the needs of Bahá'í community life as it was developing in Washington D.C. They planned feasts, held holy day festivities in their homes, taught children's classes, gathered the correspondence and sent out mailings, took care of the sick, and nurtured souls. As mentioned previously, Leone St. Claire Barnitz, one of the daughters of Leona Barnitz, worked for many years as a personal secretary to Mrs. Agnes Parsons, helping with her many administrative services to the Faith. In future chapters, we'll cover much more of the work that these stalwart believers took part in. Each had their particular role and specialty, but they were always busy performing some kind of service to their Beloved.

- 6 -

Accepting the "Most Challenging Issue"

By 1906 the Washington Bahá'í community was growing rapidly. Vibrant and active, its members were involved in a variety of activities going on several times a week. However, there was still one tenet of the Faith that needed immediate attention. The unity of all races, one of the central principles of Bahá'u'lláh's teachings, was not outwardly manifested in the community. The community was primarily composed of people of white European-American ancestry, with a few Persian families in the mix. Here is where Pauline, Joseph, and the Knoblochs began to play a very significant role in the history of the American Bahá'í community. They have been given credit by many Bahá'í historians such as Gayle Morrison, Robert Stockman, and Christopher Buck for being among the first to make a consistent effort to introduce and teach the Faith to people of African descent.

Pauline had grown up in the South—Wilmington, North Carolina—where near total segregation was the norm. Schools and churches were, for the most part, exclusively segregated. Restaurants, hotels, and many other public community spaces insisted on the use of separate bathrooms and drinking fountains for the black population, if they were allowed to use the facility at all. Lynching was more common than not, and malicious, inaccurate, negative stereotypes of the black population were continually propagated and reinforced by a white "society" afraid of losing its self-appointed "power." Growing up in this environment produced an unfounded, but certainly intentional, fear in Pauline of black people. She says herself:

> Long before hearing of the Baha'i cause, when I was a little girl in Wilmington, N.C., teaching and environment had made me regard colored people with something like terror. I had known of the frightful retribution visited by whites on negroes for offenses of which I assumed they must be guilty. At about 14 I was brought back to Washington, my birthplace. Walking

> one day in the shopping district, I found myself watching not the shop windows, but the passers-by. Many had Ethiopian marks but were almost white or even blue-eyed. "Why!" I softly exclaimed, "before long we shall not be able to tell colored people from white. How terrible!" Years passed and the problem, for us at least, passed with the years, but not the fear.[1]

By this time in Pauline's life, she had been studying the Bahá'í scriptures and knew of a statement of Bahá'u'lláh's concerning the oneness of humanity in the Hidden Words:

> *O children of men! Know ye not why we have created you all from the same dust? That no one should exalt himself over the other. . . . Since we have created you all from the same substance it is incumbent on you to be even as one soul, to walk with the same feet, eat with the same mouth and dwell in the same land, that from your inmost being, by your deeds and actions, the signs of oneness and the essence of detachment may be made manifest.*[2]

These beautiful words began to melt the prejudice in Pauline's heart. In her own words, she tells the story of how she overcame that fear:

> Following the crisis in an illness of my baby son, I went to the market for the Thanksgiving supplies. Returning to the street I met a heavily-set colored woman, her arms full of bundles, making her way amid the snow and ice in spite of flopping shoe laces which she could not stoop to adjust. Something in the picture brought to me the spirit of universal brotherhood. I knelt in the snow and tied the wayfarer's shoes. She was astonished, and those who saw it appeared to think I was crazy. I did not mind this, and from that moment was possessed with the conviction that I must create a work of brotherhood among the colored people. . . . Some words of Baha'o'llah had sunk deep into my consciousness. These no doubt were the motivating power which changed the current of my whole life, prompting me to uproot the prejudice of childhood and render loving service to all humanity.[3]

The first place Pauline looked to teach the message of the Bahá'í Faith to people of African descent was in her own home. She began to share the teachings with those that she knew best. Again, in her own words:

> Forthwith I went to call on my washerwoman, Mrs. Carrie York, who had raised three generations of children. Her true Christ spirit attracted me to her home as a good place to begin. To Carrie I explained the principles

> of the Baha'i teachings, the prophecies of the Bible and their fulfillment. An understanding of this was given to her and she was the nucleus of a class, meeting in her home, composed of friends and neighbors. We used the [Kitáb-i-Íqán], the "Book of Certitude," revealed by Baha'o'llah. This was the beginning of a Baha'i mission which multiplied into a number of such groups in several Washington regions.[4]

Pauline goes on:

> The meetings at Carrie York's so far as my experiences were concerned, proved to be the candle-stick from which the Light was spread. To these classes came ministers and teachers and people of various grades of intelligence, many of remarkable refinement. Often the discussions crowded midnight; then because of conditions in that pre-taxi era, one of the men would see me safe [sic] home, keeping at a respectable distance behind, despite urgent appeals to walk at my side. My husband disapproved of these adventures, but did not seek to prevent me. He watched, expecting this fire of zeal to burn itself out. In the end he became a tireless worker in the same kind of service as well as in many other branches of work for the diffusion of Baha'i Teachings.[5]

Next was Pocahontas Pope, her sister Alma's seamstress. Pauline claims that Pocahontas Pope was being taught by her sister, Alma, in the meetings at Carrie York's home. Pocahontas then "decided to open her home and invited friends and neighbors. This was the second of our Washington houses of faith," she explains. "Her husband was a minister, filling pulpits here and there; a fine man to enliven the interest with pertinent questions."[6] Stockman explains in his notes that 'Abdu'l-Bahá extolled Mrs. Pope as the first among her race to accept the Faith. Stockman figured since 'Abdu'l-Bahá knew she wouldn't have been the first Bahá'í of African descent, He must have considered her to be the first Native American Bahá'í. Her name also hints at this possibility as many African Americans can also claim Native American heritage.[7] However, in a letter Pocahontas received from 'Abdu'l-Bahá, which is quoted in Pauline's recollections, she put in parenthesis that He was referring to her being of "the colored race." Pauline goes on to say:

> Since Alma, now a believer, and I were very young in the Cause (and in knowledge) we had ample opportunity to recognize the confirmations of the Spirit of God, the answers coming without difficulty. One fruit of these meetings was a tablet or letter by Abdul-Baha to Pocahontas, in which He said:

> *Render thanks to the Lord that among that race thou art the first believer, arisen to guide others. It is my hope that through the bounties and favours of the Abhá Beauty thy countenance may be illumined, thy disposition pleasing, and thy frangrance diffused, that thine eyes may be seeing, thine ears attentive, thy tongue eloquent, thy heart filled with supreme glad-tidings, and thy soul refreshed by divine fragrances, so that thou mayest arise among that race and occupy thyself with the edification of the people, and become filled with light. Although the pupil of the eye is black, it is the source of light. Thou shalt likewise be. The disposition should be bright, not the appearance. Therefore, with supreme confidence and certitude, say: "Oh God! Make me a radiant light, a shining lamp, and a brilliant star, so that I may illumine the hearts with an effulgent ray from Thy Kingdom of Abhá ..."*

> During this same period, another home was opened to us, Rhoda Turner's. These meetings were outstanding in three points: First, white believers and friends also attended. Second, we had the privilege of introducing some of the then prominent Bahá'í speakers such as Hooper Harris, a real southerner, Howard McNutt, Lua Getsinger, Isabella Brittingham, Madame Dreyfus-Barney and others.[8]

After Pocahontas Pope and Mrs. York became Bahá'ís, they started holding meetings in their homes to which they would invite their friends. The Hannens would come sometimes as teachers. After a while though, Joseph and Pauline started inviting black friends to meetings in their own home—not a common practice at the time.

In Washington D.C., much like any other city in the United States at that time, people were not accustomed to seeing black people visiting white folks' homes for a social call. Even within the Bahá'í community, the idea of the oneness of humanity was a big stretch for those who were mainly attracted to the Faith because of its fulfillment of biblical prophecy or its teachings on spirituality. And for those who were able to accept the concept in theory, it was difficult to put it into action and prepare to be ostracized by friends and family.

Stockman reports that, "By 1908 fifteen black Americans had accepted Bahá'u'lláh in Washington. The interest spread. Soon a black minister in Greenfield, Massachusetts wanted to learn about the Bahá'í religion, and Corinne True wrote to Pauline Hannen to ask her advice about reaching Chicago's black population."[9] The community in Washington was beginning to diversify. They now had believers from a variety of cultural backgrounds as well as a range of economic levels. Also, in 1908 Mrs. Agnes Parsons, a member of the higher social class, was becoming interested in the Faith. She eventually became known as the "mother" of the Washington community, even though she wasn't the first Bahá'í in the area by any means. The role was bestowed upon her by 'Abdu'l-Bahá when He asked her to be an adviser to the community. Although she never would have dreamed it, she was destined to play a key role in the race relations of this often divided community.

In his book, *Some Bahá'ís to Remember,* O. Z Whitehead explains that Mrs. Parsons was forty-seven at the time she first heard about the Faith in 1908. She was living with her husband, Arthur Jeffrey Parsons, and two sons, Jeffrey and Royal, "in the large house of conventional elegance which she and her husband owned in Washington DC."[10] Until that point in her life she had mostly associated with those in her upper-class society. In 1910, she was invited to go on a pilgrimage to meet 'Abdu'l-Bahá. She had decided to base her decision about becoming a Bahá'í on her meeting with Him. When she returned she was a Bahá'í! Having considerable wealth and prestige in the wider Washington community, she was able to help the local Bahá'í community in many ways throughout the years. Including, for example, making it possible—through her generous financial support—for the first Bahá'í children's classes to take place. However, the same privilege that allowed her to support the Faith in many of its teaching endeavors, also presented its own challenges and obstacles. Her upbringing and social circumstances did not favor the work that needed to be done to bring racial harmony to the Washington community. Yet, because of her enduring love for 'Abdu'l-Bahá and her absolute obedience to His instructions, she answered the call with heart and soul. As directed by 'Abdu'l-Bahá, she organized the first Race Amity Conference and other activities focused on fostering racial harmony; her efforts brought wonderful successes to the Bahá'í Faith and much happiness to 'Abdu'l-Bahá.

Teaching among those of African descent was coming along quite well and several families were having classes and teaching their friends. However, there was not much mixing of the races; the Hannens, as well as a handful of other white Bahá'ís, held meetings in their home that were open to all and attended meetings in the homes of their African American friends. During this time, the Hannens befriended a man who was destined to become one of the foremost Bahá'í teachers of his era, Mr. Louis Gregory. Louis, a very accomplished African American, then introduced the Faith to some of his white friends, Mr. and Mrs. Dyer, who became vital participants in teaching those of African descent. They too began to hold regular weekly meetings in their home. Pauline recounts what happened as a result of those wonderful souls' services in this field:

> As a result of the meetings at the Dyer's, made up of inquirers of both races, Mrs. Coralie Franklin Cook, now a believer, realized the need of more space. Through her influence, we were offered another center for work. This was the Conservatory of Music (colored), Mrs. Marshall in charge. It was an ideal meeting place with spacious communicating rooms

and spiritual atmosphere enriched by superior music. Many earnest souls had been endeavoring to do their part in spreading the message of the Oneness of Humanity, often bringing their friends and inquirers to these meetings of Unity, as well as to the regular Washington Bahá'í Assembly meetings. Could any save the power of Bahá'u'lláh's Teachings bring such peoples of divergent minds and creeds together in such love and amity? His Words have the power to melt the hardest of hearts, if we but allow its warming influence of love to enter in.

In 1910 in a tablet to me (Pauline) 'Abdu'l-Bahá said:

> *Convey wonderful ABHA Greetings to Mr. Gregory and Mrs. Dyer and exercise toward them on my behalf the utmost kindness, for they are sanctified souls. They have opened their homes for the meetings and are kind and compassionate to the colored race." (July 5, 1910)*[11]

The above-named Coralie Cook, and her husband George, were both professors at Howard University with very impressive credentials. She was Chair of Oratory and he held the positions of Professor of Commercial and International Law and Dean of the School of Commerce and Finance. She became a Bahá'í in 1913. In an essay written by Gwendolyn Etter-Lewis, printed in *Lights of the Spirit*, one can read of the numerous accomplishments of Coralie, many of which had the aim of assisting young African American women reach their potential. The essay states that, "The Cooks heard about the Bahá'í Faith as early as 1910 through Joseph and Pauline Hannen . . ." and quotes a letter Coralie wrote to Mr. Hannen, dated 18 March 1910:

> You may be sure that the booklet from Mr. Wilhelm was received with grateful pleasure. I could not put it down until I had read it thru. The cover design is unique and the entire contents wonderfully appealing. If you can find speakers so impressive as those we listened to Sunday night it will be a *joy* to me to gather a company to listen to you. My friends were very generally impressed not only with the wisdom of your teaching but with the earnestness and *sincerity* of the teachers.[12]

The essay continues, "Coralie recognized the importance of exposing young Black women to people who could appreciate their potential and simultaneously provide them with a positive outlook on life. The well-being of Howard's female students was her foremost concern. They regularly organized Bahá'í meetings on campus mainly for the benefit of students." [13]

The following quote from Coralie touches on the style of teaching that Pauline in particular was well suited to, and for which she was much appreciated. Coralie mentioned in a letter to her, "Your many kind words and *deeds* have been a great spiritual help to me. . . . I am just beginning faintly to grasp the fact that I need the Bahá'í Faith far more for my daily tasks among unbelievers than I do when sitting at a board meeting." She continued, "I am praying for patience and wisdom to live my life so that I may not bring discredit upon the Teachings that have brought such joy to my weary heart." This spirit of giving and care was a key feature in the manner with which Pauline shared the Faith with others, and is expressed in many of the correspondences the recipients of her kindness left behind. Her sincerity bore many fruits, such as Coralie and her husband George.[14] In a letter written by Louis Gregory, included in Christopher Buck's biography of Alain Locke, Gregory states that George Cook, "although never formally declaring himself a believer, gave valued cooperation to the friends [Bahá'ís] in efforts to spread the Faith." The letter goes on to say, "On many occasions he expressed with earnestness and enthusiasm his appreciation of the great principles enunciated by Bahá'u'lláh for the perfecting of the human race, and unhesitatingly offered his home for Bahá'í meetings."[15]

In a short span of time, Pauline and Joseph had developed a nice group of African American friends—especially around Howard University—which was close to their home. Louis Gregory, later appointed as a Hand of the Cause of God, was among them. Since he called my great grandmother and grandfather his spiritual parents, I feel I can claim him as part of my own heritage as well.

- 7 -

A Radiant Pupil

Mr. Louis George Gregory found the Bahá'í Faith around the same time as Mrs. Agnes Parsons, and, together with several others, was unquestionably a dynamic force in the early years of the Washington D.C. Bahá'í community.

Mr. Gregory's attraction and eventual acceptance of the Bahá'í Faith will always be my favorite story about my ancestor's activities in the Faith, and the one in which I am most delighted. The following is Louis's account of how he became a Bahá'í, written in 1937, and sent to his teacher Pauline Hannen, in a manuscript titled "Some recollections of the early days of the Bahá'í Faith in Washington D.C."

> My first information about the Revelation of Bahá'u'lláh came in the latter part of 1907, just thirty years ago. Mention of it came from one who might have been regarded as traditionally foe. At the time I was a Federal employee in the Treasury Department. There were two fellow clerks, white and very elderly, occupying with me the same room, with my door between theirs. One of them was a one-armed veteran of the Civil War and a Native of New England, inheriting all traditions. The other was an intense partisan of the South, untouched in spirit by the influence which overcame slavery, but yet a man of unusual culture. It is amusing to recall how any question about the Civil War, innocently enough asked by me, would bring them into verbal conflict. They were both to me warm personal friends such as I hope never to forget in time or eternity. It was the southerner, Mr. Thomas H. Gibbs, who knew a little about the Bahá'í Teachings and was most urgent and insistent that I attend a meeting, which I had no inclination to do: as although I had been seeking, but not finding truth, had given up, because he had exacted a promise and I thought to do him a favor. I went one cold, blustery, extremely unpleasant night to the address he gave me, a room in the

old Corona building opposite the Treasury Department and long since demolished and supplanted by Keith's Theatre. The only occupant in the room when I entered was Mrs. Pauline Hannen. She gave me an unusually cordial welcome, identified me as a friend of Mr. Gibbs and told me that I would hear something very wonderful, though difficult. It would afford me an opportunity similar to that which would have been mine had I lived on earth as a contemporary of Jesus Christ. She urged me to get a full understanding of the message of today, that through it a work would be possible that would bless humanity. She kindly gave me three pieces of Bahá'í literature, *The Hidden Words, Daily Book,* and a small tract written by Charles Mason Remey. Soon thereafter entered another lady, Mrs. Lua Getsinger, referred to as "our teacher." A little later came two colored ladies, Miss Millie York and Miss Nellie Gray. So uncomfortable was the night that no one else came.

Mrs. Getsinger gave the Message historically recounting the appearance of the Báb and Bahá'u'lláh and of the great persecutions and martyrdoms in Persia. Her recital was brief but vivid. Mrs. Hannen invited me to another meeting. It was held at the home of the two colored friends previously mentioned, among poor people. Mrs. Hannen was the speaker and her loving service was impressive. She then invited me to her home where I would meet either herself or her husband for further teaching. Mr. Hannen thus became my teacher, a service in which he was aided by his wife. Over a period of over eighteen months I went to their home on Sunday evenings, sacrificing time previously given to social life. During this period Mr. and Mrs. Hannen went on their pilgrimage to the Holy Land. As they were my sole connection with the Faith, my interest waned during their absence. A long time afterwards I learned that they had kindly mentioned me to the Master who had instructed them to continue teaching me, assuring them that I would become a believer and an advocate of the Teachings. Upon their return they remade the connection. Through the very unusual kindness of these dear friends my mental veils cleared away and the light of assurance mercifully appeared within when they had taught me the Greatest Name and how to pray. I became a confirmed believer about June 1909 and thereafter cooperated with the Hannens in arranging meetings and trying to give everyone its message.

One curious thing was that by far the majority of my friends thought I had become mentally unbalanced. One of my old teachers, a professor of international law and a very affectionate friend, almost wept over my departure from orthodoxy and with others warned me that I was blasting all hopes of a career. *The Washington Bee,* a well known colored newspaper, on one occasion gave me two columns of ridicule which remained unanswered. Others knowing my controversial habits of the past said,

> "He must have religion since he does not answer that!" There were always some who were willing to investigate and the opposition seemed to promote inquiry.[1]

Pauline's recollections of that night are as follows:

> One night at Carrie York's, a handsome, intelligent-looking colored gentleman (yes, I mean just that), holder of degrees from several universities, entered that home. Abashed by so much scholarship (I had spoken to him before), I was flushed and nervous, but thought Baha'o'llah and Abdu'l-Baha sustained me and I taught the lesson without confusion. The visitor was so impressed with the Words of Baha'o'llah as revealed in "the Iqan" that he could not let it go. This was Louis Gregory. For a year or two he would attend the various meetings and at the close of the week would come to our home. He told us afterward, "I came wondering whether you and Mr. Hannen could talk intelligently on other subjects or only on Religion. I discovered you both are interested in many topics, but after a while you would both automatically return to the Baha'i Teachings. I thought there must be something in it after all." We had been praying that someone among the Negro Race would arise to serve them more effectively. We believed Louis to be the answer.[2]

The decision to become a Bahá'í was not an easy one for Louis. He was ridiculed by his friends who thought he was "mentally unbalanced," and joining a group of predominantly white people had a tangible effect on his standing in the Black community.

When the Hannens returned from pilgrimage Louis's interest grew again, and on 23 July 1909, he sent Joseph and Pauline a note of gratitude for their role in leading him to the Faith, and confirming his belief in its truth:

> It comes to me that I have never taken occasion to thank you specifically for all your kindness and patience, which finally culminated in my acceptance of the great truths of the Bahá'í Revelation. It has given me an entirely new conception of Christianity and of all religion, and with it my whole nature seems changed for the better . . . It is a sane and practical religion, which meets all the varying needs of life, and I hope I shall ever regard it as a priceless possession.[3]

One of the objections that many of Louis's friends expressed to him was regarding the practice of segregation in the Bahá'í community. Even though black Bahá'ís were teaching other black friends the Faith, and a few like the Hannens, Lua Getsinger, and the Knoblochs were holding meetings with both black and white friends, there were still many meetings taking place where only white Bahá'ís and their friends were welcomed. Concurrently, the United States was soon to go through one of its worst years ever in terms of racial violence. The year 1919, in Washington D.C., was known as the "red summer" because of the bloodshed due to racial prejudice. Given the atmosphere, the issue of integrated meetings in the Bahá'í community was being debated. Louis put into his own words his assessment of the situation:

> One matter that caused much difficulty in adjustment was handling of the American race problem, especially in Southern atmosphere of such a city as Washington. Some of the friends, reading the command of Bahá'u'lláh which read: "Close your eyes to racial differences and welcome all with the light of oneness," interpreted it to mean that all barriers of race should be put aside in every meeting that was planned for teaching the Faith. Others knew the principle as wise and just, but felt that the time was not yet ripe for its application. One difficulty was finding places, either private or public, that were willing to welcome all races. In the same family, one or more members being Bahá'í and the others not believers, the mixing of races would cause a family disturbance. Even where the believers were free from prejudices some felt that it would upset inquirers after the truth if they were confronted too soon with signs of racial equality. One of the friends went so far as to state that some of the Bahá'í principles would not be operative for a full thousand years! On the other hand, others were [insistent] that such principles should be upheld and applied even though the world should go to smash. As for a thousand years in future, there might be another Manifestation with laws for another day. But the laws for this Manifestation were for this day and must be applied.[4]

This issue would not be resolved in any short manner, and in Washington D.C., took years of difficult and courageous efforts on the part of Louis Gregory, the Hannens, the Knoblochs, and others to rectify. As Louis explained in the above passage, there were some among the community who were quite zealous about teaching the Faith and felt that if done "correctly," many people would become Bahá'ís. To their way of thinking, these prejudices were so ingrained and reinforced by a racist society that many would not even begin to investigate the Faith if it meant having to accept black people as equals. These Bahá'ís felt if the seekers could first come to accept the beautiful teachings of Bahá'u'lláh, which offered so many solutions to the world's problems and were such a comfort to the soul, then perhaps they would gradually come to accept His teachings on the equality of the races.

For several years this disunity existed in the Washington community. However, despite the prevailing attitude, teaching in the black community progressed steadily through the efforts of some of the friends. Through Mr. Gregory's efforts many highly educated African American's showed a serious interest in the Faith. Morrison tells us:

> In 1909 he [Louis] had written to the Hannens that he wanted to arrange a presentation of the Bahá'í teachings to a large meeting of the Bethel Literary and Historical Association. The hoped for meeting turned into a series of meetings, the fourth of which Joseph Hannen assessed in a report to the new national journal, *Bahá'í News,* the following spring.
>
> "The Bethel Literary and Historical Society, the oldest and leading colored organization in the city, devoted its session of Tuesday, April 5, to the Baha'i Revelation, Mr. Hannen and Dr. Fareed speaking on the subject of 'The Race Question from the Standpoint of the Baha'i Revelation.' This Society, of which Mr. Louis G. Gregory is President, has given three previous sessions this season to the Baha'i Teachings, and this has exerted a powerful influence in the work among the intelligent circles of this people, whom we are commanded to reach and help as brothers and sisters."
>
> In another report, Mr. Hannen mentioned two recent meetings arranged by the wife of a Howard University professor, at which Roy Wilhelm and Percy F. Woodstock, Bahá'í visitors from the New York area, spoke to interested groups of black intellectuals. Such a ferment of activity, focusing on individuals whose education and professional status made them eminently respectable on every count except color, could not be ignored by the white Bahá'ís. Obviously some action had to be taken to accommodate these people.
>
> The Washington community held its first formal interracial meeting during this period and proudly announced its success in the first issue of *Bahá'í News (1910).*
>
>> On the evening of March 6th, an important gathering assembled at the home of Mr. and Mrs. Hannen, representing the joining in one meeting of the white and the colored Baha'is and friends of the city. Considerable work is being done among the latter, and a regular weekly meeting is held at the home of Mr. and Mrs. Dyer, 1937 13th Street, N.W., on Wednesdays. [These were friends of Louis Gregory whose names he had given to Pauline as someone interested in the Faith and willing to start a class in their home]. In February of last year, Abdul-Baha commanded that to prove the validity of our Teachings and as a means of removing existing prejudices between the races, a Spiritual Assembly or meeting be held, preferably at the home of one of the white Baha'is, in which both races join. This is the first meeting of that character, and is to be repeated monthly.

> There were present about 35 persons, one-third of whom were colored, and nearly all believers. It is planned that every fourth Unity Feast [forerunner of the Nineteen-Day Feast], beginning April 9, should be held in such manner that both races can join. This is a radical step in this section of the country and is in reality making history.[5]

This Unity Feast has been reported in several publications because of its significance as the first feast with interracial participation. In *Bahá'í News,* Joseph reported that it was "notable because it was the first where the white and the colored Bahá'ís united, [it] was held and proved to be wonderfully blessed and successful. Several leading men and women of the colored race attended. Mr. Gregory gave the Message most eloquently. Mrs. George William Cook [Coralie] expressed in a few well-chosen words her approbation of the Cause. Several of the friends read Tablets and the children again chanted melodiously in Arabic. Miss Knobloch was the hostess of the evening. Our thanks are due to Mr. H. S. Cragin and Miss Stamper for the use of their home . . ." [6]

Robert Stockman confirms in his book the significance of these events not only in the American Bahá'í community, but in the nation as well. In reference to Louis Gregory's contribution to these efforts, he writes:

> Because he was the president of the Bethel Literary and Historical Society, the city's oldest black organization, Gregory was able to bring the Bahá'í Faith to the notice of Washington's black intellectuals. His awareness of the emphasis on racial integration implicit in the Bahá'í sacred writings caused him to write to the Working Committee about segregation in the Washington Bahá'í community. As a result, in March 1910 the Washington Bahá'ís began to hold racially integrated meetings. The significance of this act must not be underestimated; at that time Washington DC was a thoroughly segregated city. Although some churches may have held racially integrated meetings, very few if any were committed to creating a single religious community out of blacks and whites. The fact that the first Bahá'í community in the United States to reach out to black Americans did not establish a separate community for black Bahá'ís was an act of enormous significance for the future course of racial integration in the Bahá'í Faith. It presaged efforts which by the end of the twentieth century had so increased the religion's black American membership that perhaps thirty percent of the American Bahá'í community was of African descent.[7]

Some of the distinguished individuals attracted to the Faith at that time—Booker T. Washington, Langston Hughes, and W. E. B. Dubois among them—

are mentioned in several Bahá'í historical accounts. Alain Locke, a professor of Philosophy at Howard University, and considered by many to be the Dean and founder of the Harlem Renaissance, and the first African American Rhode Scholar, became a Bahá'í in 1918 according to his biographer Christopher Buck. Locke had a profound influence on the African American community and his theories of cultural pluralism, which he promoted over a hundred years ago, are now regaining popularity. Buck gives credit to the Hannens "playing a key role in Locke's conversion to the Bahá'í Faith."[8] Their determination to create an atmosphere of inclusion attracted many among the African American community in Washington, and some of them quite distinguished.

As the years passed, Louis Gregory and the Hannens developed a very close relationship, which can be seen in the many letters they wrote to each other. Louis eventually became so involved in teaching the Bahá'í Faith that 'Abdu'l-Bahá sent him all over the American South, as well as other parts of the world, to spread the Message and promote racial harmony. During those trips, he regularly corresponded with Joseph and Pauline; their friendship is evident when, in a letter written in 1911, Louis called Pauline "My dear Bahá'í sister."[9]

It didn't take Louis long before he plunged into the teaching work even more fully. Morrison writes, "In 1910 he made his first teaching trip, stopping in eight Southern cities, including Richmond, Virginia; Durham, North Carolina; Charleston, South Carolina; and Macon, Georgia. He recalled that, 'in every city people were found who accepted the great Message, however crudely and abruptly given, and the spirit was powerful,' but communities were not established at the time, because 'the system of follow-up work was not then developed.'"[10]

Morrison goes on to say, "His second area of endeavor was Bahá'í administration. Well suited by his education and legal training to become a leader in the Bahá'í community, he was the first African American elected to a Washington D.C. Bahá'í office in February 1911, less than two years after he became a Bahá'í, when a special election was called to fill a vacancy on Washington's Working Committee."[11] Louis wrote to Joseph Hannen on that occasion:

> I have your kind favor of the 4th, advising me of the action of the Working Committee of the Bahá'í Assembly in electing me to membership. My emotion upon reading it was a commingling of pleasure and embarrassment. There is joy, because I know that this action springs from a noble impulse on the part of the committee. It evinces breadth and the Guidance of the Spirit. Who knows how far-reaching the effect will be in advancing the Cause of God in the future?
>
> The embarrassment is due to the fact that what is truly a great honor should be given one so unworthy. I agree to serve temporarily, until someone with a wise head and noble heart may be found, who may thus more fitly represent my race."[12]

When 'Abdu'l-Bahá, after forty years of living under house arrest as a prisoner of the Ottoman Empire, was finally released from travel restrictions, He left the Holy Land for the first time and traveled to Egypt. It was from Ramleh, near Alexandria, late in 1910, that He sent Louis Gregory an invitation to come "in the spring." Mr. Gregory reserved passage on a ship sailing from New York on 25 March 1911. He was able to plan an extended trip that included stops in Europe as well as in Egypt and Palestine. Many fellow-Bahá'ís in Washington, well aware that Louis Gregory was the first black American to have the privilege and opportunity of pilgrimage at the express invitation of 'Abdu'l-Bahá, shared his excitement. On 22 March, Mr. and Mrs. Andrew J. Dyer's regular Wednesday Bahá'í meeting became a surprise farewell party, attended by more than fifty Bahá'ís and guests. Even though the Wednesday meetings were comprised primarily of black friends, on this occasion a number of white Bahá'ís participated. Joseph Hannen wrote of the evening in *Star of the West*:

> Mr. Gregory was given the seat of honor, at the head of the long table, and his chair was surmounted by a horse-shoe of flowers. While refreshments were being served, speeches were made by a number, including Dr. W. B. Evans, Principal of the Armstrong Manual Training School; Judge Gibbs, former U.S. Consul to Madagascar; Professor W. H. H. Hart, of Howard University; Professor G. W. Cook, of Harvard University; Mr. Edward J. Braithwaite; Mr. Duffield; Miss Murrell, of the faculty of Armstrong Manual Training School; Miss Grace Robarts; Mrs. Claudia S. Coles; Mr. Charles Mason Remey; Professor Stanwood Cobb; Mr. And Mrs. Hannen. Mr. Gregory responded in a feeling manner to the good wishes expressed. [13]

The following is from Pauline's personal recollections:

> Several years afterward Louis Gregory, in response to a letter of request received permission to visit Abdul-Baha in Palestine and made the Holy Pilgrimage. To this day he addresses me as "Little Mother." On the eve of his departure we made a banquet at which both races were represented. It was a joyous occasion for all, but for Joseph and me a solemn one. Our pupil was now to meet his Great Test. Would he turn out to be the answer to our prayer? Mr. Hannen was toastmaster. I asked him not to call on me, as I was so deeply moved I felt it would be impossible to articulate. After all, however, he thought it best to get me to my feet and prepared the way with a toastmaster's joke. Then among other things he said: "One is present who is the spiritual mother of two big sons, one white and one black." Trembling I rose [sic] and these were the potent words of my response: "Mr. Gregory, you are on the eve of meeting your Greatest Test.

When you return to us you will not be the same. You will be changed. You will be a different Gregory, never again the same."

A few months later Miss Margaret Doering, a believer resident in Stuttgart, Germany, where Louis Gregory visited en route homebound from Palestine, received from Abdul-Baha a letter attesting the fulfillment of that prediction. Abdul-Baha wrote:

> *Your letter arrived, and its contents showed that Mr. Gregory, by visiting the Blessed Tomb, hath received a new power, and obtained a new life. When he arrived at Stuttgart, although black of colour, yet he shone as a bright light in the meeting of the friends. Verily, he hath greatly advanced in this journey, he received another life and obtained another power. When he returned, Gregory was quite another Gregory. He hath become a new creation. Reflect on the Grace of the Kingdom of Abha and see how it enlightened such a person. It has made him spiritual, heavenly, divine and a manifestor of the graces of the world of humanity. This man shall progress.* [The translation of this passage is from Star of the West, vol. II, no. 7, p. 6]

Louis has since carried the Baha'i Teachings from east to west, from north to south. . . . This fulfills a hope of Abdul-Baha expressed in a tablet of 1909 written to Joseph and me after His release by the Young Turks from imprisonment under the persecuting Mohammedans. [To be clear this Tablet was addressed to Louis Gregory but the sentiments were expressed to the Hannens while on pilgrimage]:

> *I hope that thou mayest become a herald of the Kingdom and a means whereby the white and colored people shall close their eyes to racial differences and behold the reality of humanity, which is the universal unity. In other words, it is the oneness and wholeness of the human race, and the manifestation of the bounty of the Almighty. Look not upon thy frailty and thy limited capacity; look thou upon the Bounties and Providence of the Lord of the Kingdom, for His Confirmation is great and His Power unparalleled and incomparable. Rely as much as thou canst upon the True One, and be thou resigned to the Will of God, so that like unto a candle thou mayest be enkindled in the world of humanity and like a star thou mayest shine and gleam from the Horizon of Reality and become the cause of the guidance of both races.*[14] [This is the updated authorized translation.]

Another example of the closeness of the relationship between Louis Gregory and the Hannens can be found in a letter written 19 September 1912 from

Louis to Pauline, telling her about the approach of his marriage to Louisa Mathew, a white believer, to whom 'Abdu'l-Bahá had encouraged him to propose. Mixed marriages at that time were almost unheard of and certainly in the southern states like Virginia and Maryland, were not acceptable to most people. They were, in fact, illegal in many states. This was assuredly a test even for the Bahá'ís, who purportedly believed in the oneness of humanity. Although they held a fondness for each other, had 'Abdu'l-Bahá not suggested this marriage to Louis and Louisa, they would certainly not have entertained the idea themselves. In his letter to Pauline, Louis reported:

> My marriage to Miss Mathew will occur at noon on Friday, Sept. 27, in the parsonage of an Episcopal Church, N.Y.C. But please do not mention this except with the utmost discretion, as we do not wish any sensational newspaper articles written at the time and are exerting ourselves to avoid such things. How I wish you or Mr. Hannen might be present. Only a few persons will be asked to attend, no formal cards being issued.[15]

Certainly, his willingness to share this important event in his life, which he only shared with a few intimate friends, shows his great trust and confidence in the Hannens. He added this postscript in his own handwriting:

> My fiancé and I find ourselves growing into wonderful harmony and are seeking guidance to higher spirituality. Last year we visited 'Abdu'l-Bahá in Ramleh and the Holy Tomb at AKKA and although greatly attracted to each other not even divinely realized its future bearing. Last Sunday we prayed for Guidance at your mother's grave after reading the visiting Tablet—the light grows brighter and brighter—we were happy and content with the Will of God.[16]

In September of 1912 Louis wrote another letter to Pauline, sharing the details of his marriage to Louisa. With 'Abdu'l-Bahá's praise and much prayer, they were successfully wed in a quiet ceremony, using the utmost discretion, as 'Abdu'l-Bahá had advised, in order to avoid criticism. Louis wrote, "Our prayers have been heard and answered and we are very happy." He wrote four pages describing the ceremony in detail for his friends who were unable to attend.[17]

The character of these letters illustrates the deep care and respect Louis held for his spiritual parents in the Faith. From these and other historical accounts of the Washington Bahá'í community, one can see the effect the Hannen and Knobloch families had, when in overcoming their own personal prejudice, they responded to the call for unity of the races. Their efforts to encourage the oneness of mankind; establishing bonds of friendship and trust; inviting people of color to their homes, and, in turn, visiting them in their own homes;

brought about such wonderful victories for the Faith. Joseph, in his own words described the significance of his association and friendship with Louis Gregory in a letter dated December of 1919:

> Let me say that you can never ask anything of me that I shall not gladly grant. For you have done much for me, if I may have been privileged to be of some little importance in your life. Often, when I wonder what I have done in my Bahá'í work that is worthwhile, my thoughts go to you and your splendid work, and I feel that it is quite worth living, to have helped to guide such a noble soul to the Kingdom.[18]

Gayle Morrison shared that this letter was so treasured by Louis that he retained it in his papers until the end of his life. The following words sum up her assessment of Louis's contributions to the Cause;

> Louis Gregory proved to be an agent of change in the Washington community. He was the first black from the "talented tenth." A cultivated and articulate Lawyer, distinguished in appearance and bearing, he was not deterred by any lack of education or social standing from assuming an active role or from challenging the community's racial practices. Under his questioning, the old, unconsidered habits of segregation had to be confronted by the community; and, once the issue had been raised, it could not be dismissed. Louis Gregory began, quietly but uncompromisingly, to lay the groundwork for changes he knew were inevitable."[19]

A Tablet from 'Abdu'l-Bahá expresses His good pleasure with the teaching work going on in Washington. In the original, the following lines were written by the blessed hand of 'Abdu'l-Bahá:

> *O ye dear ones of Abdu'l-Baha!*
> *In the world of existence the Meeting is blessed when the white and the colored race meet together with infinite spiritual love and heavenly harmony. When such meetings are established and the participants associate with each other with perfect unity, love and kindness the angels of the Kingdom of Abha praise them and the beauty of Baha'o'llah addresses them; Blessed are you and again blessed are you!*
> *(Signed) Abdu'l-Baha Abbas*
> Translated by Mirza Ahmad Sohrab, May 5, 1910 Washington D.C.[20]

- 8 -

Alma Knobloch Answers the Call

There were several significant occurrences that impacted the Hannen and Knobloch families during these years. One of them had to do with Alma Knobloch, the middle sister. In 1907 she made the life-changing decision to pioneer to her homeland, Germany. She was obviously well suited for this service as she was born in Germany, steeped in the culture, spoke fluent German, and would be able to relate well to the people of that country. She also had relatives there who would be helpful when she arrived. 'Abdu'l-Bahá had asked for someone to carry the glad-tidings of the advent of Bahá'u'lláh into that country and she accepted the call. She left for Germany in July of 1907. Her personal accounts of this trip can be found in two different memoirs and many personal letters that she wrote, at least once a month, to her sisters in the United States. This first account gives details about events leading up to her decision to go to Germany:

> One evening after retiring to my room, after prayers, great waves of spiritual Fragrances were felt most powerfully & a distinct voice was heard, mentioning services & Ahmad's name very clearly. When the call came that Ahmad should try his utmost to secure a severed soul who would go to Dr. Fisher in Stuttgart to assist him in teaching the Cause, Ahmad showed his Tablet, which was written in Abdul-Baha's own Hand & trembling to Fanny to read, she immediately said, "Oh Ahmad that is meant for Alma, if she will go I will pay her way." Fanny sent me a copy of the Tablet & I felt as though I already knew about it & wrote and said I would go. Telling the Buffalo believers about it & showing the Tablet—they said, "Oh no—that is not meant for you. That is meant for someone else. Abdul-Baha has sent you to us." [Remember that Alma had just recently made a move to Buffalo, NY and was having good success there teaching the Faith. The friends were not happy to see her leaving so soon.]

In about a week or ten days, trying to do the best I could, keeping some of the many engagements & canceling some, [I] reached home leaving only a week to get ready. Berth was secured, & the time went all too quickly. Ahmad called to see how things were progressing & asked if I had my steamer ticket. Replying to the affirmative, I asked would you like to see it? He replied yes—and I showed it to him. The day before leaving, wishing to have everything in place, looked for the ticket. It was nowhere to be found. Remembering having shown Ahmad a new book, carefully paged through the book many times—but no steamer ticket. Fanny telephoned to the Steamship Agent & explained the matter & they promised to inform the Steamship, it would be all right. How it rained that day the 17th of July 1907 Dear Mother, Pauline, Joseph, Carl, Mr. Ed Struven, Ahmad.

After the steamer H. H. Myer was in motion & had left the pier [I] was called into the Purser's office & identified by Mr. Schoemaker the Agent of Balh [?] who explained the situation & gave necessary recommendations. This was proven later, after several ladies had asked me if I had secured my card for the table—which I had put off as long as possible not having my ticket, naturally thought that I would be placed at the most undesirable place. At last I went in & asked for my card. Looking at me for a while, [he] then turned & gave me a yellow card. I had noticed that all on deck had received red cards. It took all the courage I had to go in to dinner & was one of the last ones, was rather surprised when handing my card to the waiter, that they should show me such marked respect & was ushered to the head of one of the two long tables, the Captain at the head of the other. My time for active service of the Cause had begun.[1]

A full account of her teaching work in Germany, "The Call to Germany," can be found in *The Bahá'í World, Vol. VII*, pp. 732–45. I will include a few parts of this account to give an idea of the many successes she accomplished for the Faith while she served in that land:

> There are some experiences in life that one never forgets. Running upstairs one day to speak to our saintly Mother, I stopped at the threshold of her door with awe—mother was praying. This heavenly sight was indelibly impressed upon my heart, and there was no need for questioning. Quietly withdrawing, I, from that time on, never became deficient in the one great hope that Germany might become illumined with the Light of Truth, and be permitted to take her place in establishing it in the world.
>
> The opportunity came while I was teaching in Buffalo, N.Y., in 1907. My dear sister, Fanny, made it possible for me to take this trip. The following are some of the words of Abdul-Baha concerning the undertaking.

> *O ye beloved Maid-servants of God, the bounty of the True One hath elected you from among the maid-servants in order that ye may engage yourselves in the services of the Kingdom, spread the Verses of the Lord of the Realm of Might, become the cause of guidance of the souls.*
>
> *Truly, I say, Miss Alma Knobloch will show forth and demonstrate on this trip that she is a beloved maid-servant in the Threshold of Oneness, is wise and intelligent, and spiritual in the Kingdom of the True One.*
>
> *A great service is this, for it is conducive to the descent of the eternal outpouring and the cause of everlasting life. All the affaires of the world, though of the utmost importance, bring forth results and benefits for a few days, then later on they disappear and vanish entirely, except service in the Divine Kingdom, attraction to the Fragrances of Holiness, quickening of the souls, vivification of the hearts, imparting joy to the spirit, adjusting characters and the edification of the people. I hope that ye may become assisted and confirmed to this.*
>
> *Upon ye be Baha El Abha*
>
> *Signed Abdul-Baha* [This is dated 26 September 1907 and can be found in the National Bahá'í Archives]

While traveling on the ship, Alma had many opportunities to teach fellow passengers about the Faith. This in turn led to many opportunities to make contact with interested people in Germany once she settled there. After a short time in Bremen with Miss Bredemeier, who showed a good interest in the Faith, Alma moved on to visit relatives who lived in Germany.

> My uncle, Wilhelm Knobloch, a retired Professor of very high standing, carefully read the manuscript of the Iranian tablets which had been translated by my sister Fanny, by the wish of 'Abdu'l-Bahá. (These were later printed by her.) My uncle listened to the explanations that I gave concerning the teachings of Bahá'u'lláh and 'Abdu'l-Bahá, and about the fulfillment of Prophecy in the Latter Day. He was profoundly touched, and a few days later, made known his desire to serve the Cause. My heart leaped with joy, although outwardly I remained calm. I knew that his Mother had been a very saintly woman and also a Templar. This sect was founded on the Bible verse Malachi 3:1 "And the Lord whom ye shall seek shall suddenly come into His Temple." This faith spread throughout Germany and the founders thereof settled in Haifa, at the foot of Mt. Carmel expecting the coming of the Lord in 1863. Both my uncle and my aunt were most kind and helpful in introducing me to their circle of friends. These I found to be sincere and progressive in their attitude toward the Principles of Bahá'u'lláh and they all developed a greater consciousness of the Oneness of Mankind.

Several very pleasant weeks were spent at Leipzig. My new friends assured me of their good wishes and saw me off to Stuttgart, my real destination. There I was expected to assist Dr. E. Fisher in teaching the Cause.

In Stuttgart, on Aug. 9, 1907, a very beautiful lady greeted me with the Greatest Name, and from that moment we became friends. Miss Doering and I were inseparable throughout my fourteen-year stay in Germany. Dr. Fisher and Mr. M. Geenschweig appeared and greetings were exchanged.

Dr. Fisher had done some very fine preparatory work and had interested a number of very fine souls in the Bahá'í Teachings. Miss Doering arranged for a group of young girls at her home where also lived Frau Palm. This group was happy to receive the message from 'Akká and Frau Palm became attracted and a believer. From all sides, doors opened and invitations were received to go and teach those who were interested in the Faith.

It is pleasant to recall the hours spent at the Air Health Bath. . . . This was an ideal place to tell of Spiritual Truths. To me it seemed surprising how many became interested. Many looked forward to those talks and later made visits in our home. A number of these young ladies became beautiful believers.

The weekly group held at the home of Frau Palm, grew in strength and numbers. By Sept. 1907, Miss Doering and I had occasion to visit Heilbronn and meet some people who were friendly toward the Cause. There, the parents of Miss Schaffer gave us a hearty welcome. From there a delightful trip was taken into the beautiful Schwabisch Alps. We visited Miss Scheuerle and family at Pfadelbach. They were deeply touched by the story of the messenger of God at 'Akká. Miss Scheuerle is an outstanding young woman of high esteem in her noble work. We returned from the trip with grateful hearts for all the kindness shown us and for the divine assistance received.

In October, Frau Med. Rad v. Burkardt returned to Stuttgart and invited Dr. Fisher and me to dinner at her palatial home. This unusually highly developed lady of great culture was deeply interested in promoting the Cause of God. She translated the Hidden Words into German.

Some of the Art students of Stuttgart became attracted and especially enthusiastic were Miss A. Schaffer from Heilbrönn and Miss Doetrich from Konstanz of the Boden Sea. They became earnest students of the Bahá'í Cause. From this time on the Club became our headquarters. Our Nineteen Day Feasts were held there for several years.

A committee of nine men with Herr A. Eckstein as chairman, formed the first working committee of the Bahá'í Cause. A hall was secured at the Burger Museum and I was asked to take charge of the teaching.

The Friday evening meetings at the Burger Museum increased in numbers and interest in the Teachings became widespread. Several groups were formed at which the Words of Bahá'u'lláh and 'Abdu'l-Bahá were translated. I spent four evenings a week with them at the various homes. . . .

That fall a unique Public Meeting was held, in Stuttgart. Herr Eckstein, a member of the Swedenborgian Club, a German, Mr. Dreyfus of France, and a Mr. Sprague of England, each made a talk in his own language. The meeting was well attended by well educated people. The Principle of Bahá'u'lláh concerning the need for a Universal Language and the need for establishing world contact was well brought out. All three speakers gave eloquent talks on the Bahá'í Faith. At the close of the addresses open forum was held for freedom of discussion. . . .

It was a great help to have some of the Bahá'í literature which had been translated into the German and published. We longed for more, and were delighted when Professor Christale translated, "One Year in India" into Esperanto. This was in great demand at the following Esperanto Convention. Other translations finally followed. The Peace Movement in Stuttgart became interested in the Bahá'í Movement and asked for literature.

One of our first German contacts, Mrs. Palm, moved to Tübingen and we were glad to have a new opening to give the message. She arranged several meetings for us. Miss Doering and also Carl Nategh could join in these weekend trips. [At this point Pauline and Joseph's son Carl had come to Germany to stay with his Aunt Alma and attend high school.] We also enjoyed visits to Miss Spidel at Ludwigsburg. About this time I commenced to receive letters, cards and communications from influential men, writers of note, and those interested in civic uplift. They encouraged me with books, pamphlets etc., expressing their appreciation of the efforts and help of the noble Bahá'ís.

'Abdu'l-Bahá and four of His Persian secretaries arrived unheralded April 1st, 1913. Our joy was beyond measure! We had been working and serving at the break of the New Day and now the Light of the Sun of Truth had flooded the land and we were grateful. 'Abdu'l-Bahá's Words gave new impetus to the Cause in this country and a number of meetings were held.

Friends came far and near to see the Master. There was a constant flow of visitors at the Hotel Marquart. There, 'Abdu'l-Bahá received them with such love and graciousness that they became radiant with joy and happiness.

On 'Abdu'l-Bahá's arrival I asked Him for two meetings; one for the Youth Group at Esslingen and one for the ladies.

Miss Köstlin, who had been doing a marvelous work at Esslingen, arranged a beautiful meeting there, to welcome 'Abdu'l-Bahá. It was held April 4th, 1913 in the afternoon. This date is commemorated each year in memory of 'Abdu'l-Bahá's visit.

The following evening 'Abdu'l-Bahá graciously addressed a large and distinguished gathering of friends who had come from far and near. The meeting was held at the Museum, a most exclusive and elegant Hall. The Master called me to select a subject for the evening and I told Him "On Women." Smilingly, He questioned, "On the German Women?" I answered "No, on Women in general." His face beamed with that radiance that brought divine fragrances and He said, "Very well, very well." 'Abdu'l-Bahá enlarged on the women in Iran. His address was highly appreciated, especially by those noble, esteemed ladies, who had so marvelously assisted us in our early work. Our gratitude was boundless for the blessings received during 'Abdu'l-Bahá's visit and also during His week's stay after His return from Budapest and Vienna.

To me, one of the most outstanding events occurred when I called on 'Abdu'l-Bahá one morning and asked Him to attend our Bahá'í Meeting that evening. He said that He would if it might be scheduled for 4 P.M. that afternoon. Overjoyed, I rushed to inform the Believers and to make the necessary arrangements, it was then noon and now the time was very short. The ladies at the Frauen Club were most obliging in letting us have all the rooms and in preparing for the Unity Feast. We expected about 150 and over 160 attended. The ladies of the Club beautifully decorated the tables and the rooms with gorgeous flowers.

'Abdu'l-Bahá arrived at four o'clock and walked thru the rooms giving greetings to the friends before taking His place at table. His face shone with pleasure and a happiness that was divine. All the believers beamed with love and joy. The lecture was translated by Mr. Herrigel and all felt the inspiring Spirit which permeated the atmosphere and penetrated the very soul of all present. Each felt baptized with the power of the Spirit and the Fire of the Love of God. The rooms were filled with the fragrances of the Abhá Kingdom.

The following morning when I called upon 'Abdu'l-Bahá, He said that the meeting was blessed. "It will never be forgotten in the future generations. The Supreme Concourse of Angels were pleased and rejoiced. It was an illumined meeting, giving eternal life to mankind. The Apostles of Christ did not know that the Last Supper would be commemorated throughout the next two thousand years."

Professor Christale, President of the Esperantists of Europe invited 'Abdu'l-Bahá to speak at one of their meetings. This 'Abdu'l-Bahá kindly consented to do and a large meeting was arranged at their Club. 'Abdu'l-

Bahá's address was very significant in that He especially stressed the Principle of Bahá'u'lláh, the need for an international language. The professor, in expressing his deep appreciation and thanks for 'Abdu'l-Bahá's presence, brought out the need for an international language, since 'Abdu'l-Bahá spoke Iranian. This was translated into English and finally translated into German.

We all felt that a new life had begun and that now the Cause in Germany was established. Before leaving 'Abdu'l-Bahá said, "The Cause has thrown so universal a reverberation through the pillars of the earth that the Divine Power of Bahá'u'lláh shall encircle the globe. Be assured."

Within the week after my return to Stuttgart, I took an extended Northern trip, stopping over in many places that had been visited on previous occasions. A number of these friends had met 'Abdu'l-Bahá in Stuttgart and expressed their love and esteem for Him. Making Leipzig my permanent home, I went from there to a number of places. At Leipzig, regular weekly Bahá'í Meetings were held at an attractive hall near the university.

A number of influential people became interested in the Teachings in the central and northern part of Germany and we were happy to respond to their call, in order that they might hear more about Bahá'u'lláh and 'Abdu'l-Bahá. One of these cities was Bautzen, our saintly Mother's home. This palatial homestead became illumined with the Light of Truth and several became believers. Some of the Roessler family received glorious words from 'Abdu'l-Bahá. The Tablets were highly appreciated.

Although the world war [WWI] darkened the horizon, the activity of the believers was not interrupted. We increased our services in many ways. Bahá'í Literature cheered the hearts of many. My trips became more extensive but were confined to Germany. No government restrictions were made and our hearts were grateful.

A very eventful occasion was the dedication of a monument in memory of 'Abdu'l-Bahá and His visit to Bad Merkenheim. It consisted in a life-size head of 'Abdu'l-Bahá in bronze on a granite stone about six feet in height. It is placed next to the rose arbor and thus had a mass of exquisite roses for a background. The ceremony was very impressively conducted by the donor, Consul and Mrs. A. Schwartz. . . .

Our hearts were filled with love and profound thanks for the Tablet received from 'Abdu'l-Bahá, at this time. It is as follows:

April 9, 1920

. . . Therefore it is certain that the Teachings of the most High Bahá'u'lláh will in that region and country spread to the utmost, and souls from Germany will be like unto candles, enkindled and radiantly streaming beams into all directions. Therefore, I am giving thee the

Glad-tidings that the favor is directed upon thee and the Rays of the Sun of Reality are the adornments of your hearts. There is no greater confirmation than this."
'Abdu'l-Bahá Abbas
In humble submissiveness
Faithfully in His Service
Alma S. Knobloch
Cabin John Park, Maryland (signed)[2]

The Bahá'í World, Vol. IX, states that, "Alma worked incessantly, always effacing her own strong personality and accenting the Spirit of Bahá'u'lláh."[3] According to an article in Wikipedia, from the time Alma arrived in Germany in 1907, when there were just a few Bahá'ís in Germany, to the time that 'Abdu'l-Bahá visited there in 1913, the Faith had grown to over 300 members in Germany.[4] A truly remarkable accomplishment! Robert Weinberg, author of a book about Lady Blomfield, also acknowledges, "Alma Knobloch . . . built on the small nucleus of believers that Dr. Fischer had confirmed and raised the largest Bahá'í community in Europe by the end of the first decade in the 20th century."[5]

While Alma was living in Leipzig, she had the good fortune to befriend a future Hand of the Cause of God. Hermann Grossmann heard of the Faith from an American couple, the Obers, who had given a talk while passing through Germany following their pilgrimage to Haifa. When these friends returned to the States, the Grossmans and another couple made daily visits to Alma to learn more about the Faith. He and his wife Anna went on to become integral to the growth of the Faith in Germany, and their son, Hartmut Grossmann, later became a member of the Universal House of Justice.[6]

Because Louis Gregory had strong connections with the Hannens and Knoblochs, when 'Abdu'l-Bahá requested Louis Gregory visit Germany, Alma was excited to welcome him and held a reception in his honor. Morrison wrote, "Miss Knobloch assured his welcome in a land where non-European minorities were few and where, scarcely more than twenty years later, racialism, which Shoghi Effendi has termed one of the 'chief idols in the desecrated temples of mankind,' was to be enshrined by the Nazis in their country's political philosophy."[7]

As Alma mentioned in her memoirs, when war with Germany was declared in 1914 she stayed in Germany and continued her teaching work. Her memorial in *Bahá'í World,* Vol. IX, mentions that she suffered with her "German brothers and sisters, descended into the damp cellars with them, hungered and froze with them, renounced her American citizenship (which she later resumed), in order to be free to travel in the service of the Master; and indeed, the need of spiritual food was great at that time."[8] Yet in the many letters she wrote home to family during those years she was always reassuring her loved ones she was fine and had plenty to eat, even though food was rationed. She wrote glowing reports about how the German government took care of the people and knew just how much food was needed per capita. She even told of classes the government sponsored to teach the women how to cook most nutritiously with the least amount of food. According to these letters money and food was tight, but it didn't hamper her efforts to teach the Cause. She spent much of her time visiting wounded soldiers in the Red Cross hospitals and sharing the message with them. She wrote of many Bahá'ís who served on the front and were lost to the war. The hardest part for Alma was that during the two years the United States was in the war, she didn't receive any letters from her beloved family in America.[9]

The following letter from Charles Mason Remey, while he was visiting Alma in Germany, was sent to be published in *Star of the West.* It gives another perspective on the conditions and events that occurred during war times:

> Stuttgart, Germany, August 22, 1914.
> To the friends of Abdul-Baha in Washington, D. C., through the kindness of Mr. Joseph H. Hannen.
>
> Dear friends in His service:
> For three weeks there has been practically no opportunity to send letters to the friends in America. On account of this terrible war, communications are cut off in all directions, and here in Europe all conditions are most difficult; but now some Americans are going from here to America, so I will try to send this through their kindness.
>
> George Latimer and I were in Leipzig with Miss Alma Knobloch when the first hostilities began. There were some people in Leipzig who were attracted to the Cause, and the work bid fair to progress; but with the commencement of the war all was thrown into confusion and it was impossible to carry on any propaganda work in that city. Therefore, we decided to come on here to our objective point in Germany—Stuttgart. After much difficulty we got through and were followed in a few days by Miss Knobloch.
>
> Here in Stuttgart we found our Baha'i friends in great material trouble, but in a state of great spiritual attraction and enkindlement. Their beautiful spirit has been a lesson and a blessing to us.
>
> Although we are suffering humanly because of the suffering about us, yet our own difficulties are nothing compared with those of our German friends. There is hardly a household that has not a father, a brother or a son at the front, and each day brings the news of many killed and wounded—you may imagine the rest. I think of our Baha'i brothers

going thus to battle! They do not want to kill. They have only love in their hearts, but the conditions necessitate their sacrifice.

Yet despite all this human agony and misery, nowhere in Europe have we found such real spiritual warmth, peace and joy of soul as here in Stuttgart—here where the friends are all in the very vortex of material distress. Every night and every afternoon a meeting is held, and the spirit of the Covenant of God is always manifest in our midst. Through distress the hearts of the people are turned towards God, and many new faces are appearing in the meetings.

Dr. Habibollah and Mirza Azizollah, two young Persian Baha'is from the American College in Beirut, Syria, are also here in Stuttgart. Abdul-Baha sent them on their way to London, with a mission to perform in connection with the Baha'i Cause there; but they have been obliged to remain here in Stuttgart. . . .

Pray for the Baha'is in Germany, and pray for these multitudes who are soul hungry and are seeking the peace of God's Kingdom. May the friends here be enabled, through the Spirit of the Center of the Covenant, to carry God's Message to all of these hungry souls.

Love and greetings to all.

In His Covenant,

(Signed CHARLES MASON REMEY)[10]

Although the letters that Alma wrote during the war years are filled with interesting information and touching stories of her visits with the soldiers and her many sacrifices, space does not permit including them all. However, there is one letter I feel is especially interesting because it includes an explanation of how she was able to be so successful in her teaching efforts. The letter is included in its entirety as it gives a flavor of the many letters she wrote during that period. It also has an endearing portion where she talks about her own looks—she was, after all, known by some members of the family to be rather unattractive physically.

Alma to Fanny Munchen April 9, 1915
Allaho Abha!

My own precious sister Fanny!
Your good letter of March 12 was received today, & you can imagine how very glad I was to receive it. I had a good laugh about your description of my hair. Frl. Döring had always been scolding me about my poor way of dressing my hair. Well I will try my best to improve & please you both if possible. I must have caught your thoughts, for every time that I went through the business part of this beautiful city I stopped & looked at the

different photo places & thought it rather unnecessary expense that you would perhaps disapprove, still I did wish to surprise you with a decent picture of myself although I am not good looking & have no charms, still I manage to attract some people after all.

Rest assured I have plenty to eat. It is true we have each received a bread card with coupons for ½ pound bread, & I believe I am just like the rest, when told to be saving with the bread, I have more longing for it, & eat more than before. Everything in Germany is most carefully kept account of, so they could make careful calculation how much wheat & grain was on hand & how much would come per head, & there are no high prices & each one is provided for up to children to 1 year. There is plenty to hold out until the next harvest & the poor people are cared for, & everyone else. This could not be done in England, for they have not even control over London, much less other places.

Because prices have gone up some & it costs more to live, in my last letter I wrote that I try to keep within 100 marks per month, not counting extra expenses, but it takes more with the closest figuring. Have kept account of my expenses since I am here. No one knows how difficult it is before the Cause is well established in a place. I invite people to tea, call on the sick & of course bring them something, visit the poor & distressed & try & help them, visit the hospitals & now of course the Red Cross (Lazaretts). This all costs a great deal in all directions & I try & save on myself in some way the best I can.

To get acquainted in a place so as to spread the Cause is not an easy matter, not having any one to introduce me at any place & must work my way up through winning the confidence of the people first. This of course is not done in a few days or weeks. It is quite a different matter after it is established & visitors come & the Believers invite their friends to meet & hear their guests. I often wonder how it was possible that I could accomplish as much as I did, & still I am not at any time contented with myself. Later on, public lectures can be given in Germany as they are now given in America, but to make Baha'is it takes personal work.

Glad you sent Onkel Moriz the booklet. The man that printed it has accepted the Teachings & also his family. Their son was here Easter on a visit. He had been on the Front since Sept. & a few weeks ago he received a shot in the hand. I was asked to meet him. Well, I wish you could have seen him, a fine healthy, fine looking young man of about 22, rosy cheeks & smiling bright eyes. When telling his experience, he would smile so sweetly. He was with very good people in Belgium, who treated him very good, also in France. Conditions are not always as they are reported in any papers for they are continually changing. It takes cool nerves he said to do one's duty as best one can. The overall number of the others is very great, but they often fail to hit the mark. The English soldier is very good. He stands still when he finds that he has lost, but the French flees or gives himself up, not the other. He thought the soldiers from India were very handsome, fine built men, & they use rifles & shoot as the others. They are very meek when they give themselves up. Herr Domerhuber will be glad when the war is over, but is perfectly willing to serve until the end. I have received beautiful letters from the different ones from the front. They were so thankful for the Cards with the Glad-tidings & have asked for some for their comrades. I have never received so many Easter Cards & letters as this year. Frau Metzeroth wrote so kind & loving & signed herself d. truce Mutter. Her son is well & never lonesome & is at Stuttgart for Easter. She went to see Parsonal for the 3rd time. My trip with Battgers was very fine & wished you could have been along. Oceans of love,

Your devoted sister, Alma

Please do not worry about me & I have plenty to carry me through summer if careful.[11]

Before Alma returned to the United States, she visited Austria, Switzerland, London, and Paris. She taught wherever she went and wrote letters to all of her spiritual children.

Unfortunately, when the Nazi regime came into power, the Bahá'í Faith was banned in Germany, the Bahá'í centers were abandoned and confiscated, and the Spiritual Assemblies disbanded. According to Wikipedia,

> Following the fall of Nazi Germany, an American Bahá'í, John C. Eichenauer who was a medic of the 100th Infantry division then at Geislingen started searching for the Bahá'í community in Stuttgart. He drove through Stuttgart looking and asking for Bahá'ís and was able to find an individual by nightfall/curfew. The next day saw the first meeting of Bahá'ís since their disbandment in 1937. Two other American Bahá'ís, Bruce Davison and Henry Jarvis, in Frankfurt and Heidelberg respectively, also connected with the Bahá'í community in Germany. At the beginning of the partition of Germany there were about 150 German Bahá'ís in the American section and they became registered with the American authorities. The National Spiritual Assembly was re-elected in 1946.[12]

In one of the Tablets of the Divine Plan, a letter written to the Bahá'ís of the United States and Canada revealed on 11 April 1916, 'Abdu'l-Bahá writes of the contributions of Alma:

> *Likewise, Miss Knobloch traveled alone to Germany. To what a great extent she became confirmed! Therefore, know ye of a certainty that whosoever arises*

in this day to diffuse the divine fragrances, the cohorts of the Kingdom, of God shall confirm him and the bestowals and the favors of the Blessed Perfection shall encircle him.

O that I could travel even though on foot and in the utmost poverty, to these regions, and, raising the call "Yá Bahá-ul-Abhá" in cities, villages, mountains, deserts and oceans, the divine teachings. This, alas, I cannot do. How intensely I deplore it! Please God ye may achieve it.[13]

- 9 -

Loss of a Matriarch

In addition to the loss she felt when her dear sister Alma moved to Germany, another more permanent loss visited Pauline in 1908. The passing of Amalie Knobloch, her "saintly" mother, the matriarch of the family, to the Abhá Kingdom was a great loss to her and to the community. Amalie was sixty-six when she first heard of the Bahá'í Faith and was convinced by her daughter as to the truth of this heavenly message. She was highly praised by 'Abdu'l-Bahá for raising three daughters, "*each of whom has arisen to serve the kingdom like unto thee and is engaged in the guidance of the souls. In the Assembly of wisdom they are lighted candles; they sacrifice their lives in the Path of God; they are gardening in thy orchard and irrigating thy rose-garden.*"[1]

Amalie and her late husband emigrated from Germany in their adult years and as a result, they were unable to master the English language. Amalie's service was not in giving speeches and leading activities in the community as her daughters had managed so magnificently, but rather she would go to meetings, and sit, and smile beautifully at the friends, and her wonderful spirit enhanced the welcoming atmosphere of every gathering she attended. Pauline shares in her account to Ahmad Sohrab that her mother was present at all of the visits she and her sister Alma made to the homes of their African American friends. Both Alma and Pauline spoke of their mother's loving support when they faced difficulties. The word they used most often to illustrate her character was "saintly."

The most detailed account of Amalie's passing was one Pauline wrote to her sister Alma, who was living in Germany at the time and was not able to be with her beloved mother during her last days. It is presumed this letter was sent with Fanny when she met Alma and went on Pilgrimage with her to 'Akká. In the letter Pauline pours out all her feelings in an effort to reassure Alma that everything possible was done for their mother. The details of the following event sheds light upon why many thought of Amalie as a saintly woman:

Alla o Abha
My precious Sister Alma!
God willing I will try and write you as nearly as I can all about the last two weeks of Mamma's life upon this mortal earth.

On Wednesday night our sainted Mother was taken with violent pains in the back and thighs, she wept, and Fanny brought her coffee as usual, the pain had ceased—and in the morning Mamma said she was nearly alright, nothing but an attack of the Gripp. Fanny left for the office, but felt very uneasy and returned home at noon to find Mamma on the bed in the workroom, but Mamma said she is not so sick, only weak. Fanny came for me, and I too had gone to bed with the Gripp, but in a very few minutes I was ready, bought the medicine and went over at once. Dr. Parsons came and said: a hard case of Gripp, but thought if she stayed in bed until Sun. Mamma would be well. At this time it had been decided that Joe and I were to leave for Acca Oct. 15th and Mamma was so very happy that she might get well as quick as possible so she could take care of one of the Boys. This trip of ours made it necessary for Fanny to go away at once, her health was such that she had to go or I would have two, instead of one to nurse. Well, Fanny left Saturday thinking Mamma was much better, and of the two Fanny seemed most ill. I went to the house prepared to stay until her return, or until Mamma should be up and about. On Sunday Mamma was worse because the food would not stay on her stomach, and she had a chill. On Mon. Aunt Mary said we must try various forms of food until we find something she can retain. On Tues, the chill did not come, but fever set in until it increased to 106.

During the Wed. just one week from the time she was taken ill she had a most wonderful Dream. She called me to her bedside at 2 in the morning, and asked for coffee. I went downstairs, made fresh coffee and took it to her. After taking a sip she told me of her dream. She started by saying the Angel of Death had called her and thinking of me and my trip to Acca, she thought, Poor Pauline, poor Pauline, and asked God to let her stay long enough to do this one more service. In a little while she felt a most wonderful peace, and perfect stillness. She felt as though she were near Heaven. Suddenly there was a terrible upheaval and the whole World seemed to be in the throes of death, and she cried out! It is indeed the Day of Judgment and the People of the World are heedless. Just then, a dark something appeared in the room, and gradually took form. There stood a man with two glass symbols, one in each hand. There he remained motionless for a while, listening to the awful noises of the elements. Suddenly, with a terrible Crash of the symbols he shouted, "Divide! Divide! Divide!" Then turning to Mamma he said, "Are you ready?" Without awaiting the answer, he left.

Mamma said she remained still for a second, and did not feel that she was ready just yet because of our trip. She tried to pray once then again, and finally, the third time she cried out to God: Yes, Oh yes, I am ready, but if Thou O God doesn't see wise I beg to remain a little longer for this one more service, but now and forever let Thy Will work through me. Not my will, Oh Lord, but Thine be done.

I spoke cheerfully to her, telling her it was not the Angel of Death, but a spirit testing her, and that she must eat and take her medicine so that I might begin to get my things ready. All that day she was bright & happy and talked about the Assembly and my trip, of Alma, and her wonder at God's great Mercy to us all.

Toward evening she became delirious at times, & again she would explain in a loud voice, "Glory be to God, the Ruler of the seen and the unseen." Again, "Praise be to Thee Oh Baha, that Thou hast lifted the veil from our eyes, and hast made us to see Thy beauty." Again, "Oh the Glory of Unity if only the People could see it as I do, they would not notice any faults, All is perfect."

She was so bright, and at times witty, that Dr. Parson and I thought the dream had no power over her. She ate her food, longed for one thing or another to eat, which showed such an improvement that we believed the danger was past. During the night she was with the Angels all the time, and when she spoke to me she said: I am surrounded by an atmosphere which only angels can enjoy. At another time that night she said, I have seen the Glory of God and now I want—out of here. The wonderful part of it all was that when Mamma spoke of spiritual Truth, she spoke English, and when speaking of the things of this life, she spoke German. Wasn't that strange? Perhaps this was because the Truth was revealed to her in English.

On Sunday, she was much better than she had been for several days and again we thought unless there should be a change for the worse, she would mend rapidly. During the night Mamma had wonderful Dreams and awakening said: I want to go out of here. [She] spoke of our Assemblies as Heavens, always praising God for His Love and Mercy. But I realized she had been called, and that we were powerless to hold her even though we insist upon nourishing and giving the medicine. I could scarcely wait for day light, being alone with Paul. I had to wait to send for Aunt Mary. She had called twice Sat. and Sun., then phoned Joe to wire Fanny who had been very ill at Atlantic City, to come at once.

When Aunt Mary came she said: Your Mother is not so ill, but she wants to go home. We must have a Nurse full of life and Fanny to come to change the current of her thoughts.

Mamma was just living, and that was all, she was very low, in her conscious moments she asked, when would Fanny come home, we expected her at five o'clock, but the train was delayed again and again Mamma would say: Oh I can't wait any longer. Believe me Alma, between 12 o'clock and the time Fanny came I lived a hundred years. Everyone in the house was praying to God to give her to Fanny for one day and night. From five until 8 there were no signs of life, no pulse beat, and to all appearances she had left this earthly home for the Heavenly home. Aunt Mary and the Nurse said so but I did not believe God would punish me like that when I had made such a terrible sacrifice for Fanny's sake, nor did He, for the Greatest Glory and Bounty descended upon us after this. While we were waiting, watching and praying that Fanny would arrive in time, the elements were at war, thundering, lightning, the wind blowing a perfect gale, and with every crash of thunder, Mamma would lift her gentle face, illumined with the light of the Holy Spirit and whisper: I must go now, I can't wait any longer for Fanny. I would tell her she must wait, for that is what life is made up of. Then she would smile and say: Yes, yes. I will do anything you say.

At last, at last, the carriage drove up, Fanny came, our hearts were lifted up with joy and prayers of thanksgiving. I put my lips close to her precious ears and said: Shall I bring Fanny up? She opened her eyes wide and feebly pushing me to go, saying: Quick, quick. I want to bite a piece out of her. Don't say I ran down, no, I fairly flew and Thank God Mamma knew her. Many times during that dreadful night Mamma spoke to Fanny of different things and on Tuesday morning we three had coffee and cake together, Mamma taking just a wee bit, after resting a while, looking at the nurse, she said, "Dirty, dirty. I don't want to be dirty." Then although a bath and change of bedding had been made in the early morning, the Nurse and I bathed her, put on a fresh gown and sheets and pillow and made her comfortable. Then her gentle spirit slipped away for us for a little while, and we all thought it was over—when suddenly she awoke and without warning she began to give the Message to the Nurse, with a strong clear voice telling of the beauties of the Baha'i Revelation, saying that although she could not understand now, but when she heard of it again, she should remember that she (Mamma) assured her, while leaving this world that it is the only Truth—and now take Christ to your Patients. Then she turned to Fanny placing her hands on Fanny's bowed head and said: This will be a great test for you, don't waver, be firm, be steadfast. Then smiling up at me, she told Fanny to see that my new dress be made up pretty, and to make me look nice. Of course I said, Mamma I don't care for dress, at which looking at me so gently she said: I do want you to look nice. I left the room just then and she turned to Fanny and said: I will see the Master first and said more to Fanny. By this time I had phoned for Joseph for I realized we were receiving Mamma's blessing.

When I returned Mamma turned to me and said: Joey is perfect, he has no faults, stick to him, stick to him! What you see as a fault is nothing, sometime he will realize the great nothingness of it all, and it will be a puff and it will be past. He is good my Joseph. Pauline you must nurse Fanny and care for her, be a Mother to her, to my dear Fanny. Then came a vision, and we were asked: Which of you have that beautiful Shell? I smiled and said: Was it Fanny with a shell containing a Pearl of great price, which she is to share with the people of the World? Her face was luminous and she replied: Yes! Yes! That is it. Then her eyes opened wide and turning to me she said: Do you see the crowds of people, great crowds looking at you? They are afraid of you. I said: No Mamma, I can't see them, but why do they fear me? She looked so disappointed because I was so earthly and said: Not You, but the Truth in you. You will not waver, you will be firm. She gave several uneasy gasps trying to use the Greatest Name. When I put my ear to her mouth, she whispered: "I cannot say it anymore." Then I spoke into her ear saying: Don't worry Mamma, dear. We will say it for you, when you tell us to. We said Alla o Abha aloud again and again until the lines of trouble left her face and she was in peace. We did this many times, until she breathed her last breath. Every time she regained consciousness for a moment she would say: Alla o Abha and Fanny and I or Joseph and the Nurse would repeat the Greatest Name until again she had slipped away, even Mr. Remey would say it aloud for her and she looked so peaceful and happy.

To Aunt Mary she said: Oh here is our Angel. You have always been our Angel for nearly 25 years. You are blessed Aunt Mary. You know the Truth. "God is One, Truth is one, Spirit is One. The Master is the Great Light and many pure and lofty souls are upon this Earth who reflect this Glory."

This was said to Aunt Mary at the time when Mamma had blessed Fanny, the Nurse and I, we were all gathered around her bed, then she laughed and said, what are you all waiting for? Something that will never happen! So we dispersed and told her, we just had a nice little reception haven't we? Mamma then said some funny things to make us laugh, and we really did laugh, but I can't remember what was said. Then with a clear distinct voice she said, "Be happy. I tell you be happy. You would be if you could see what I have seen, and now I want out of here. But the Nurse keeps me back with her medicine and I want to go. Now, now I am doing the Master's work, my death in and He lives in me." [sic] Then she was exhausted and lost consciousness.

In a little while Joey came into the room, and we all thought too late. But, as he neared the bed, Mamma blinked, then opened her eyes wide and in a clear voice said: My Joseph. He kneeled by her side and said: Alla o Abha. Then she placed her blessed hands upon his bowed head and Oh such a prayer as Mamma offered up to God. It was heavenly and inspired. By this time it was nearly 12 o'clock and she became restless again and I asked if she wanted anything. In a weak voice Mamma answered, "My Boys." Carl was the first to arrive. He wept bitterly, but Oh the joy in Mamma's face when she said in a weak voice: My dear, dear Carl. You are a fine boy and you must work hard for the Master. Suddenly in a loud vibrant voice, so distinct so that those downstairs could hear as well as me, she lifted her hands and cried out to God to listen to her prayers for her little boys. Then she prayed, but Oh dear Sister, I cannot remember what she said, it made us all weep, so wonderful, so full of spiritual strength and power. When she saw us weeping she said: Be happy! I tell you be happy, then made some fooling joke at our expense and again we were all laughing, then quietly Paul came into the room, and her face was full of mischief as she said, here comes our little Rogue, full of life and fun. Then she placed her hands upon his bowed head, perfect silence reigned for a second then again her voice was lifted up in prayer to God; a wondrously touching Prayer for our little Paul.

After this we had lunch, Mamma having dropped into a deep sleep and to all appearances was dead. Fanny remained while the Nurse, the boys and I had luncheon at the table. The Nurse said, I do not understand all your Mother said to me, but this <u>I do know:</u> it was the Truth of God. Never in my experience as a Nurse have I ever witnessed or even hear tell of such a glorious death bed scene; to see such a pure soul leave this world with such joy and great peace, and to see the transfigured faces of you and your Sister when you would repeat that name for her. I shall never, never forget it as long as I live and <u>I shall use that</u> <u>name</u> too. I have said it to your mother <u>too</u> when you girls were resting or you had stepped out of the room, and she knew it and was at peace."

Really, it did not seem like death, but rather the passing of a Saint. When Fanny went to lunch, the Nurse went into the next room for a nap, she had remained at the bedside all night. Again I was alone with Mamma when she breathed the Greatest Name and gaining strength through it she said: are we all alone? And when I answered Yes, she said: listen carefully, when I pass out the Friends will say: Oh she was a Saint, she was a grand woman, such a good woman and things like that, but remember, I am no better than they, and now there is something I wish to have done yet in this world. When it is all over, give Paul and Carl five Dol. each and see that they start a little Circle among the Baha'is like the one you started in Wilmington, and ten dollars will be a starter, then tell Joseph to write up something in which he will mention the work of the Germans, how they established the Colony in Haifa; how the Germans are waking up spiritually through Dr. Fisher and Alma and how I, a German fully and completely accepted the Teachings of Baha'o'llah, and had a Baha'i Burial Service etc. He will know.

Then she shivered and said, "Brr, it will be very cold when you go to Acca. Alma is here. I see her, I see her. Dear Alma, she is doing the Master's work." That was the last time she spoke to me, and I think the last time she knew me. Then she asked me to pray for her, the Greatest Name nine times aloud. Again she fell asleep. When she awoke Fanny was kneeling by her side. She, taking one of Fanny's hands and placing her other hand on Fanny's head, she said: My dear Fanny, this will be hard for you, but do not waver. Be firm, be happy. I am happy and now I want out of here. Your love for me and my love for you holds me here. I want out of here. Both Fanny and I were kneeling at her side. Fanny smiling sadly asked: Do you want to leave us now mamma? and she nodded yes. Then I quickly said: We will not hold you here any longer. Mamma dear, you are going. Fanny then said: Have you no message for Alma? She looked at Fanny so pityingly and replied: Alma will become wholly spiritual. She is entirely under the care and protection of Abdul-Baha. What can I say more than this? She is blessed.

Then Fanny sang her two wedding songs for her. It sounded like an angel singing and Mamma looked very happy. Then she was still for a long time, only now and then struggling to pronounce the Greatest Name, and we would say it aloud for her, but she did not know us anymore.

About half past two Mr. Remey was announced and Fanny went quickly to welcome him and asked him up to take a last look at our dear Mother, believing Mamma to be too far away to be disturbed by his coming, but, wonder of all wonders, she struggled, then winked and blinked and by the time he knelt down and kissed her forehead she was looking at him with a face bright with the Light of God and said the Greatest Name so that he could hear it. He said it several times aloud for her while she slipped away. She regained consciousness again and repeated the Greatest Name feebly, but the third time her voice filled the house with Alla o Abha so that the folks downstairs heard it and were speechless with awe. That was the last time I can recall that she spoke aloud and was conscious.

After this we used the Greatest Name all the time. Fanny and I were alone with our beloved and it seemed to us as though Mamma's soul was being lifted heavenwards on the waves of the Greatest Name.

Was this not a very wonderful death? From Monday until half past three Wed. her blessed fingers were already turning blue before she breathed her last. . . .

Joe and I decided in the event Mamma should leave us, we would hasten the plans to leave for Acca to meet you on the way. Poor Fanny had nothing to do but submit. We made all the arrangements and did all we could to spare Fanny extra pain. She did only those things which I could not do. [In fact Joseph and Pauline decided to let Fanny go in their stead and they went a year later.]

So often during that last week Mamma would call me her dear little Mother, now you are my Mother and I am your little Baby. The Afternoon when Mamma's gentle spirit left the body we covered her with a sheet until Aunt Mary came. Then we three, Aunt Mary, Fanny and I prepared the body with the greatest reverence. Fanny and Aunt Mary bathed the body according to the Bahá'í Burial Service, each bathing one side of the body while I prayed aloud in which they joined. In the water was Oil of Cedar and Camphor, then a white Dressing Sacque and drawers, a white Rose and the Hidden Words in her hands, a sheet pulled over her, the window open, thus we left her to rest while we made the arrangements for the Funeral and Services.

The friends were very much surprised that Fanny and I seemed so happy instead of sad and really we believed the Church People thought us crazy, for they said to us, "even, Jesus wept at the grave of Lazarus." Alma dear, Mamma had expressed the command, "to be happy" so firmly and with such power that it was not in us to be other than happy.

On Friday morning at half past nine we came downstairs dressed in Mamma's black clothes except Fanny's waist and Jacket, which belonged to Clara. The Parlor Hall stairs were packed with Friends, principally Members of the Assembly. Uncle Moritz sat with us of course. The service was opened by Mr. Remey with the Greatest Name, then I started and all joined in chanting the First Commune. Mr. Remey then read some Hidden Words and prayer, then, all having a typewritten copy made by Joseph of the Burial Service, all responded to this. Then Ahmad chanted a Prayer of Baha'o'llah. Then five carriages filled with Friends and the Hearse winded their way to Prospect Hill Cemetery. Here Mr. Remey read a prayer, after which the two Boys, one at the head and one at the foot of the grave dropped three beautiful roses each, one at a time while they softly used the greatest name. Then each of the Family dropped one. Finally, everyone present did likewise, each having received a rose from Joe. The roses were "From Cushman to Mamma" and they covered the casket nicely. We then left the Cemetery . . . Mr. Remey and Ahmad remaining until all was done. They arranged the many floral pieces.

Everyone we have met since, have said it was a wonderful privilege to be present at such a service, and thought it the sweetest Funeral Service they had ever witnessed. Aunt Mary in speaking of it said it was more like the birth of a child than that we were mourning for the dead. A number of the friends were weeping, but there was no sound save that of the

Service, and absolute peace, yes even joy. We did not cry, and have not cried as yet. The moment we are inclined to cry, wonderful memories of her last words arise and self is forgotten in her joy.

Alma dear, if you felt hurt because I was silent so long, you will surely forgive me when you have read this long letter.

There is but one thing now to make me completely happy and that is when you two write and can say, "I have seen my Lord."

God bless you both, although He has already abundantly blessed you. This is my earnest prayer.

Affectionately,
Pauline[2]

The Tablet that 'Abdu'l-Bahá wrote for those who attended her funeral seems to capture Amalie's spirit and the spiritual influence she had in the family:

Through the Maid Servants of God Lua, and Mirza Ahmad
To the friends and maidservants of the Merciful who were assembled together on the 14th of October 1909, at the memorial service of Mrs. Amalie Knobloch, the one who has ascended to the Kingdom, of God.
Upon them be Baha El Abha!
HE IS GOD !
O Thou Almighty! O Thou Forgiver!
These souls have ascended spiritually to Thy kingdom, are begging Thy Bounty and Favor and are in need of forgiveness and providence.

O God! Thy Mercy is unlimited and Thy Favor is all-encircling! Immerse Thou these souls in the Ocean of Thy Generosity and Compassion. Shower upon them the Rain of Thy Mystery!

Thou art the Giver! The Generous, the Pardoner and the Clement!

O ye friends and maidservants of the Merciful!

Thank ye God that ye become assisted to be present at the Memorial Service of the Bird of the Rose garden of Immortality, Mrs. Amalie Knobloch, chanted the supplications, prayed and communed at the threshold of God, pleaded forgiveness for many souls and read Tablets and Heavenly Verses. All the inhabitants of the Kingdom of Abha were made happy thereby and became engaged in mentioning you.

You must never forget the beloved maidservant of God Mrs. Amalie Knobloch, always remember her and supplicate for her inexhaustible bounties.

Upon ye be Baha El Abha! (signed) Abdul-Baha Abbas

Translated by Ahmad[3]

In 1910 the friends in Washington received this wonderful Visiting Tablet, which was to be read at the tomb of Amalie Knobloch. Revealed by 'Abdu'l-

Bahá while Fanny and Alma were in Haifa after their mother's passing, this precious gift was no doubt a comfort to the family members who were left without their loving mother. This is the same Tablet Louis and Louisa Gregory read on a visit to Mrs. Knobloch's gravesite before they were wed. Joseph even wrote in the very first *Bahá'í News*, "The Visiting Tablet revealed by Abdul-Baha for Mrs. Amalie Knobloch has been read over her grave by a large number of the Baha'is of Washington on different occasions. March 13, Mr. Roy C. Wilhelm was accompanied to the tomb by a party of the young people; March 27, Mr. and Mrs. Kinney, Dr. Fareed and Mrs. Getsinger were visitors, with the Sunday School children completing the party. The obedience of the friends to this command to read the Visiting Tablet, is notable and a great blessing attends this act."[4] This Tablet is still shared today with friends in the Washington area who plan to go out teaching, and they are encouraged to read it at her gravesite.

THE FOLLOWING IS WRITTEN by ABDUL-BAHA'S HAND
"The believers in that City in which the Maid-Servant is buried must all go to her Tomb and read this Visiting Tablet.
(signed) ABDU'L- BAHA ABBAS
Through His Honor Mirza Ahmad
VISITING TABLET
Revealed for the Attracted Maid-servant of God, Mrs. Amalie Knobloch, who has ascended to the Kingdom of God!
HE IS GOD!

O, thou Pure Spirit, Amalie Knobloch! Although thou didst soar away from this terrestrial world, yet thou didst enter into the immeasurable, illumined universe of the Almighty. While in this life thou didst hear the Divine Call, beheld the light of Truth, became alive by the Breaths of the Holy Spirit, tasted the sweetness of the Love of God, became the Maid-Servant of the Lord of Hosts and the object of the Bounties of His Highness the Desired one.

Thou didst lead the erring ones into the Path of Truth and bestowed a portion of the Heavenly Food to those who are deprived. Thou didst consecrate the days of thy existence to the Service of the Fragrances of the Paradise of Abha. There are many souls perfumed and many spirits illumined through thy services!

O, thou divine, beloved Maid-servant! Although thou didst disappear from the mortal eyes, yet thou didst train and educate thy daughters, each of whom has arisen to serve the Kingdom like unto thee and is engaged in the guidance of the souls. In the Assembly of wisdom they are the lighted candles; they sacrifice their lives in the Path of God; they are gardening in thy orchard and irrigating thy rose garden. Happy is thy condition, for thou art enjoying Eternal Life in the Kingdom of Everlasting Glory and hast left in this world kind and loving Remembrances. Happy are those souls who visit thy luminous resting place and through thy commemoration receive and acquire spiritual Power!

(signed) ABDU'L-BAHA ABBAS.

Translated by Mirza Ahmad Sohrab, February 24, 1910, Washington, D.C.[5]

- 10 -

Fanny and Alma Meet the Master—Pilgrimage Accounts

At the turn of the century, pilgrimages to the Holy Land were obviously quite different than they are today. Without the modern conveniences of air travel and bus rides, the trip at that time was extremely arduous. Many accounts of early pilgrimages told of exhausting and sometimes dangerous voyages on steamships, followed by days of further travel over dusty roads. In order to go to 'Akká to meet the Master, one had to first obtain permission to go, which is not unlike today. In those days, upon arrival, the pilgrims were met by Persian friends and escorted to the home of 'Abdu'l-Bahá, where they would often stay for the duration of their Pilgrimage. Afterwards they often met with members of the holy family, 'Abdu'l-Bahá's wife or daughters, who would then prepare them for their visit to the holy sites.

The groups that went on such visits in those days were quite small and were able to have an intimate audience with 'Abdu'l-Bahá Himself. They developed relationships with members of the holy family that often lasted a lifetime. 'Abdu'l-Bahá took great care to nurture and instruct the early believers in such a way that when they returned home they were better prepared to spread the teachings and further the aims of His Father's Cause. The pilgrims spent the majority of their time in 'Akká where 'Abdu'l-Bahá was still a prisoner and unable to go far from the city limits. Pilgrims would stay in the same home with the holy family and, to some extent, suffered the same hardships. However, the spiritual benefits of such an experience far outweighed any challenges one might face.

From 7–13 November 1908, Fanny Knobloch along with her sister, Alma and a good friend, Ida A. Finch (who was the daughter of the Phelps family that had been a part of their Bahá'í circle of friends from the beginning) were blessed to take part in one of these early pilgrimages. Originally their tickets had been intended for Pauline and Joseph, but due to the passing of Amalie in 1908, the Hannens decided to give the tickets to Fanny and Mrs. Finch and postpone their own visit for another year. They also felt that it might help Alma ease the pain of losing her mother if she could spend time with her sister Fanny and, of course, be with her beloved Master. As Alma was already living in Germany at the time, Fanny met her in Naples, Italy along the way.

The following account, written by Alma later in her life, is full of her feelings of expectation about meeting 'Abdu'l-Bahá and the holy family. It includes some of her preparations and a glimpse of the trip from Germany to 'Akká, as well as many heartwarming stories of their times with 'Abdu'l-Bahá and the women of the holy household. It should be noted that when reading her accounts of 'Abdu'l-Bahá that these are "pilgrim's notes" and words attributed to Him are neither authenticated nor authoritative, but rather they are her own recollections and impressions:

> While at Leipzig a letter coming from Fanny was received telling that our mother had passed out [died] & to meet her at Naples & join her and Mrs. Finch to visit the Beloved at Acca. I immediately started for Stuttgart, saw as many of the believers as possible, many petitions for Abdul-Baha [were given], & in two days was on my way. Herr Eckstein & his sister accompanied me as far as Zurich & safely placed me on the train for Rome where I spent several most delightful days, reaching Naples a day before Fanny arrived. Here we stayed four days, taking several delightful trips of interest, of which Pompeii was one.
>
> At last the time came to leave for Alexandria where we were met by believers who showed us so much affection and kindness simply because we were on our way to the Beloved Master. In two days our steamer left for Haifa. What joy and expectation! Would we find all we expected? Our expectations were high—Perfections in a human body—His surroundings reflecting His Divinity, His followers super humans giving forth the Light & spreading the Fragrances of God's love. His family purified from all dust of the world, beautiful flowers in the Garden of the Abha Kingdom. A heavenly Home of peace in a prison town, Acca inhabited by only State prisoners of a very low life, surrounded by a high wall & soldiers guarding the entrance to the city gate. All these & many more, all of which had left their deep traces. Reaching Haifa we were met by believers who showed the same loving kindness & giving forth the same beautiful heavenly light as the believers in Alexandria. We were made comfortable at the Hotel Carmel & later called for to visit some of the Daughters of the Master & His wife, the Holy Mother who was staying in Haifa at the time. Meeting these ladies showed clearly that true refinement consisted in purity of soul & heavenly sentiments & these ladies possessed all these

qualities & more too. Real nobility & refinement, cleansed & of pure gold. The Holy Mother gave us helpful instructions & truly deserves the name "Brilliant Leaf." One of her sayings is: "Be like a leaf that is blown by the breezes." We met two of the Daughters, Zia & Ruha & they fully came up to our expectations.

At last we were to start for Acca. One of the members of the Family had gone to Acca to tell of our arrival & the Master sent for us. The Holy Mother & an old Persian believer who makes herself useful in the capacity of nurse & Ruha's little girl accompanied us on this most memorable visit. The Holy Mother telling us of her trip from Persia & her first trip to Acca & being accepted in the Holy Family, & the wish of Baha'o'llah that Abdul-Baha should marry her & he finally consented, being the wish of His Father.

This trip was very interesting, reaching Acca just at sunset. Shortly before reaching the City Gate, a caravan of camel drivers with a number of camels had settled down for the night & the men in their accustomed religious devotions a most picturesque sight. We had passed several trails of camels leaving for the desert packed with merchandise, disappearing between date palms. Reaching the city Gate of Acca, which [was] guarded by soldiers, & asked something of the men who were driving our carriage. They answered in reply, "Abbas Effendi"—& we drove through the gate into that ancient city. Such narrow streets—the men stood close up to the walls & crevices of the old buildings as our carriage drove through & entered into the court yard of Abdul-Baha's house, a large two story square building, porticoes all around the second story where the ladies' apartments are.

We ascended the long flight of steps & were greeted by Menevar [sic], the youngest daughter of Abdul-Baha who took us to our rooms & saw that we were comfortable. Supper was served & we were told that the Master regretted not to be present at our arrival, but had an appointment with the Governor & would see us in the morning. Everything seemed most interesting & marvelous, but the keynote of our expectations was the meeting of our Beloved; would He come up to our expectations?—We had heard such wondrous & marvelous things about Him & we had placed Him high, very high on a pedestal! We arose very early & Fanny said, Abdul-Baha it is said walks on the roof, perhaps we will see Him.

At last we were called to the living room where the family gathers in the morning, & tea is served, & prayers chanted, a heaven of peace, birds flying in & out, children of the Holy Household permitted to come in at will & leave when they felt inclined—We suddenly heard quick decided firm steps, it gave a thrill to all present—He entered the room & it was as though a darkened place had been suddenly flooded with light & perfuming fresh air—we three pilgrims arose—Fanny was the first to rush up & the most harmonious clear voice rang through the place, Welcome! Welcome! How are you! Are you well? Did you have a pleasant journey? Mrs. Finch then stepped up & extended her hand & received equally the same hearty welcome. Then my turn, advancing & Abdul-Baha gave the warm hearty, Welcome! Welcome! One felt an overwhelming power of Majesty & dignity—love & authoritativeness. There was no trace of doubt but that we had found our Lord & for Him we were ready at all times to give up life, soul & spirit—we had reached our goal—Heaven.

Abdul-Baha took His accustomed seat in the corner having asked us to be seated. [I] well remember watching who would take the seat next to Him. Mrs. Finch sat down, then Fanny & I next to her—Abdul-Baha's personality seemed much too powerful, a search light beyond this world, & in whose presence one felt secure & sublimely happy, never had we thought it possible to attain to such real pure happiness, neither here or hereafter. It was all far beyond our highest expectations, it was beyond our comprehension & understanding. Our visions became clearer, our thoughts brighter, our feeling keener—our sense of happiness greater & we had but one thought: to become empty vessels as to be able to receive a large portion of this Divine Outpouring.

We were lifted into another world, receiving boundless blessings, at the same time realizing our responsibility.

Abdul-Baha inquired about our journey & health & if we had rested well—inquired about the different believers & our assemblies. Fanny was asked about the Washington Assembly & the different believers. He was pleased to hear that they were in perfect harmony & unity & received the loving greetings with real pleasure. Then He inquired about the believers in Seattle. Mrs. Finch said not all were in unity, some were. Abdul-Baha replied when you return they will be in perfect unity. Then He asked me how are the believers in Stuttgart? Are they united? My reply was that they were in perfect unity & love, they send their heartfelt love & greetings. They were very grateful for the Teachings & always had a good attendance at the weekly meetings, many group meetings were held in which the friends translate the Holy Utterances of Baha'o'llah & Abdul-Baha. Also a group weekly meeting at Esslingen & Zuffenhausen.

Abdul-Baha said He had made a program for every hour of our stay. The ladies of the Household sat along one side of the room on the divan [sic]. An old venerable Persian member of the family chanted prayers & an old believer from Persia sat on the floor & served the tea from a large samovar. Birds flying in through the windows & hopping on the floor picking up the grains of sugar. Abdul-Baha had some Tablets which He looked over & corrected.

We returned to our rooms & breakfast was served in the dining room. A Chinese served the meals. The ladies called on us & assured us of their love & delight that we had come that great distance, the Holy Mother expressed her great regret not to be able to talk in our language & told of some of their experiences during their prison life in Acca. Meneva [Monavvar] translated.

Dinner was served at noon in five [illegible]. Mirza Moneer Zein translated for the Master. All showed the highest respect & veneration. Fanny sat at the right of Abdul-Baha & I at the head of the table & Mrs. Finch on the other side of me. The Persians that took meals with us were His secretaries & distinguished guests. In the afternoon some of the old Persian believers called, telling of their life in the services of Baha'o'llah. During our stay there were several groups, mostly of 9 venerable old teachers who had served Baha'o'llah & who gave brilliant accounts of their experiences, how they had been put in prison—tortured, their eyes sparkling with mirth & telling jokes to one another, also showing the marks on their necks—remnants of torture or from the heavy iron chains that were placed around their necks & ankles with large heavy iron balls. Oft-times three were chained, placed together. Whenever one moved the other was made uncomfortable when lying down or trying to sleep, each turn of the body of one or the other discomfort the other.

In the morning when we met in the living room, Abdul-Baha greeted us & inquired of our health. He told me that He had revealed a Tablet for me. I gave Him a photograph of Herr & Frau von K, she had asked me to beg of Abdul-Baha that she might be able to meet people who would become attracted to the Cause. Abdul-Baha replied that in this age it will be the women that will establish the Cause of Baha'o'llah. He told us that in some Religions it is taught that after death we enter into a place of purification called Purgatory where souls are cleansed so as to make spiritual advancements. So too our stay here is a preparatory place, & He hopes each day we will make progress, as a gardener cares for his plants, or the doctor looks after his patients & is pleased to see the progress & advancement, as a loving father who cares for his family & looks after their welfare & is happy to see their development, so He too hopes we will make daily progress & attain spiritual capacity & make wonderful progress. This is my hope. We strained every nerve so as not to be a disappointment, knowing & fully realizing now that every thought is registered we could control our words, but had to learn to control our thoughts also.

In the morning in between the group callers, Shoghi & his little sister called, later Shoghi called alone bringing his slate & pencil. Fanny & Mrs. Finch were busy with their writings & I did my best to entertain the little visitor of about 9 years old. He would hand me his slate & say Spinglish. The letters did not please him & were quickly wiped away, numbers also—still he came and would bring his slate & hand it to me. At last [I] was able to amuse him by drawing sketches. The sun—moon—that he left on his slate, then a farm house, trees, bushes & chickens & a little boy trying to catch the chicken by the tail feathers—He placed his hand over his mouth & shook with laughter. These were not erased.

One morning while kneeling on the floor beside him, Shoghi seated on the chair at the table with his slate in front of him, the door opened & there stood our Beloved Master. I quickly arose, feeling a little embarrassed. He gave a sign of pleasure & withdrew. In the morning, when we were in the living room, Abdul-Baha [was] correcting some Tablets the old Persian had chanted & we were drinking our tea. Shoghi came in & walked up to the Master & showed Him his slate & pointed to me—all smiles—he was pleased, but I did not feel as though I had done my best & felt rather ashamed at the poorly designs. There was some lesson to learn in this, which became a little clear after the Ascension of Abdul-Baha, & Shoghi Effendi was appointed Guardian of the Cause.

One morning Shoghi & his sister came & we were just about finished with breakfast, & not using sugar. I gave them both a piece of sugar, Shoghi refused but the little girl took it, Shoghi talked to her, but the more he talked the tighter she held it. He became very earnest & finally she slowly laid the sugar on the table. Fanny asked their nurse about it & she said they had been told not to accept anything from the Pilgrims, so Shoghi was doing as instructed. Obedience.

One meal was especially enjoyed because Meneva & her cousin, the young man who took care of the Shrine of Baha'o'llah, . . . had brought us some flowers. Meneva translated, Abdul-Baha showed great pleasure & enjoyment. The cousin Afnan told of the severe times they had when Abdul-Baha was expected to be taken away at any time. He was attending the American College at Beirut & a ship was anchored nearby that was to take the Master away. Every morning the first thing was to see if the ship was still there & the last thing at night. The nervous strain was very great on the family during those days—officers coming to the house at all times & inspecting everything, trying to find something to show up against Him. They asked the Master to sign a paper to make Him a perpetual prisoner. He told them if there was no hereafter they could, but Abdul Harmud would experience that, for the real life is Eternal.

When the officials returned to Constantinople, some were killed, others fled & Abdul Harmud was banished & the Young Turks set up the new government. It was shortly after we left Acca that all the state prisoners were given freedom. This recalled my first prayer vision when coming into the Cause.

The visit to the Garden of Rizwan was greatly enjoyed. The Holy Mother & Meneva & also Dr. Fareed went with us. They took refreshments along & we had tea in the garden. What a glorious spot—such brilliancy of colors & variety of flowers & trees which gave refreshing shade & fruits. The fountain in the center with its four streams paved with white marble. A plant, on the bench marked the place. Also in the garden house, the chair on which Baha'o'llah used to sit. Casmin had flowers on it—such deep reverence was shown to everything connected with Baha'o'llah & the Master. The old gardener Casmin took such delight in showing us about & telling of the early days, when magnificent Mulberry trees were in danger. These Mulberry trees are most significant, the two trees have grown into each other that one can scarcely see where the branch extends out, or in which one it has grown in, making "the canopy made without hands." And the "Temple made without hands." We were given flowers & fruits & leaves, the ladies told many interesting accounts concerning this garden during the early days.

There is a large truck garden adjoining the Rizwan garden—acres and acres of vegetables which are used by the Master & in His extensive household & much of it is sent to Damascus to market.

Our visit to this Shrine is far beyond words. We were received in the living room of some of the relations & tea was served, then we passed through a court garden & entered the Shrine. It would have been needless to tell us where we were—& that it was customary to remove one's shoes—we knew we had entered sacred grounds. We kneeleth [sic] down near the door & supplicated as never before for all our dear ones. The Holy Mother chanted a prayer which seemed as though heaven had opened & we heard the celestial Angels lifting us from this earth, up to a higher plane—overwhelmed by this wonderful, spiritual atmosphere. A magnificent Persian rug covered the Center of the floor around which stood different colored lamps & vases which are used at special celebrations, also beautiful candle holders.

Fanny asked to return & pray for her dear ones & I returned with her, this time only venturing to the doorstep. These penetrating spiritual forces must certainly vivify the souls & rejuvenate the spirit. On our way there we met some of the Persian pilgrims & Aban Abner gave us some of his flowers he had brought from the Holy Shrine & saved . . . for the Master.

On our return, entering the gate of Acca, Abdul-Baha was in the street & some of His disciples, so it looked, stood a respectful distance. This impressive picture is indelibly inscribed upon my memory, never to be forgotten, the Majestic Royal Figure. His attitude showing His respect to the Ladies that spoke far more than words can express, and we fully appreciated having had the honor of visiting the Garden of Rizwan & the Holy Shrine with the Ladies of the Holy Household, the Ladies of the Center of the Covenant.

All three of us were overwhelmed from our afternoon's experiences. No one spoke a word. Abdul-Baha excused Himself for supper, had an appointment & I for my part felt relieved & grateful, could not have stood any more of spiritual food, for we received both at table. There was a large floral center piece that had been sent to the Master. We were very quiet & soon retired, each meditating over their experiences of the day, & fully realizing that we had been placed into an entirely different environment.

The following morning in the living room when the Master greeted us [He] said, "I will reveal a Tablet for your mother through which she will be remembered throughout eternity."

Each day was filled—different groups of Persian teachers called & gave talks on various topics, of which we took notes. . . . The talks Abdul-Baha gave us at mealtime were answers to some of our questions without asking—some thoughts we perhaps had years ago.

One morning the Master told me that He would have my Tablet translated & I was happy. He also revealed another Tablet for me & had copies made of several Tablets to German believers, this was given me in a book form. He also told us that the believers in Acca/Haifa were excited over the fact that the teacher from Germany was here. During the visit of one of the group visitors of Persian teachers, one of them asked, which one is the German teacher? Higra Ali [sic] to me said, "This one—she is so quiet."

The visits of the ladies were heavenly, telling of their life & relating experiences, especially with the missionaries in Acca, how they tried to win them over to their Faith. The Greatest Holy Leaf did not talk as much as the others. Ruha Khanum said several times that she wished she could go out into the world & teach as we can.

Fanny several times asked if she could entertain the Ladies in any way, feeling so sorry that they were housed up & had no changes. So one afternoon Dr. Fareed came to us & said the Ladies would be pleased to have us spend a time with them in their apartment—the Greatest Holy Leaf's room. We were delighted to accept the invitation. We were shown things of great interest & then Dr. Fareed asked Fanny to show the ladies how they danced in America. She quietly responded. This looked so utterly out of place that I laughed very heartily. Finally one of the daughters said,

"It seems to amuse you more than it does us." Then we were asked to sing some popular (American) songs & also German songs. Fanny also sang a Danish song & we also sang some of the colored plantation songs.

The following afternoon we were shown the pictures of Baha'o'llah & the Bab by the Greatest Holy Leaf & we knew by this that our visit was drawing to an end.

We lingered long & felt we were in a hallowed place & felt very humble & grateful. Every moment of our stay seemed valuable & we were trying to take in as much as it was possible to do, realizing that everything had its value & importance, something that was meant for a lesson for us. Naturally the strain was great, we were being remodeled. One day Fanny said, "Alma, we will not cry when we have to leave will we?" "No" I answered—"We will not cry. It makes the Master feel badly."

Casmin brought us flowers from the Rizwan garden, wrapped in cabbage leaves to keep them fresh. They were beautiful. . . .

The Greatest Holy Leaf gave each of us 9 pieces of candles which had been used in Baha'o'llah's Shrine, some of the sand in a white silk bag, & the Most Brilliant Leaf gave us a string of pearl bead prayer beads & a silk handkerchief that is used to tie over the head. Abdul-Baha presented each of us 5 stones with the Greatest Name. We felt intoxicated, experiencing so much love & kindness. It was almost more than we could bear, our cup was filled to overflowing.

The morning of our leaving, 9 of the women believers of Acca came to bid us good-bye & said they would pray for our success & protection at the Holy Shrine & asked for our prayers. Fanny & Mrs. Finch were ready to leave—but I longed to remain—remain always, had found the real home—but we had been told that, the Master was closer to those on the front; a king is more interested in those soldiers in the fire line, than those near him; that oft-times those far away are very close to the Master & some of those who are near are very far from Him, that we were very fortunate to have been chosen to serve the Cause. Future generations will wish they could have been in our places & will esteem us. . . .

The carriage was waiting for us. We slowly drove out, looking back & letting the transformed prison—now a paradise & heaven—its beautiful brilliant flowers and all, leave a lasting impression. The ladies on the upper balcony almost out of sight—still feeling their presence. The carriage rolled through the gate & through the narrow streets—so narrow that the men stood up close to the houses as we drove through here & there where a group of men smoking their long tube pipes . . . and then through the gate of the city hall. [My] heart pained me—we were leaving the most precious place in the world. Abdul-Baha had told us to visit Port Said, Alexandria, Cairo, Paris, London & Stuttgart—I was to return to

> Stuttgart & make that a strong Center. To tell the believers in Alexandria & Cairo that the light in us was His love to them. They had begged of us to ask the Master to come & visit them, & in reply He said So God Willeth.[1]

When the three pilgrims left 'Akká they visited Haifa and then went on to the other places 'Abdu'l-Bahá had instructed them to visit, and carried with them the spirit and love from 'Akká. I have left out some of those stories but I pick up again with a bit of Fanny's memoirs. The following is one of the more amusing stories, and is best told in Fanny's style:

> Below us were large flat-bottomed boats—Orientals making much noise—men in some of the boats loading bags upon the backs of others to carry up on deck, others at the same time carrying quantities of freight down to boats below. These boats, because of rough water, were swaying and crashing against each other. Looking down upon this noisy, picturesque scene, we wondered how we, ourselves, would ever reach one of those boats. But there had been no need to worry, for suddenly a huge oriental unceremoniously grabbed us like a bag of meal, with our heads facing frontward and bodies hanging, carried us down the steps between the freight carriers and dropped us into the arms of waiting boatmen. There were eleven men in the boat to row three little women with hand baggage to shore! Again, when landing at shore, we were picked up and carried in the same manner over a pile of coal. We heaved a sigh of relief when we felt the cobblestone of the road beneath our feet.[2]

A formal account of Alma's, Mrs. Finch's, and Fanny's pilgrimage entitled "*Flowers Culled from the Rose Garden of Acca,*" was compiled by the three pilgrims shortly after their trip. It was published in a little booklet upon their return and shared with fellow Bahá'ís and friends, as were many of the accounts of pilgrimages at that time. I have not included that account, however, for those interested, it is currently available online.

The following statements are extracts from the memoriam section of *The Bahá'í World* for Fanny Knobloch. It is a good summary of some of their most memorable impressions of the pilgrimage.

> What joy to meet Shoghi Effendi (later to become Guardian of the Faith) and his little sister, and Bahíyyih Khánum, the Greatest Holy Leaf, as well as the other members of the Holy Household. Of Bahíyyih Khánum, she wrote, "A strange and unknown feeling possessed me while in the presence of Bahíyyih Khánum, the Greatest Holy Leaf. Possibly it can be described as a feeling of awe, a feeling very unfamiliar to me. However,

later, I realized that I had been in the presence of the greatest, the most holy woman in the history of the world—the Greatest Holy Leaf! The daughter of the Manifestation of God, Bahá'u'lláh." . . .

Only one who had visited 'Abdu'l-Bahá could understand what it meant to be with Him. For nine days the three pilgrims experienced a happiness beyond expression because of their close contact with Him. When they were leaving, He said to them, "*You are not weeping? Do not weep! Many friends weep because they wish to remain longer.*" Miss Fanny replied, "No, we have received so many blessings and are eager to go out and share them with all who are ready to listen."

Nodding His blessed head, 'Abdu'l-Bahá replied, "*The general does not love most the man in the back of the ranks. He loves most the man in front. If you knew the value of these days, you would not eat, you would not sleep, you would not walk. You would run and give to all the Glad Tidings!*"

After leaving 'Akká, the three travelers went to Cairo, Egypt, to see once more their beloved teacher, Mirza Abu'l-Faḍl, then living in that city. Upon their departure, he gave to Miss Fanny his most precious possession, his prayer beads, saying to her, "My Lord gave them to me."

Their steamer then took them to Marseilles. From there they sped to Zurich, Switzerland, and then to Stuttgart, Germany where Miss Alma had labored for two years and continued for yet another twelve, serving the Cause of Bahá'u'lláh. The two sisters addressed a large meeting, bringing to the German friends 'Abdu'l-Bahá's message of love.

After several days Miss Fanny then hastened to Paris, according to 'Abdu'l-Bahá's wish, then to London, to convey His greetings, and back again to America, after an absence of three months.

Upon her return to America, she shared her experiences with friends in Washington, Baltimore, and New York, always working for the establishment of the Faith.[3]

- 11 -

Pauline and Joseph Meet 'Abdu'l-Bahá— Pilgrimage Accounts

In 1909 Pauline and Joseph had the opportunity to follow in the sisters' footsteps and embark on a voyage to 'Akká to visit 'Abdu'l-Bahá. Several accounts in the form of letters written by Joseph and Pauline while on pilgrimage, detailing their trip in its entirety, from New York to 'Akká, through Germany and back home, were discovered in the archives during my research. Both Joseph and Pauline wrote home about the same experiences, he to his mother, and she to Fanny and the boys, each giving their own perspectives. I have included excerpts from each of their letters, and have highlighted some interesting aspects of their differing views when necessary. As previously mentioned, all of these accounts are pilgrim's notes; the sections attributed to 'Abdu'l-Bahá are not authoritative scripture and should not be considered an authenticated rendering of His words, but rather they are the hearer's recollections. We'll start the voyage with Joseph's view:

> On Board S. S. Koenig Albert 418 miles from Gibraltar
> February 7, 1909
> Beloved Mother,
> Tomorrow will be our first chance to send off a letter so behold me this fine Sunday afternoon busily engaged in writing a few of the many messages to you which have forth gone since we parted. First of all, we are well and happy; are having a wonderfully pleasant voyage, and drawing near to our first destination—Naples.
>
> Tomorrow afternoon we will be in Gibraltar—our first stopping point; there we may get off & see some of the sights, if we arrive before dark. We arrive Naples Friday of this week, & if all goes well can leave that night for Port Said. This we shall hope to do, so as to arrive at Akka with all

possible speed, & then stop at Naples etc. on our return. Perhaps a little history of our trip thus far may be in order: Beginning with our departure Jan 29, so far off it now seems, & yet so near! We were met at the station by young Sigard Russell, of whom we probably spoke before going. He has been to Akka twice. He accompanied us to New York, where we met Mr. MacNutt. On the way it first rained, then sleet & snow fell, so that by the time we reached our destination there was quite a blizzard. Mr. MacNutt took [us] over to his home in Brooklyn—a beautiful place. On the way we stopped at the home of a Believer where a Ladies meeting was in progress. Despite the weather some 8 or 9 were there who welcomed us lovingly. Pauline told about the Sunday School & the work among the colored folks. Then in the evening we went to the meeting at Miss Juliet Thompson's studio. Quite a large gathering greeted us, including some well known names & familiar faces. I spoke—they said quite well. Prof. Barakatullah also spoke & Miss T. [Juliet Thompson] & Mr. MacNutt read tablets. It was a beautiful send off.[1]

Here I interject with what Pauline wrote about Barakatullah, because Joseph was too humble to mention it, "Prof. Barakatullah spoke beautifully and told this large audience that in our home, the home of Brother Joseph & his wife he had received the first real rays of the light of truth. He was so earnest in his gratitude that a number spoke to me afterwards saying, how strange that you should be his spiritual parents, we believed he had received the Teachings here."[2] Pauline continues with more detail about all of the guests who went out of their way on an unpleasant, snowy night, to give them a wonderful send off.

Here she writes about their boat experience, which was rather trying:

Saturday after leaving New York, we soon had dinner. All were at the table then, at supper only a few, but we went even though we much preferred not. . . . It made me sick just to see the dishes so uneasy, slipping and sliding, so as fast as I could & throwing my coffee overboard, there was no room for my supper, my stomach was busy getting ready for a sea voyage. Sunday I went to breakfast but much preferred to remain in bed, ate a little, kept it but felt wretched until shortly before dinner some German boys joined & we sang to beat the band. We ate our dinner but didn't want it, our stomachs though seemed to think it was alright and retained it. Since this we have really enjoyed our meals."[3]

Joseph writes:

Tho it is February we have sat outdoors all of each day. After the second day the temperature has been that of spring—& one day like summer.

We were just a little bit sick. I lost the first supper that's all. We have not missed a single meal & now enjoy—hungrily every one.

We are about 28 second class passengers, probably 150 first class. Our part includes Germans, French, Italians & Americans, one colored undertaker from New York. Oh yes! A Swiss lady & baby. We are well liked & our part of the ship is like a happy family, so attractive is the fact of a mutual end to be reached. The First Cabin folks are awfully stylish & not as happy as we are, if one might judge by appearances.

Today I gave the message to five or six of our fellow passengers, nearly all who could understand English. A young German, Mr. Obermeyer, & the colored man Mr. Thomas, seemed much interested, the former especially.

We are both getting fat & the salt air seems to agree with us. We do not notice the motion of the boat at all. . . . Everything is so nice, we shall reluctantly leave this ship save for the joy of proceeding to dear Abdul-Baha![4]

The next letter Joseph wrote was from Hotel Milan & Schweizerh of Naples on 13 February 1909, in which he describes the trip up to Naples. We skip over that and go to his next letter about Port Said:

Dearest Mother,

Here we are where we have always felt it would be just a step to Akka. Really it is quite a trip, as we sail from here this afternoon at 5 and may reach Haifa in 24 hours or perhaps not for 36 hours. Then there is a carriage drive of several miles and then—our great and longed for destination. . . .

Arriving here we had no trouble at all in locating Ahmad Yazdi, who is most loving and kind. We also met Abraham Ali and Taki Menshadi. At the hotel is a Miss Holzbecher, an American Believer, who hopes to go to Akka soon. We are surely overjoyed to be again with the Friends. This is a most interesting place, truly. The climate is moderate, trees and flowers are in leaf & blossom, as in mid-summer and I do not need my overcoat. On the Ocean the weather has been almost warm at times, with a chill at night but only moderate.

We are perfectly well and I believe we really have gained flesh on the journey: surely we have gotten well rested and the world "as we have known it" effaced temporarily so as to leave a clean slate for the Akka Lessons.

Love and kisses from your devoted, Joseph[5]

In his account Joseph casually mentions the beggars they have seen in their travels, whereas, after reading Pauline's version of the same scene, it is clear this issue touched her on a deeper level, and stuck to her soul. She wrote:

From the moment we landed until we returned we were beset by beggars on every side; some we felt sorry for, some we shrank from, some made us angry, but such a sight, never, never will I forget it as long as I live: such rags, such a degraded looking people, devoid of all signs of spiritual joys, or of any joy for that matter. My dear boys if you could see this new world, you would be the happiest children in the world to know this is not my home. Give me America, just America & I'll be happy.[6]

The next letter is Pauline's. The subtle differences in the nature and character of the writers can be detected. I was brought to tears many times as I read her words, partly because of the memories it brought back to me of my own pilgrimage, but also because of the nature of the things that touched her heart.

Letter to Grandmother, Carl and Paul, Cairo, Egypt March 4, 1909
My Precious Ones,
What shall I say, where to begin. We have lived ages in a few weeks, my last letter was written on board the Prince Ludwig. (Early in the morning we arrived at Port Said) Such a noise, you can't imagine, thirty or more row boats filled with strange looking men shouting, and calling for passengers for their particular boat to land us. This awful noise and confusion was and is the only unpleasant feature of the trip. After a while we were safely landed and with the help of a man engaged by Joseph, we were taken to the home of Ahmed Yazdi. He is (just) a real Baha'i, and we loved him at once. Also the clerks in his store are Baha'is and this made it easy for us to speak freely. He sent his clerk with us to a neat little hotel, where we found an American believer, Miss Holtzbecker, who has taken a great fancy to us and was a great help to us also. She is now preparing to go to Akka next week. We walked all around Port Said and out the narrow streets and along the beautiful beach front where we gathered shells for our baby Paul "Thabet." And for our big son Carl "Nategh" (the first name sounds like sabet). It was such a beautiful place to pray and we did.

We had to wait until the next afternoon for the steamer. During the early afternoon, a sand storm began to gather and by three o'clock the whole city looked pink. The air was filled with sand, and we could not see half a block away. We secured a row boat, which landed us safely on the Russian steamer about five o'clock, which was to leave that evening, Thursday, but on account of the sand storm, and very rough sea, we had to lay in the harbor for 26 hours, leaving on Friday evening instead. The sea was so rough that all the passengers who were booked for Jaffa had to go on to Haifa. Such a lot of sea-sick people you never saw. But it was no wonder the boat rocked every which way, trunks, and satchels were flying back and forth like crazy things.

The steamer seemed like a rubber ball tossing on the waves. The front of the boat would shoot its nose into the air and then plunge into the sea as it seemed, then tip to one side then to the other on a slant like this [illustration] in other words the edge of the upper deck touched the water. Once while Papa and I were sitting in the middle of the boat, on the upper deck on the floor, all of a sudden we had a toboggan slide in a great hurry to the railing of the boat and while straightening ourselves up a little and laughing at our hurry we were hurried back again and poor Papa had a good rap on his head, but it was so very funny that we could do nothing but look at each other and burst out laughing. In the midst of the fun, we were sliding again, as fast as the wind to the side of the boat again. This time we managed to scramble to our feet and by the time the boat tilted again we were holding fast to something. Strange to say we were not ill, not the least bit, and we rather enjoyed this novel experience.

When we reached Haifa, the sea was so very rough that no boats came out to reach us or to take us in from ten in the morning until five that night. We believed, as the Captain said, we must go on to Beirut, because if the men would venture out in their row boats the landing would be very dangerous. At five, we saw some row boats coming towards us. Oh joy! We hastened to our things and Papa looked at me so longingly and said, you must show your pluck now. I was not in the least afraid, but it was indeed a dangerous landing, but thank God after being pulled and thrown and pushed we finally found ourselves walking on firm ground once more. We were so glad to be walking on mother earth that we refused to take a carriage to the hotel, but we had some men carry our baggage.

On arriving at the Hotel, the Manager sent for Mirza Jallal, the Son-in-law of our Beloved Abdul-Baha. In about an hour he arrived with Mirza Moneer. After a very little talk about the various friends, we were startled speechless by the announcement, "Our Lord will receive you, after you have had supper and one of us will call for you." They saw we were unfit for further speech and left us. We hastened to our rooms, washed and dressed. I put on my silk dress, ate supper though we did not wish for it. While still at the table Mirza Moneer came. I saw him come in. We put on our hats and coats for it was cold, and started for that wonderful meeting. After ten minutes', very quiet, and prayerful walk, we came to the gate of Madame Jackson's house and looking ahead of us on Mt. Carmel, a great eye as it seemed, but really a light on Mt. Carmel, was shining down on us and this we were told was the Tomb of the Bab.

The Heavens seemed to be a mass of stars shedding their light upon us as though even the stars were happy for us. But how did I feel? Like a timid little bird, expecting I knew not what, but the end was very near. We were ushered into the parlor, where we removed our things. Then

Mirza Moneer came back saying, "Come." I followed first, then Joseph. I stood upon the doorsill for one instance as though it might have been the edge of a precipice, looking upon our Lord who said something, perhaps Welcome, but at the sound of His Voice, I flew at Him, my arms about His Blessed neck my head on His Shoulder. I was breathing very hard, really panting, and the uppermost thought was Father, Father, Father. I seemed like a weather beaten birdie having passed through storms and at last had reached the heaven of rest. Just as I began to feel that I was losing consciousness, this wonderful Father led me to a chair. Then I was quiet and more composed and saw Him embrace and kiss your Papa, your son and brother. He will tell you how he felt.

We sat to one side of the room with Armeen, his dear Father, Mirza Moneer, Mirza Jallal, I don't remember any more, oh yes another son-in-law and in one corner sat our Lord's little grandson, and our beloved Lord, very well, face beaming the inexpressible love light in His Eyes. He spoke of your recent visit (Fanny) and how happy He was to have you, and that you were sincere servants, then spoke of Alma's work and among the other things, said she was the Conqueror of Germany, and her conquest would last throughout all eternity, while Napoleon conquered many lands and people during his day, but now these lands belonged to others, etc. He spoke with great joy of the Beloved in America and of the Cause, especially the Washington friends. I can't remember all that was said that night, but after a little while, He arose, took me by the hand, and led me across the large inner hall or court (you remember Fanny) to see the ladies, at the same time calling Monavvar. He seated Himself upon the divan and I next to Him with my hand encircled by His warm hand. In a few minutes, the Blessed Mother came in. He slipped out, while other ladies and I had to tell them about the Beloved in America, etc. Our Lord returned to Joseph, embraced him, and called him His Son, His own Joseph, and said he (we) should come the next morning and be His guests, and then said good night. Joseph talked to the men for a while, then sent for me, and we started for the Hotel. Happy beyond expression, but very quiet, we said very little, and slept very little, thinking over the wonderful events of the day. Personally, Our Beloved Abdul-Baha was a great and pleasant surprise; His wondrous forehead, clear skin, soft white beard and moustache, the hair is thin and white but not often seen, warm soft and small firmly grasping hands, and last but by no means least, His wonderful, wonderful eyes. They express as no other eyes can, unspeakable love, sympathy, power and authority, submissiveness, and oh the merry twinkle; I never saw anything like it. As to His Spiritual power, our knowledge increased day by day and we wondered how the people could be so blind, and not know Him, only to see Him walking with six or more pilgrims, following at a short distance. His bearing, that of humility and power combined. He is. He is, yes He is ABDUL-BAHA THE PERFECT.

The reason I say Abdul-Baha, instead of Lord or Master, is because He gave us a talk on this subject. To give it without the setting and in brief it is this; lord is one title or attribute of God, Master is one attribute, Abbas is another and, etc. Abdul-Baha is the combination, total of all perfections.

To go on, the next morning we packed our things, left some clothes to be washed, and by this time Dr. Fareed came for us and took us for a walk, and then to the home of Ruha, but she was in Acca at this time. We took all the gifts out and had them ready, but not till Monday morning did we present the gifts. Abdul-Baha walked in saying good morning and asked how we slept, made us feel comfortable and at ease, then I began and placed each gift one at a time, mentioned the names of the givers and the messages where there were any to give. He thanked very sweetly for their expressions of love and asked for the many letters we had brought and then said, "You are a letter from the Friends in America, a long expressive letter. You are their gift, they have sent you," meaning both of us. "When a merchant wished to sell grain he sends samples of his goods to be examined, and you are the samples, and it is very good." Then Joseph said, "We wish to say to our Lord that the goods is really much better than the sample." His eyes twinkled as He replied, "if the goods are equal to the samples it is very good. You are dear to me." To go on again with my story, or at least try to, it was not until Monday morning we gave the presents, but we arranged them Sunday morning, had just completed the operation when Mirza Moneer came in to us saying "Our Lord awaits you out front." Quickly our hats and coats were put on and when we came to the front door, who should be standing at the gate but Our Lord, with a little bunch of violets which He handed to me. He helped us into His carriage and He got in back of us with Mirza Moneer and in front was the driver, an old believer.[7]

I want to interject here with some of Joseph's words about aspects of this event that Pauline did not mention. He wrote in his letter,

We are told that we arrived at one of the greatest moments in the History of the Cause, i.e. when Abdul-Baha for the first time had availed Himself and the believers of their liberty by going to the Tomb of the Bab on Mount Carmel and holding a Public Meeting and Unity Feast there. This is Saturday. We reached here in the evening, and yesterday were privileged to attend another meeting, at which the second half of the oriental pilgrims, now at Akka were taken. We met a number who had traveled for months from remote regions on horses and donkeys, camel back or afoot, so that our three weeks looked insignificant tho the distance of 5696 miles from home makes up for some of the distance.[8]

Now we resume Pauline's account of this very special celebration on Mt. Carmel:

> As we were winding our way up the steep mountain roadway, every one silent of course, Our Lord spoke, saying to me: About two years ago you had a vision in which you were going up this steep mountain and at the top you met many strange people at the feast. Today you will see this vision literally fulfilled, in a moment. He said think and then you will remember all. I did not recall this dream until I reached the top and greeted many pilgrims who had just arrived from different parts of Persia and India and Russia, believers who had traveled for three months on camels, donkeys or walking as best they could. Seeing these shining faces, the dream came back to me. After resting for a while and talking about America and having a friendly chat, one very old and beautiful believer read the greetings sent by the Washington friends to our Lord. Their faces expressed perfect joy and Joseph and I were very happy. I chanted the Commune and the Arabic chant, and they were delighted and this servant was most happy to be able to do something to please these wonderful people. In a few minutes Abdul-Baha appeared at the door and said come. We all followed Him, Joseph and I were mixed with the others, but in a second Our Lord stopped and motioned for me to come and then to Joseph to come near Him, and quietly we followed Him into the Holy Tomb of the Bab on Mt. Carmel. It was very solemn and I felt utterly unworthy to be there. All stood while Our Lord chanted the Visiting Tablet in a clear ringing voice. Then He knelt on the floor and all of us did likewise. Then we retreated slowly out into the garden. We went into the same room where we had assembled in the first place, where the feast was prepared for us. With the exception of Joseph and I, all were seated about the feast spread on the floor in real oriental fashion, and Abdul-Baha walking back and forth to serve us and to see that we all were happy, pushing some cheese in front of Joseph or patting him on the back and saying eat and now and then letting me take His Hand in mine and look at me with such unspeakable love and tenderness. He spoke to us, but Joseph has it all written out. I will not attempt to give His teachings here, but nevertheless it seems to me the greatest lesson was that of love. He embraced Joseph several times and kissed him too, once on the crown of his head as he was kneeling at His feet. Once He called us both to sit beside Him on the divan. Being a

woman I was denied the privilege of being kissed by Him, but His Hand grasp, I felt many times, and to hear His Voice, as He entered one end of the house, to come to us at the other end, my daughter, my daughter, my daughter, until He reached us and I was at His feet. He has shown us so much love that we can never do anything now but show love to the creatures of God.

When Joseph asked how he might serve more and differently He smiled sweetly, He said, "Go on just as you have been doing. Your services are acceptable." [These words were translated and recalled at a later time.] I begged that my tongue might be loosened to glorify the Cause. He said, "You have great love, the utmost love for the Cause. That same love is service to the Cause. You serve the Beloved of God and this also is a service. Because you remember God, this also is a service. You shall be confirmed to render great services. Be Confident." When we think of the great love He has showered upon us, our hearts must melt with love for everyone. Oh, I can hear Him, now saying "my son, my daughter" in English too. First He said "My son" two or three times in English and "My daughter" had to be translated. Then this humble servant wished with all her heart that He might call her something in English. A very few minutes afterwards, He stepped into the room and said, "My daughter." I could have cried for joy, but I didn't.

When we were about to leave the Tomb for the carriage, we had been sitting about in groups on the grass, talking when all became silent and all stood reverently watching our Lord coming towards us from the gardener's house. He stopped, picked a rose, and while doing this Mirza Moneer said, "I prophecy. He is going to pick it for you" (talking to me). Sure enough, walking slowly towards the road leading to the carriage not seeming to see anyone or anything until He came to where I stood, He handed me the rose, smiled and walked on until He came to the edge of the parapet or wall. Here all Haifa lay at His Feet, and at ours. In that moment, it seemed to me all the world was His to do with as He chose, yet like Christ, He chose the humblest, yet most mighty position of non-resistance. He stood like a statue for quite a while, as it seemed, the bearing of One who has conquered the world. Like the gentle Christ, when he was being crowned with thorns and persecuted, with only one to stand by him, John, yet he said, "I have overcome the world." As Our Lord stood there, the embodiment of humility and power, that saying of Christ became clear to me. As He turned He motioned to us to precede Him to the carriage, which was about a block away, higher up the mount. As we seated ourselves, we looked back to view another wonderful sight, Haifa, at the foot of Mt. Carmel, the Tomb bathed in sunlight. Our Lord, walking firmly up the steep mountain path towards the carriage, at a little distance came about 25 pilgrims, heads bowed, hands crossed over their breasts, Jews, Zoroastrians, Moslems, Greeks, etc. When He reached the carriage, He stopped and faced them, motioning them to come nearer and then He spoke. This we did not understand of course, nor was it interpreted for us. But it made a wonderful picture. Then He got in the carriage and we went home, not a word was spoken.

On several occasions we saw Him walking on the rough mountain roads with ten or twelve men following Him, and now and then He would stop and speak to them. On one of these trips He said to them, [that] when [He] arrived at this place forty years ago, there were only a very few little huts about and now see the many houses, to this side, the German Colony over there awaiting the coming of the lord. After He passed through this land they came to settle. This was news to us because we had been taught that they came in 1868—guess that was the Monastery.

Another time Dr. Fareed, Joseph and I went for a walk and on our return we saw Our Lord crossing the road a block away. We were coming this way [arrow pointing right] and we had crossed like this [arrow pointing up]. I saw that He had a bunch of flowers in His hands as He waved His other hand. Joseph began to go at a lively trot to overtake Him, but foolish me, I said to Ameen, "No I won't run for then He will give me the flowers and I would rather the other Pilgrims should have this pleasure." What do you think, when we reached the gate, He stood near the house smiling, and Joseph was coming toward us with the most beautiful flower in the bunch, a perfect iris. Every one marveled at its beauty and wondered where Abdul-Baha had gotten it, and Joseph had a beautiful rose (for himself.) The point is this: He had a flower for each pilgrim and one for Joseph and one for me.

Abdul-Baha visited Tiberius during which time we were sent to Akka, the Holy Tomb of Baha'o'llah, and the Garden of Rizwan, the never to be forgotten trip.

Fanny, the ladies one and all send their love and wish me to tell you they often speak of your visit and what a joy it was to them. They are indeed wonderful people, especially the Greatest Holy Leaf, who was especially affectionate to me, which gave me great joy. She was quite distressed that we had to leave so soon, and sent word by several of the Persians to Our Lord, asking Him to send us back again before we left for home. But He told us it was not wise, because we would cause the people to wonder at our being there so soon again and be means of trouble. Don't ask me how I felt when I had to leave the peace of the Holy Tomb. It seemed as though I could not leave, though I knew I kept the others waiting, I believe a long time. I did not hear them go out nor would it have made any difference, it was heavenly and I longed to stay. At first it seemed my whole being seemed like a surging sea, my head buzzing and I found myself wondering at this condition. All of a sudden I seemed to see Abdul-Baha on my right hand, and the eyes of the Greatest Holy Leaf on my left, and all was at peace, such peace that passeth all understanding. At last realizing it was time to go to the others outside, I backed to the door, but my heart failed me, I must step back for one more prayer, and I did so. Oh such joy cannot be imagined, it must be felt. After putting my shoes on and we were about to leave, a relative of Baha'o'llah or the gentleman who lives next to the holy Tomb and cares for the Tomb, came to us with two little bunches of violets that had been in the holy of Holies for two days, and presented them to us. These we have pressed and will bring with us. At the Rizwan we received two pomegranates that had been on the chair where Bahá'u'lláh had sat, in the room where He lived while at the Rizwan. How strange it seemed to be walking about the Garden where He, the Most Glorious, walked and taught His beloved. The mulberry trees with its twisted branches and the natural seat.

On arriving at this Garden, all were surprised to find that other pilgrims were there ahead of us, ten or twelve of those whom we had met at the holy Tomb of the Bab. They were just being served tea when we arrived on the scene. We also were served and then explored the gardens. After receiving a number of beautiful flowers, we went to the carriage. All the pilgrims gathered about us to bid us God speed, and we started for Haifa. Forgot to say that while in the Garden, we were permitted to go in the Blessed Room, in which His Blessed Perfection sat and rested or wrote. We were told to enter, but neither of us had the physical power to go further than the door sill. We prostrated ourselves in awe and prayer. I was dimly aware of a large, possibly an armchair, the seat of which was covered with fresh fragrant beautiful flowers. It was indeed a very strange experience to know of a Powerful Presence and not able to see but an unmistakable feeling of His Presence. Similar to the experience in the Holy Tomb only this time there was not that struggle for peace and understanding. We received that at the Holy Tomb, and when we gazed upon the Photographs in Akka, of Baha'o'llah and the Bab, that experience defies expression, at least on my part.

Another experience, silly perhaps, but not for me. I was very serious when a piece of lemon was handed to me, from the lemon tree, growing in the Rizwan Garden. It was eaten with the solemn prayer on my part, that, like as in the Story, I might eat with equal joy the sour as well as the sweets offered by God.

Just remembered the story of the peacock at Akka. One day while in the presence of Our Beloved, and feeling extremely unworthy, He said, "when you visit Akka notice the feet of the peacock, they are ugly. The peacock proudly struts about with his beautiful tail feathers spread out. He is proud, but the moment he glances at his feet the tail feathers drop. So you must keep your faces and hearts turned to God always, never look upon your unworthiness."

The drive along the beach was delightful although somewhat sad because the shore was lined with wreckage from an Italian steamer that had been dashed against the rocks at the foot of Mt. Carmel. Many hundreds of oranges, washstands, beds, tables, railings, doors, floors, great bales of cotton, and hay there—I must stop just this minute to mail this or I fear you will never get it. Continued in our next. So much has happened during the writing of this letter, I fear it is very bad, but perhaps in Algeria or Naples I may find time.

Pauline

Your homesick little Mother. . .

Thabet be a good brave boy and pray for us[9] . . .

Pauline's next letter:

March 12, 1909.
Dearly Beloved ones,

. . .

We had just left Akka, and the wonderful Believers who were loath to part with us, then the wonderful Tomb of Baha'o'llah and the dear little Rizwan Garden where we had tea, now this drive to our home in Haifa, where perhaps the dearly Beloved Abdul-Baha would not be seen until the next morning. We went to our room to rest, Joseph did take a nap, but I (poor me) was nearly heartbroken with unutterable longing to return to the Holy Tomb or to see the Master's Face. In the depth of despair, I cried out, oh Lord, come to me now or I shall perish. Scarcely had the prayer been spoken in my innermost heart, when a voice from the back of the house rang out loud and clear, "My daughter, my daughter, my daughter," until our Lord stood in our room and I was at His Feet weeping telling Him how I missed Him, etc. But in my heart I was ashamed to have disturbed Him, He had just returned from His trip to Tiberius, and was, and looked very tired. He was very gentle and kind to me, said He had been with us to the Tomb in Spirit and had prayed for us, and because of us He had returned that evening. Be sure, though my body was absent, my spirit was with you. After this little speech I arose from my knees. He shook hands with Joseph, patted him on the back and said, My son, and left us without further speech, save to say, I am very tired, so will leave you, goodnight. This night Joseph and I both had a dream in which we were told we must prepare ourselves to leave on Sunday. On waking in the morning we both spoke of it, but Friday passed, and Saturday yet no word had been said, but we knew as though the word had been said. On Sunday morning, our Lord called on us and after the regular talk He arose and said you will be leaving this afternoon. Remember, I shall be with you always, I love you very much, in dream He had spoken to us.

One afternoon, while Abdul-Baha was out for a walk with a group of Believers about Him, which is in itself a Christ picture, He turned to His followers and said, "when I came here forty years ago there were only a very few houses. Now see the size of it, the many beautiful homes and well-kept grounds since Baha'o'llah and His followers passed this way . . ."

One afternoon I was visiting the ladies when Abdul-Baha came in and sat down beside me. This was in answer to an unspoken wish, but I did not say what I wished to say, but after His saying, "speak to me," I thanked Him for the magnificent flower He gave me and said in English, this flower is called a flag, but it was more beautiful than any I had ever seen, and that I hoped He would make me a flag bearer in this Most wonderful Cause. He smiled and said, "The opportunity may present itself, this was a very pretty thought of yours." I answered and said, "You can make the opportunity if you see wise." Again He smiled and said, "En shah'llah. Because of your great love for the Cause, I love you very much." ['Abdu'l-Bahá's words are Pauline's recollections.]

I am telling only the little events, because Joseph had taken the messages and talks in shorthand. These you will have when we return. I will tell one more thing then leave the scenes of that inexpressible life for some other day when we meet. After our Lord left us, I packed the things while Joseph went to buy the tickets. We had dinner, but our Lord was not present. After a long, long wait as it seemed, He came to our room to say goodbye. It seemed to pain Him to send us away. Seeing this, I used every effort not to cry and thanked God I did not. My eyes were dim with tears, but they did not flow. My goodbye was like the meeting. He permitted my head to rest on His shoulder for a minute, called me daughter, kissed Joseph and called him son, said I will be with you always, remember these days, then He left us. In a minute or two I was told to come and say goodbye to the ladies. I ran quickly thinking to have it over with before I broke down, but on reaching the door, saw our Lord walking very slowly with bowed head on the very path I must walk to reach the ladies, I stepped back a little, that I might not disturb the thoughts of this heavenly one battling with the inclination to run after Him and falling at His Feet and just once more seeing those eyes, oh those Eyes of love. But I conquered this selfish thought, but when He went into the house and I finally went to see the ladies, my strength was gone. I wept and wept and have done so a number of times since. Abdul-Baha has given us much work to do and now we go forth to live a new life.[10]

Before continuing with their accounts of the trip home, I want to add a few words from Joseph's letter again about his impressions of 'Abdu'l-Bahá. He wrote,

> As to our impressions of the Master—it is difficult to write adequately, but our highest expectations have been truly exceeded. Pauline feels that He is a Father in the truest sense of the word. He has called her His Daughter and me His Son and again "My own Joseph." For me I felt that many vague conceptions of greatness have been brought together and the result is—Abdul-Baha! It is as if one were looking at a landscape through a glass, and finally got the right focus, when everything stood out clear and distinct. I see for the first time the Christ-type and am rejoiced.[11]

Later on, long after returning to America, Pauline took the time to type up some of her favorite stories of her time with 'Abdu'l-Bahá. It must be remembered that these are pilgrim's notes. She wrote:

> I was a very earnest, ardent worker among the colored people. To my knowledge, I was the first to work among them, and then later my sister, Alma Knobloch, and Joseph, my husband. Alma had gone to Germany so her work ceased with the colored people in Washington, but Joey and I continued without her.
>
> At that time the colored people were not so fond of my husband, as he was the intellectual type. When we went to Akka in 1909, it was with a hopeful heart that Abdul-Baha would understand my work among the colored race, because I had many drawbacks. There were many to tell me I was wasting my time, that I would do much better and more creditable work among my own people. When the boys of the neighborhood knew that colored people were coming to meetings at our house, they would throw bricks and stones and overripe tomatoes and vegetables in our vestibule, and also unhinge the front gate. I would sit by the door in the hall and quietly hide these things back of the vestibule door, so that the friends never knew. My husband would unhinge the gate and put it in a place of safety until the meeting was over, replacing it later. All these happenings really brought joy to my heart and I believed, contrary to the others, that Abdul-Baha would understand it all when I saw Him. During our visit in 1909, one morning Abdul-Baha came to our room very briskly and said, "How are you? Are you happy? Are you well?" He then made

several other remarks, after which He turned to my husband and said, "Tell me about the race question in Washington."

After having spoken at length on this subject, He swiftly left the room and walked in the large circular central room. Hearing Him walking briskly, we followed Him and stood close to the wall, together with several Persians, and watched this majestic figure pace back and forth. The power of the holy spirit was almost too much for us. We practically shrank against the wall, overwhelmed, when suddenly like a bow from an arrow [sic], He came towards us. We did not know what was going to happen. Placing His hand on my husband's shoulder and looking into his eyes with great power, He said, "May you be the means of uniting the colored and the white races." Then He walked out and left us.

Here is the moral. It was for me a clean, deep operation, and I learned, and have never since forgotten, the lesson, "He doeth whatever He willeth and commandeth whatsoever He desireth." Many times after that I knew the wisdom of Abdul-Baha turning and giving this command to my husband.

My husband did all in his power to obey the command of Abdul-Baha, and eventually became much beloved by the colored people. . . .[12]

My husband, Joey, was a very fine looking man. He loved life and loved to touch shoulders with humanity. For some unaccountable reason, he began to lose the hair on the top of his head, . . . This was the source of great annoyance to him. It touched his pride deeply, that he should be growing bald at such an early age. The only thing I know of that would give him a jolt was to have someone, or hear someone, refer to his bald spot.

One day while we were in Haifa, Abdul-Baha came into our room and after a general talk, I suddenly remembered a promise made to one of the believers in America. I jumped up quickly and fell at the knees of Abdul-Baha, who was seated, and supplicated very earnestly for this believer, that He might come to this holy spot. In an instant I was conscious of my husband on his knees just a little in back of me. I pulled him by the hand and coaxed him to come up to the knees of Abdul-Baha, while I stood up. Joey added his supplications to mine. As quick as a flash, Abdu'l-Baha stooped forward and kissed Joey upon his bald spot, and looked up at me and smiled, just as though saying to me, "Are you pleased?" Which of course I was.

When Abdul-Baha left us, I put my arms around my husband's neck and said, "Oh, Joey, Abdul-Baha has kissed great capacity into that head of yours. You will be a great servant when you return."[13]

Another significant bit of news that was conveyed in Joseph's letter home was that 'Abdu'l-Bahá approved of their decision to send Carl to live with his aunt Alma and finish high school in Germany. It seems he found himself in a challenging position with a few boys in D.C., and 'Abdu'l-Bahá agreed it would be best to remove him from the situation. As soon as Fanny received word of 'Abdu'l-Bahá's consent to their plan, she arranged for Carl's travel to Germany, and as a result, Pauline and Joseph would be able to see him on their return journey. Pauline writes:

> The Master has given us so much to do that I am anxious to start and see the work progressing. For one thing, I can't imagine how we will instruct the children concerning the Ishrakat, but He told us to do so, and no doubt in the world, He will give us the Light. Also the work among the colored people, and to establish a Spiritual Meeting for Believers only, where the colored are to take part as well as the whites.[14]

Before returning to their waiting family, Pauline and Joseph had a few more meaningful stops along the way. The first stop their route took them to was Alexandria, Egypt where they met with some lovely Bahá'ís who showed them great hospitality. It was interesting to learn that one of the Bahá'ís there owned a store and several clerks were Bahá'ís as well. This made it easier for Bahá'ís passing through town on their way to Haifa, to find the local Bahá'ís. Once they arrived there, word was sent out to other members who arranged for meetings and wonderful hospitality.

After a wonderful visit in Alexandria, they boarded another ship, and traveled third class to Italy. They left Venice at midnight and took a night train through Switzerland and the Alps into snowy Germany where they had a wonderful visit with Alma and Carl, or Nategh, as they now called him. Joseph wrote this about their reunion with Carl:

> Of course the most important news is Carl's arrival. We expected him about this time, but it was a wonderful coincidence to say the least, that he reached here at 8:40 p.m. March 17th and we came in 22 minutes later or at 9:02. This by no means prearranged as we had absolutely no intimation of his plans but needless to say it made us very happy to see him at the station and vice versa. He made the long journey safely and is quite well. We have gotten him in the best school in Stuttgart where he started on Saturday. He is boarding in the same house with Alma, will be well looked after by several good people, so that with all arrangements consummated we are quite happy in that direction. Carl seems to like it, and while surroundings will be new and work difficult at first, I think he will take hold and make good.[15]

Pauline wrote soon after, "Alma is very happy that the people are pleased with us. All are fond of Nategh and said they would help to look after him and pray for him, for they feel that he is their charge from Abdul-Baha." She also mentions that the professors liked him, even though they usually weren't fond of foreigners. It was tough for him having to catch up on his French and also learn German enough to complete school, but he did it. Pauline writes:

> The work of the Cause here is really to be wondered at; the friends are so full of love and attention and really spoil us. I am a source of great amusement to them with my German, but I don't mind since it makes them happy and they seem to like us very much. I have spoken twice at the meetings and the folks said I spoke wonderfully well and I really believe I did too. The way I spoke in German was a revelation to me more than anyone can guess except Alma.[16]

From Germany, Pauline and Joseph journeyed to London, Paris, and then finally home to their loved ones.

Their pilgrimage to visit the Head of the Bahá'í Faith, the Center of the Covenant, the Master, was a galvanizing experience in the lives of the participants. Meeting the Master in person gave them the confirmation and assurance they needed to dedicate the remainder of their lives to His service. Their complete obedience was never in doubt through the rest of their endeavors. The questions they asked show their still deep attachment to Jesus and their Christian roots, but the answers helped them to turn steadily toward their new beloved, Bahá'u'lláh. Remember that Joseph was still a very active member of his congregational church and superintendent of their Sunday school, even though he had accepted Bahá'u'lláh as God's new Manifestation. Other questions that were answered shed light on how they might serve when they returned home. After her pilgrimage, Alma continued to spread the Faith to many parts of Germany and beyond. Fanny and the Hannens returned to Washington and taught the Faith to friends of African descent, and particularly to Louis Gregory, who carried the torch even farther than they could have imagined. Joseph took up the cause of helping the Persian friends and sowing seeds of friendship between Persians and Americans. He also put his secretarial skills to work and tirelessly served in many different capacities. Pauline was very involved in teaching children's classes, following the instructions 'Abdu'l-Bahá had given her, even though she admitted to feeling unprepared and unworthy to do so. Her example of obedience inspired others to follow in her footsteps. All four of the returning pilgrims became sought after public speakers due to their clear and deepened understanding of the message of Bahá'u'lláh. Their lives were by now firmly rooted in this new heavenly garden.

Joseph wrote a beautiful tribute in his account to Ahmad Sohrab, illustrating the profound influence his meeting with 'Abdu'l-Bahá had:

It had been my privilege before this year to visit the Assemblies in Baltimore, New York, Philadelphia, Buffalo and Chicago. These trips were fittingly culminated by a trip to Akka, taken through the grace and power of Abdul-Baha, in February of this year. En-route we visited the Friends in Port Said, Cairo and Alexandria, Egypt, Haifa and Akka, Syria, Stuttgart, Paris and London. Everywhere we have seen the transforming power of the Word of God. For there has been neither Christian nor Gentile, Greek nor Jew, bond nor free, Mohammedan nor other dividing line; all were like brothers and eager to show their love by servitude. No world conquerors could have had a more triumphant journey than was ours. Customs, habits, prejudices—all were subordinated to overpowering love, and we could see the power which shall conquer the world when it is a little more diffused, as Praise God, it will be and is being! We left home with a belief; we returned with a knowledge. Once we had heard; now we can speak of the many millions whose representatives we have seen and conversed with: formerly of every religious creed; now all believers in Christ as the Son of God. All happy as we ourselves, in the fulfillment of their prophecies and its miracle of Unity in the Manifestation of God—Most Glorious! This is the greatest fact in the world's history. What are you going to do about it my brother?

And of Abdul-Baha; that perfect servant of God and of Humanity in His Name: words fail to do Him justice, as they must always until we can "speak with the tongue of angels." In Him we found the perfect man, the loving father and the spiritual king of the Universe. No little need of us, His humble guests, but received His loving thought. No spiritual problem too abstruse to be solved instantly. Truly "never man spoke like this man;" whether for the tender cadences of love in His tones, which awoke echoes that shall ever reverberate through our hearts; or for the power which filled our souls and of which we shall ever partake and still have "a portion for the portion less." A hundred lifetimes seemed centered in those nine days with Abdul-Baha and His household of Saints, and yet "twas as but a dream in the night in its passing."

O Lord! I thank Thee that Thou hast vouchsafed that I might live now, rather than at any other age of the world history, that I may be just my little self, trying to serve Thee in thy Cause each day, rather than the mightiest hero of this mortal world. And I pray that I may be enabled to be faithful to Thy great trust until I shall transfer my servitude to a higher realm with Thine elect and with my dear one's soul thy Holy angel Mrs. Amalie Knobloch, who has gone a little while before us to the Rizwan of El Abha![17]

The following Tablet to Joseph was received after his return from Haifa. It must have added joy upon joy, and further confirmed what they had already experienced while in the Master's presence:

O thou who art firm in the Covenant!
Thy letter dated July 12th, 1909 was received. Praise be to God that you have traversed the countries of Africa and Europe, visited the Friends of God, delivered to them the messages of Abdul-Baha and upon your return to America you associated with all the Beloved and in all the meetings engaged in the commemoration of God. You must thank God for this Bounty and Favor to which you have attained. Any soul who in this day arises to serve the Cause of God, undoubtedly the Confirmations of the Holy Spirit will surround him.

Ye have written that the colored Bahá'ís have gathered in one meeting with the white Believers, destroying the foundations of racial differences and the barriers of color. When a gathering of these two races is brought about that assemblage will become the Magnet of the Supreme Concourse and the Confirmations of the Blessed Perfection will surround it.

I supplicated toward the Kingdom of God and asked forgiveness and pardon for the mother of Mrs. Hannen and Miss Knobloch. Upon thee be Baha'ul' Abha!

O Thou Almighty! O Thou Forgiver! Cause Thou the entrance of Thy beloved maidservant, Mrs. Amalie Knobloch, from the world of matter to the World of Spirit. Forgive Thou shortcomings; overlook mistakes; do not look upon errors. Deal according to Thy Generosity and Bounty. Verily, Thou art the Forgiver and the Bestower of Favors.

O thou Joseph, the speaker of the Word, the firm! Convey the wonderful Abha Greetings on my behalf to Mary Alexander and exercise toward her the utmost kindness. The article which was published in one of the newspapers was received and read. I ask God to confirm and assist thee under all circumstances.

Upon thee be Baha'u'l Abha!
(signed) Abdul-Baha Abbas[18]

- 12 -

The Persian-American Connections

This chapter is dedicated to an area of service very dear to the heart of Joseph Hannen—building relationships between the East and the West, the orient and the occident, especially, Persians and Americans. Because the Bahá'í Faith originated in Iran, events taking place in that country held a great deal of interest to the Bahá'ís of the West.

Sidney Sprague, an early American Bahá'í, lived in Tehran for a year and had experienced the poor economic and educational conditions. Sprague returned to the United States and gave a series of talks regarding his impressions and concerns about those conditions. Action was taken, and on 30 October 1909, during a meeting held to discuss the idea, a committee was formed consisting of Ahmad Sohrab, Fred Woodward, and Joseph Hannen. These three men were to draw up a constitution and a prospectus for the formation of a society to address these issues. The intended goals of the society were to help Iran with its educational and economic development.[1]

The following year 'Abdu'l-Bahá sent a Tablet to the friends in America to be read at the National Convention in 1910. Reproduced in *Bahá'í News* for the friends not in attendance, the Tablet urgently stressed the need for building good relationships between Persia and America. In part, it said:

> *From the inception of the world until now there has been no uniting bond between Persia and America, and communication and correspondence never transpired between these two countries. Now consider what a Joy and bliss have united these two regions in the shortest space of time! What a real and ideal tie hath bound these together! What spiritual communications have been revealed! And now is only the beginning of this early morn and this is only the result of the twilight preceding the dawn. Soon will the star of this unity shine forth and flood all the horizons with its light, and perfect connection and real oneness be obtained in all the regions of the earth. But the speedy realization*

of these hopes is dependent upon this: That the beloved of God in the West shall arise in unison with perfect strength, girding the loins of endeavor in service and putting forth their greatest effort in the way of unity and love. They must not rest a moment nor take a breath of ease . . . May ye be salutary water for the thirsty, an evidence of guidance for the seeker, protection and support for the helpless, a shelter and home for the wanderers, the treasury of the Kingdom for the poor; the source of hope and happiness for the disappointed; the remedy of the heart and soul for the ailing. May you manifest the utmost of kindness to the human race; to weep with him who mourneth and to laugh with him who rejoiceth; sympathizing with the helpless; in communion with the wanderer; a friend to the friend and foe.[2]

'Abdu'l-Bahá reminds the friends that despite the very challenging circumstances for the believers in Persia, they nevertheless found ways to contribute to the building of the House of Worship in Wilmette, demonstrating the love the Persian friends had for their American brothers and sisters. Several Bahá'ís, including Joseph, founded an organization, or "Society," as a direct response to 'Abdu'l-Bahá's encouragement to build bonds of friendship. The result was the creation of the Persian American Educational Society, also at times known as the Oriental Occidental Interdependence Society, or Persian American Interdependence Society. The following articles were written for the *Bahá'í News* magazine by Joseph. He explained the purpose of the Society, how its efforts relating to assistance for Persian Bahá'ís were promoted by 'Abdu'l-Bahá, and what kind of support was needed from the American Bahá'ís. Published in Volume I, No. 5, the first year of its circulation, the article shows the extent to which Joseph was involved with the Society's activities. Portions of the article are shared here:

THE PERSIAN-AMERICAN EDUCATIONAL SOCIETY

One of the most important developments in the Baha'i world during the current year was represented by a meeting held in Washington, D. C., on January 8th, at which time the Persian-American Educational Society made its formal announcement and appeal for co-operation. Since that time, 39 active and 13 associate members have been enrolled, one draft for $300 has been forwarded to Teheran and another remittance is to be made during the current month. Considerable interest aside from that represented by contributions, has been aroused, and promises of additional memberships have been received. The work of the Society may now be said to be fairly under way, and a concise statement may be timely for the guidance and information of the friends.

During the summer of 1909, Mr. Sydney Sprague, who had been for some time a teacher in the School of Tarbiat, in Teheran, Persia, visited this country, which is his native land. At various points he delivered lectures on the country and the work, and a large number of people became interested. The School of Tarbiat was founded some years ago by Persian Baha'is, and was planned to meet the need of non-sectarian education along modern lines, . . .

As to the School of Tarbiat, the following Tablets have been revealed:

> *. . . The problem of the School of Tarbiat is of the utmost importance. It is an essential obligation and duty incumbent upon all the friends to serve that school. This is the first school that the friends have founded in Persia, and all the people know that it belongs to them. Neglect and carelessness in the management of its progressive affairs is a blow to the Cause of God. Therefore everyone must give extra-ordinary importance to the school of Tarbiat and assist it from some standpoint, either through enlightened ideals or the introduction of modern system of education, either by liberal contributions or continual encouragement and assistance. To be brief: It is the hope of this Servant that in the course of time this school become distinguished from among all the schools of the world. Now consider how important is this matter.*
> *(Signed) ABDUL-BAHA ABBAS.*

The Society has received the approval of Abdul-Baha, the following Tablets having been revealed recently, addressed to Mirza Ahmad Sohrab and to the officers of the Society, respectively:

> *In the last two mails, detailed answers have been written to thee. Now the papers that you have forwarded pertaining to the Persian American Educational Society have been received. Truly I say, although the importance of this Society at present, is apparently unknown, but if it remain firm and steadfast in the future it will become the Association of the union of the realm of man, it will thoroughly combine and harmonize the East and the West and accomplish a great service to humanity.*
>
> *The believers of God must give great importance to this Society and arise to perform its fundamental principles and essential duties with heart and soul. I send my congratulation and felicitation to this blessed Society and ask from the bounty of His Highness the Incomparable, confirmation and assistance, supplicate and entreat at the Threshold of Oneness and beg, from the Kingdom of ABHA preservation and protection, providence and safety. If this Society acts with independence and exerts itself in bringing about relations between the East and the West, it will become the foundation of the oneness of the world of humanity. Firmness is essential, for if small affairs can not be accomplished*

without firmness and steadfastness, how much more are these qualities needed for the undertaking of great matters! The friends of God must encourage each other to be firm and steadfast, to reason and consult with each other so that day by day this Society will progress.

Persia and America are in great need of such a Society, even to matters pertaining to material relations between these two Countries, especially America. This Society will become the cause of spreading the American industries in Persia and the great profits, which in the past other nations have collected through the introduction of their goods and implements in Persia, will then go to America. Now consider thou, what great profits will be the result! Moreover the spiritual powers will assist and help, the Breaths of the Holy Spirit will be spread, the Breezes of the Paradise of ABHA diffused and the rays of the Sun of Truth will display wonderful influence.

Convey, on behalf of Abdu'l-Baha, to all the friends of God and the maid-servants of the Merciful in America the wonderful greeting of ABHA and congratulate and felicitate them for the organization of this Society.

Upon thee be Baha El-ABHA! (Signed) ABDU'L-BAHA ABBAS.

(Revealed in Haifa, Syria, April 3, 1910. Translated by Mirza Ahmad Sohrab, Washington, D.C., May 18, 1910.)

From the foregoing, it will be realized that the cooperation and assistance of all the friends is necessary, in order that the Society may be able to do effective work, to realize the ideals of the organization, to open the door of opportunity to our merchants, to spread knowledge in the Orient, and to facilitate the means of industrial, commercial, educational and agricultural interchange. As Abdul-Baha writes, the final and important results of the activities of this Society will accrue to America. In these Tablets He has opened a great door of intercommunication between the East and the West, and has clearly detailed the policies and aims which must be followed in order that it may become a fitting servant in the world. To make the Association firm and permanent, as Abdul-Baha desires, we need the active energetic cooperation of all true lovers of progress, of humanity, of all the friends of truth and philanthropists. May we all become assisted to perform this command, and make this Society a Society of the union of the Realm of Man!

In a letter recently received, Mr. Sprague states that the news of the formation of the Society has greatly cheered our brothers in Persia, who are proceeding to form a local Executive Committee in Teheran, which, with the Executive Committee here will administer the affairs of the body. They naturally expect a large number of scholarships, and must not be disappointed.

Dr. [Susan] Moody writes from Teheran, April 27, 1910, that "On the first day of Rizwan, three meetings were held in various gardens and about six hundred tomans ($600) were collected to found the school for girls. This is a great sum for these times, and shows how eager the people are to progress." She adds: "They have been much stimulated by the loving work of the P.A.E.S. and we hope the interest there continues to be of a practical turn. There is great necessity and also high sense of honor in regard to the love of all the friends in this matter." If Persia in her hour of need can do these things, how much greater should the response of favored America be! The Orient last year sent over $8,000 to America toward the Mashrak-el-Azkar, and in a small way we can show our appreciation of this munificent gift by helping to educate their children. . . .

The official headquarters of the Society is at 1800 Belmont Road, and its address is Post Office Box 192, Washington, D.C. Communications and memberships are earnestly solicited, that the desire of our beloved Abdul-Baha, as expressed in his Tablets, may be carried out, and that speedily. It is a great privilege which is offered, rather than a favor on the part of those who help, yet the grateful thanks of the beneficiaries will resound in the praise of those who respond.

Joseph H. Hannen
Washington D.C. May 26, 1910[3]

The above article offers an indication of the scope and planned activities of the society, as well as the especially high regard and hopes ʻAbdu'l-Bahá had for its success. In volume I, no. 17, of *Star of the West,* another article by Joseph appeared describing the considerable progress made by the society within a year of its inception. A new constitution had been developed and plans were being made to adopt it at a future meeting. Circular letters calling for books for the library at Tarbiat School were mailed, and weekly journals in Tehran and Cairo were publishing articles about the activities of PAES. There was talk of Shiraz opening another Tarbiat School. A proposal was put forward for comment, suggesting that a Persian Bahá'í student be sent to America and that the Society would offer support and assistance. They concluded that, "The circle of activity and the influence of the Society is widening daily. It is assured that with the active co-operation of the friends and the assistance of all far-sighted men and women, it will soon become what Abdul-Baha prophetically says: '*The greatest Society of the world; produce inexhaustible results and benefits; become the tree of the oneness of the realm of humanity and cast its all-encircling shade over the people of the East and the West.*'"[4]

From 16–17 June 1911, the Persian American Educational Society held a successful and well attended First Annual Conference in Washington D.C. A glowing five-page article was written, again by Joseph Hannen, for *Star of the West* (Vol. II, nos. 7 and 8), the new name for *Bahá'í News* magazine. The article boasts, "Probably the central figure of attraction—an interest shared, and justly so by the able founder, Mirza Ahmad Sohrab—was Ghodsia Khanum, the little lady from Persia, whose arrival in this country for the purpose of obtaining an American education was well-timed for the purpose of the Conference. Illustrated interviews with her were published in the leading newspapers, and her reception at Rauscher's Hall, Saturday, June 17th was a notable feature of the Conference."[5]

A group picture, published in *Star of the West* along with the article, shows Joseph proudly standing in the front row next to Ahmad and Ghodsia. The article, reported in Joseph's typically detailed style, includes an impressive list of speakers from various organizations with common aims who supported the conference. Joseph even recited an original poem, written for the conference, illustrating his duel interests in education and Persian affairs. It was highly praised by 'Abdu'l-Bahá. A list of committee appointments, new officers, and resolutions it hoped to accomplish were included. One of those resolutions read, "That this conference record its appreciation of the untiring efforts and effective work of its Secretary, Joseph Hannen, in the preparation of his report and in the business of the Conference." It continues, "That the recommendations embodied in the report of the secretary of the Persian American Educational Society are here-by adopted," making it clear that Joseph had a critical and influential role in the society. In addition to his role as secretary for the society, Joseph also served on the Program Committee and the Press Committee for the Conference.[6]

In 1912, when 'Abdu'l-Bahá made His long journey to America, one of His first public addresses was to the Persian American Educational Society Conference. The talk was given on 2 April 1912. Maḥmud wrote in his diary:

> That evening 'Abdu'l-Bahá attended the annual meeting of the Orient-Occident Unity Conference at the public library. It was a vast gathering and the hall was filled to capacity. As the Master entered the hall, the audience was awe-struck. All stood and remained standing until He bade them be seated. It was amazing to witness how spontaneously these people paid Him their respect, even though most were not Bahá'ís. He spoke on the importance of the relationship between the East and the West, the unity of people and about the Revelation of the Greatest Name. His talk was so moving and inspiring that afterwards everyone wanted to meet Him but because He was so tired to greet everyone, He decided to return home.[7]

Over the next few years several letters between Joseph and Dr. Susan Moody demonstrate Joseph's involvement in managing the gathering of funds, as he was the person to whom she would write when there was a particular need to be filled. Dr. Moody sent numerous reports detailing events that had taken place at the Tarbiat School with the aim of generating greater response and contributions. In Joseph's tenure as the society's secretary, he reported on the contributions it accrued, as well as the projects and further developments the society hoped to initiate with the funds. The reports often appeared in *Star of the West* and each expressed his passion for this endeavor as he appealed for support from the growing Bahá'í world. In one report written in 1916, Joseph details a variety of activities and services the society was pursuing. Activities included sending boxes of books to the Library at the Tarbiat School in Iran, and also "catalogues of agricultural, mining, telephone and railway machinery and supplies," which they hoped to display in Iran, with an interpreter on hand to explain the equipment's usefulness. If they could successfully interest the people of Iran in American technology, such as it was, then developing commercial relationships might be the logical next step. Their high aspirations for the work of the society in bettering relationships is shown in this statement included in Joseph's report, "The appointment of five Americans as Financial Advisers to the Persian Government, recently arranged through the State Department, will, no doubt, stimulate our work. These advisers sail for Persia during the current month, and this official recognition of American prestige will naturally be followed by a public desire to know more about our country, which this Society will be able to gratify."[8]

In 1916 an article reported the appointment of a "Central Executive Board, with headquarters in Washington, composed of the following: Charles Mason Remey, Chairman; Arnold Belmont, Vice-Chairman; Jos. H. Hannen, Secretary; Mirza Ahmad Sohrab, Treasurer; Stanwood Cobb, Edwin C. Reed, Mrs. L. J. Young-Withee, Mrs. C. S. Coles, and Mrs. E. C. Dunlop, Assistant Secretary."[9] In typical fashion, Joseph ended his reports with quotes from 'Abdu'l-Bahá, reiterating the importance of the friends giving their support to this important work. His desire to be of service and be obedient to the desires of 'Abdu'l-Bahá was evident in his tireless work for the society.

Many requests were presented to Joseph in his post as secretary for the society. One such letter came from a young Persian friend: "Please pay special attention & do your best to get me a position there so that I can come to that free country. . . . My intention is to spend the rest of my life in the service of the Cause & be with you and other spiritual friends in that free land."[10] Other letters address a situation concerning several Persian boys who had, with the help of the society, been sent to school in America, but had been found to be misbehaving. Joseph's help was sought in determining the root of the matter and dealing with it.[11] Another situation involved two women in Iran whose home had been broken into, and who had been severely beaten. On this occasion Joseph was writing to various Bahá'í Assemblies asking for their support in signing a petition to the Persian government in defense of the assaulted women. On yet another occasion, Joseph was called upon to assist a gentleman from India who was stranded at Ellis Island and in need of funds or some assurance that he would be financially supported before he could enter the country. A few letters seem to indicate he was involved with the purchase of Persian rugs, and assisted various people in arranging transactions.[12] Again, Joseph to the rescue![13] Much of the correspondence also involved Mr. William Hoar in some manner. A Bahá'í from New York, he corresponded with Joseph on many occasions regarding multiple situations, especially when there was need of financial assistance for the society.

Such was Joseph's commitment to building relations with Persia that there was a short period in 1918 when he actually took on some of the duties of the Persian Legation, or Consul, in Washington, in order to help out his dear friend Ali Kuli-Khan, who usually held that position. He wrote in a letter to Juanita Storch, dated 18 July 1918, using the impressive letterhead of the Legation, ". . . the Legation is without attachés, other than our wonderful Khan, and so I am helping him out . . . writing some of his letters which must be typed. It is 'on the cards' that I may become Honorary Secretary of the Legation, or Consul at Washington, when the Government can be reached to make the appointment. I care less for this, however, than the opportunity of serving Persia, and helping a dear and wonderful Bahá'í Brother."[14] Two folders of letters at the National Archives indicate that Joseph and Khan had a special relationship. Frequently through the years Khan would ask favors of Joseph on confidential matters. On one occasion, he needed Joseph to secure a lawyer for a Persian minister who had been in some kind of trouble. At times Khan would confide in Joseph when dealing with matters concerning Persians who were considered Covenant-breakers. The fact that he would write to Joseph about these issues, and many others, indicates the deep level of trust and affection shared between these two unique figures in the history of the Faith.

Meanwhile in Haifa, 'Abdu'l-Bahá was facing very challenging times with those who were considered Covenant-breakers. These individuals claimed to be believers, but for reasons of jealousy or want of power and money, turned against 'Abdu'l-Bahá. They were continuously instigating serious mischief, trying to persuade others that 'Abdu'l-Bahá was not the true authoritative leader of the Faith; even going so far as to send representatives to America to influence the young Bahá'í community to turn against 'Abdu'l-Bahá. The following letter from 'Abdu'l-Bahá to Joseph, dated 26 April 1919, hints at these difficulties:

> *Concerning the matter of receiving Orientals regarding which you had inquired, affiliate and associate and exercise the utmost kindness to the Hindus, Chinese and Japanese Orientals for they have no bad intentions and are not ill-natured; but assuredly do not receive and associate with any Persian*

or Arab who may come to those regions without having an autographic letter of recommendation from me and bearing my signature. He may perhaps go to those regions in order to intrigue, to sow the seeds of sedition and to create difference and enmity. The blessed souls, however, will undoubtedly carry with them a letter of recommendation from me.[15]

The situation became particularly challenging for Joseph, due to his involvement in the Persian community of Washington and the many friendships he had developed over the years. Joseph, desiring to be obedient to any instructions of the Master, wrote to the grandson of 'Abdu'l-Bahá, Shoghi Effendi, asking for further clarification and guidance. In a letter dated 7 July 1919, Joseph writes:

> In connection with my last Tablet, and particularly with reference to the matter of receiving Orientals: Won't you please ask the Beloved for me, for instructions as to these individual cases: there are several Persians who have been in America for some time, former employees or protégés of Mirza Ali Kuli-Khan, and with whom He has asked me to keep in touch. . . . These do not attend Bahá'í meetings, and seem in no sense inimical to the Cause. Also, there has arrived in Washington a new Persian Minister, . . . and as I have been friendly and helpful to the Legation officials heretofore, I am awaiting an invitation to call on him, and perhaps to be asked to render what services I can to Persia, as a friend, of course, and with no idea of receiving any compensation. May I be allowed to make these visits to the Legation, and to be friendly to the Persians mentioned? My sole object in life is to obey the Beloved's Commands, and I do not ask in a sense of desiring to evade or avoid obedience, but I have felt that the prohibition of association undoubtedly refers to stranger Persians, or others who may come to the Assemblies, or approach us as Bahá'ís or friends of the Cause, rather than to those who have been here for years, and are well authenticated, or to the Legation staff at Washington.[16]

A return letter, dated 15 October 1919 and written in Shoghi Effendi's own handwriting, addressed these questions. He writes:

> My dear Bahá'í brother!
>
> Your two welcome letters, dated July 4 and Aug. 11 have been received and their good tidings have been fully submitted to the Beloved.
>
> With regards to those Orientals whose names you mentioned in the first letter the Beloved's message is the following: "Exercise toward the Persian minister and the Persians of whom you have written in your letter the utmost love and kindness and in order to please them do all you can to help them. But be vigilant & awake lest one there should be a follower

of Ezelis or a covenant–breaker! The instant that you feel that a person among these Persians in an Ezeli or a covenant–breaker, assuredly and immediately avoid his company for he is the essence of evil.

On the other hand, those whose devotion is manifest—& Mirza can investigate this matter—show to these the utmost love and kindness."[17]

\- 13 -

'Abdu'l-Bahá Comes to America

One of the fondest wishes of the friends since the Faith began to take root in America was to have 'Abdu'l-Bahá visit and meet the new believers. Unfortunately, 'Abdu'l-Bahá, as a prisoner of the Ottoman Empire, was unable to leave the vicinity of 'Akká or Haifa. However, in 1908, due to the Young Turks Rebellion, His imprisonment finally ended, and the earnest attempts and campaigns to bring Him to the United States reached a feverish pitch. The Hannens were among those who helped to circulate petitions and letters urging the Master to come. In response to their requests, 'Abdu'l-Bahá sent a message, printed in 1911 in *Star of the West*, Vol. II, no. 4. Here is a portion of that Tablet:

> *Now the friends and the maid-servants in America have written innumerable letters and all of them are pleading that 'Abdu'l-Bahá make a trip to that country. Their supplications and entreaties are insistent. In view of the differences among the friends and the lack of unity among the maid-servants of the Merciful, how can 'Abdu'l-Bahá hasten to those parts? Is this possible? No, by God!*
>
> *If the friends and the maid-servants of the Merciful long for the visit of 'Abdu'l-Bahá, they must immediately remove from their midst differences of opinion and be engaged in the practice of infinite love and unity. . . .*
>
> *O ye friends and maid-servants of the Merciful! If ye are yearning for my meeting, and if in reality ye are seeking my visit, ye must close the doors of difference and open the gates of affection, love and friendship. Ye must pulsate as one heart, and throb as one spirit. You must be like the waves, though they are innumerable they constitute the all-encircling sea. . . .*
>
> *Verily, verily, I say unto you, were it not for this difference amongst you, the inhabitants of America in all those regions would have, by now, been attracted to the Kingdom of God, and would have constituted themselves your helpers and assisters. Is it meet that you sacrifice this most glorious Bounty for*

worthless imaginations? No, by God! Should you reflect for one moment, you shall become enabled to destroy, instantly the foundation of this difference by absolutely refraining from backbiting and faultfinding amongst yourselves. Adorn with infinite love and concord the assemblage of beatitude, bring about the meeting of happiness, establish the banquet of the oneness of the realm of humanity, loosen your tongues in praising each other, and then anticipate the presence of 'Abdu'l-Bahá in your midst. . . .

I beg of God to confirm you in union and concord that you may become the cause of the oneness of the kingdom of humanity. Live and act in accord with the Divine Teachings, be abstracted from all the attachments of the human world, characterized with merciful characteristics, release yourselves from the nether world, become heavenly souls, spiritual beings and the angels of Paradise.

Upon ye be Baha-el-Abha
(signed) 'Abdu'l-Bahá Abbas
Translated by Mirza Ahmad, April 28th, 1911[1]

The American Bahá'ís certainly had their work cut out for them. All the differences of opinion, large and small, had to be consulted upon and worked out in order to create the unity the teachings of Bahá'u'lláh called for. It is one thing to want unity, but it is another to actually achieve it. Eventually, though, they must have made some headway in that direction because 'Abdu'l-Bahá finally agreed to come to America.

In his book, *239 Days,* Allen Ward gives an account of 'Abdu'l-Bahá's travels in America and the effect it had on communities and individuals from coast to coast. Ward writes:

'Abdu'l-Bahá thus made it clear that He did not set His course toward America to seek His own glory or to spread His own message. He said, when He reached His destination, that it was His "purpose to set forth in America the fundamental principles of the revelation and teachings of Bahá'u'lláh. It will then become the duty of the Bahá'ís . . . to give these principles enfoldment and application in the minds, hearts and lives of the people." 'Abdu'l-Bahá's name means the Servant of the Glory, and He came to America in that capacity—the Servant of Bahá'u'lláh, appointed by His Father as the Center of His Covenant and the Perfect Exemplar of the Faith of Bahá'u'lláh. He came to reinforce the efforts of those few early believers in America and to give them a living Example of what it means to be a Bahá'í. In short, He came to unify and to deepen those early believers and to teach them the significance of firmness in the Covenant that Bahá'u'lláh had made with the Bahá'ís. He came to set in motion teaching efforts, the effects of which would be felt around the world. He came to sow seeds that would germinate, sprout, grow, and bear fruit for a millennium—that, in fact, would hasten the advent of the millennium.[2]

Another publication chronicling 'Abdu'l-Bahá's travels through America is *Maḥmud's Diary*, an account of one of the Persian companions of 'Abdu'l-Bahá who assisted and translated as needed throughout this momentous journey. Earl Redman's book *'Abdu'l-Bahá in their Midst*, *Juliet Thompson's Diary*, and *'Abdu'l-Bahá in America: Agnes Parsons' Diary* are some other excellent accounts of His sojourns through America. Because she lived in Washington D.C. and hosted 'Abdu'l-Bahá at many of the gatherings in that city, Mrs. Parsons' account is of particular interest. Another notable book is Robert Stockman's *'Abdu'l-Bahá in America,* which was published at the time of the centenary of 'Abdu'l-Bahá's visit in 2012. As all of these authors have done a marvelous job of capturing the essence of 'Abdu'l-Bahá's journey, I have chosen to concentrate on the parts of His travels that directly concern the Hannens, Knoblochs, and Barnitzes and especially His visits to Washington D.C.

The importance of the details that the following accounts record for history was mentioned by the Guardian of the Faith, Shoghi Effendi, when he addressed the American Bahá'ís in a letter dated 21 April 1933 saying, "The joys which the announcement of His arrival evoked, the publicity which His activities created, the forces which His utterances released, the opposition which the implications of His teachings excited, the significant episodes to which His words and deeds continually gave rise—these future generations will, no doubt, minutely and befittingly register. They will carefully delineate their features, will cherish and preserve their memory, and will transmit unimpaired the record of their minutest details to their descendants."[3]

In addition to being present at all of the events and addresses in that city, Joseph also played a key role due to his expert skills as a stenographer. In fact, Pauline often made reference to his ability to write very quickly what took her half a day to record. He put these skills to good use during 'Abdu'l-Bahá's talks, whether formal or informal. Many of the talks printed in *Star of the West* credit Joseph for taking the stenographic notes. The full text of the talks will not be presented in this book, as they can be found in other sources such as *Star of the West* and *The Promulgation of Universal Peace.* I am, however, including the full text of some personal accounts that both Pauline and Fanny wrote to Alma, who was living in Germany at the time and missing all the exciting events taking place in America. Their accounts and personal recollections are rather touching as they include the personal and heartfelt emotions not captured in Joseph's more formal reports. The great love the sisters felt for 'Abdu'l-Bahá is undeniable in these precious accounts. I remind the reader again that any words attributed to 'Abdu'l-Bahá in quotes are the recollections of the writer, and not considered authentic.

'Abdu'l-Bahá's imprisonment in 'Akká ended in 1908. For the first few years after His release He chose to remain in the vicinity of 'Akká but later moved to Haifa. It was during those years in which He was residing in 'Akká that the family made their pilgrimages. In 1910, He traveled to Egypt as He had promised the friends He would do. There He tasted His first real freedom since His family had been banished to Baghdad in 1853. He remained there until He made His first historic visit to Europe in September of 1911 when He left for London and then Paris the following month. He spent the winter of 1911 in Egypt, and the following spring, on 25 March 1912, He boarded the *S. S. Cedric* and began the long journey to America. At a stop in Italy many of the passengers left the Cedric in favor of a trip on the maiden voyage of the *Titanic*, and the friends in America had gathered enough funds for 'Abdu'l-Bahá to do the same. However, He chose to return the tickets and gave the extra money to charity, and He continued His trip on the *Cedric*.[4]

At 9:00 pm on 10 April 1912, 'Abdu'l-Bahá's ship anchored in New York Harbor, and by 11 April, He began His historic travels through America. His days were filled with public talks and an endless stream of visitors. I have not found any evidence to suggest that Pauline or Fanny traveled to New York to see 'Abdu'l-Bahá while He was there, however, Pauline still had her network of friends to keep her informed:

> My own dear sister Alma,
> Though we have perhaps kept you in suspense for a time, yet it was for the purpose of giving you the most of this wonderful visit of Abdul-Baha to our country. I will begin with New York and what I have heard from there.
>
> Very early in the morning great multitudes were assembled at the wharf to meet Abdul-Baha, but the steamer did not arrive until 1 p.m. When it finally appeared eager eyes searched the decks to single out the Beloved One, but He was nowhere to be seen. During this eager searching, the gangplank for freight was put forth and suddenly to the astonished few, who should be standing at the other end of the gangplank but Abdul-Baha, <u>alone</u>. When first seeing the masses, some of the friends thought He looked worried, but in a flash His Face was wreathed in smiles and He bowed right and left, then disappeared. Then many who had received a permit to go on deck the steamer to meet Mr. Woodcock's family, really to greet Abdul-Baha, . . . were allowed to come aboard. Then word was sent to the waiting crowd of Believers and friends to go to the home of the Kinneys and Abdul-Baha would see them all there. This was a terrible blow to them, some obeyed and some did not. Since then I have heard that the majority, even those who did obey, do not believe it was

the Word of Abdul-Baha, but some of the Friends who desired to shield Him. Be that as it may, there were a great many who remained and they say there was a great Reception. In the meantime the company gathered at the home of the Kinneys and the place was packed. Finally Abdul-Baha came and while many were watching the front door for Him to enter, He led His party down in the basement through the laundry room and up to where the friends were gathered, still leading the way. He passed through the two crowded rooms straight on to an alcove. Here He rested for a while on a couch. After a little while He addressed them. Then a funny thing happened, naturally the tension was great. To relieve this Abdul-Baha smilingly bid the visitors to be seated oriental fashion. There was such laughter and fun seeing the efforts of these elegantly gowned women and men trying to sit on the floor, and Abdul-Baha's hearty laughter at their expense, that all were at ease in a moment and He had won the hearts of all present. In New York, His mission seems to have been among the Believers and when He returns to New York it will be more for the public. But there are two events that are noteworthy and of a public nature. The first was His public appearance at the Church of Percy S. Grant, an Episcopalian. Abdul-Baha and His little party were assembled in the rectory, just off from the pulpit, while the first part of the service was being conducted—the pastor, after reading a most appropriate text, I have forgotten what it was, and while a most wonderful song was being rendered; Abdul-Baha was led up to the Bishop's chair, at the top of which was placed a Laurel Wreath, the Victor's Crown with long purple ribbon streamers. This was done by the Minister himself. Then when Abdul-Baha spoke He chose for His text the one the Minister had opened the service with.

It is said that it was a most solemn service. It must have been. In connection with this service one of the Friends told of Abdul-Baha's love for a joke. (At the convention this joke was told.) After the service someone who was awestruck, because Abdul-Baha had not been present when Rev. Clark read the Scripture Lesson, yet He Abdul-Baha seemed to know to the letter and went right on with the text. The person asked Him, "Tell me, how did you happen upon the same text?" A twinkle, full of mischief came into His Eyes, and He said, "Would you really like me to explain this miracle?" "Oh, yes, please do." Then Abdul-Baha leaning forward with a mysterious manner and in a stage whisper said, "Because Dr. Fareed told me what he said."

The next thing of public interest was His visit to the Bowery Mission, in the slums of New York. At the Hotel where Abdul-Baha was stopping was a maidservant who seemed strangely moved by Abdul-Baha's presence, and was ever near when He came or went, perhaps neglecting her duties. Naturally she was near when Abdul-Baha left for the Bowery Mission and expectant upon His return.

After Abdul-Baha's address to those poor, degraded, benighted and ignorant men and boys, holding out hope to them, encouraging them to be better men and boys, showing them that being poor was no reason for falling into the path of ignorance. He said, "See how God loves you and wants you to receive His highest gifts for He, God has chosen poverty for you as for His Son, Jesus Christ. All the saints of God chose poverty in order that they may attain His spiritual bounties. The Bab and Baha'u'llah in this day have chosen poverty and shame that the glories of God might become manifest, et*c*." At the close of His address He desired to greet each one, as they departed. He took His place by the door and as each man passed, He gave each a warm hand clasp leaving a shining quarter (25 cents) in the palm, and then the next, and so on until every man and boy in the hall had received one. When the party returned to the hotel, who should be standing, reverently waiting, but the maid-servant. When Abdul-Baha saw her, He smiled a welcome and putting His hand into the green bag, gave her all that was left of the quarters. The girl was dumbfounded and turning to a man servant said, with tears in her eyes, "I am going to use all this money as He would like me to." In a very few moments without ceremony Abdul-Baha's private dining room was opened and regardless of those in the room, with tears rolling down her cheeks she walked up to Abdul-Baha and said, "I can never thank you for your great kindness, but I hope to be a better girl and will leave this Hotel at once, and start anew." Only Abdul-Baha knows just what she meant as she shook hands and departed.

On the eve of Abdul-Baha's leaving New York, He said to some of the friends, "just as soon as I leave New York, articles denouncing me will appear in the daily papers." Sure enough the next morning after His departure the first ugly article appeared denouncing Him.[5]

In another letter, Pauline writes:

May 10, 1912
My Beloved sister,
You have been kept waiting a long time before the events of Abdul-Baha's visit to America were recorded for your special benefit. Surely now you have forgiven the long silence because I have been writing steadily every minute I could since beginning to relate the happening. One item of more or less interest not to be incorporated in the long letter is this: In New York Abdul-Baha has been shown the greatest kindness by the ministers,

which is just the opposite here so far. On the other hand, the Friends in N.Y. flocked about Abdul-Baha, principally blaming and accusing one another to Him until He was weary and worn out. Finally one evening He, Himself, invited about nine men chiefly concerned in this unrest, prepared the meal with His own hands, served them and left them to talk and unite. After a time He returned and one of them started in again with complaining. Abdul-Baha is supposed to have said, in great weariness: "I have invited you all, prepared the food for you all, and served you all, that you might serve one another. I return and you still come to me with complaints." This was a grave admonition to them, and it seems they have profited by it, for the interest in New York is widespread and a dignified body is now gathered together, far outnumbering the old assembly. God grant that the seed thus sown in other hearts may be productive of great results to the Glory of New York City.

He, Abdul-Baha, addressed a very large gathering of at least 1500 distinguished men and women, the elect of N.Y., in the Ballroom of the Astor House. This being a gathering of the Peace Advocates, Abdul-Baha spoke on the subject of Peace, the following I think worth mentioning. I copy it from a newspaper.

> "Peace is light; war is darkness. Peace is life; war is death. Peace is guidance; war is misguidance. Peace is founded on good; war is a satanic institute. Peace is conducive to illumination; war is destructive of light. Peace and amity are factors of existence; war is decomposition, or lack of existence. Where ever the banner of peace is raised it is conducive to the welfare of the world." Etc.

Another extract to please you, "Baha'is believe in the equality of women and men, for until women have an equal voice in the affairs of the world, war will not be abolished."

So much sickness and visiting had to be done that my long account had to be put off for awhile. I'm writing on it and will soon send it along. My mind will rest easy that you know all I can recall with interest.

Affectionately,
Pauline[6]

When 'Abdu'l-Bahá and His party made their way to Washington D.C. ten days after His arrival in America, Joseph, being an officer of the Persian American Educational Society, was privileged to be a part of the small welcoming group.[7] During 'Abdu'l-Bahá's first stay in D.C., Joseph did much of the preparatory work before His arrival; arranging gatherings, and answering correspondence concerning meetings and promotional efforts. In addition to taking notes during 'Abdu'l-Bahá's talks, Joseph also wrote detailed reports of the Master's visit for *Star of the West.* Miss Leone St. Claire Barnitz was another who desired to serve in any way she was able. As she was the personal secretary to Mrs. Parsons, she was given the job of escorting visitors who came to see 'Abdu'l-Bahá, into His presence, and recording each of their names and the topics that were discussed.[8]

An article in *Star of the West* details 'Abdu'l-Bahá's time in Washington, and it is this account, written by Joseph, that is often quoted in various books about 'Abdul-Bahá's visit as it is one of the earliest accounts published. Because Joseph's complete report can be found in *Star of the West,*[9] I have included many of Pauline's and Fanny's personal accounts, which are longer, more detailed, and give a more personal rendition of the events. They present the little details that touch the heart, and give one a feeling for what it must have been like to be in the presence of 'Abdu'l-Bahá.

Pauline recounts of 'Abdu'l-Bahá's arrival:

> As Fanny has already told you, here in Washington we were all keyed to the highest pitch of expectation. It had a very strange effect upon most of the Believers. They were either very happy or so nervous that they were easily angered or quick to cry or fume. It took very little to upset us, even Carl and Paul were strangely affected. Paul seemed to want to run away all the time. Carl on the other hand, was unsociable and stayed very close to me. We had every reason to believe that our Beloved would arrive Wednesday, the night before the "Persian American" Conference. On that assurance we sent for Carl [who was living and working in Pittsburgh at the time], but Abdul-Baha did not arrive until Saturday. Carl might have saved a week at work, but we see now that the nervous expectation was the preparation necessary for those here. His coming was no small matter to the Friends. Because of the great amount of advertising on behalf of Persian American Educational Society and their distinguished guest of Honor, Abdul-Baha, we believe the clergy became alarmed and before Abdul-Baha arrived the ministers took counsel, and as a unit agreed to warn their congregations against the Servant of God. They also sent a delegation to the newspaper offices and made them promise not to publish His talks—and most particularly urging that no mention of Him be made on the religious sheets of the Saturday and Sunday papers. In a measure they succeeded in preventing Abdul-Baha's Addresses from appearing but not the mentioning of His Name.
>
> So we were highly strung because of this united effort on the part of the clergy against us. This was certainly not the attitude we would have desired, but what would happen? No one could even guess, except for the fact that He is the master of every situation. Saturday was the day

> for sure now, and since we had received word from N.Y. that Abdul-Baha desired that there be no demonstration at the station, the Believers modestly refrained from imposing. I said to Fanny and Carl, they are not Believers of Washington, so they might violate this wish by going to the station and just see Him, nothing more. But He arrived before the time we were expecting Him. Carl was dressing to go with Fanny, Paul had disappeared, when Joseph came in radiantly happy saying, "He has come! I saw Him! But He paid no attention to any of us except Khan's two children, these He took in the carriage with Him, then only did He wave us an acknowledgement." Joseph thought He looked so very tired. Joseph saw Him again as He was entering the home of Mrs. Parsons. Poor Joseph didn't know what was happening, our nervous tension snapped, that is, Carl's and mine, Carl's keen disappointment was too much for me in my weakened nervous condition, and I broke down at last and cried and cried and cried. Of course, I was unfit for the Reception and Fanny, dear heart, would not leave me. You understand Alma, no one was to blame for anything, in fact it was my dream come true, but it is to show you the intense excitement existing among the friends before His arrival. I had my cry first, others had theirs afterwards. Carl went with the Barnitzes after the reception and went to the Hall with them. Joseph had to go early to arrange things at the Hall (in fact he was rushed to death for nearly a month beforehand.) Paul and I were together. Fanny had gone home to dress and came alone, so our little family was quite scattered at the great moment.[10]

Fanny wrote her impressions of the evening program:

> Sat. night—my such crowds of people—all quiet as in church. Several speakers were heard and anxiously even the Persians. Mr. Hoar, Joseph and all on the platform gazed toward the door. Khan kindly began an impromptu address to fill in time—then—suddenly everybody arose—Abdul-Baha majestically came down the center aisle, accepting Mr. Hoar's proffered hand. He instantly stepped to the reading desk slightly leaning against it. He began to speak, Dr. Fareed interpreting for 15 minutes. The audience seemed spell bound. Then at its close those nearest grasped His hands—but the whole audience began moving forward—and then we were asked to form a line down the aisle and Abdul-Baha would shake hands with us as He passed and—from where I stood it looked like a sea of heads. Winding in and out was the dear white head of our Beloved.[11]

Pauline wrote to Alma her impressions of the next event, which was at Studio Hall at the usual Sunday School hour:

> Sunday morning the little ones were divinely happy. Colored and white were assembled. One little colored boy, a Believer's son, about five or six years old said, "He kissed me and I am going to try never to be bad again!" His little sister, a few years older had her hat on, so Abdul-Baha shook hands only. She cried afterwards but was comforted when she was told that she should see Him again Wednesday. Then she burst out, "I won't have any fancy hat on then, you bet. O, how I do love Him!"[12]

Fanny wrote of an event at the Universalist Church:

> Sunday afternoon we visited the Universalist Church. This was packed to overflowing, a goodly sprinkling of colored folks. All eyes were turned toward the door. Abdul-Baha bathed in rays of sunlight walked through the center aisle, everybody standing respectfully, then introduced to the Pastor. He, with a sigh of contentment dropped into the chair (clerical chair). Our Baha'i Brother, Prof. Mayo presided at the organ and a Baha'i young lady—a noted singer sang the solo. Abdul-Baha spoke, walking back and forth. Then because of other engagements He asked to be excused. The pastor in announcing this at the beginning of the service said we would dispense with the opening service, until after the Great Teacher of the orient had departed. Then we should remain seated until the services close. Yes we fully intended to but, when Abdul-Baha stepped down, the pastor asked Him or rather said, "The members and Friends of this Congregation greatly desire to meet and shake hands with the revered Teacher." Instantly Abdul-Baha remained standing, leaning against the floor of the pulpit. All those hundreds of people filed passed Him, each receiving a warm clasp of the hand. The stream of people was three and sometimes four abreast as they came up to Him. Two young colored women, not wishing to push forward, they were farthest and were about to pass on, all the time eagerly looking into His face, when suddenly without seemingly having seen them at all, He reached way over to them, catching the sleeve of one, the end of the others coat. He pulled them to Him, smiling at them, He gave a clasp of the hand—did they realize how fortunate they were? Yes, they smiled while tears dimmed their eyes as they passed on.[13]

Pauline wrote:

> That afternoon, at the Universalist Church where Abdul-Baha spoke and Fanny has so beautifully described, three or four things I noticed with surprise. First, that Abdul-Baha made the sign of the cross as He seated Himself in the pulpit chair. I was so astonished, I thought it must have

been my imagination, asking the stranger seated next to me if they had noticed it and they too had seen it. Then when Abdul-Baha had finished speaking, He did the same thing, then we were sure we were not mistaken. In this way, no doubt He showed His reverence to the Christian Church. But the minister failed to do this.

The third incident Fanny mentioned, but being on the ground floor she could not observe what we did from the balcony; namely the two colored women, whom Abdul-Baha drew towards Him [were] a Believer I know (Mrs. Marshal) and her sister. What Fanny evidently missed was the flash of joy that passed over His weary face as He drew them nearer to His side and called to Ameen to translate something for Him as He held their hands. What He said I have not yet found out, but believe I will pretty soon. Out of perhaps thousands of people who filed before Him, why should He have singled out for particular attention these two colored women? The one is a missionary, the other who is her sister, is an excellent musician of our own city.

(The fourth) In front of the church were two men with leaflets, which they gave to all as they left the church. Through this little paper they were warning the public against Abdul-Baha, and you and Fanny, Joseph, Mrs. Finch and Mr. Remey came in for a roasting. This same man distributed these same leaflets to all who attended the great gathering at the Library, Saturday night. So your names have been widely circulated though you are in Germany, and Mrs. Finch in Seattle. This man selected something from your notes, I believe a lesson by Hayder Ali (Flowers Culled from the Rose-Garden of Abdul-Baha). You see the Cause is growing very fast and the clergy are alarmed and aroused.[14]

Joseph continues:

Receptions were held at the home of Mrs. Parsons every afternoon at about 5:00 o'clock, from Monday to Friday, inclusive. The large parlor, seating 150, was crowded each afternoon and the interest grew as the week advanced. Many persons prominent in social, official and diplomatic circles were present, beside numbers of well-known men and women of literary and scientific attainments.[15]

Joseph left out an event personally significant to him and Pauline, feeling it was not appropriate to include in a formal report. However, I found evidence of this event in Mrs. Parsons' diary in an entry for 23 April. She writes, "On Tuesday, after seeing several people in the morning 'Abdu'l-Bahá and Dr. Fareed went for a short drive, stopped at Mr. and Mrs. Hannen's and afterwards they went to Howard University where 'Abdu'l-Bahá made an address before a large audience of professors and students."[16] Although Joseph didn't mention this stopover in his report, Pauline found it exciting and wonderful. This particular call held a special interest for her due to a dream she'd had. In her recollections, she describes this dream:

> Do you believe in dreams? I do in some. Many and many a time I dreamed that Abdul-Baha drove up to our door and entered the house. I never believed it could happen. At the time, the Mohammedans [sic], to interrupt His mission, which they thought undermined their religion, had confined Him in prison in Akka. But step by step the dream did come true. The young Turks overthrew the Old Turks. Abdul-Baha was released. In 1909 Joseph and I made the Holy Pilgrimage to Palestine, enjoying to the full unique experience which other pens will describe. At Haifa we found ourselves riding in the same carriage with Abdul-Baha, the beginning of a personal relation which enriched our part in His reception when He visited America.
>
> And now came the crowning glory of the dream. Abdul-Baha was to deliver an address at Howard University, the institute of higher learning maintained for colored people under control of the federal government. Among those occasionally attending our meetings at Mrs. Dyer's was Mrs. Coralie Franklin Cook, whose husband was Dean of the university. She had invited me to her home on the campus, where we had many delightful meetings with professors and students, and in due time Mr. Cook arranged large gatherings to which noted Baha'i speakers were invited. Joseph and I were to attend the exercises; the arrangements having been made by Mrs. Agnes Parsons and others in charge of Abdul-Baha's Washington itinerary. Driving Abdul-Baha to the campus (not in an automobile, though she owned one—but in a horse drawn carriage) Mrs. Parsons was to call for Joseph and me.
>
> "Oh, can it be true, is it true?" I exclaimed again and again to my husband, "that our Beloved is calling for us tomorrow?" He drove to our door, as I had dreamed. On this drive with Him—Abdul-Baha instructed my husband: "You will listen attentively to my address. It will be an important message to the white and colored races. Record it if possible." Joseph was all attention and he recorded the address. [It is in *The Promulgation of Universal Peace,* p. 41.][17]

In a different letter, Pauline wrote to Alma about this special opportunity to be with her Beloved:

> Tuesday was another terribly exciting day, nerve racking. Please don't forget, Alma that I was physically very weak from the long confinement

(nine weeks in bed with the gripp) and unfortunately my nervousness affected all of us because we are so sympathetically bound together. We were ready and expecting Abdul-Baha at quarter of eleven, though we were told He would come about half past eleven. But we were such geese, we were cherishing an inner hope and prayer that He might step out of His carriage only for one minute, and meet us in our home—as a family, but when it grew late we were worried for fear He would not come at all. When the carriage did come it was too late to think of His coming in the house, so we all hurried out to the carriage. Here all shook hands and while Ameen was reading your message Abdul-Baha saw Mrs. Columbus (our neighbor) back of Mother, even before Mother, and His hand was extending toward her, before Mother asked Ameen to introduce her. Mrs. Columbus was deeply touched, had tears in her eyes. Says she feels that she will be blessed in touching such a good man, He is a prophet. Ameen went on with your message, and Abdul-Baha seemed very much pleased. What He said I don't know beyond "Very good. Very good." Ameen was outside the carriage addressing Fanny. Joey and I were in the carriage. He held the picture very close, that I know.

Regarding that ride, I was happy because I was near Him. Abdul-Baha gave Ameen a bottle of attar of rose to open and anoint each of us, Abdul-Baha also. Then He directed His conversation to Ameen and seemed most anxious about something. In due time Ameen turned to Joseph and said, "The Master is very anxious that you take down every word He says at the University. It is very important that you do this and have it printed in the papers. Do what you can to bring this about." Joseph took this to be a command and you may be sure it was no easy task. (The ministers had gone to the newspapers and unitedly asked that nothing of Abdul-Baha's words be published. And they didn't.) But one paper did accept this article; The Evening Star, but printed only part of it. The colored papers are going to print it. This was the very best he could do because of the minister's influence with the papers here. Not a word was said to me nor did I utter a sound. I was happy to be near and we saw He was troubled, no *weary* is a better word.

We reached the Chapel just as the students were coming. Prof. Cook led Abdul-Baha in the back door and upon the platform and we had the real pleasure of seeing the Chapel rapidly filling with 1400 students of both races, as well as visitors from the neighborhood. Mr. and Mrs. Cook had already been greatly tried by the President of Howard University, who is soon to be made bishop of the Methodist body, Dr. Thurkield. They were both in agony of soul for fear the students would manifest the distrust shown by the President, and their honored guest Abdul-Baha would receive a cold reception. But, praise be to God! After the introduction, by one of the members of the faculty whose name and position I have forgotten, Abdul-Baha arose and instead of an icy reception, they gave Him a hearty applause, which Prof. Cook says they only give what they consider a distinguished speaker. When Abdul-Baha finished the address the applause broke loose, enough to shake the Chapel and gave the "University Clap," which, Prof. Cook says is the greatest honor they could give Him. Even then the applause kept on until Abdul-Baha arose in order to silence them. When silence reigned He said, "I will show you my great appreciation of the honor you have shown me in the Oriental manner." He put both hands to His fez and bowed three times.

They were evidently delighted after singing "God be with You till We Meet Again." The people crowded around Abdul-Baha wanted to clasp His hand or touch His robe. When He finally managed to get near the steps it gave me another brief but intensely happy moment. As He started down the little steps I grasped His hand and elbow to help Him down, unnoticed it seemed at first, in an instant His grasp tightened in my hand, as though for support. At the bottom He let go as instantly as He had tightened. Whether He knew who it was, mattered not to me, for one brief moment, I did support His Holy Presence, a thing never dreamed of by me.[18]

The following account of the trip home from Howard University is thrilling, and gives an indication of Pauline's undeniably resilient spirit:

When we reached the carriage, He called Mr. Gregory to take the seat next to Him and said Assad'u'llah and Ameen fill His carriage. This hurt me a wee little bit, but I have since found out why it was done, or at least I am satisfied. We went in the carriage hired by Mr. Gregory for that occasion, though we did not know it then. We went in the carriage with Mirza Mahmud. We were having a most delightful time with him when suddenly our carriage was run into by a big dray wagon. The trace on one side was broken off, the horse, free to kick and smash us to pieces any moment. He was loose and running away. The driver held the reigns, which made the poor horse even more frantic. He was plunging on every side. I was the first to see the danger and realizing that Mirza Mahmud would be the first to get the full force of the horse's hooves if the carriage got too close. I opened the door, gave a forward leap and called the men to follow suit. I started for the horses head but a man ran up from the other side and made me step back. It was quite some time before they could quiet the poor animal; the horse was terribly wounded and bleeding profusely.

Though we did not know it at the time, we were right in front of Khan's house. I was not hurt in the least. I won from Mirza Mahmud and Joey sweet praises. But best of all, that afternoon, at the reception at Khan's, Abdul-Baha again singled me out asking how I felt and praising me for my quickness. Mirza Mahmud will never forget me I am sure. Every time we meet he mentions this subject of the accident in Mr. Gregory's carriage, as he believes it was. Not until Mr. Gregory came out and paid the man were we aware of the fact that it did not belong to Mrs. Parsons. I forgot to tell you that Saturday night when Mr. Gregory came to greet Abdul-Baha, the latter petted him on the cheeks and said "Mr. Gregory, Mr. Gregory." He is surely favored for something special.[19]

On Tuesday evening, the Bethel Literary and Historical Society, the leading African American organization in Washington, was addressed, and again the audience taxed the capacity of the venue where the meeting was held. Joseph had the opportunity to give several talks about the Bahá'í Faith to this group previous to 'Abdu'l-Bahá's visit, and had been actively involved with this organization. The following account of Pauline's reveals several issues not often reported in other accounts of the time, and hints at how 'Abdu'l-Bahá's visit affected the Hannen family circle:

Tuesday night was memorable, because of the change of attitude towards our Beloved, Abdul-Baha, due to the dictates of the Ministers Association. This body of people had met before Abdul-Baha's arrival and decided that it was their duty to warn their congregation against this man, Abdul-Baha, who would soon be in the city. They sent delegates to the papers of our city telling them they must not publish His talks. That is why our papers had so little, yet that little was in His favor, but they dared not write much. You see then in what a delicate position this placed the colored minister Rev. Ross. The ministers having warned their flock, the audience was large and expectations keyed up to the highest. They of course expected Abdul-Baha to expound on His Religion and urge them to accept. Instead Abdul-Baha, the perfect man, filled the place according to the work of the Society. The Society being a Literary and Scientific body, chose for His subject Science. When He was finished with a most wonderful talk the audience was speechless and silent. The basket was passed for collection after which they had a right to discuss the subject. When this was translated to Abdul-Baha, He took a roll of bills from His pocket, six dollars I believe, and with His little band left us, after handing the money to the President of the Society. The air was tense with vibrations of reverence, as well as disappointment. Then the

> debates began and to our joyful surprise we found many loyal friends to stand up for and defend Abdul-Baha against the ignorant accusations of the minister, Rev. Ross and a white missionary who were reined against Him. Our Carl was intensely interested in these debates, for and against the Teaching and said he wished there were more occasions of this kind. Except for the novelty of it, I would have preferred that all should show Him the same reverence and respect. This body represented that class of people, "who have eyes but see not, who have ears but hear not." There were many who were deeply touched and brought together because of the attack by the clergy and missionaries. But this much is to be born in mind that when He came in all arose to greet Him and when Abdul-Baha left all arose in respect and reverence. He swayed the hearts of people with the rod of love.[20]

On Wednesday afternoon one of the most beautiful functions of the week was successfully planned and carried out. At Studio Hall, more than 100 children—with as many adults, parents, and friends—gathered. 'Abdu'l-Bahá received and embraced each child, seeming most happy in their presence, and then delivered a wonderful address. 'Abdu'l-Bahá presented each child, before He left, with a gift. Fanny wrote of this event:

> Pauline and I, at the suggestion of Ahmad, had the pleasure of arranging for a mother and children's afternoon in our Sunday School room. Only mothers and children were to be present, but you might as well forbid the sun to shine as to keep others away. At six a.m. Carl and I met at the market, bought all we could carry of Dog Wood and Bridal Wreath and Fruit blossoms and white lilacs. We carried these to the Hall. Then visited other markets, hired a man to help carry. Pauline and four of our girls were busy decorating. We helped—all the decorations were white and green with great clusters of bright golden colored tulips. Four canary birds were placed among groups of palms. Pauline said they nearly split their little throats singing that afternoon. Carl and Paul, from the money Mamma left them wanted each child to have something blessed and distributed Cat Eye Pearls in various colors. One hundred were blessed and distributed among the children. Well before Abdul-Baha arrived, Pauline requested the adults to remain seated, the children to rise and turn around so that their dear little faces would be the first to be seen by Abdul-Baha. While waiting, Sunday School songs were sung. Pauline told a story just to keep the little folks quiet. Then the signal from out of doors, "He is Coming!!" Oh dear. I shall never forget it.
>
> The children standing, facing Him sang: "Softly His Voice is Calling Now" while slowly smiling, touching His forehead in greeting, in Persian

saying: God Bless you. He seated Himself among the blossoms and the singing of the birds; another singer rendered a beautiful solo. Then Abdul-Baha spoke. After this Pauline ushered the smallest lads, and mothers with infants in their arms received a blessing each. I had removed the hats but one little colored child, belonging to Jennie's family, you remember those folks don't you—this little girl when standing between Abdul-Baha's knees had on a Lingeria Hat. [She was the granddaughter of Carrie York.] He tried again and again to get it off and did not give up until it came off—then laughingly He toyed with each of the four kinky braids which stood like little horns—it was too funny—we think He probably had never seen a real little Negro like this, very dark. In her surprise she rolled her eyes of [?] and think of it, after patting the curly head kissing her on hair and forehead several times, He turned to the only child of the wealthy and aristocratic Mrs. Parsons drawing him near and patting him just at the moment when the difference would be most pronounced.

One tall young colored woman with a new born babe in her arms, returning from Abdul-Baha's presence—the aisle was narrow at one point so I came forward to guide her saying, "Did your baby receive its blessing?" With a face radiant with happiness the mother replied excitedly, "Yes Mam and He gave my baby a name." I asked them to write it down on a card for me and I'll get it later.[21]

The following is a report Pauline wrote of her recollections regarding children's classes in Washington.

While in Washington, DC, in 1912, Abdul-Baha delivered an address at our Sunday school, reported in the *Star of the West*, Vol.3, No3, p.19. Several features stood out. My son Carl, speaking for himself and his brother Paul, supplicated Abdul-Baha to accept a box of agates of various colors, generally designated as cat-eye pearls. When Abdul-Baha had finished His address He offered a prayer, first asking that it be not recorded but should be felt by everyone. Then He handed the beads to Mirza Ali Kuli-Khan, to be given to all the children and adults alike.

When the agates had been distributed, Abdul-Baha requested that the children remain seated, and passed through, shaking hands with each one, until He had left us at the exit; a cherished memory for everyone privileged to participate.[22]

More of Pauline's impressions:

I have since found out who the little colored baby was that was named on that occasion by Abdul-Baha. Its father is a beautiful believer and being a porter on a Pulman car, was so fortunate as to be on the same train with Abdul-Baha on His first arrival here (Mr. Anderson).[23] [Some descendants of this man attended the Centenary Celebration of 'Abdu'l-Bahá's visit in Washington D.C. in 2012.]

The following story confirms Pauline's thoughts about the influence these stones might have on their recipients. I was thrilled when I came across it, recalling the story Pauline had told of the cat-eye pearls. Years later she reported:

> One day during Abdul-Baha's visit to the Washington Sunday School conducted by Mr. and Mrs. Joseph Hannen, a number of cat-eye pearls were placed in His hands and then distributed among the children. One of the visiting children, a colored child, was a recipient of one of these pearls blessed by Abdul-Baha and was told by Him that she would become a great singer.
>
> Many years passed and then one day an exceedingly attractive young lady visited the office of the "*Star of the West*" in Washington. Glancing around and speaking to Mrs. Hannen, she expressed surprise and pleasure at really being there in the Baha'i room. She then gave an account of how she, as a small child, had attended a reception given to Abdul-Baha and each child had received a cat-eye pearl from His hands. Abdul-Baha had said at the time, "You will become a noted singer." Hurrying home, she told her mother to put this pearl away very carefully—that it was precious, for it had been given to her by Abdul-Baha. The mother did so.
>
> Years passed and then came the time when this young girl was about to leave for Europe for a required course in a Conservatory of Music. Her means were limited, yet she had implicit faith, and requested her mother to give her the cat-eye pearl. This she carried with her as something very precious. In speaking of this, she took occasion to say that while securing her musical education there were times when she did not know where the next bread would come from. Then she would take out her pearl and hold to it as a token of assurance that she must succeed. In telling it, she smilingly added, "And strange, assistance always seemed to come."
>
> She graduated with honors and at this time, when giving this account of her experience, she was a noted singer on concert tour through the United States.
>
> "I was not a Baha'i during this time," she continued, "but on my arrival in New York in the course of time I attended a racial amity meeting where I met some beautiful Baha'is. I was taken back very vividly to my meeting with Abdul-Baha. I became deeply interested in the Baha'i Revelation, and am now a confirmed Baha'i.[24]

In Alma's handwriting is a note saying, "In 1942, Mary Anderson sang at the White House. In 1943, we heard her over the Radio. The announcer said as he announced her, Miss Anderson wishes to say that I have dedicated my voice to my Lord. Come what may, Mary Anderson had been announced as the best contralto in the World & many other praises. Her voice was indeed most beautiful."[25] History records that it was Eleanor Roosevelt who insisted on having Marion Anderson sing at the White House, although it broke many social barriers and met with much resistance by some.

I remember as a young person that, Wyatt Cooper—the head gardener at the House of Worship in Wilmette, IL during the 1950s and 60s—cultivated a special pink rose, which he named the Marion Anderson Rose. In fact, there was a special program organized in which Ms. Anderson came to the House of Worship to accept this honor. It is a memory that has stuck with me for many years, and now I know why.

Joseph continues with the rest of 'Abdu'l-Bahá's itinerary:

> On Wednesday evening Abdul-Baha visited Mrs. Dyer's home, where the meetings are held regularly on that night. More than 100 persons were present and were made happy by His address.[26]

Pauline's excitement is evident in her account of the evening:

> Wednesday as you already know, Abdul-Baha blessed the home of Mrs. Dyer, where we meet on Wednesdays. The place was packed to the utmost limit with loving friends of all races. Abdul-Baha was so happy to see this happy mixed audience. When He was seated some of those standing in the hall were told by Him in English, "Sit down, sit down." So it came about that He had only room for His feet, because of the friends seated on the floor in front of Him. I did not see it for I was outside, but it was told that Abdul-Baha picked out the blackest man in the audience . . . who had been sitting at Abdul-Baha's feet (not a believer) caressed his face and head with such tender love that some were moved to tears, not so the man, his face was radiant with joy and happiness. Another incident, this I saw, being crowded back against the wall to make for His coming I managed to mount a chair and in this way save my face and see too. Here in this mass of humanity we saw Abdul-Baha recognize a colored school teacher, who had visited Him, Abdul-Baha, in Ramleh. His face was radiant as he told one of us later, "just to think of Abdul-Baha knowing me again." Then Abdul-Baha turned to Mr. Dyer's son-in-law, petting him on the face and head, saying in English, with a merry twinkle and a meaning smile, "I am glad to see a white man among the colored." Someone who stood near said, "He is colored," believing Abdul-Baha had

made a mistake. There were many white men present—why pick out the colored man and call him white? It is true, he is very light, but because of the expression on Abdul-Baha's Face, I thought He knew the question of color, but was having a joke because his name is "White." Though no one told Abdul-Baha his name, I firmly believe He knew. Then Mrs. Dyer ran forward begging Him to bless her husband who had just returned from the Valley of the Shadow of Death. Abdul-Baha waited in the porch while they brought Mr. Dyer out. He was able to walk with the help of others. He is much better since.

(Abdul-Baha also called on Mrs. Dyer's daughter, Mrs. White, the next day. She was too ill to attend the meeting.)[27]

Many of the books written about 'Abdu'l-Bahá's historic visit mention various people of note whom He met. Pauline describes some of these encounters:

It was at Khan's reception that I saw a number of people of note, among them Alexander Graham Bell, inventor of the telephone. In New York by the way, Rockerfellow [presumably Rockefeller] was very ill and unable to visit Abdul-Baha and begged that Abdul-Baha would visit him. Abdul-Baha went to Rockerfellow, who is deeply impressed. Also Andrew Carnegie had an interview and is delighted with Him.

In Washington, one of the little things that counted for much happened. Mrs. Dunlop met with a terrible accident, was nearly burned to death. Though suffering intensely from bodily burns, it was nearly killing her that she could not see Abdul-Baha. Through Khan's mother-in-law, Mrs. Alice Breed, it was brought to the attention of Abdul-Baha, and without a moment's hesitation He promised to go the next Monday. Before they had a chance to straighten up the rooms, He came to her little flat and stayed with her ten minutes. She was really beside herself with joy. I haven't seen her since a week before Carl came, then it made me sick to see her patiently suffering.[28]

Friday morning the ladies of President Taft's Unitarian Church were addressed, with a large crowd in attendance. Later that day He addressed another large crowd at the Daughters of the American Revolution building. Fanny was quite impressed with this venue as she reports in her account. This event also may have been of particular interest to the Barnitz family, as Leone spent a good deal of time there researching her genealogy, eventually becoming a member of the DAR. Joseph reported:

Friday evening, the last public meeting was addressed at the Continental Hall of the Daughters of the American Revolution. This is one of the most spacious halls in Washington, and the very finest location possible. It had not been contemplated to have such a large meeting that evening, but the interest became so intense that it was deemed necessary. Saturday evening a reception was given, under the auspices of the Persian American Educational Society-Oriental-Occidental Unity—by Mrs. Parsons. This was the culmination of the visit, from the standpoint of meeting the representatives of social and diplomatic life, large numbers of whom had become interested, through Mrs. Parsons' afternoon receptions, as well as through an afternoon reception held at the Persian Legation on Tuesday.[29]

Before 'Abdu'l-Bahá left for Chicago on Sunday, Joseph and Pauline, along with a party of ten, journeyed there by train as they were attending the Fourth Annual Temple Unity Convention, where Pauline was a delegate that year. Carl went with them as far as Pittsburgh where he returned to his electrician apprenticeship. After her family left, Fanny's feelings had altered slightly. She said, "Pauline and Joseph had suggested my calling up the Parsons' home, and if possible to arrange to take Abdul-Baha out for a drive, but while it seemed likely this could be done my desire to do so was gone after our folks left. Instead, Paul and I went to a show Sat. night and Clara joined us out at the zoo Sunday morning. I do not know when Abdul-Baha left the city. The impression was that He would start for Chicago Sunday."[30] After all that intensity, Joseph and Pauline's younger son Paul was probably ready for some special attention from his loving aunt "Dona" Fanny.

- 14 -

Chicago and the Temple

The Bahá'í National Convention held in Chicago in 1912 was particularly momentous. It was the only National Convention 'Abdu'l-Bahá attended, and it was at this gathering, He laid the foundation stone for the holiest Temple of the West on the shores of Lake Michigan in Wilmette, Illinois. Joseph wrote a glowing and detailed report of that special convention in Vol. III of *Star of the West.* He described the opening session as a garden with many kinds of flowers and birds of all sounds and temperaments, providing a splendid description of the atmosphere surrounding the friends during this exceptional meeting.[1] Both he and Pauline addressed the convention more than once, giving reports of 'Abdu'l-Bahá's talks in Washington. Both Joseph and Pauline were in attendance on the final day of the convention when 'Abdu'l-Bahá was present and addressed the crowd Himself.[2] In one of her letters to Alma, Pauline describes her feelings upon arriving at the convention:

> On our arrival in Chicago, Sat. morning we were met by a large number of believers from Chicago, Maine, California, Colorado, New York, Minnesota, in fact delegates from everywhere, such a lot of people. Some I had corresponded with and who were so grateful for some forgotten service I had rendered them. To me it was a most wonderful meeting, of course Joey had been there twice before and it didn't mean the same to him. I could easily imagine how it will be when we leave this world and loving friends come to greet us, no wonder that the dear ones long to go at the last moment when they receive a glimpse of such a heavenly vision.
>
> I didn't want to leave the big flock but being human, Joseph said I must spare myself for the Convention proper, and go to our home while in Chicago, the home of Mr. and Mrs. Lesch. Their daughter Helen had come to meet us and took us home. Here I took a nap before lunch, and felt better though very tired.[3]

Pauline and Joseph arrived several days before the convention started, allowing them time for sightseeing. Her account of their time in Chicago includes some precious details of several teaching experiences with their dear friend Mr. Gregory:

> After lunch the same day, Sat. April 24, we started down town to Mr. Scheffler's Office, the central meeting place for the Friends during the convention. Joseph and I went alone, leaving Mrs. Lesch to attend to her duties. In arriving at the Office we found that nearly all the many Friends had rooms provided for them & therefore nearly all had gone.
>
> Here we saw Miss Engelthorn again, a very dear Believer who had spent some time with us in Washington. She was very tired, had been on the jump continuously, meeting the different trains, steamers, finding homes for all the guests. I found Mr. Scheffler a very charming young man indeed. We were introduced to others whose names I cannot recall. They were all busy in one way or another, so Joseph & I took ourselves off to the Lake Shore which is not many blocks off. . . .
>
> After dinner we attended the most wonderful Unity Meeting ever witnessed by "yours truly." Here an immense Lodge Room had been transformed to enchant the eye with its many flowers, bedecked tables and tiny bunches of Arbutus, the modest little spring flower, at each plate. Before & after the meeting (so eloquently described in the article written by Joseph for *Star of the West*, which will soon appear so I will not attempt to describe it) we had such wonderful Meetings with the Friends from various parts of the United States, people whom we had served through correspondence & then lost track of. Some we had served here & forgotten about it, but then remembered. Here we again met Godsia, the Persian lady who came to America to get an American Education. She was so very happy to see those of us from Washington, especially Joseph, Mr. Gregory & myself. We were introduced to many, many Friends, whom now I can only recall as part of a great rolling ocean of spiritually illumined faces. I spoke a few words and read a Tablet, but the place was so immense & I so small that to me it seemed like a tiny voice coming up out of their midst. Many heard me, but just as many more did not. At least I was self-possessed and did my very best so I don't feel badly because some did not hear me. The next morning, Sunday, when nearly all the audience was in front of me, instead of all around me, my speech as well as reading was praised by many. This morning service was even more spiritual & powerful in its influence upon the hearts of all attending. One thing most conducive of this wonderful atmosphere was the great abundance of heavenly music rendered by the Chicago Friends under the direction of Mr. Windhurst. Violin, organ & harp were the instruments used to

vibrate & send the voices heavenward. How I wished all my Family as well as Friends might have shared this shower of heavenly blessings with us. After this Meeting I met Mrs. Paul Dealy, who was entirely blind. You remember we had the son William with us for quite a while. She was so happy as well as myself to have this meeting. It had been my intention to visit her but this had not been brought about. Poor soul, she fully expected Abdul-Baha to restore her sight, and I asked the nurse if anyone had prepared her for the possibility of disappointment. I told her, as far as I knew Abdul-Baha very seldom applied His powers in that way. It hurt me to think of her disappointment should He not restore her sight. The nurse said they had tried to prepare her for this but she was headstrong and wanted her physical sight above all else. I of course had no time to say much because of the many Friends who were crowding around her, on this little platform where she was placed out of harm's way. Though blind, she was very popular.

. . . After the Dinner most of the party went to the Douglas Settlement where Joseph & Mr. Gregory have spoken before. Now we were to hear Mr. Gregory give the Message, but the weather was so fierce that we expected no audience but ourselves. This being a good work towards bettering & uplifting the colored race, we wanted in this way to show our real interest in their work & progress. Mrs. Wooly, who is at the head of this Douglas Settlement work, is a white woman and a well-known character in Chicago, also in other movements concerning Women in particular. She is an elderly, gray haired lady, not pretty at all, but a very charming manner & splendid speaker. She received our bedraggled party with a hearty welcome & explained that she feared no one would venture forth on such a day, but people like the Baha'is who were so filled with the singleness of purpose & love & zeal for a Cause of highest principles such as the Cause of Baha'o'llah seemed to express. . . . She regretted that she did not know of Mr. Gregory's coming in time to put the announcement in the colored people's papers, so less know of his presence with us this afternoon, otherwise, she believed even the weather would not have detained them. As it was, she bade us a hearty welcome, and the small number of colored people who had braved the elements for the regular Sunday meeting would be well repaid by listening to Mr. Gregory, the speaker of the afternoon. . . . Our own party nearly filled the room, but some colored people had arrived, among them a colored minister. I don't remember the order of our speaking but I think Joseph was first, I second, & Mr. Gregory gave the talk. However that may be, Joseph's talk was inspired as he enlarged upon the Race Question & illustrated his talk by telling them of the black & white keys of a piano, their difference being lost in the one great keyboard hidden within the piano, yet the black &

white keys in front were used to express half tones and whole tones. An entire piece played on either the one or the other could not compare in harmony & exquisite sound produced by using both keys. Of course I cannot recall all he said, but this was most striking. It was a gem. Mr. Gregory's theme was a splendid one . . . ,

Mr. Gregory . . . told the old and even new story of the beginning of every new civilization & how it had its inception through the power of the spoken words of the Messenger of God, then he spoke of Moses & the slaves of that time . . . etc. Of course he did well, & I think I spoke well too because Mrs. Wooly referred every now & then to something Mrs. Hannen had said. I told them principally of Abdul-Baha's love for the colored people, manifested in Washington & the reason for many humiliating & shameful persecutions during His 40 years' imprisonment which was due to the fact that He manifested love alike to the people of Abha regardless of creed or nationality. He is now teaching the people of the Occident that they must make no distinction because of class, creed, or color.[4]

Although the Hannens arrived in Chicago on 24 April 1912, 'Abdu'l-Bahá did not arrive until 29 April. Most of the talks He gave while there were taken down via stenograph by Joseph from 30 April. He gave three major talks that day, which, according to Maḥmud in his diary, reached audiences of two to three thousand people each. The first was at Hull House in Chicago, then on to the Handel Hall, "especially to bring together the blacks and whites." The day's final talk was at Drill Hall, Masonic Temple, at the conclusion of the Temple Unity Convention. Both Pauline and Joseph spoke several times throughout the convention, recounting 'Abdu'l-Bahá's talks in Washington D.C.[5] These talks can all be found in *The Promulgation of Universal Peace,* and many were also printed in *Star of the West.* I've included Pauline's personal reflections of that momentous day:

We were seated in the tent on the Temple Grounds where Abdul-Baha was expected, awaiting His arrival. The atmosphere was charged with excitement, everyone tense. Suddenly my husband rushed forward to me and grabbed me by the hand. I naturally followed, unquestioning. When we got out of hearing he said, "A believer told me that if we hurry we can see Abdul-Baha, for He is expected at Hull House any minute." Needless to say, we made haste to hear Him there. On our arrival, we discovered that Abdul-Baha had not yet appeared. We had the opportunity of watching the excited audience, but notably the face of Jane Adams. We watched and watched, and could not take our eyes from her face. It was natural that she should be displeased and greatly disappointed at having Abdul-

Baha delay His visit for so long a time, and she had to do her very best to take care of the vast audience who had come to hear Him. That, however, was not what attracted our attention to her face. It was the expression of infinite sorrow and worry that stood out. We, having met Abdul-Baha so often and under trying circumstances, knew that His face was so radiant. Her sorrows, no matter what they were, were nothing compared to those experienced by ['Abdu'l-Bahá], who had been a prisoner and exile since the age of nine, until released by the Young Turks in 1908, and now, after all these hardships, was making this world tour with such vigor and joyousness, His eyes sparkling with fun and humor.

Suddenly the atmosphere was completely changed for, notwithstanding the unbelievably long hours, with speeches and private talks from early morning till late at night, Abdul-Baha entered the room with vigorous, majestic step, and walked briskly to the platform.[6]

According to Maḥmud's Diary, "The Master spoke on the subject of the unity and oneness of humanity; that God has given faculties and powers equally to all and that the different colors of humankind are like the various colors of the flowers of a garden, which increases the beauty and charm of the garden. His eloquent and impressive talk thrilled the listeners."[7]

As they were leaving Hull House, Pauline writes:

Abdul-Baha and His long green bag of small change was a familiar sight to the Baha'is. On leaving Hull House, my husband and I rushed out to see Him as He came forth. As He stepped into His automobile, He pulled out the familiar long green bag. I knew what was going to happen. He was going to pass quarters to the poor people all around us! One of these quarters, which I knew was intended for the poor only, fell just beneath my uplifted heel, and I saw it. My heart longed to possess what I knew was not intended for me. I hesitated just a second, when a man's hand quickly reached under my heel and took the quarter. I was relieved that I had not succumbed to the temptation to cover the quarter with my heel, which would have been an easy thing to do, but not the right thing![8]

Perhaps the most significant historical event of this time period took place on 1 May 1912 when 'Abdu'l-Bahá visited the site of the future Bahá'í House of Worship on the shores of Lake Michigan in Wilmette, Illinois. Here He met many of the Bahá'ís who had come from all parts of the world to witness the groundbreaking ceremony. Pauline shares:

The account has already been given in the *Star of the West,* Vol.3, by Mr. Jackson [Jaxon] of the dedication of the Temple grounds by Abdul-

Baha on May 1, 1912. I wish to add an incident that was both funny and significant.

The program was entirely spontaneous and various friends were asked to represent various nations and races, each one being called upon to come forward and get a shovelful, if possible, of the earth from the hole in which the cornerstone was to be placed. Mr. Jackson, representing the Indian race, worked most diligently with the big shovel, hoping to bring forth a full shovel of earth. When the shovel appeared into view, however, there was a lump of earth about the size of a man's fist. Everyone laughed uproariously, including Abdul-Baha, because he had made such a tremendous effort. Mr. Jackson also laughed.

Then my name was called and an earnest supplication went up from my heart that I would do better than that for Germany. When I came forward Abdul-Baha said, "Mrs. Hannen, Mrs. Hannen, Mrs. Hannen!" (three times), which filled my soul with confidence and faith. I put the shovel in and when I brought it forth I had a shovel full! I could scarcely lift it. Abdul-Baha exclaimed, "Bravo! Bravo! Kheili Koob! Kheili Koob!"[9]

One more story of note in Pauline's recollections about this treasured time in Chicago concerns a more personal episode that she believed was a miracle. We are told that miracles are only truly real to those who witness them, and, to her, this occurrence was truly miraculous:

I think it was due largely to the fact that a specialist had told me that one morning I would wake up and my hearing would be completely gone, that the friends selected me as delegate to the convention held in Chicago. I could not hear children's voices on the street or the sounds of automobiles, but still I could understand Abdul-Baha and His interpreter.

While in Chicago I went out day-nurse visiting with Mrs. Betty Herrick and she said to me, "How would you like to make up Abdul-Baha's bed? That privilege has been assigned to me." I joyfully exclaimed, "Oh, I'd love it!" She took me to the hotel where Abdul-Baha was staying (The Plaza). His bed had already been made up, but there was a deep dent in the pillow where His blessed head had lain, and there was a turban on one corner of the bed, by the pillow.

I said, "Oh Mrs. Herrick, may I put Abdul-Baha's blessed turban on my head? There is no one here but you and me—Perhaps it will bring healing to my ears. I have no intention of asking Abdul-Baha personally." "Certainly," she said. I reached over, took the blessed turban with trembling hand and held it to my face, breathing a prayer to Baha'o'llah that if it would be His will that I might be given hearing in order to do better work for the Cause, I would be so grateful, but if not, I would joyfully

> accept a soundless life and find some other way to serve than by teaching by word of mouth.
>
> At this moment Lua Getsinger, with two or three of the friends entered the room and saw me with the turban in my hands. Suddenly she exclaimed, "Oh, here is Abdul-Baha's coat. Let's each of us place it around our shoulders and say a prayer!" This we did, each saying a silent prayer.
>
> Not until a few weeks after arriving in Washington, I was suddenly aware that I could hear about as well as I ever had. My hearing returned so naturally that I was not aware of it. As proof of the fact that the hearing returned I went to the hospital and the specialist was so amazed at the condition of my hearing that she called other physicians and attendants, saying, "I want you to see this. This lady says I can do anything I like with her head, but not probe her ears; I might disturb something that she considers a miracle of spiritual healing received in 1912 (this was 1928). Now will you look? There is scar upon scar on the ear drums and I do not understand how she can hear anything with ears in this condition. Now let us test her." Different tests were used and she found the hearing very good.[10]

Before leaving Chicago, 'Abdu'l-Bahá spoke at the following venues, where Joseph took notes: 2 May, Hotel Plaza; 2 May, Hotel La Salle for the Federation of Women's Clubs; and also at the Bahá'í Women's reception. He gave several other talks over the next few days, but notes were taken by other people.

- 15 -

Pittsburgh and Philadelphia, PA

From Chicago, 'Abdu'l-Bahá traveled through Ohio with a stop in Cleveland to spend the night on May 6, and then on to Pittsburgh on May 7 and 8, before making His way back to Washington D.C. for a second short visit on 9–10 May 1912. An exciting event took place in Pittsburgh, which was of special importance to the Hannens. Carl, their son, was living in Pittsburgh at the time studying to be an electrician, and had the opportunity to see 'Abdu'l-Bahá while there. Pittsburgh was also home to Hand of the Cause of God Martha Root. She worked as a journalist and it was to Pittsburgh she would send letters to relatives and friends, after she embarked on her historical world travels to spread Bahá'u'lláh's message. Carl served with her in the same community for a time, and she was part of the encounter with 'Abdu'l-Bahá, which he writes about in his letter. First though, Pauline describes to Alma her great joy upon hearing about this event:

> This is a hasty note—I am writing this to you at once, half-cocked perhaps, but I am so very, very happy, that I feel ready to burst. The secret of my joy is that Abdul-Baha has taken our big boy to His heart, as He has taken all of us who have been to Akka; I mean that close personal touch. Let me explain. Last night when Joey came home he said, "Would you like to go to the station, and take a chance of meeting Abdul-Baha?" I said, "Of course, but we won't speak to Him, just look." So immediately after supper we started for the train. We were first to arrive, next thing I saw Khan and his wife and secretary, then Mrs. Parsons who was very gracious to us. In a few minutes Khan had received a pass and we were allowed to go through the gate to meet the train. Here we had to wait about ten minutes, a very happy though socially a mixed company. When the train pulled in we all looked for a sleeper, but the first thing you know, there was Abdul-Baha smiling at us from a day coach window. He looked

so contented and happy as He shook hands with us from the car window. When the party came out of the train, who should be among them but Zia Bagdadi of Chicago. The first thing he said to me was, "O your boy, your boy, he was so very happy last night (Pittsburgh). Abdul-Baha caressed and petted and I believe He said kissed him, and said beautiful things to your son that the tears were just raining down his cheeks in streams." This was too good to be true so I asked, "Are you sure that it was my boy?" "Yes, of course, he was Mr. Hannen who was there to study electricity and Abdul-Baha gave him a beautiful talk on that subject." Zia said to me and Mrs. Parsons that Abdul-Baha had said of Carl, "This is a very dear son of mine." Zia said that after Carl left, Abdul-Baha said to the Persians, "He was born of pure blood, pure seed, he is pure birth."[1]

One of the special letters that I recently received from the National Archives is this letter written by Carl to his parents, telling them of his wonderful encounter with 'Abdu'l-Bahá. Keep in mind this was written by a seventeen-year-old boy and his recollections of 'Abdu'l-Bahá's words cannot be authenticated. However, they are too precious to leave out. He wrote the letter the same day that it happened:

Dearest Mother:
5/7/12
Abdul-Baha is here. He arrived 12:15 & I was at the station to meet Him. Then He came to the hotel & have been here ever since. When He arrived at the hotel He had lunch of [sic] some of the Dahl's place & bread & then He rested for a while. Next He had interviews & at 4:50 o'clock I went in & He said Welcome, then I told Him I was studying electricity so that someday I could go to Persia. He said; "Electricity is a very good science; you must study & become learned & then go to Persia. God willing your name will go down in history as a great Electrical man." Then He said, "You have a beautiful city here." I said, "Tell Him I am from Wash." He said, "It is all one country. I hope you will not be from Wash or Pitts but from the kingdom of God, not worldly but heavenly, not of the kingdom of man but of the divine kingdom." Then He put His arm around me and said in English, "You are my son. Bless you my son, bless you my son."

Oh yes. Just as I went in He said in English, "I love you, I love you very much, so much that I came from Persia to see you." & I said, "I love you very much too." & He said, "Kaile Kube" [sic], & smiled at me. Dr. Bagdadi trans. & I sent his love to you and Pa.

He will be here tomorrow & I am going to stay home & come down to the hotel, as He is going to speak at the University.

Yesterday & this morning it rained pitchforks but it stopped just 5 minutes before He came. I am very happy & only wish you were here too. He will leave tomorrow for your burg so you will see Him again. I bought Him 2 packages of chocolate & Hil bought some too.

Well goodbye,
Your spiritual and earthly son,
Nategh[2]

That was Carl's first quick letter about the visit. Five days later he wrote another letter after receiving a response from home requesting more details:

My own Dearest Mamma,
I have spent I guess the most glorious days of my life. When Abdul-Baha arrived, Mr. Dahl, Miss Root, & myself of Pitts. a Mr. Hill & Zia Bagdadi were here to meet Him. He did not meet Rev. & Mrs. Lee. They did not appear. No one took down His parlor talks. At the meeting Hil & I stood by the door handing out literature & right after He finished speaking we went up to His rooms so we did not hear any remarks. I think that is all you asked.

When He arrived Mr. Dahl went from the station to the hotel in the taxi sitting right next to Abdul-Baha. I went on a car & arrived about 5 min later. Mrs. Dahl, Mrs. Burt, & Hil* had been in his rooms to greet Him. Just as I came in they all came down. (The rooms were on the 7th floor.) & Hil & I went out to lunch. When we got back we waited an hr. in the hotel library while Abdul-Baha took a nap, then we went up & sat in one of the rooms. Mr. Dahl had lunch with Abdul-Baha. Right after we went up we found He was fond of chocolate, so, Hil & I went out & bought some. At about 3 He gave interviews to a few who wished it & Mr. & Mrs. Dahl & Hil went in & when they came out Dr. Fareed told me to go in so I went in & you know about my interview [in previous letter]. Then we sat around till six & went out to supper. When we came back & saw that the hall was ready & then took a walk until meeting time. There were about 400 there I think & Hil & I gave out lit. A stenog took down the talk & I have asked Mr. Dahl for a copy for you. After the lecture we went up the stairs and Abdul-Baha talked to about 15 of us very wonderfully but no one took it down & then we went home.

Wednesday morning, I went to the hotel about 7 o'clock & found Mr. Dahl & Miss Root already there. Abdul-Baha was sitting at the table &

* Hilbert, the son of Mr. and Mrs. Adolf Dahl, in later years designed much of the landscaping at the House of Worship in Wilmette.

> when I entered He said in English "Good morning & How are You?" & I replied, "All right." Then He talked a long time to us telling us how much He liked us & our town (Pitts) & our country, nearly ½ hr. later Mrs. Dahl came in. He told us we should meet on Sundays so we could come together as Miss Root cannot get off any night; for nearly 1 ½ hours He talked to us & then went in to pack as He left the hotel at nine. Then we went in the front room & sat down & after a while He came in & sat down next to Mrs. Dahl & took her hand in His & held it a long time & all of a sudden Mr. Dahl fell down on his knees in front of Abdul-Baha and put his face in His lap & cried & cried. At nine He left & Mrs. Dahl & I stayed & took the flowers . . . [3]

Carl continues his letter, detailing several items he found left behind in 'Abdu'l-Bahá's room, which, at first might seem of little consequence, but considering how the believers felt about 'Abdu'l-Bahá, even an empty candy wrapper touched by His hand was an important keepsake!

Allen Ward gives the following account of the events in Washington on 'Abdu'l-Bahá's return visit in May:

> . . . He rented an apartment at 1340 Harvard Street. From there He went to the Parsons' home where there was an assemblage of people waiting for Him.
>
> On Thursday, May 9, people came to Him all day long. Many ministers invited Him to speak in their churches. When a few spoke against Him, He observed, "I deal with people very gently that they may not turn away and raise the least objection. Yet these ministers have accused us of atheism . . ."
>
> On Friday, May 10, He spoke at a women's meeting, visited a settlement house for children, and went to Mrs. Alice Barney's for supper, where He talked late into the night. The next day 'Abdu'l-Bahá left Washington.[4]

Pauline's recollection of an encounter she had with 'Abdu'l-Bahá on this visit to Washington follows:

> Dear Alma,
>
> Were you happy because of my happiness described for your special benefit of our meeting with Abdul-Baha at the Station on His second arrival in our city[?] Oh it was so dear and natural of Him.
>
> Thursday night at half past eight, Abdul-Baha spoke. This time He stated His claim without equivocation, am sending you a copy of it. It was wonderful beyond expression—His power, and freedom from the cares of what people say or think of Him. You may have heard that just

after leaving the city the ministers in all the churches spoke openly or referred to Abdul-Baha's mission, denouncing Him. Joseph and Mr. Hoar made a reply which was published, a copy of which I enclose. This won for Joseph much praise and he was very happy.

The next morning Joey and I had another blessing unexpectedly. Ahmad asked a few to be at the Persian American Unity Office by 10 a.m. because Abdul-Baha had promised to pay a visit there. You bet we were there, ahead of time. Our Beloved had promised to visit there. Our Beloved arrived, I almost believe He was surprised to see us all. He shook hands all around, so genial. Then seating Himself smiled comfortably saying "How are you! How are you!" Then a silence for a moment, looking lovingly at Joseph He said, "It seems you have become our secretary." He then asked for coffee. Ahmad went for it. While he was gone Abdul-Baha seemed to rest a little then opening His glorious eyes wide He smiled at Joseph and said, "How are you Secretary General, are you happy?" You bet Joey was ready to pop, being called Secretary General. Then someone mentioned the next room as the possible office in the near future, inviting Abdul-Baha to step in there. Here seeing Him stride about in the nearly empty room, where there was plenty of room, I thought of a huge power caged in a human temple, having a little more freedom than in the other room. Here we all stood around as He walked with such strength and power. Here Mary Little showed Him some pictures of Ahmad. Though the time was inopportune, I guessed it would be my only chance to have Him hold Papa's and Paul's picture if nothing more. [possibly pictures of her deceased father and brother] So Ameen handed them to Him. He looked very attentively at them and in English said, "Very good, very good, very good." Then held them in His hands quite a while as He stood in silence. Others were arriving, the Khan family, then Mrs. Parsons. The little girl of Khan's had a tiny doll in her hand and insisted that her mother give it to Abdul-Baha to keep. Of course Madame Khan hesitated but the little one insisted. At last she explained to Khan, and Abdul-Baha accepted it, loved and petted her and turning to us said, "She has given to me her dearest possession." When Abdul-Baha started for the other room, He said, "You have given this baby to me, I accept, now I give it to you." But she steadfastly refused to take it back, saying, "I don't want it, I want Him to keep it." Finally, Abdul-Baha handed it to Khan, but the little one was not going to take it back.

Abdul-Baha took His seat and bade us all, "Sit down, sit down!" Just as we were seated Ahmad came with the coffee. Part of this He drank, then He addressed us. This speech you shall have, in time. Then He arose to leave, bidding us all goodbye. Then Ameen mentioned to Him our request about the drive. (We were going to take Him to Mamma's grave.)

He smiled most beautifully, after a moment's hesitation, saying that His time was short, and the day a very full one, since He was leaving in the morning for New York. Your invitation is accepted. It is as though I were going, but since every minute is taken up, I can not go. In English He said, "Thank you, thank you very much!" While saying this, He walked over to us and took our hands and said through Ameen, "I am very much pleased with you both, so much so that a drive will make no difference." Then He shook hands with us again and left. Joey discovered that He had left half a cup of coffee and asked me if I wanted to drink it. You bet I did take a swallow, and thought of you and Alma, Carl, Paul and mother. [I] wished that we be athirst with the desire of servitude.

Your Schnuddle[5]

For the next few months 'Abdu'l-Bahá traveled around the eastern United States, visiting many cities, periodically returning to New York, before traveling to His next destination. During one of these return visits, He gave a talk at the Mohonk Peace Conference at Lake Mohonk, New York. From there He traveled to Philadelphia (8–10 June), where Fanny Knobloch arranged for Him to speak at a Viavi Conference. Pauline joined them in order to be part of the various meetings. Below is her account in a letter she wrote to Alma detailing several of the activities:

Fanny will send you my letter to her about my visit to Philadelphia to be with our Beloved once more, mostly to tell about my teaching in the Viavi Office. [Viavi is the company for which both Fanny and Joseph worked.] This is preparation for the meeting, Sunday with Abdul-Baha.

I was the house guest of Mrs. DeNean, Assistant Viavi Manager. She made this class possible with the result that many of those present went to hear Abdul-Baha at the Rittenhouse Hotel, the two Church services, Unitarian and Baptist Temple.

Abdul-Baha said that Philadelphia would be glorified because of the Spirit of Baha'o'llah's Message. He said write down this date and what He said, so that someday we would recall that He had made this statement.

The church services were given over entirely to our Beloved. Needless to say it was marvelous. When the collection plate was passed, Abdul-Baha contributed generously, as is His want.

At the hotel many guests presented themselves, black and white, rich and poor alike. At one time there were so many guests and no chairs. Some wished to leave in order to make room for the new arrivals. But Abdul-Baha, smiling, bade them remain and motioned around. Since there were no chairs, many sat on the floor, (ladies too.) Abdul-Baha laughed heartily saying, this is indeed a symbol of the unity that is being established between the East and the West. Occidentals sitting on the floor and Orientals are seated on chairs. Then when He resumed His interrupted talk, it was almost a repetition of His address at Howard University to which He referred before. Feel pretty sure we will get it later because there were those who were taking it down in short hand. This was the longest talk in the Hotel Parlor and addressed mainly to a colored man, may have been a Believer.

Abdul-Baha asked about the Baha'i work in Philadelphia to which Mrs. Revell responded, very earnestly, just what was being done. He gave quite a long talk which I cannot recall except that He made a great point of the Nineteen Day feasts. They should make them of great importance and how to prepare themselves for it. Believe He said the Bab had instituted these meetings. Must make sure of that. Abdul-Baha spoke a great deal of the Apostles of Christ and their persecutions and that now churches were built in their honor. He himself had witnessed a crowd of people praying and kneeling about on a rocky hillside and on inquiry found that they were Christian Pilgrims and paying homage to those early Disciples. They had been told that an Apostle had sat down to rest on one of the rocks, and so they were hoping that they might happen to stand or kneel on that spot.

After the morning service I believe it was, Mrs. Revell was so excited jumping up and down clasping and unclasping her hands, saying, "He is coming to our home." Inviting the friends, as well as yours truly, hugging and kissing me, dear darling. I knew just how she felt, for I too had had the experience. Needless to say I went, took Mrs. DeNean with me. The spirit was powerful, as Abdul-Baha visited each room in the house. He saw me on the stairs and called my name as usual. When the opportunity presented itself, I delivered a message from Madame De Lagnel and He gave me a glorious message of hope for her. Col. De Lagnel was in a glorious state of happiness, etc. I was to be very kind to her.

Can't tell much more, o yes, Jessie said Abdul-Baha had called her a "laughing angel," and so she is.[6]

- 16 -

Special Visit in Dublin, NH

After traveling the next month and into July, 'Abdu'l-Bahá journeyed to the summer residence of Agnes Parsons in Dublin, New Hampshire. He stayed from 24 July to 16 August, allowing time to speak at length with the many visitors who traveled to visit with Him. Allen Ward writes:

> His days were spent in talking in detail with the persons who came from nearby and from distances, in speaking to local gatherings, and in writing the endless Tablets (letters) to people around the world. Again, He was taking time to deepen the friends, to inspire them, to raise them up, to teach them the spiritual meaning of life, to prepare them for the tasks that lay ahead, and to show them how to develop true happiness.[1]

While in Dublin, 'Abdu'l-Bahá made an unscheduled visit to nearby Harrisville to see Joseph, Pauline, and her sister Fanny, who had recently returned from a visit to Stuttgart, Germany. They then joined Him for two heavenly days in Dublin. After the visit, Pauline wrote a letter to Alma giving us a precious glimpse into the feelings she and Fanny held regarding this special opportunity. (She is writing about Fanny when she uses her nickname "Dona.") Joseph also wrote an account of this visit for *Star of the West*. The following is a melding of these accounts:

> At a mean altitude of something like 1,700 feet (and that, if one may be pardoned an apparent anachronism, is *no mean* altitude) the historic village of Dublin lies, a gem amid the verdure-clad hills of New Hampshire, and recently shining with particular luster because of the presence of Abdul-Baha, The Servant of God, and the consequent centering of the spiritual rays, which focus from all the world where He is.

. . . the traveler is reminded of Haifa, in Syria, and Abdul-Baha agreed to the resemblance, adding, "It is warmer there!" for even in midsummer the air in Dublin is delightfully cool and the nights almost cold.

. . . Reaching Harrisville late in the afternoon of Tuesday, July 30, 1912, our first and joyful surprise was to be met . . . by Abdul-Baha, who had come over from Dublin with Mrs. Parsons for that purpose, the latter also welcoming an expected guest. Mirza Vali'o'llah Khan was on hand to interpret and to add to the home-coming aspect of the occasion. First bestowing His guests in a waiting automobile and seeing to their comfort and happiness, Abdul-Baha joined Mrs. Parsons and Mrs. Ford in a carriage, and we were rapidly whisked to the Dublin Inn, a quaint and exquisitely-appointed hostelry just suited to the surroundings. Such is the magic of this place that in the vastness of the hill-country even the "honk, honk!" of the auto, seemed subdued, and the sense of being part of a scene of primal magnificence was not disturbed by the means of transportation, the electric lights and modern conveniences which abound. Dublin has long been known to the friends as the summer home of Mr. and Mrs. Arthur J. Parsons, and now for a time it is the Spiritual Summer Capital—of the Republic of Religions—God's Covenant with man of which Abdul-Baha is the Center!

At the inn we found Mrs. Hoagg and Mrs. Cline, of San Francisco, and we learned that Mr. George Latimer, of Portland, Oregon, was also a visitor. As we had come from Portland, Maine, and Washington, the meeting of extremes was evidenced by the fact that the little party of pilgrims were from Portland, Maine, to Portland, Oregon, San Francisco to Washington, thus spanning the continent from two points, a demonstration of the power of the Word of BAHA'U'LLAH. Then in the party with Abdul-Baha were representatives of Persia, Syria, Russia, and Egypt. A cosmopolitan gathering truly, and one which is attracting much attention in that section; although the naturalness and simplicity manifested by all makes them seem quite at home. This was manifested by Abdul-Baha at the station; the Master of the situation, issuing His orders quietly, passing around among trainmen and officials, the scene might well have been in Akka or Haifa!

As soon as we were comfortably ensconced at the Inn, Abdul-Baha visited us, and there ensued one of those delightful meetings which characterize such occasions. He asked if we were well; if we were happy, if our rooms were comfortable, and exhibited the tender solicitude of a host to His guests, or more properly, a father to His children. Then ensued the following:

Abdul-Baha: "In returning, I will certainly go to Europe."

Miss Knobloch: "To Stuttgart?" Abdul-Baha: "Perhaps." (Laughing)

Mrs. Hannen: "They are supplicating for it."

Abdul-Baha: "See how much we have moved from one place to another. How far New York is from here: Washington, Chicago, Philadelphia, the many places we have visited. And now these ladies have come to invite me to come to California. They are supplicating that I should come to California. Now these two have come to insist that we shall go; and letters are coming about it. A letter came yesterday from the Spiritual Assembly, asking how it came that we went to other places and not there. Now Mrs. Hoagg is going to build an aeroplane [sic] and take me there. What do you advise? Shall I ride on it?"

Mrs. Hannen: "It would not be very safe."

Abdul-Baha: "When I ride on it, it is the Ark of Noah. This aeroplane will become the Ark of Noah." (This was accompanied by an exchange of smiles which showed Abdul-Baha's keen sense of humor.)

Abdul-Baha: "Tonight I have promised to be present at the house of Mrs. Parsons at 8 o'clock."

When told that we were happy to have had Abdul-Baha with us, the reply was, "I am very happy also."[2]

Pauline's version of the same events:

Again we have been to heaven, Joseph, Dona and I. The most wonderful part of it all was that we were invited, Joseph and I without asking. Joseph, while on his way to us stopped in NY to see our Beloved. While there Abdul-Baha said I want you and Mrs. Hannen to spend a day and night with me in Dublin. When we left here Dona was all excited inside, very solemn outwardly, Joey and I delighted. When we arrived at the station, imagine if you can the excitement that seemed to get me by the throat when on looking out the window I saw Mrs. Parsons, but my eyes like a flash left her face as though drawn by a magnet, and were fixed upon a miracle. Our Beloved Abdul-Baha was standing, so majestic and powerful and yet the perfect Father Face radiant with love and life. He had driven from Dublin to Harrisville to meet His children to see that we were comfortable having a Persian brother accompany us. As we rushed forward to meet Him, with His own Hands cordially extended, He said hardily, "You are welcome. You are welcome." Through the interpreter we were told that rooms had been secured for us at the Lower Inn. We were His welcome guests.

He left ahead of us in Mrs. Parsons' carriage saying He would come to the Inn later. The auto in which we were, soon passed their carriage, as we seemed to be flying up and down and around about, the wind cutting our faces like whips of ice. Though we were nearly frozen, the joy within made it indeed a joy ride towards heaven. Just think 30 of July and so cold. Abdul-Baha had on his fur lined coat. On our arrival at the inn we were told two friends were waiting for us. We soon found them to be two believers from California, Mrs. Hoagg and Mrs. Cline, both of whom we learned to love very dearly.

We went to our rooms to fix up a bit. I started down stairs, thinking to visit with the ladies while Joseph washed up and Dona straightened out the room. At the head of the stairs looking down, whom should I see coming in but Abdul-Baha. Fanny said she was already down. After shaking hands with us He called, Mr. Hannen, Mr. Hannen, Where is he? I said he is dressing but will be here in a minute. Never the less I flew back to let him know of Abdul-Baha calling for him and hurried back again. Just as I started to sit down by the door, [someone] who was sitting on the sofa with Abdul-Baha said, Come right over here. Abdul-Baha took this up so brightly as usual, saying in English, "Sit down right here," patting the place next to Him. Come sit down! Oh it sounded so loving. I ran over and clasped His hand in mine and He let it rest there quite a while knowing it would cause me happiness. Really I felt as happy as a little child and grasping the Beloved's hand tightly said, "I love you so much, oh so very much!" Oh the tender smile of the Father to the child.

Then Abdul-Baha asked, "have come from Green Acre?" We both answered at once, "No. Portland—Portland, Maine." Then I told Him of my long illness and that Fanny had brought me with her to Maine to get strong.

Abdul-Baha smiled at me, said in English, "You have a good sister, a <u>very</u> good sister: You have many sisters and brothers, (turning to Mrs. Hoagg and Mrs. Cline) These are your dear sisters from California. You must love each other very much."

Then Joseph came in and Abdul-Baha went forward to meet Him, affectionately saying, "Mr. Hannen, my Mr. Hannen" with such a hardy, joyful, ringing voice. (Joseph's notes fit in here.)

Then Abdul-Baha bid us good-bye and told us to go into supper. He asked the proprietor if He might look at the rooms, which He did while we waited for Him. . . . Finally He left the inn. We thought He had gone. While at table He sent for Joseph, they walked back and forth a while. Joseph saying something, but I have forgotten. When he came in he said, Abdul-Baha invites us to His cottage in the morning and to have lunch there. We were very happy. The next morning He again spoke of Green Acre and if we were going? One of us answered we were only going there because of His Holy Presence, now we would not go. Abdul-Baha smiled saying, "This is much better here, much better here." We of course thought so too.

First Mrs. Hoagg, then Vali'o'llah and Ahmad made us very happy about this time, saying Abdul-Baha said to us last night when He came in, "These three are real Baha'is."[3]

Joseph's account includes several lessons 'Abdu'l-Bahá shared during the morning visit mentioned above:

"In reality, the length or shortness of the meeting has no influence whatever. It depends upon capacity. A piece of dry wood, as soon as it comes in contact with fire, receives the ignition, but a piece of wet wood, even if it stays in the fire a long time, is not ignited; it will only produce smoke and fumes. No matter how long a piece of stone is in the fire it will not dissolve. Therefore the length of time has no sway whatever. There must be capacity. Although the length of time of the meeting with Mr. Hannen is short, yet it is my hope that its results may become manifold. From here with a shining face, a merciful heart and a heavenly power may you return and become the cause of the guidance of the people; to be the cause of the firmness of the souls in the Covenant.

I desire to answer some letters that Miss Knobloch has sent. They have been here for some time, but there has been no opportunity whatever to answer them."

After a time of dictation to Mirza Ahmad Sohrab: "I am writing while you are silent. Is this permitted? [To Miss Knobloch and Mrs. Hannen.] You enjoy it because the letter is to your sister. It is fortunate for her that I find time to answer today. Letters come by bundles, but there is no time to answer them."

Abdul-Baha finished dictation, and surveying the mountains with a convenient field-glass, commented on the beauty of the panorama. It was indeed matchless—superb. In the distance a chain of mountains stretched, lofty Monadnock the highest, the others reaching as far as the eye could see. In English He said: "Good mountains; good green; good meadow; good plain; good view. Speak to me. Speak to me!" Told of the study of the Ighan, in the Wednesday night meetings in Washington, His comment was, "Very good! Very good! It is very good to memorize the logical points and the proofs of the Holy Books. Those proofs and evidences which establish the fact that BAHA'U'LLAH is the fulfillment of the Promises of the Holy Books. These proofs ought to be collected and memorized. As soon as someone will ask you—What are your proofs?—you may cry out at the top of your voice and say: 'Here they are!'"

A question was asked based upon the familiar reply to those who say there is good in all things: "What shall we say when they ask, 'Of what use are the flies and mosquitoes?'"

Answer to the question: 'What is the use of your creation? What benefit have you given to the world?' The same benefit that you have given to the world, the mosquito has. You say that the mosquito harms, and sucks in the human blood; but you kill animals and eat them. You do not suck blood, but decapitate the animals. Therefore, you are more harmful than the mosquito. By this, I mean that man commits greater sins. But that which is the reality of the matter is this: The world of life, the world of existence is connected, each with the other. All the created beings are the members of this stupendous body. Each one is a member, and that member should not remain imperfect. If that member is, for instance, harming the human body, but it is useful from some other standpoint, because it is one member of the members of this creational book, is it allowable that a member of the members of this great world be imperfect? For instance, we do not know what is the use of, this nail. It grows and it is cut again. We see that we have the nail; but we do not know that there are a thousand wisdoms within the creation of this nail. For instance, men ask: Why should we have the beard; why should we have the moustache? They shave. But in reality there is a great wisdom in this. It is healthful. The skin receives the oxygen through the beard."

Asking for further questions, the problem of contributing for the care of Baha'is who may be sick or infirm, was presented; in view of the fact that there are many demands at times and the friends are able to do but little, generally speaking.

Abdul-Baha: "The Friends must strive and show efforts and assist. Whosoever is a believer and assured, firm in the Cause, there is no doubt that he will contribute towards the assistance of the poor. This is an evidence of the faith. But if a person comes in contact with another who is in the utmost need, and he sees that he can help, and if he fails, this is an evidence of the weakness of his faith. If his faith is firm and strong, it is impossible for him not to assist. There is no greater trial than the test of riches. Whosoever you see that he is helping and assisting the poor ones according to his ability, know of a certainty that his faith is strong. Continue according to your ability, not beyond your power, and tell him to content himself with it. Not that he may receive your assistance and not look out for himself. He is not able to work, that is why he needs assistance; if he were able to work it is not allowable to assist him. Lazy people should not be assisted; otherwise everybody would leave his work and expect others to support them. There would be no end to it. But there may be someone who is either unable to work or is striving to find some work and is not able to find it; it is not really a shortcoming but he cannot succeed. Such souls are to be assisted. The aim is this, that the friends of God must assist each other, and in assistance be greater than all the other communities of the world. If one of the friends find out that another has no food for this evening, for instance, he should not rest, he should not sleep till he finds food for him. All the members of humanity are in need of each other."[4]

Pauline's letter:

We had dinner at the cottage of Abdul-Baha, prepared and served by our Persian brothers, Abdul-Baha having excused Himself because of a previous engagement with Mrs. Parsons, was of course not present. Here again was enacted a sparkling scene, as He came towards us shaking hands with one another of us asking our pardon in the most humble manner possible for leaving us and capped the climax when with bowed head He said, "I am ashamed, but I must go." Though I felt keenly disappointed when He first spoke of going, when He said, "I am ashamed," a big lump rose in my throat as I thought will we ever learn the lesson of humility and evanescence such as Abdul-Baha alone seems able to manifest. That sight is a glistening gem in my spiritual heaven. Oh He did look so wonderfully sweet and lovable as He walked off, disappearing into the green woods with Dr. Fareed a few steps behind.

The dinner of splendid soup, fallow lamb, fried potatoes, bread, coffee and rice pudding was heartily enjoyed, accompanied as it was with a vivid account of the wonderful supper at Roy Wilhelm's, by Ahmad, punctuated here and there with jokes by the others present. The time passed only too quickly before Joseph had to take his leave, Abdul-Baha having asked him to stop by Mrs. Parsons' on his way to the station. Between His leaving and our going to Mrs. Parsons' our time was well spent in listening to Said Assad'u'llah tell of his persecutions . . .

On arriving at Mrs. Parsons' we found Abdul-Baha seated in a large parlor and Ameen was reading the news to Him from our American papers. After a little while He left us as the first guests were arriving in their carriages. I should judge that about fifty were gathered when Abdul-Baha and His Persian party came in and began to address this fashionable audience.

He looked heavenly as He sat, His blessed white head against the red curtains alive with the sunlight piercing through as though it too were eager to show its devotion by bathing Him in its light. He gave the message, starting with Abraham and going on showing the influence of these messengers of God upon the people of the world. After the meeting He called us into a smaller room where a few were gathered and gave another short but impressive talk, showing the marked difference between the perfect happiness as existing in the animal kingdom and that of the human kingdom. Proving man is much lower than animal unless he become confirmed by the Holy Spirit.

Then He shook hands all around and said good-bye to us. When He took my hand in His warm clasp He said, "I love Mr. Hannen very much, he has served me faithfully and well. And you too I am well pleased with." Then I, like a baby filled up, but fortunately Abdul-Baha had passed on out of sight. Oh dear if you only could imagine the great, great ache in my heart as I realized His unbounded generosity and Patience with me and I had not served Him faithfully and well.

All must work, work hard and carry out His instructions to us to the letter, that we may never drink the cup of bitterness, realizing that we have not worked faithfully and well. Don't put it off thinking, tomorrow not today, for tomorrow may never come. God has been more than merciful to me a sinner, and has given me another chance. Believe me, I shall put forth every effort to teach all I can.

We were waiting for the carriage to come for us, when suddenly Abdul-Baha appeared on the porch where we were, one end of which was wired in giving it the appearance of a wired cage. In this place Dona, Mrs. Hoagg, Mrs. Cline and a Persian seated themselves enjoying the wonderful mountain scenery, while I stood off at a distance, just by the door, fighting, fighting back the tears that would flow. Then Abdul-Baha found us as He came out. After a quick glance at me, I thought, surprised, He walked to the end of the porch and into this wire cage. Oh, Oh! I shall never never forget how He looked as He walked about this enclosed porch, silent, deep in meditation or prayer despite all of us looking, watching (yes, I too was praying for greater opportunities and greater capacity). How I longed to throw myself at His feet, begging forgiveness and mercy for my past sins and greater capacity to serve in the future. When that heavenly Earnest Face was turned my way, and His Eyes lifted Heavenward, I could hardly stand it and my soul cried out for sacrifice in His Path. Suddenly He stopped His walking, faced the Friends standing around and said, in penetrating voice, I could feel the power of it, though not near. He said, "God has provided means, good means." No one knew what He meant. No one had spoken. Was He answering our silent prayers? I felt that someday we shall understand. It could have been an answer to my ardent silent prayer, it fit in, but I don't know.

The walk was continued, then He asked the California Friends about the Friends in California and if they were alive. Mrs. Hoagg said some were; others were earnestly striving to serve as best they knew how. Then Abdul-Baha began to speak and I moved up closer in order to hear His wondrous Voice better. (He told us that we need to teach and be busy like

He is all the time. Follow the precepts and teachings of Baha'o'llah and teach. Day by day it will get better.)

Here Abdul-Baha began to walk again in great majesty and power (in Heaven though on earth.) Thinking it high time for our carriage: He said to Mrs. Hoagg,"You phone and see what has delayed them." She returned saying it has just come. While she was gone I had slipped away again, that Abdul-Baha might not see my aching heart and tear stained face, believing as I did, this is our farewell.

Mrs. Parsons came out just as I reached the door, she of course saw my distress and was so sweet and tender, placing her arm about my waist in sympathy. I shall always love her for that tender touch, though she can't guess how much it meant to me, because just then Abdul-Baha began to shake hands with the ladies and I was sobbing so I cried, "Oh dear! O dear! He's coming." and I tore myself loose from Mrs. Parsons clasp and ran through the house to the waiting carriage. I was ashamed of my tears. He didn't come! As the carriage drove out into the road, we all looked and saw a Heavenly Messenger gazing after us, so earnest, so thoughtful.

I cried nearly all the way home but it had a good effect. I slept so peaceful as not in months and months. In the morning we awoke, the rain coming down in torrents but our spirits were joyful and happy and I felt well and strong. I told of this condition of mine because of what followed.

Dona said "they think we left on this morning's train, and I truly believe if Abdul-Baha knew He would let us have a few minutes more with Him. Shall I phone and ask permission?" Though my heart was pounding at the prospect I nodded, "yes." The answer was "yes, come." "When?" Dona asked, "What time?" He said, "Any time, just come!" We were beside ourselves with joy, as we ordered the carriage for ten o'clock. There was a damper though, namely that the two ladies would not be with us.

Just as we were leaving the Inn the sun broke through the clouds as it seemed to me, to bid us God speed. In fifteen minutes we were there. Dr. Getsinger admitted us, Mr. Latimer came in and one or another of the Persians would say how do and depart. The members of the household were all busy with one thing or another. A bright fire was glowing in the hearth, warmed us bodily and our hearts were full of song. Suddenly that One Matchless Voice called, "Mirza Ahmad, Mirza Ahmad." And you can imagine Ahmad flew.

Then a real strange and yet pleasing conversation took place between Abdul-Baha, Whom we heard but did not see, ordering the market, through Ahmad and the grocer. It made us feel so homey. After this was settled we were told Abdul-Baha would be down in a few minutes.

He came so briskly into the room greeting Dona first with such love beaming from His Countenance, such a perfect Father. When I stepped forward (because I was back of Dona) I wondered at the particularly merry twinkle in His Eyes, and a quick motion as though to say, "You too are here." Dona noticed the same look, we believe now, His Eyes said, "You are here after you were so sure yesterday was the last good-bye?" Whatever it was, He at least was pleased and we were radiantly happy.

. . . Then He turned to us and said, "How are you?" Because He was looking at me, I said, "Very well and very happy, and I feel anxious to go to work." Here a little talk was given in English saying those who arise to work in this Great Day of God, how they are assisted by the Supreme Concourse, and are confirmed, etc. Unfortunately, none of us took it down but the lesson we did learn was to strive with all our strength in this Great and Wonderful Day of God.

Now Dona and I can't recall just how the talks were given, because now and then Abdul-Baha would address one or the other of us and Mr. Latimer, now and then something to Vali'o'llah, Khan, Dr. Fareed, Ali Akbar or Said Assad'u'llah.

It was during this visit Dona told about Carl Hannen and Hilbert Dahl taking a colored minister for a ride in their canoe.

Once I said, "tell Abdul-Baha, I am so very much ashamed of my weakness yesterday, but I believe the tears washed some veils away and I am very happy."

Abdul-Baha looking right at me said, "You are strong, you are firm, you have the love of Baha'o'llah in your heart. You must withstand all the people of the world. The Supreme Concourse are behind us, when the love of Baha'o'llah is in our hearts, if all the people arise against us, one Baha'i could withstand them. In brief, when you return, you must return with the utmost great glad tiding. Wherever you enter you must cause such happiness there, that I can feel it here."

. . . We think He began this talk by giving us the following prayer. However, that may be He asked us to take it down, and then He asked us to bring them up for Him to sign it. Fanny had written the talk and prayer and I took it to Abdul-Baha. Now she has His precious signature.

He said recite this as you enter the cities. In the assemblies say:

O God! Assist me with the hosts of the Supreme Concourse and make me firm and steadfast in the Covenant and Testament. I am weak in the Covenant and testament; confer upon me strength. I am poor; bestow upon me wealth from the treasures of the Kingdom. I am ignorant; open before my face the doors of knowledge. I am dead; breathe into me the Breath of Life. I am dumb; grant me an eloquent tongue, so that with a fluent expression I may raise the call of Thy Kingdom and quicken all of them in firmness to the Covenant. Thou art the Generous, the Giver and the Mighty! [This version is from *Star of the West,* vol. III, no. 14, 23 Nov. 1912, p. 5]

Once, speaking for both of us, I said: "Tell Abdul-Baha I am so very grateful and do sincerely appreciate His bestowing this wonderful bounty upon us, this heavenly visit." Dona nodding and patting herself, said, "I too, I too!" Though I was so earnest, tears welling up anew, yet I could not help noticing Dona's radiant face, and subconsciously thought how bright her face, how wrinkled up mine is. She was beautiful to look upon and Abdul-Baha evidently thought so too, as He said looking at us, with such a beautiful smile, "I met you with great kindness and happiness, you must become the cause of happiness of the hearts."

That was not all but that much is true at least. I believe it was about here where Abdul-Baha began to laugh and chuckle as He said: "Your sister strives nobly. Everyone is astounded that such a little girl possesses such power. (He laughed heartily as at thoughts.) All the people are saying, 'How can such a little girl be the means of guiding those who scarcely enter this door.' (Here again He laughed heartily, greatly amused.) Whomsoever I send anywhere has been assisted. That which is needed is Divine Confirmation and <u>she has that</u>."

Alma, at last your size has become a thing of praise and fame.

During this visit Abdul-Baha ordered grape juice to be served saying, "It is cold, but it will make you warm, drink!" I said, "May it symbolize our firmness and steadfastness as we drink it all." He smiled saying, "Enshallah!"

I believe it was about this time Abdul-Baha said to Mr. Latimer, "It is part of wisdom that you leave with the guests." Meaning Fanny and I. Oh how I wanted to take him in my arms and comfort him. I had been there myself. Though His lips quivered, the sweet smile stayed, it was unexpected.

Mr. Latimer asked if there was a message for Portland. Abdul-Baha said, "You have my message. That is for all" namely the prayer and the talk.

Abdul-Baha arose briskly and left us, but we, Fanny and I were supremely happy. While waiting for the carriage Vali'o'llah Khan told the story of how his brother at 18 years of age, gave the Message to a man of great knowledge and wisdom and convinced him, all because Abdul-Baha had told him to teach.

When the carriage arrived we were told to go to Abdul-Baha on the side porch. He is waiting. Fanny went first and she thanked Him. He held her hands close to His heart, the other resting on her shoulder and though I was standing near, I did not hear. She does not remember except that it made her unspeakably happy, and she seemed to be melting with bliss as she did grasp the words to the effect that He hoped her work would be such that the report would reach Him.

This time I did not cry, but asked that my life be a sacrifice in His Path. Before this He has always answered, "God willing." This time I don't know just what the quality of that Voice, but it seemed akin to something in my own soul as He said slowly, "Allah o Abha." I was joyful but not moved to tears. For the first time I seem to understand that note in His voice. It was a "Lost Chord." You remember that song. Sometime I shall hear it again, I felt sure.

Then came the picture of the All Loving Father as He held out both hands to Mr. Latimer, embracing him, patting him, calling him "my son, my dear son!" What else was said I don't know; it was too sacred for one to watch. I only know that when Mr. Latimer lifted his head from Abdul-Baha's blessed shoulder he had tears like Dona—was struggling for self-control. Then all the members of the household gathered to bid us God speed and such a heavenly picture. As we drove away, all the men grouped on the steps and on the side porch, Abdul-Baha smiling, so bright and happy saying, "Goodbye, goodbye," waving His hand and with a burst of merriment He called out, "Au revoir." It gave me the feeling that we would see Him once more. I thought of His departure from New York. Whether we do or not, that picture will ever be fresh and beautiful in our minds, pure as the morning dew.

We took Mr. Latimer to our Inn, where dinner was served. He took a carriage to some station and we, Dona and I went to Harrisville and there ended that heavenly visit and now we begin life anew.

Account of the days spent in Dublin, NH. July 30 and 31, Aug. 1, 1912.

Your little Schnuddle[5]

'Abdu'l-Bahá ended His extended stay in Dublin, and once again resumed His rigorous travel regime, going to many states, and even Montreal, Canada. His journey took him all the way across the country to California and back again.

- 17 -

Final Visit to Washington D.C.

'Abdu'l-Bahá, having traveled all the way to California and back, returned once again to Washington D.C. for His third visit. He arrived on 6 November 1912 at 8:45 in the morning. The following series of letters, which Pauline typed, describe her experiences during 'Abdu'l-Bahá's third and final trip to Washington. As these letters were not with the original material in the archives, it is unclear who her intended audience is. They were found in a box that was kept in the family for years, and finally donated to the archives circa 1997. The letters are very carefully organized and given page numbers, which indicates she might have intended them for historical purposes; and yet, as they are in the form of letters to the family, perhaps she felt the family would be interested in her accounts for posterity. Although many other books have been written about these events, none that I know of have the detail and personal touch that Pauline puts into her writing. The way she organized her letters so meticulously highlights how significant 'Abdu'l-Bahá's last visit to Washington D.C. was to her personally, and to the family. I only wish I had seen these much earlier in my life. Some portions of the letters have been left out. Letter number one follows:

> Again we have been blessed with the presence of His Holiness, Abdul-Baha, in this beautiful city, the Capitol of the United States. This time it seems to most of us, that the visit is far more significant to us Believers than the twice before. This time His power and Authority was manifest, even to those who do not understand His Marvelous Mission.
>
> Though I have been very busy serving during these last days, and received wonderful praises from our Beloved I fear I will be unable to recall more than half that has happened because I was like one in a dream, silent and dazed, and only now am I waking up slowly but surely to the

magnitude of the Heavenly Bounties showered upon us. Not only upon our family but to the whole of Washington.

As Joseph and I left the house at quarter of six, Wed. morning Nov. 6th, 1912, it was still dark and oh what a strange, weird and marvelous sensation, to be walking to the Station to meet our Lord. To see nature responding to the Breath of God, as dawn appeared on the Eastern horizon, the light gradually spreading over the still city. In this mysterious morning hour we walked as it were with God.

At the station we found several of the friends already assembled with radiant faces, for they too had felt the power of the newly awakened day. Here let me mention the names of the Friends gathered for future days' remembrances. Ghodsea Khanum, Valie Ullah Khan, Said Assadullah, Mrs. Marie Hopper, Mary Little, Mr. Barnitz, Dr. Getsinger, Mr. and Mrs. Gregory, Elizabeth Hopper, Mrs. Allen, Mrs. Parsons, and Joseph and I.

Naturally He was the center of attraction and the focus of all eyes. By this time of course the party had become a little colony because of His own party. Let me see if I can remember those who came in with Him; Dr. Fareed, Ahmad Sohrab, Ali Akbar, Mirza Mahmood, Dr. Harper of Minn, Min. and Mrs. Wise of California. After a while we reached the carriage of Mrs. Parsons, here Abdul-Baha stood smiling and seemed so pleased to see His children gathered around Him. Some claim that I received the most wonderful smile of all, be that as it may, I know that that smile which He bestowed upon me just before entering the carriage electrified me. I was a land apart from this—another world.

. . . After this He went down to greet those of the Friends who did go to the house. But Mrs. Parsons said to me afterwards, He looked and was so tired that she begged Him to go and rest for the Friends, she was sure would not mind coming at another time. He greeted the friends assembled telling them that He was happy to see the faces of the Friends of Washington, etc., and that they should come to see Him any time the next morning. He would speak that night at the Universalist Church.

Joseph then told of the wish of the Rabbi to have Abdul-Baha sit in the Pulpit with him on Friday night and give a short address. He did not answer at once, and we were conscious that His spirit was with Baha'o'llah, as He gazed apparently at the ceiling or the gas light. He was in reality communing with God. After quite a few minutes He said, "Good." Then Joseph asked for an appointment for a colored Minister from Pittsburgh, PA, Carl's Friend. "Yes, at 11 tomorrow morning." By this time it [was] nearly quarter of eight, and the meeting at the Church a great number of people had already gathered and by the time Abdul-Baha arrived the Church was crowded downstairs and quite a number in the Gallery. There was quite a sprinkling of colored Friends, too.

Rev. Schaick payed [sic] a most beautiful tribute to our Beloved but unfortunately no one took down his remarks. Joseph expected to get his paper after the meeting was over, but someone had gotten it just before he came in. The vast audience was spell-bound, surely one might have heard a pin drop, so intent were the people upon the words which fell from the lips of "THE MASTER." I have forgotten to say that before Abdul-Baha left Chicago we had received a telegram saying that Abdul-Baha would address the colored Friends at our house. Can you imagine how our hearts were filled with unspeakable joy, to hear that the Manifestation of God would honor our humble home? [Pauline's pilgrimage notes indicate that she was aware that 'Abdu'l-Bahá was not a Manifestation of God, as the phrase is understood in the Bahá'í writings, so she is presumably not employing the phrase here to imply that this was His station.] So one other thing Joseph asked before leaving the Presence of Abdul-Baha this evening was, what evening or time would Abdul-Baha come to our house . . .

I have forgotten another item in that busy day. I begged Joseph to supplicate for Mrs. Dyer's daughter who was very ill, and He would be going to Philadelphia the next day, if possible. It is at Mrs. Dyer's home we meet every Wednesday night. Word came to me saying He would visit her that same afternoon, after His drive. Poor Mrs. Dyer was beside herself with joy, and so was I, for I would have another glimpse of my adored One. He came and blessed the sick daughter, rubbed her forehead and cheeks and told her she would get well, and held her hands so tightly clasped in His for quite a while as He prayed in silence, after which He said, "Give her plenty of fresh air & light." Mrs. Dyer supplicated for those of her family both in this world & the next, and great comfort. He then hugged & caressed as well as slapped the chest . . . [illegible] As we were waiting for His carriage I picked a strand of hair from His robe & gave it to Bessie, the granddaughter with whom Abdul-Baha simply shook hands, & she was radiantly happy.[1]

Letter No. 2, detailing 7 November 1912 in Washington D.C.:

The second day when Washington was bathed in the glory of the Holy Presence of Abdul-Baha, I awoke with a joyous heart, thinking of what this visit might mean to this city. After breakfast I went about my home duties as usual, not expecting to see our Beloved until that evening at the home of Mrs. Parsons, where Abdul-Baha was to address us. But a telegram and a special letter came in our care for Abdul-Baha and at once I made ready to deliver it, still not expecting to look upon His Heavenly Face. On my arrival at His House I found quite a few of the Friends gathered, waiting for an interview with His Holiness. Be sure I was most delighted that the telegram took me there for in a few minutes I was told to go to Abdul-Baha's room which I did. After delivering the Telegram and letter He bid me be seated and made me very happy the way He smiled at me. I then asked Him if He would honor our humble family circle by partaking a meal with us. He said, "This means a great deal of work for you, and it is my mission to serve and help, not make trouble. I testify before God, (Here He raised His Hand above His blessed head as though He were taking an oath), that you and Mr. Hannen are true Baha'is, I love you both very much and am well pleased with you. You are firm Believers, not shaken by every contrary wind that blows. You are different from other Believers." By this time I was on my knees before Him, dazed, almost stunned by His attitude, I think more than the words. I may not have the words exact, only the meaning gathered, but His Hand raised above His Head in such a solemn attitude needed no one to interpret. [These accounts are not authenticated but rather what Pauline recalled and felt.] I was too awed for tears, only a very few, but I had sense enough left to thank Him in some poor fashion and say that it would be an honor, not hard work to have Him to Dinner, or a cup of tea if He so wished on the 19th anniversary of our wedding. "In that case put off your Anniversary until after the meeting at your house and I will eat dinner with you, in honor of that day." I forgot to mention the fact that Joseph had already supplicated that Abdul-Baha might bless us both on that special day, and Abdul-Baha had said I will give you a special blessing. This Joseph did in the carriage going from the Station to the House with Abdul-Baha. That is why I had the nerve to supplicate Him, to dine with us. When I went downstairs, I was walking on air, overcome with the magnitude of this Bounty. The next sensation was the trembling of my knees, I could hardly stand, yet I must be especially kind to all because of His unbounded generosity to us. How I lived through that morning I scarcely know, except that Mr. Remey kept me very busy at the phone and notifying the Friends of the Banquet to be given in Honor of Abdul-Baha, the Center of the Covenant, Saturday night at Roushers, 8:30 P.M. Perhaps you wonder now, how Abdul-Baha could receive the colored Friends at our house Sat. night, take dinner after the meeting, and be at the Banquet too. I am still under the influence of that morning experience, still addled. Well soon after I came downstairs Mr. Remey came to me saying that the Friends were eager to give such a Banquet, and only two evenings were left, Sat. which is your meeting and Sunday which will not suit our purpose. The Master said if you were willing to change your plans and have the Friends Sunday instead of Saturday, He would consent to be present at the Banquet. Providing there were four or five colored Friends present. Of course I made no objection to this plan. And was given work to do at once. I was to notify the friends as they came in and to help receive the money.

After a while Abdul-Baha came downstairs and addressed those Friends who were gathered in the House of the Lord. No one was present to take this talk down, but what we all remember most distinctly, was that He was well pleased with the Washington Friends. He said "it seems that the Ministers here in this City are not pleased with me and have organized to work against me. This news makes me very happy. Praise be to God through that means the Cause will spread very rapidly. I only hope a number will arise and shout at the top of their voices denouncing the Cause calling the Friends by all manner of names, then must you be rejoiced, then must you sing for pure happiness, because then something will surely happen, the Cause will become well known and the Supreme Concourse will be rejoice with you [sic]. In Persia when the clergy arise against the Baha'is, a Feast is prepared in honor of the occasion and they chant praises of glorification that they are thus honored." While these are not the exact words, it is about what He said for He has since repeated the greater part of that talk. The one thing most evident was His keen enjoyment of that day which is to come to us, for which we must pray, in order that the Cause may be more widely spread. It was a short talk and He then went for a drive and we went home except for a few that remained.

One incident worthy of notice was this. Mrs. Coles and Mrs. Marie Hopper live together in an apartment. Their colored maid was present, and was so radiant after her interview with Abdul-Baha that she begged Mrs. Hopper to ask Him to come to their house for dinner that she might serve Him. Mrs. Hopper said not to Dinner, but we will supplicate that He take a cup of tea with us. She went to Abdul-Baha, told Him of this girl's great desire, and He answered saying, "Yes I will take a cup of tea with you if you will invite a few of the colored Friends to be present." Well they were just radiant, of course and I was invited to be present, and I begged her to invite Mrs. Cook of Howard University, which she did gladly. That was to be on Friday afternoon at half past four. Now I will leave the rest until I write about tomorrow, Friday I mean. Two points to notice here. One, it was my wedding anniversary day; secondly, I will take tea with you if you have a few colored friends present. By this time it was raining hard and we were glad to rest a while. The phone kept me very busy all afternoon until the time for the meeting at Mrs. Parsons'. Here we were kept busy receiving contributions for the Banquet & notifying

> the friends. That evening Joey worked the typewriter until half past one a.m. I spent the evening at Mrs. Coles sending notice to all the friends about the Banquet. I did not get home until nearly twelve. I [my] legs were stiff & pained me from running up and down the stairs . . .[2]

When reading Pauline's personal accounts of her time with 'Abdu'l-Bahá, and His praising her and Joseph, one might think her writing egotistical or self-glorifying. However, based on years of studying Pauline and hours of reading her letters and those of her sisters, her closest confidants, and taking into account the statements made by my relatives and ancestors, my father in particular, who always said that Pauline was the true Bahá'í, that she had a saintly character, showed forth the purest motives, and that her actions were always filled with love, I can only conclude that she was quite the opposite of self-indulgent. The letters that Fanny wrote to her were always encouraging Pauline to step up into the limelight more because she was so wonderful at answering seekers' questions. She was humble and shy by nature, but when asked to speak on a subject pertaining to the Faith in large groups, she was able to overcome her fear and performed wonderfully. She was not boastful or egotistical, but rather, as she described, she was stunned and overcome with emotion and wonder when 'Abdu'l-Bahá praised her. She could hardly believe that He was saying these things about her. Although the quotes are not authenticated, and she readily admits she may not have copied the exact words spoken, the meaning is certain in her mind.

Pauline's account of the third day:

> We have come to the third day and most bewildering day in the history of my life. There have been marvelous days but none of the type of experience which befell us on this our 19th wedding anniversary.
>
> On awakening in the morning my mind was full of the meeting to be held at the Jewish Synagogue that evening at which time Abdul-Baha would have the opportunity to give the Jews the wonderful Message of Baha'o'llah. Oh how many times had I prayed that these people might hear the wonderful story, in fact ever since Mirza Abul Fazl expressed such a very great desire to do so. Now at last the time was at hand and our precious Joseph was the instrument used by God to bring this about. For surely no one ever worked harder to accomplish a thing, than did Joseph to have the Rabbi open his Church for Abdul-Baha. So the day began with a flutter of anticipation and an earnest prayer that the Jews would feel kindly towards our Beloved. While in the midst of these thoughts the phone rang and it was Ahmad Sohrab asking me to come as soon as possible to the Master's House for the Master had some work for me to do in the House of the Center of the Covenant, without my asking or

supplicating I should say. This day of all days to be asked to serve Him, no matter what the service might be, no matter how insignificant it might prove to be, He had sent for ME. Really I can't imagine how the Latrobe was finished nor how I got my clothes on but by quarter of nine, I was at the House and sent word upstairs that I was there. Word came down: make yourself comfortable, He will send for you. Abdul-Baha was interviewing Mrs. Dixon at the time. Then came the word, the Master wants Mrs. Hannen. Up I went full of gratitude and bubbling over with joy and happiness just to know that my name had passed His Holy lips.

After a warm hand clasp, and heavenly smile, asking after my health and if I was happy, this Arch Servant of God paced the floor a while talking, saying about the following: "Yesterday there were many friends here at the House, some of them came up to Me many times, others who had never had the personal touch and longed for it went away disappointed and still others remained about the house all day. There was no system at all, therefore confusion reigned. Now it is My wish that you take this in hand, be here every day while I am in the city, be very kind to all the people and you arrange matters so that there be no confusion and you see that the people have the opportunity of a personal interview." Then He had me stand to one side while Ahmad called Mrs. Dixon upstairs. He told her practically the same thing. Then He took our hands in His, placed them (our arms) about each other's neck and while patting both [of] us on the back. He smiled very happily saying, "You must love each other very, very much." We were so overcome with joy serving that the hug and kiss was an expression of the inner exaltation, which needed this human touch to keep us on the earth. It was not long before we arranged the work between us and were kept busy arranging the interviews in such a manner that all should be happy. As you may guess, there were a number who had appointments made through different interpreters for the same hour. For the most part, the Friends took our word for it that we had been appointed for that special work, but there were some who refused to listen to me and tried to pass me by. Two or three times one or another of the Persians had to tell those who were pressing them to get them to Abdul-Baha, saying that Mrs. Hannen and Mrs. Dixon have that matter in hand through the command of Abdul-Baha. Once I was standing at the second landing with outstretched arms, keeping several back who insisted on going while someone was already with Abdul-Baha. I had just succeeded in quieting them when who should appear in the Hall back of me, but our Beloved Himself. There was no more trouble after that with any one.

This morning was full of little incidents showing the heart hunger of the many friends, both believers and strangers. Oh how they yearned to be near Him, or even just a glance at Him. Once I ran up to His room to ask permission for someone and He was in bed with Zia Bagdadi rubbing His wearied limbs. I disappeared at once without saying a word. When I came down several begged to go up and just peep and when I said Abdul-Baha was resting they said nothing more to me but got after Ahmad to let them go up. I saw them go and was not pleased. I also saw them come down with shamed faces, for of course they saw what I did, namely Dr. Bagdadi bending over the bed, Abdul-Baha of course we could not see. I tell this only to show that the Arch Servant of God has not a moment to rest in peace, even while at prayer He is disturbed by the eager hungering souls. Surely He has sacrificed His life, His sleep and rest for the creatures of God. May my life be a sacrifice in His path. This same morning Madame Khan had a Photographer at the house, and had the picture of her little ones taken with Abdul-Baha in His room.

That afternoon I rested until after four o'clock, the time set for the Tea at Mrs. Coles' Apartment. I was there in due season and gradually the guests began to arrive. I thought where are the colored Friends? I saw only two, Mr. Gregory and Mrs. Cook, and the room was full of white Friends who had seen Him many times before, like myself. Just as I thought this, Mrs. Coles exclaimed, perhaps He is not coming. We would be happy just the same for His spirit is surely here, even now. In a minute Mrs. Hopper and Lorraine came in ALONE—they had gone to call for Abdul-Baha and found Him very tired and told Mrs. Hopper that He would be sure to come in the morning about ten o'clock. As she was going downstairs, she thought, "Who am I that I should press Abdul-Baha, when He has so very much to do." She ran upstairs again to Mrs. Parsons saying, "Oh Mrs. P. I give it up, I can't press the matter—Just at this moment Abdul-Baha appeared at the door saying, "Mrs. Hopper, Mrs. Hopper, I will come at ten in the morning, there is a great wisdom in my not coming now." When she saw the room full of white people and only two colored, her eyes were opened. She called Mrs. Haney and I into the Bedroom and told us of this interview and said, "When I saw the room full of white friends, I saw the wisdom, don't you?" He had said, "I will take tea with you if you have a few colored friends present." The hearts of these two beautiful people was [sic] so filled with unselfish joy that they wanted all their friends to share it with them, and through this spontaneous love had to learn the lesson to obey exactly, not what they thought but just what Abdul-Baha says is the Will of God. So I did not get my cup of tea with Abdul-Baha on the day of my wedding anniversary, as I had fondly believed, though He had said, "Postpone your Anniversary until after the meeting, then I will eat dinner with you."

I went to the meeting at Mrs. Parsons' realizing more and more His Mercy as well as Bounty. Oh how patient He is with us, His little children.

There was very little time left after the meeting at Mrs. Parsons' and the meeting at the Temple. That never, never, NEVER to be forgotten Meeting. Oh how very grateful we are to God to have witnessed such an event . . . such Power and Majesty, such a Perfect Master of a terrible situation. The word MADE FLESH pealing forth in the synagogue of the Jews. For the first time I feared the Manifestation of Love and feared for Him as well. Sounds strange doesn't it? But true nevertheless. On the platform with Abdul-Baha and Dr. Fareed were Rabbi Simons, Mr. Blout, the president of the Temple and one or two others. Joseph and I had a high seat in the Synagogue, sure enough for we were way up front in the Rabbi's pew. They went through their regular service which was very long, though, to me very impressive but for what followed, I would have really enjoyed it. After some time the Rabbi had the time for his talk and told the whole story of a play in a Theatre, the story of the Rothchild's family. During the recital of the second or third act Abdul-Baha gave the sign that He had a message, a spiritual Message which He wished to give or leave, for it seems Dr. Fareed had told him that the Rabbi was relating this play and there was no spiritual sermon about it. To make a long story short, Abdul-Baha was finally introduced by the Rabbi. At first the people payed the closest attention until Abdul-Baha began to prove the validity of Christ. First there was a cough here and there, then groups began to cough and whisper a little louder and louder as He went calmly on until finally the din was so, so great that even those of us who were very near the front could scarcely hear Dr. Fareed. There was also excitement on the platform. The President Mr. Blout was laughing and talking and trying to make the Rabbi stop Abdul-Baha from going on with the speech, while the Rabbi himself was in hot water because he had been the one to bring this about against the President's wish, for Mr. Blout had refused to have Abdul-Baha, while Rabbi Simons urged His Cause most beautifully. And now that Abdul-Baha had a Message to give to the Jews, He gave IT and the congregation was such an unruly one, such a noisy one, Joseph (who had made the greatest effort), Mrs. Parsons and I had assisted to bring it about (this meeting), felt more or less responsible and sorry for the Rabbi. There were many of us there who would not have been at all surprised to see our Beloved thrown out of the Temple by some of the older Jews. Painful as it was on the human plane, the power of the Spirit was so great that most of us were unable to stand it with any comfort. As the Baha'is came out of the Temple, there was a great scatteration, no one wanted to talk, our hearts were full of a new wonder, a new realization of the power of the Truth of God. It was indeed a two edged sword that night, but Abdul-Baha Himself was very greatly pleased and laughed heartily in the carriage as they drove home. He said to Mrs. Parsons, "You must not be worried over this meeting. Baha'o'llah was with Me. I had a Message to give and I gave it. The result of that meeting is now in the Hands of Baha'o'llah. He will care for it according to His will and Wisdom." In spite of these words of comfort, she spent a sleepless night as did many of us.

Not for anything in this world would I have missed that meeting. While in the Temple, I seemed to be living, not in this generation, but two-thousand years ago. When the Blessed Christ drove the money changers from the Temple, the excitement and astonishment must have been the same then as we witnessed this night, two-thousand years later. Dr. Fareed and others of the party said nothing of this kind had ever happened during the entire tour, it was new even to them. The following I have not dared to breathe, but you two may know of a secret experience of mine. Joseph and I were in the second row, almost at the feet of Abdul-Baha, Who looked at us steadily but made no sign of recognition. When Mirza Abul Fazl was here I prayed so earnestly that he might give the Glad Tidings in the Temple, for it was his earnest hope. Now when I beheld Abdul-Baha sitting there, my heart was again lifted in prayer, not so much that the hearts may receive the Word of Abdul-Baha, no, that was not my prayer, but instead, looking straight up at our Beloved's Face, I prayed "Oh God, now is the chance, oh let the whole Message be given tonight to the Jews of this Temple. Let the wonderful Message be given that all may hear it. Oh God, move the hearts of these people gathered here." Again I prayed that the Jews be given the Message.

How little, how very little do we realize the meaning of prayer. Oh how ignorant I was of what might flow from those Divine Lips, and the results following, was proven when I prayed just as fervently, that God have mercy upon these poor people who left the Temple, which of course would not have happened, had Abdul-Baha spoken in the usual manner.

Please do not think for a moment that I fancied Abdul-Baha really read my thoughts and was answering my prayer this way. But I had a big, big secret lesson all my own. My first prayer, that they receive the Message in full so that those with prepared hearts might be brought in touch with the Glad tidings direct. The second to run away and hide when we saw how it was refused and perhaps our Beloved's life endangered. But on second thought, or emotion, was the victory over my soul, for joyous would I have followed Abdul-Baha to death itself.[3]

Pauline's fourth letter in this series recalls the events of 9 November:

Again another day of Glory has arisen to bless the City of Washington and its inhabitants. For it is indeed a bounty of God that Abdul-Baha was shedding the Fragrances of the Holy Spirit among us.

This morning as usual I went bright and early to the Heavenly Duty given me to do by the Center of the Covenant. But before leaving the house I had occasion to call up Mrs. Hopper to explain the absence of Mrs. Dyer at their tea the afternoon before, when lo and behold the maid said that Abdul-Baha had phoned a few moments ago saying that He would be at the house in three quarters of an hour, making the tea at half past nine instead of ten o'clock. Poor me, I was so distressed because the afternoon before when Mrs. Cook was so disappointed in not seeing Abdul-Baha I had said if you come to His House you will surely have the chance of an interview, knowing of course that I had the privilege of letting her go to the room of Abdul-Baha. Now I knew that this cup of tea with Abdul-Baha would mean so much to her in the future. I was sorely distressed. Having told her to come just as early in the morning as possible, I hastened my own departure praying that I might be in time to send her to Mrs. Coles'. God was indeed good to us, for who should get on the same car with me at 7th and U St. but Mrs. Cook. It was out of her way to take that car but something she said compelled her to walk that far and get that car. I saw her out of the car window, and heard her say to the conductor, does this car go to 18th St.? He answered yes, just as I called back to her to get a Fourteenth St. Transfer. She did without question. When she took her place in a seat next to me I explained to her the need of her going AT ONCE to Mrs. Coles'. We thought this very wonderful, and the Hand of God. This time Abdul-Baha did arrive on time, and oh such a heavenly blessing as she in particular received. He called her His daughter several times and placed His hands upon her head and blessed her. She is radiantly happy and her heart is now on fire with zeal to earn and teach this wonderful Message. I was not present because of my duties in the House of Abdul-Baha but I heard of the heavenly meeting and of her special blessing. That I was supremely happy you can well imagine for she is especially dear to my heart, also her husband, who is a bright jolly Professor of Howard University, in fact ranks next to the President Newman. Fanny, Prof. Cook has asked after you several times as also Ahmad and Dr. Fareed and some of the Persians. They seemed to think you should have been here instead of way up there in Portland.

That morning everything went on very smoothly and happily. The interviews were nicely arranged and all were happy. At the same time I was busy at the phones receiving names of friends who wished to be present at the Banquet that night. I think I have told you that each morning after the interviews Abdul-Baha gave a short talk to all the friends assembled in the parlor and hall. He would then go for a walk or drive. This morning we had the pleasure of seeing Him seated on the front porch with several children around Him and Mrs. M. Haney took two pictures of Him, one of which turned out very good indeed; the other was not so good of the children. Then He walked up and down in front of the house for quite a few minutes while the rest of us peeped through the windows and doors. No one dared to disturb that heavenly picture by going out of the house. He called Mr. Remey in a few minutes, saying that He had heard that the expense of the Banquet would be too heavy for most of the Friends, and some could not pay anything. Now why not give the money you have collected to the poor and let me give this supper alone. Mr. Remey came into the parlor a few minutes later telling us this and that he, Mr. Remey, had said to Abdul-Baha, "Most of the Friends are very anxious to give this supper in Honor of Thee, and while it might prove a strain upon them now, the time will come when they will be very proud of having taken a little part in this supper. The poor we will always have with us, and both laughed." Abdul-Baha then said, "Good! I will be present."

This afternoon which was Saturday, Nov. 9th there was very little for me to do but my regular household duties and to buy the perfume for you, Fanny to be placed with greetings from you to Abdul-Baha, at the side of the plate of Abdul-Baha at the Supper. It was hoped that He would anoint the believers with it. Mr. Remey had asked me to come early in order to receive money from those who might wish to give it. This as you know is not the kind of work I like but I was on hand. It was also my duty to take charge of the musical programs. Mrs. Fuhrman as the pianist and all the friends who knew the songs would follow my lead. Joseph had been invited by Mrs. Parsons to be present at a small gathering at her house of society men and take down the talk if possible. Just as he got there he met Rabbi Simons, who had just spent a most delightful hour with Abdul-Baha. He told Joseph that he agreed with Abdul-Baha in His Universal Doctrine of Truth and that he was trying to teach the young people in his Congregation to listen with reverence to religious thoughts of others and investigate the reality of Truth from every source, etc. But the older people of my Temple are not easy to move from the old beaten path. With the help of God I believe he will be able to lead the younger generation to more liberal religious views. He asked Abdul-Baha to try to teach the Christians to be more Christ-like toward Jews, and Abdul-Baha answered "I do that All the time." Abdul-Baha is pleased with him and advised some of the Baha'is to go to His Temple and mingle with the Jews. He told Mrs. Parsons to be very kind to Rabbi Simons because he had shown great kindness to Him, Abdul-Baha. This is the first fruit of Joseph's effort with the Rabbi. Praise be to God! May a beautiful harvest be the result of that Powerful Speech given by Abdul-Baha from the Pulpit of the Jews.

There was a meeting at Mrs. Parsons' house that same evening before the Banquet, but I of course could not go. I was needed elsewhere. As I came out of the dressing room to go to the Banquet Hall, Mr. Remey hastened toward me begging me to stay right by the landing and take in all the money I could. He gave me a little bag to put the money in and a pencil and paper to put down the names of those who had given. While I was not particularly anxious for this honor, it turned out to be very pleasant after all, for by this means I had a pleasant word from nearly everyone who came in, and indeed the Friends were charming. I wore that dress that Miss Doring and Alma gave me.

By this time He had bid us be seated. After He had finished His short address of welcome, Mr. Remey stood in the middle of the Hall and read the greetings from the Washington Friends to the Center of the Covenant. After which Abdul-Baha arose, Mr. Remey having given Him the bottle of perfume, Fanny, and while Abdul-Baha went around the Table anointing the Friends, generously, the rest of us sang "The Lord is in His Holy Temple let all the earth keep silence before Him." This we sang a number of times. Then we were seated and the servants began to serve the food, which was very good, but I fear most of us had our thoughts so completely centered upon Abdul-Baha that we scarce knew whether we ate or not. Though some of the friends were in tears of pure joy, I was not moved that way, as I have already said I was dazed, more like a stick of wood than anything else I can think of. Though many said to me afterwards, Mrs. Hannen, you look radiant, so full of joy and happiness that it makes us happy just to see you. Why they said this I can't imagine, for Joseph was always punching me saying cheer up, you look so blue. But I found out afterwards why he thought I was blue. It seems that by the time Abdul-Baha had gone only half way round, He held up the perfume bottle, turned it upside down to show Mr. Remey it was empty. I did not see that, or I might have been very much upset. As it was I was basking in the glory of the most wonderful, most enrapturing visions of the spirit of Abdul-Baha. I was lost to the world and its surrounding. For it seems that the most marvelous picture of the heavenly Messenger, the most spiritual vision was given us because of His having to wait for more perfume. Praise be to God it gave out too soon! Otherwise that heavenly picture would not have been ours. As Prof. Cook said, there was something about Abdul-Baha never seen in any man. This from one entirely without emotions proves that I am right; this is unexpected, manifested glory for all those present. I saw Him like that as He stood on that stone walk at the Holy Tomb of the Bab overlooking the Bay of Acca and the German Colony of Haifa. The power of the Holy Spirit was upon Him.

He was the living Prayer beyond any doubt, to those privileged to be present. But Fanny & Alma I still have not seen Him as you two saw Him just as you were leaving Acca.

When more perfume was brought He finished anointing the friends while now and then we sang a verse or two of some song.

While we were being served the good things to eat, Abdul-Baha made a tour of the tables, picking up a box of caramels here and there, the favors given to each one. He opened this box taking two out at a time; seemingly He was praying all the time, placing two in each Believer's hand. You may imagine those two were more precious than all the rest put together. One I sent to you Fanny and Alma, Joey will send one of his, Paul gave Mother one of his and Carl received my second one, so all of you will partake of the blessedness of that Lord's Supper. When Abdul-Baha had given to all, He seated Himself at the table and asked for some warm food to eat. He was tired and hungry, it was so natural and human that all of us ate the rest of our food with greater relish. After He had finished eating and washed His hands He again gave us an address which I will include with this letter. Then saying goodbye He left us. Naturally the friends found it most difficult to leave, exchanging words of love and joy and praise for Mr. Remey because of the great work he had done to make this meeting a great success. After a while Abdul-Baha came out of the little room and shook hands warmly with all the friends and then left the building. Mr. Remey had arranged for a flash light picture, but it did not turn out at all. The man had forgotten to take the cap off the camera. Dr. Getsinger gave a napkin on which Abdul-Baha wiped His hands to Joseph so we have another lasting memory memento. Thus another history-making day in the Cause was ended. Tired, yes, but infinitely happy.[4]

Before we continue with Pauline's account of 10 November, the most special day of all for her, I include these words of Allen Ward, which briefly describe that special day, including the talks 'Abdu'l-Bahá gave in the Hannen home.

On Sunday the entire day was occupied with interview after interview, until He went to the home of Mr. and Mrs. Joseph H. Hannen, 1252 Eighth Street, N.W., for a meeting. He looked at the interracial gathering and said:

This is a beautiful assembly. I am very happy that the whites and colored are together. This is the cause of my happiness, for you all are the servants of one God and therefore brothers, sisters, mothers and fathers. In the sight of God there is no distinction between

> white and colored; all are as one. Anyone whose heart is pure is dear to God whether white or colored, red or yellow . . .

Then He told them of Isfandyar, a man of African ancestry, who served Bahá'u'lláh in Persia, before His exile:

> If a perfect man could be found in the world, that man was Isfandyar. He was the essence of love, radiant with sanctity and perfection, luminous with light. Whenever I think of Isfandyar I am moved to tears although he passed away fifty years ago. He was the faithful servant of Bahá'u'lláh and was entrusted with His secrets. For this reason the shah of Persia wanted him and inquired continually as to his whereabouts. His Holiness Bahá'u'lláh was in prison but the shah had commanded many persons to find Isfandyar. . . . If they had succeeded in catching him they would not have killed him at once. They would have cut his flesh into pieces to force him to tell them the secrets of Bahá'u'lláh. But Isfandyar with the utmost dignity used to walk in the streets and bazaars. One day he came to us. My mother, my sister and myself lived in a house near a corner . . . our enemies frequently injured us . . . I was a child at that time. At midnight Isfandyar came in. My mother said, "O Isfandyar, there are a hundred policemen seeking for you. If they catch you they will not kill you at your fingers. They will cut off your ears. They will put out your eyes to force you to tell them the secrets of Bahá'u'lláh. Go away! Do not stay here." He said, "I cannot go, because I owe money in the street and in the stores. How can I go? They will say that the servant of Bahá'u'lláh has bought and consumed goods and supplies of the storekeepers without paying for them. . . . But if they take me, never mind. If they punish me, there is no harm in that. If they kill me, do not be grieved. But to go away is impossible. . . ." Isfandyar went about in the streets and bazaars. He had things to sell and from his earnings he gradually paid his creditors. In fact they were not his debts but the debts of the court, for all our properties had been confiscated. Everything we had was taken away from us. The only things that remained were our debts. Isfandyar paid them in full; not a single penny remained unpaid. . . . his color was black, yet his character was luminous, his mind was luminous, his face was luminous. Truly he was a point of light.
>
> . . . it is evident that excellence does not depend upon color. Character is the true criterion of humanity. Anyone who possesses a good character, who has faith in God and is firm, whose actions are good,

whose speech is good,—that one is accepted at the threshold of God no matter what color he may be. In short—praise be to God!—you are the servants of God. The love of Bahá'u'lláh is in your hearts. Your souls are rejoicing in the glad-tidings of Bahá'u'lláh. My hope is that the white and the colored will be united in perfect love and fellowship, with complete unity and brotherhood. Associate with each other, think of each other and be like a rose-garden. Anyone who goes into a rose-garden will see various roses, white, pink, yellow, red, all growing together and replete with adornment. Each one accentuates the beauty of the other . . . . Although different in colors, yet—praise be to God!—you receive rays from the same sun. From one cloud the rain is poured upon you. You are under the training of one gardener and this gardener is kind to all. Therefore, you must manifest the utmost kindness towards each other and you may rest assured that whenever you are united, the confirmations of the kingdom of Abha will reach you, the heavenly favors will descend, the bounties of God will be bestowed, the Sun of Reality will shine, the cloud of mercy will pour its showers and the breeze of divine generosity will waft its fragrances upon you.

. . . How beautiful to see colored and white together! I hope, God willing, the day may come when I shall see the red men, the Indians with you, also Japanese and others. Then there will be white roses, yellow roses, red roses and a very wonderful rose-garden will appear in the world.[5]

Pauline's own words describe that special day in letter number five:

At last it is Sunday, the day of all days for the Hannen family, for did not Abdul-Baha promise a special blessing, a marvelous Anniversary Gift, namely to come to our house and bless it and us with His Holy Presence and to partake of a meal with us? God is more than merciful to us His creatures.

Again I am running ahead of myself. This beautiful Sunday morning, Sunday Nov. 10th, 1912, Joseph and I started early to the House of the Lord. . . . It was a wonderful morning for me, because the power of the Spirit was manifest to such a degree, that although I hurt the feelings of some by not letting them run up just when they wished, yet before the morning was over we were all good friends. There is such a spiritual power present when Abdul-Baha is around, that none of us are normal. There is one thought, Abdul-Baha, there is time for no one but Abdul-Baha, we have eyes for no one save Abdul-Baha. . . . We were all very happy, though physically it tired me to try to calm the excited ones. But the first callers I sent up were Mr. and Mrs. James Sharp and our dear Joseph. Joseph tells me that they were served with tea, while Abdul-Baha talked with them. Joseph took notes of the talk and you will read for yourself what took place. Mrs. Sharp said she was not satisfied, for she had several questions to ask but Mr. Sharp didn't give her a chance. For this I was sorry, but since it was her own husband, there was nothing for me to do. Mr. Sharp expressed himself as very well pleased, and was surprised at the breadth of general knowledge which Abdul-Baha possessed. They did not stay for the parlor talk, and perhaps it was just as well because it was quite late before Abdul-Baha could come down. The next to go up were the Friends from Baltimore in a body and to me this was a beautiful sight, for they were radiant and happy. One of the Baltimore Friends, Mrs. Thompson, had a question to ask for a Minister in Baltimore and asked me if she might go up again and ask it. I suggested her having Joseph go up and take down the answer, if Abdul-Baha should give one. This was arranged. You should have seen them when they came downstairs, you might have imagined that they had been to some comic play, the way they were laughing. It seems the Minister had prepared a test question and answer which took them by surprise and made them all laugh heartily. The question was, "Do you trust Jesus Christ ALONE as your personal Savior?" In answer, Abdul-Baha went to Ahmad Sohrab and gave him a good slap on the cheek saying, "That is the answer to the second part of the question." We gather from that action, that He saw the Minister was trying to trap Him. Had He said "yes" then the Minister would have said, "what about your claim for Baha'o'llah then?" Had Abdul-Baha said "No" then the Minister would have said, "There you see He is displacing Jesus Christ." Whatever Abdul-Baha meant in reality we of course do not know, but it was quite evident to those present, beyond any doubt that Abdul-Baha was very greatly amused. The first part of the question of Rev. F. S. Downs of Baltimore was, "Do you believe Jesus Christ to be the only begotten Son of God."

Abdul-Baha [answered] that as Baha'is we believe that His Holiness Christ is the Word of God. We believe His Holiness Christ is the Spirit of God. We believe that His Holiness Christ is the collective center, that collective Reality which, like unto the sun, shines upon all the contingent beings. We believe that His Holiness Christ was the Savior of the world. He guided all the people and He delivered them from the darkness of ignorance and superstition and caused them to attain to that which is the highest desire of the soul.

To me this is a most beautiful answer to anyone who may inquire regarding the Divinity of Jesus Christ. As usual Abdul-Baha gave us a short but very impressive talk, His voice ringing when He wished that ten

> Ministers might arise, in their pulpits caring [sic] against us, then would the Cause spread. But this time we were so fortunate as to have Joseph there to take it down . . .[6]

On the evening of November 10, 'Abdu'l-Bahá did finally go to the Hannen home for dinner and gave the talk mentioned earlier. This visit was the manifestation of a dream Pauline often had, and was a confirmation of all of the teaching she did in the African American community. For this writer, it has been truly inspiring to reflect on the events leading up to, and culminating with, 'Abdu'l-Bahá visiting the home of my great-grandparents and grandfather, and praising the services they were rendering to the Cause!

On 11 November 1912 'Abdu'l-Bahá traveled to nearby Baltimore with a large group of friends from the Washington community. Below is the final letter of Pauline's personal accounts of 'Abdu'l-Bahá's third visit to D.C.:

> For some reason, Joseph had to get up at half past five o'clock this morning, in order to have a few words with Abdul-Baha regarding a message from Him to the Christian Commonwealth. (By this morning, I mean Monday, Nov. 11th.) I was greatly tempted to go along but thought I had received so much already that it was a pity to take up even one second of the few remaining moments left to Abdul-Baha before leaving the city. But Joseph was showered with blessings this morning. First of all, before he went up to Abdul-Baha's room he found someone was even earlier than he. After a little Mrs. Haney came down, simply overcome with the glories of that interview. She was weeping, but she managed to tell Joseph that Abdul-Baha had said such a beautiful thing about him, he must be very, VERY happy always. She was too full of tears to tell more just then but since, she said "I went up just as Abdul-Baha was at His Devotions, a marvelous experience. I wanted to tell Him of those I loved and esteemed in the Assembly and began, Mr. Remey, Mr. Hannen, then before I could go on He raised His hand towards heaven saying, "I testify that Mr. Remey and Mr. Hannen are sincere servants in the Cause of Baha'o'llah. They are firm, they are not like other Believers." When Joseph went up, he too saw Abdul-Baha at prayer, seated on a red prayer mat. He did not understand at first, simply thought Abdul-Baha was tired sitting on a chair and was resting in this manner, seated upon the floor. But he says Abdul-Baha embraced and kissed him and was so gentle and kind that he will always feel that love flowing through him. Joseph is not such a chatter-box like me, or he would have a great deal to tell us which he has not shared. There is very little that I saw and heard that I have not tried to repeat as nearly correct as possible, for us all to enjoy someday in the future as well as you dear ones knowing almost as much as I do at the

very time. Poor dear Joseph is so very busy that he does not have the time to think to tell me. Sometime he will tell little things and then I will try to put it in my notes.

Well to go on, he had a most wonderful time with Abdul-Baha, and then hurried off to work. I arrived at the house about half past eight or a little sooner, but had no word with the Master. Joseph told me that he had started to ask permission for me to go to Baltimore with the party, but before he had half-finished or as said, scarcely started, Abdul-Baha said quickly, "Yes, Mrs. Hannen must go to Baltimore." I was still in that stupid and dazed condition so that Joseph would often say, "Cheer up, cherries are ripe."

Abdul-Baha took Mrs. Dixon as His guest in the carriage and I can't remember who went with Him but most of the party went to the car, and when we arrived at the station Abdul-Baha was surrounded with a host of friends. Mrs. Parsons told me she had asked permission to go to Baltimore but Abdul-Baha had said, "No, you must stay with your husband, he has just come and will want you." She told Him she had accepted an invitation to take lunch with her Aunt and she would like to go. Then He laughed and said, "Since you have made an engagement to lunch with your Aunt then you must go." Wonderful and beyond the ken of man are the ways of His Holiness Abdul-Baha. Each one approached Him during that journey except me. I had more than I could grasp and there was no room for any more just then. While my eyes rested upon His white turbaned head my mind was busy with the scene at the Station at Washington. Surely such a scene would melt a heart of stone. Such worshipful faces, to me marvelously beautiful faces, flushed with various emotions, eyes bright with unshed tears, some were really weeping, others were full of joy at the many bounties received, manifesting happy love. Oh words fail to describe that picture, no artist could portray it. What was it in the faces of each one? Was it hero worship? No. For I was at the station once when it was simply packed and jammed with men and boys, also women waiting for the favorite Base Ball King. Just to have a look at him. They yelled and shouted like mad, but there was a marked difference between that manifestation of love, and that other smaller group with their upturned faces, radiant with a light not of this world. Oh what a difference between the light of spiritual love manifested in the faces, and the human hero worship. . . . While the necessary arrangements were being made Abdul-Baha made a quaint picture, sitting in this, as it seemed to me, a tiny Station, surrounded with His big family of children. . . . The rest of the crowd went on a street car to the Church at which Abdul-Baha was to speak. On reaching the Church it was found to be closed and so Abdul-Baha evidently asked for a Hotel near where He could rest while arrangements might be made. Imagine the picture if you can of Abdul-Baha with flowing robes and the band of black turbaned Persians and such a group of Americans following in the wake of that majestic Prince of Peace. . . . On the way to the Hotel, you may well imagine this strange precession created quite a sensation. Among those who stopped to look after the Servant of God, was a Catholic Priest, his face was as black as thunder as he watched Abdul-Baha and the party. As Dr. Harper and I came up to him, he turned abruptly to Dr. Harper saying, "Do you know who that foreign looking man is? Is he a Greek?" I did not wait to hear more because I was more interested in seeing our Beloved than listening to the Priest. As we reached the Renner Hotel . . . the porter came to say, "Come to the other parlor." It seems Abdul-Baha was giving an interview to a reporter and when Mrs. Allen saw this she sent word for us to come too. With the exception of the reporter the parlor was filled with His humble followers. Mrs. Parsons had left Abdul-Baha at the station to go to her Aunt and was to meet Him at the Chapel later. After this interview Abdul-Baha left the Hotel parlor and all of us filed after Him but stood modestly as we could against the houses along the block while He walked down the street with His hands behind Him, absolute Master of the situation with one Persian walking at a respectable distance behind Him. He finally called for Mrs. Dixon and they walked down the street looking in at the windows, now and then stopping to talk to her or listen to her. Then He called Edna and they walked off, after which He stood before us women folks and told us to be very kind to her and take her back to Washington with us. Then He called for Mrs. Allen and walked and talked to her. Then to my great surprise Dr. Bagdadi came up to the group and said, "The Master wants Mrs. Hannen now." I wish with all my heart and soul I could remember what those words of Life were which He spoke for me. It must have been written in my soul and reflected in my face for at a meeting last week Mrs. Allen told all the friends that when Abdul-Baha called me it must have been very wonderful because my face was transfigured. This of course she saw with the eyes of love but I was exalted in truth. What I can recall is this, "You have worked very hard to serve me during my visit and I am very much pleased with you." Then He repeated what He would pray for me. I wish I could remember but it is enough to know that He will pray for me. I felt that I was to say something but what? At last I said, "Tell Abdul-Baha that it was not work but a bounty to serve, and I would do my very best to serve Him faithfully." Then He said, "Be assured that I know you will." In a second, "I am sure you will do your best." In another second "I know and am very sure that you will do your very best." I don't believe it was so much what He said but the way He said it that lifted me to the seventh Heaven. I did not walk next to Him like the others but a step or two back of Him like the Persians. Since the night of the Temple Service I stand in awe of Him, and my love is greater but of another kind. . . .

Arriving at the Chapel we found they had been waiting for quite some time and sent Mr. Hope to find out what was keeping the party. At last Abdul-Baha arrived and as He mounted the platform I noticed that a folding door stood partly open just at His back. These doors when folded back made the Church and Chapel one. After a few moments I saw this door closed but did not see who it was that closed them. Later I was told that three Priests were in the Church which was locked, and evidently had come to hear but not to be seen by the people. Abdul-Baha saw them and quietly closed them in the empty Church. No doubt they could hear all He said but it was not as they planned. Wasn't that just like Abdul-Baha? This talk was a review of the Temple Talk.

. . . There is still one more beautiful picture. Abdul-Baha came down after His nap. It was more than time for them to leave to catch the train for New York, but as usual He was just as calm and serene, undisturbed and with kingly majesty took a walk over the rough grounds to a point from which He had a birds-eye view of the City of Baltimore. With His back to us . . . He prays for the people of the city of Baltimore. He turns at last to return to us when Edna goes to Him begging to be allowed to go with Him to New York. Then Mrs. Parsons joined them. By this time the friends are sure that they will miss that train and we would have Him with us at the station for two hours. Mrs. Woodward came over on a later train, came towards Him with a Catholic friend of hers. Abdul-Baha smiled upon her brightly and said she was the only Catholic in Baltimore who had come to see Him, and gave to her a beautiful jasmine. While talking to them the taxi was tooting and making such a noise, wanting them to get out of the road, but as you can well imagine, Abdul-Baha finished His talk first. Then what do you think! There wasn't more than ten minutes left to reach the station, which was . . . more than thirty minute's drive from Struvens, even by taxi. He quietly came towards the house, shook hands with each one and standing on the top step with all but a very few friends standing around on the street before Him, He gave them a brief but beautiful talk, saying among other things that He would pray for the friends in Baltimore at the Holy Tomb. Then He nodded a farewell and got into the waiting Taxi, calling Mr. Remey and the Persians, and that is the last I saw of the wonderful personality of Abdul-Baha, the Center of the Covenant.

Of course we hurried off to the station hoping to see Him once more should He have missed the train. But Mr. Remey told us that they were <u>just in time</u>, some of them had to run, and in that way Abdul-Baha got off on the train intended, for it was late. He knew it all the time. That is what all of us said to each other.

Thus ends the story of those marvelous days wherein the Temple of the Spirit of God was in Washington D.C. and Baltimore and the Lamb was the Light thereof.

Your happy little Schnuddle (Pauline)[7]

In the words of Allen Ward:

'Abdu'l-Bahá went on to New York where He spent the remaining days of His time in America. During His last month He gave very few public addresses but rather preferred to visit homes of individual Bahá'ís or have them visit Him in His residence. He concentrated on preparing the believers to be able to carry on the work of the Cause, to spread the Divine Teachings, to become unified in their efforts, to love each other and to serve their Lord with heart and soul. On His final day, December 5th, 1912, as the friends stood in tearful attention, He spoke these stirring words of encouragement and instruction to them:

> This is my last meeting with you, for now I am on the ship ready to sail away. These are my final words of exhortation. I have repeatedly summoned you to the cause of the unity of the world of humanity . . .
>
> The earth is one nativity, one home, and all mankind are the children of one father. . . . The obstacle to human happiness is racial or religious prejudice, the competitive struggle for existence and inhumanity toward each other.
>
> Your eyes have been illumined, your ears are attentive, your hearts knowing. You must be free from prejudice and fanaticism, beholding no differences between the races and religions. . . . the best way to thank God is to love one another.
>
> Beware lest ye offend any heart, lest ye speak against any one in his absence, lest ye estrange yourselves from the servants of God. . . .
>
> A world-enkindling fire is astir in the Balkans. God has created men to love each other, but instead, they kill each other with cruelty and bloodshed. . . .
>
> As to you;—your efforts must be lofty. Exert yourselves with heart and soul so that perchance through your efforts the light of Universal Peace may shine. . . .
>
> Consider how the prophets who have been sent . . . have exhorted mankind to unity and love. . . . Consider the heedlessness of the

world. Notwithstanding the heavenly commandments to love one another, they are still shedding each other's blood. . . .

Your duty is of another kind, for you are informed of the mysteries of God. Your eyes are illumined, your ears are quickened with hearing. You must therefore look toward each other and then toward mankind with the utmost love and kindness. You have no excuse to bring before God if you fail to live according to his command, for you are informed of that which constitutes the good-pleasure of God. . . . It is my hope that you may become successful in this high calling. . . . And unto this I call you, praying to God to strengthen and bless you.[8]

(Edited by Allen Ward)

The following is taken from a letter Joseph received about six months after 'Abdu'l-Bahá returned to Palestine, following His long and historic journey across America. He writes:

O thou who art firm in the Covenant!
Thy report was received. Through this news of the effulgence of the Kingdom of God the hearts of the divine friends became rejoiced. Praise be to God that the splendor of the Sun of Reality has cast such an illumination from the East to the West and had made possible the holding of such radiant meetings, so that the sweet melody may ascend to the kingdom of Abha!

Less than a year Abdul-Baha traveled through cities of America and crossed its deserts and from His heart and soul He raised the cry of "Ya Baha el Abha!", in gatherings and churches. He gave the Glad Tidings of the appearance of the Kingdom of God! Vociferously He imparted the news of the Sun of Reality. He explained divine proofs and evidences and with a spirit and mind overflowing with the Love of God, He sang the New Melody. Undoubtedly they will have great effect.

Consider that the life imparting Melody of His Holiness Christ—may my life be a sacrifice to Him!—became world-wide after 300 years and created the desired effect; and the Melody of the Kingdom of Abha in a short space of time, stirred the East and the West. Therefore, reflect over this Melody. What a Melody is this! What music and song are these! What a stupendous Cause is this!

Convey to all the friends all the Wonderful Abha Greetings.
(signed) Abdul-Baha
Translated by Ahmad Sohrab Paris June 11, 1913[9]

- 18 -

Fanny & Alma in Paris

In 1913, after meeting 'Abdu'l-Bahá while on Pilgrimage, and after Fanny had the opportunity to spend time with Him in America, she and Alma both had the bounty to meet Him, again during His historic travels to Paris, France. The following are accounts of these visits; Alma was first to join 'Abdu'l-Bahá in Paris:

> Paris, Feb. 12, 1913
> About half past 10 o'clock Frl. Köstlin, Herrn Eger, Frau Schweizer & I started from the Hotel to find the home of Abdul-Baha. . . . Mirza Hahoum Khan was also pleased to greet us & told me that he had met my sister, especially remembered my sister Mrs. Hannen. After a little while Mms Dreyfus & Mirza Khan came in & said the Master wishes to see us. We were happy beyond words. As we entered, our Beloved Abdul-Baha came forward to greet us, extending His Blessed Hand, which we in all reverence kissed, saying: you are welcome. He then bade us to be seated & after a few moments Abdul-Baha sitting in an easy chair said: "You are welcome. You are very welcome. You are very, very welcome. I have been very anxious to see the Believers of Germany. I am longing to see the Baha'i Friends in Germany. I have great love for them."
>
> Looking at me He said: "You have a good sister a very good sister, she is in reality a very good sister. You are a good teacher because!" Looking at Frau Shweizer, Frl. Köstlin & Herrn Eger, He said: "these your scholars are burning torches, Very good, very good."
>
> I asked if the Unity Feast could be given in the same rooms where it was held when Mirza Assadullah & the other guests visited Stuttgart. Frau v. B. had offered these rooms, she was the first to open the way for the spreading of the Teachings. Abdul-Baha said "Yes, she will be greatly blessed. She will be greatly favored, & Baha'o'llah's Bounties will encircle

her. Everyone who assists the Cause in these Days will be greatly blessed & remembered. The Teachings will become spread all over Germany. They will become illumined."

. . . After speaking to a number of the Paris Believers & the different Friends present, many having come in & this was quite a large gathering, Abdul-Baha suddenly entered & all arose in reverence & remained standing until He was seated. He then gave an address upon the Manifestations of God. Abdul-Baha then arose & all present arose & He went all around & shook hands with the friends & saying a few words here & there. As He extended His blessed Hands to me He said: "Very good, very good." . . .[1]

In the spring of 1913, Fanny returned to Stuttgart to assist Alma in her teaching work. For a while they traveled together to Switzerland to do more work for the Faith. While there, Fanny received an invitation to meet 'Abdu'l-Bahá in Paris, where she had the privilege of attending the many meetings at which He spoke. Those talks were later published in English in a book entitled *Paris Talks*, Fanny wrote:

In the spring of 1913, recovering from a nervous collapse, I returned to Stuttgart to recover my strength and at the same time give Alma the opportunity of having one of her own with her. Shortly after my arrival there, a telegram was received inviting me to Paris as the guest of Abdul-Baha. My first thought was, "How can I go in my weakened, tremulous condition?" Then a second telegram came, which started me on my way to Paris, there to be received, oh so lovingly, by Abdul-Baha. After greetings were over, He placed me in the company of a little group composed of Madame Holbach of Brittany and Mrs. Beede and Madame Blumenthal of New York. We followed Abdul-Baha wherever He gave addresses, not only in clubs but in large salons in the homes of those interested.

On Abdul-Baha's birthday, May 23, Madame Holbach and I arose at five in the morning and hastened to the flower market, where we selected the loveliest of blossom; then to a fruit store, where we purchased a basket of Spanish cherries that fairly laughed at us. Soon we were rapping at the door of the hotel salon. A well-beloved voice was heard, calling "Entre." We were just a bit timid, so next Abdul-Baha called, "Come in." What a wondrous sight! Abdul-Baha, seated at the window, which reached from ceiling to floor, was all in white, hands folded in His lap, looking out across a little park to where the sun was slowly rising in back of some tall buildings on the streets beyond. The room was in delicate shades of old rose, with long brocaded draperies at every window, creamy white glass curtains, delicate French furniture of gold and white, and flowers everywhere. Upon entering, I placed my basket of cherries out of sight as I passed the table. Madame Holbach presented Abdul-Baha with a book which she had written, entitled "Following in the Steps of Coeur de Lion," for which Mr. Holbach had drawn the beautiful illustrations. This was graciously accepted. Following the words of praise given the writer, Abdul-Baha said, "And now, you must give all your time and talent to writing about Peace." My flowers were presented. Abdul-Baha called to the Persians in a small adjoining room and soon we were seated close to our Beloved. No, the cherries were not forgotten, for with a twinkle in His eye, Abdul-Baha requested the Persians to bring them to Him. Do you get this picture? Eating cherries with Abdul-Baha in these beautiful surroundings, watching the sun rise higher and higher, whilst we were blessed by his words of wisdom.[2]

A composition book found in the Washington archives written in by both Fanny and Alma in parts, elaborates further on this visit and includes more of the teachings they gleaned from 'Abdu'l-Bahá's talks. Again, these accounts are Fanny's or Alma's recollections of His words and are not considered an authentic rendering:

Fanny's first morning in Paris, May 21, 1913
Abdul-Baha's greeting: "Oh Miss Knobloch! Welcome! Very Welcome," which was given with such loving kindness, then the two little packages, one from Miss Stäbler the other from Miss Digel, were presented & accepted with pleasure, saying: very good! Then asking: "How is your sister? Is she happy? Yes? She has done a wonderful work, for she has established a great Assembly, through her coming there many souls have been led into the Kingdom through her work. Her work is confirmed by Baha'o'llah—tell her to have no fear, to be confident, very confident, she will be assisted by the Heavenly Concourse."

Ques: Have you any preference as to the city in which she shall teach after leaving Stuttgart?

Abdul-Baha replied: "We have no preference. We leave this matter to her own good judgment, wherever an opportunity presents itself to teach the blessed Cause, there she will go. You must be very thankful to God that you are such a trium of sisters in the Cause."

Greetings from the German Believers were given to Abdul-Baha from Alma, Miss Döring, Mrs. Sweizer, Mr. Schwab, Miss Stäbler & others.

Telling of Pauline's S. School work, Abdul-Baha listened interested in all pertaining to the S. S. [Sunday School] saying: Khele Ghoo! [sic] Kheli ghoo! [very good] It is very necessary that they be renewed again, & be made active. Then Abdul-Baha asked: "If the S. S. is very important, why did they give it up? It is essential that the S. S. be upheld. First: Because the children are there taught the Words of Baha'o'llah. Second: Because the morality taught there, is the true Baha'i morality. Thirdly: Because they will become firmly established in the precepts & truths of the Baha'i Cause. Fourth: Because the S. S. is of great value it is very good & they must attend this with joy & enthusiasm."

Abdul-Baha: "I am very pleased with the Believers in Stuttgart; in reality the Believers in Stuttgart are very good. I am very pleased with the Believers in England. I am very pleased with the Believers in America. I will always pray for the Believers in America, in England and in Stuttgart so God will strengthen them ever more.[3]

Below is a story very close to my heart. On my fifteenth birthday, my grandparents, Carl and Mineola Hannen, gave me a precious locket once belonging to my "Tanta Ana" (Alma). When I came across this account in the archives written by Alma, I was delighted! She writes:

> When parting in Paris Abdul-Baha bent down & searched in His handbag for some time, & felt relieved when He found what He was looking for. A small Pho: [photo] of Himself which He gave to each one of us. A wish was granted which I had for years. My sister Fanny had given me a gold locket set with a diamond to place a hair from Abdul-Baha in it. While in Acca, Fanny one day took a hair from Abdul-Baha's shoulder. He noticed it but said nothing. Later I said to her—I wish I had the nerve to take one. Oh she replied, I will get you one, but that would not be me. . . . The following day after dinner Abdul-Baha stepped next to me shrugging [His] shoulder & standing very close & there all of a sudden I noticed the hair on His coat. What a joy to take it & carefully place it in safe keeping. This was the hair I had a jeweler place in my locket & wished [for] a small photograph to be placed in with it. My joy was great to receive this little Pho; just the right size.[4]

- 19 -

Mother of Bahá'í Children's Classes

In the National Archives index, it is noted that Pauline Hannen was one of the first believers in this country to develop material for children's classes, thus becoming known to some as the "mother" of Bahá'í children's classes. It was a labor of love for her, but not always one that came easy. When Pauline thought about teaching children, she often had to overcome her lack of confidence and genuine fear. In a letter she wrote to her husband in May of 1917, long after she had begun teaching children's classes, she expressed her trepidation:

> . . . what you have said in recent letters regarding my part of the Sunday School work, makes me fear rather than rejoice at my return. Shall pray constantly that God may drive out that fear which has taken possession of me and fill my soul with capacity to do that which is expected of me. You are the one they really love, and now you have, beyond a doubt, learned to teach them as well, the great spiritual truths. You need not bother to answer this part of the letter, for I know my weakness far better than anyone else. You have been the instrument used to bring my name forward in that work. But for your steadfastness in urging me on, I should long since have fallen by the wayside . . .[1]

As in many of Joseph and Pauline's endeavors, they were great partners and helpmates in this field of service. Although she is the one who became most known for this work, they both taught Sunday school in Washington. Marzieh Gail mentions in her book about her father, Ali Kuli-Khan, that Joseph Hannen was her Sunday school teacher and she fondly remembers how he helped her learn Bahá'í principles and quotes.[2] However, with Joseph's urging, and that of 'Abdu'l-Bahá as well, Pauline took on this service passionately, and it became the field of service for which she is most remembered.

In a 1907 report to Ahmad Sohrab, Pauline wrote about her adventures in teaching children:

> That summer I started a class for teaching the children, something of the Baha'i History. They met at this house every Saturday and it was a success to the extent that we realized a great need. So that in the Fall of 1907 the Baha'i parents felt the need of a Sunday School & promised me to send the children if Mrs. Allen would agree to take them. This she did having ten dear little Baha'i children to teach every Sunday morning in the Hall.
>
> This year after finding out that no one would undertake the Sunday School work, I again undertook the work. Starting with thirteen, then fifteen, until now there are 21 enrolled. The adults who came to see what I would do were so pleased that they asked me to start a Bible Class in connection with the little ones. During the next two weeks I found that quite a number would come to the class if Mr. Hannen took charge. I then asked Mr. Hannen & today the Sunday School is a soul inspiring institution. There are now three teachers besides myself. Mr. Hannen's Bible Class, Mr. Moore's intermediate class, my class of children ranging in age from nine to twelve years, Mrs. Barnitz has the little ones from four years up to nine years.
>
> The first visible fruit of my teaching in S. School was the quick understanding of my oldest son, who was in my class, to serve the Cause. This he did by going every Sunday morning, without a word, an hour ahead of time to call for four children who were not children of Baha'i parents & then took them home again. This was service, not easy for him but done for the Cause. This prepared him for the next service, when he was asked to serve with three young men at a Unity Feast. He was a revelation of joy to not only his father and mother, but to all assembled. The young men declared they would serve refreshments but could not get up & lead the Meeting. Our Nategh, Carl Hannen, realizing this to be the moment of action, seized it. He opened the Meeting by reading a Tablet, a little nervous at first but soon the Spirit of Abha surrounded him and he was as peaceful and calm as anyone could be. He then read a prayer, introduced Madam Ali Kuli-Khan, who was in our midst for the first time; he then called upon Mirza Khan to speak, then closed with prayer. He then announced that refreshments would be served. After this, another occasion he gave the History of the Bab from His birth to His death and burial. Therefore while visiting our dearly Beloved Abdul-Baha, we were humbly grateful but not surprised when Abdul-Baha gave him the name Nategh, which means speaker & teacher. We had not spoken of this new joy that had come to us but He knew as He knows all things. God grant he may continue to grow in grace and knowledge.[3]

Some time later, Pauline wrote another account further detailing her involvement with children's classes:

> In due course my husband, having become a Baha'i, acted upon my suggestion and cooperated in forming a class of white and colored children whom I was to teach on Sundays. First we called on two Hopkins families, both living in the same house, not believing in any religion. Pledging me on my honor not to teach the little ones anything wrong, they gave their consent for their children to attend the proposed school. Starting with 21 white children, I taught them the elements of the Baha'i Faith and memory verses from the Bible. Later we took in colored children with the white. This arrangement involved no difficulties, though when we organized classes for older people, of which my husband was moderator, colored people, whose needs were met by the various neighborhood groups, did not come, though welcome.
>
> What an inspiration, looking into the faces of those dear children, so eager, so free from prejudice, such open minds: silently I begged God to protect me from "disposing of anything not owned by Thee." How careful I must be to prove every statement made from the Words of God, or science or secular history, as the case might be.
>
> The class grew. Adults were encouraged to come and hear the little ones singly and collectively repeating the memory verses and answering questions. This prepared them for the time when they took complete charge of some of the 19-day Feasts authorized by the Washington Assembly of Baha'is. This proved a spur to endeavor in memorizing and giving talks on the Great Messengers of the past and present day Manifestations. One child was selected by the others to be chairman, and was responsible for the program, arranging for certain ones to speak, to read, to pray and select songs.
>
> It was on our pilgrimage, where we visited Abdul-Baha at Akka in February 1909 that enabled the children to show tangibly their love for Him. Among themselves they decided what to do. They asked permission to make little gifts for the poor of Akka.
>
> These gifts we took with us. In Haifa Abdul-Baha gave me instructions [on] what and how to teach advanced children.

> In that hour, you should make the children familiar with the prophecies in the Gospels and with this Revelation: that is to say, instruct them how to be teachers, so that the love of God may be established in their hearts while they are young children. They should develop spiritual feelings. You should explain to them or read to them the Ishraqat, Tarazat, Tajalliyat, the Words of Paradise and the Tablet to

> the World. You should make them memorize some of these verses. By these means they will become enlightened and well educated, for they are like unto a young tree: you can train them in whatsoever manner you like. (*Star of the West,* Vol. 9, p. 93)

It took the utmost faith on my part to attempt this program, for some of it was beyond me in their scope of knowledge. But the Power of the Holy Spirit came to my assistance, and with the cooperation of Helen Hotchkiss, a youthful Baha'i of an analytical turn of mind, a group was started in her home. When we were somewhat grounded in these advanced Teachings it became a part of the regular Sunday school, a young people's class.

We now had three classes—little children, young people, and adults. It was during these days that the little ones shone. After class work all united in closing service, when I would review the day's lesson, encouraging freedom of Speech for the little ones. When their elders hesitated, up came the hands of some from my class. From the memorized verses they had accumulated a fund of knowledge. Visiting Baha'is, who had begun to find joy in coming to the school, perhaps addressing us, were amazed by the youngest members.

One evening a Navy electrician told his experience in China. Of great import to me was his account of a meeting at the Y.M.C.A. attended by a ships officer and himself. Among other things was denunciation of the Prophet Muhammad. As the electrician told me the story he repeated the substance of what he had answered the officer. "Why!" I cried, "Where did you get such knowledge in defense of Muhammad?" He was more amazed than I. "Have you forgotten," he asked, "that you made me study Muhammad and give talks on the subject at the Unity Feasts, from five minutes up?"

When Joseph and I were in Stuttgart, Germany, in 1909, talking about my work with children, an eager listener was Frl. Koeslin. Soon after our return to America a letter came from her asking how the work was started and what was taught. For some time thereafter, I would mail the slips and lessons with an account of the program and incidents, just as we had had it the preceding month. If you desire to read the account of the result of that work—see *Star of the West,* Vol. 4, p. 155. What joy it brought to Abdul-Baha when He reached Stuttgart in 1913![4]

This Tablet from 'Abdu'l-Bahá, sent in July of 1913, not long after He returned home from His historic journey, gave Pauline even more encouragement to continue her work teaching children:

O thou attracted leaf to the Kingdom

The Sunday school for the children in which the Tablets and Teachings of Bahá'u'lláh are read, and the Word of God is recited for the children is indeed a blessed thing. Thou must certainly continue this organized activity without cessation, and attach importance to it, so that day by day it may grow and be quickened with the breaths of the Holy Spirit. If this activity is well organized, rest thou assured that it will yield great results. Firmness and steadfastness, however, are necessary, otherwise it will continue for some time, but later be gradually forgotten. Perseverance is an essential condition. In every project firmness and steadfastness will undoubtedly lead to good results; otherwise it will exist for some days, and then be discontinued.[5]

The following letter sent to Mrs. E. Grace Foster in Chicago, illustrates how other communities turned to Pauline for assistance with conducting classes:

My dear earnest sister in El Abha!

January, 1920

Please don't think I have willfully neglected answering your letter, for there have been many reasons for the delay. But the principle one is that I felt so helpless. I wanted so much to help you, but how? There is only one satisfactory way and that is out of the question, namely fly to your assistance, show you my way by handling your children for two or three classes. There does not seem to me to be a way for me to express myself on paper in a sensible and helpful manner. Nevertheless, I shall try.

First of all, you know that our Beloved wants the children to memorize the Holy Utterances and also Bible references for this day.

How to make it interesting for the children depends upon the teacher. The teacher must love the children or it would be tedious. When the children and teacher love each other the spirit will guide them to a point of contact.

One way to hold their interest from Sunday to Sunday is the promise of a story as a reward for memory work well done. (This story of course must be founded upon truth and help to impress the lesson of that Sunday upon their minds.) Abdul-Baha says Fairy Stories are not good for the child mind because it is not based on truth.

Then again the truth (Lesson) can be made most interesting by using objects to illustrate it. All ages seem to like that way.

Another way which never failed me yet . . . is to type the memory verse just the size to fit a little blank book, and each child receives one to paste in their book after they say the verse perfectly, otherwise they must wait until they can. Sometimes one or more may be playful and not attend to the lesson and when they are deprived of the little slip, they either slip off in a corner while the children prepare to leave, and then say it for me before going home, otherwise they have it ready for next Sunday, because they want the slip.

Another way to encourage them to memorize their verse well and quickly, is to set the time for them to give a Unity Feast, providing of course they can say them well. Selecting one of them to give a small part of the Message each Sunday for practice.

Now the little ones under seven or eight, depending upon their brightness, have less to learn, but they have little slips too. They are very proud to be able to open their little book and tell exactly what each verse is, even though they cannot read. This is done by cutting out little pictures to paste in the book that will recall the verse beneath it. For example: I found some tiny pictures of a dish of fruits, on a candy box wrapper. Each one received one of these little pictures to paste above their verse, just as soon as they would say it perfectly. The verse for this reminder was, "Ye are all the leaves of one tree, and the fruits of one branch." From a seed catalogue I cut pictures of onions and celery with long roots and little pictures of a book. This was pasted over the Utterance, "The root of all knowledge of God, etc." The book meant knowledge, because when they went to school they received knowledge from their books. The root reminded them of the beginning of the verse.

This looks silly written out on paper, but if you could see the children grasp the idea and make suggestions themselves for the verse, you would realize that the picture reminder is a natural childish art. If only I had recorded some of the many wise suggestions. This winter for the first time in many years we have no little class because we have no place to meet. But I am helping the Rose Tree Girls, who are made up of my girls grown up. This branch of work was started by Madame Khan.

But I want to make mention of one very important fact, make the children, no matter of what age, understand thoroughly the meaning of each word they are memorizing. Have the older ones tell the little ones what the bigger words mean. You will be surprised how difficult they find it to say what the different words mean in a simple way; they know what it means but can't express it. This is a splendid practice to help them to express their thoughts in their own way. In this way the words of every Utterance has a very definite meaning to the children and not merely repetition of words that mean nothing to the child mind.

You might teach them a prayer as we did by repeating one in unison each Sunday for opening and closing until all the children knew it. Then a new prayer was selected. We use Mrs. Waite's hymns for nearly all children love to sing.

In some of the cities they serve the children some light refreshment after the class but I have not used that suggestion yet. In Stuttgart they have the largest Sunday School at the present time, numbering about 50 scholars I believe, and only a small percentage of this number are Baha'i children. But all are instructed in the Baha'i Teachings. This is a branch of our Sunday School here. We seem very small in number, at present, because the young girls belong to the Rose Tree and the small ones are too few in number to warrant the renting of a hall where all races can meet. But I am close in touch with them just the same.

Have just found a copy of my letter to the organizers of the Junior Baha'is, who asked me to write about my work last summer in Hampden, Mass. It may be of some interest to you, but please return it because it is my file copy. They want me to write again and I do not wish to repeat the same things.

If there is ANYTHING in this letter that proves helpful would you mind letting me know so that the next one may be helped more directly. This is not because I want praise, but cooperation so that together we may find a broad and more universal system, if a system is possible, for the young Baha'i world. If they ever publish the promised Junior Paper it will be of the greatest help to us all.

Please forgive me if this letter is not satisfactory but at least I have made another attempt to try to formulate a system from my work which is without a system.

Am enclosing a set, I should say sample, of the slips as we use them. They may suggest something entirely different for you to work out, and I feel sure you will be glad to give me the benefit of your inspiration.

Will you let me know how you are getting along with your work, so that I may encourage others with your report?

Pauline[6]

Around 1917 Pauline started writing several articles for *Star of the West* about children's classes. She included in the articles many stories about the childhoods of 'Abdu'l-Bahá and Bahá'u'lláh, as well as prayers, other writings, and teachings that she felt, based on her communications with 'Abdu'l-Bahá, were important for children to learn. She drew upon direct suggestions from the Master as well as her own ideas. In a letter to Agnes Parsons, she mentions working on these articles and shares that some of the stories she tells came from Mírzá Abu'l-Faḍl and other Persian friends. This was not an activity she sought out, but rather she was asked and felt it a privilege and duty. She hoped it would assist others who were trying to begin children's classes in their communities.[7]

In August of 1917, this wonderful letter of encouragement arrived from Ahmad Sohrab, who had been with 'Abdu'l-Bahá at the time. As it has not been authenticated, we must regard it as pilgrim's notes, and assume this is the essence of what was said.

> My dear brother Joseph and dear Pauline,
> I just came from the presence of our Lord. In the course of conversation, I told him that Mr. Hannen is writing a pamphlet to be circulated in India. He said: "Mr. Hannen is serving day and night. He serves the Cause with sincerity and unique devotion. He is my son. I respect him to be always in the front. And Mrs. Hannen, she is a flame of fire, a complete torch of the Love of God. She is a wonderful woman. She is a superior woman. She has no other wish except the Cause of Baha'o'llah. Both of them are the faithful servants of the Kingdom. Truly I say they are devoting their time and energy to the service of the Cause. I have in my heart a great love for them."
>
> I thought you will be interested to know this loving praise of the Master uttered a few minutes ago in the quietness of His room.
>
> Your sincere brother,
> Ahmad[8]

The following praise in a Tablet from 'Abdu'l-Bahá must have been a great confirmation of her efforts:

> *Praise be to God! Thou art engaged in teaching and educating the children, for they have wonderfully memorized and read the manifest Verses, the Glad-tidings, the Communes, the Ishrakat and the Words.*
>
> *I hope that each one of those children may become a peerless teacher and the cause of the guidance of the people. Praise be to God! All the members are illumined with the Light of the Beauty of Abha! Convey wonderful Abha greetings to Mr. Gregory and Mrs. Dyer, and exercise toward them on my behalf the utmost kindness, for they are sanctified souls. They have opened their houses for the meetings and are kind and compassionate to the colored race.*[9]

- 20 -

Disunity Issues Continue

Although the Faith was advancing and growing in the United States, and in the Washington community in particular, there were always challenges. Every time a new issue couldn't be resolved locally, the friends would inevitably resort to writing to 'Abdu'l-Bahá for advice. Sometimes these challenges were small—should they have feast on the first day of the month, or should they have it at any convenient time, or always on Sundays? And sometimes, as we will see in the following paragraphs, these challenges were indicative of much larger, more complex, issues facing not only the believers, but the community at large.

In 1906, when the small community of Bahá'ís in Washington D.C. started reaching out to the black community to share the message of Bahá'u'lláh, there were still significant racial divides—both within the community, and in the country as a whole. Gayle Morrison addresses this subject quite comprehensively in her biography of Louis Gregory, *To Move the World*. She writes that Gregory was instrumental in exposing the blatant racial discrimination that had continued, virtually unchecked, in the community. The Hannens also played a significant role in this endeavor; working to foster racial harmony by following the directives of the Master, Who continually encouraged the black and white Bahá'ís to meet together in unity. Morrison sums up the situation:

> During the Gregorys' early years together in Washington, the interracial fellowship that 'Abdu'l-Bahá envisioned for the Bahá'ís seemed elusive, if not unattainable. The Master's visit, rather than having ended the patterns of racial discrimination in the community had brought matters to a head. The Washington Bahá'ís became increasingly divided on the issue of race. A small faction of whites steeped in the prejudiced attitudes of the time, clung to their views despite 'Abdu'l-Bahá's clear statements and demonstrations of belief. Another faction, both white and black, was emboldened by 'Abdu'l-Bahá's example to demand that evidences of

discrimination be eliminated from the community. A large number of whites found themselves on uncertain ground, hesitant about integration, fearing to challenge the unyielding attitudes of society, or even to scrutinize their own. By 1914 even the pretense of unity had broken down, and the Bahá'ís of Washington began to separate into several groups. The Gregorys found themselves having to act, as Louise put it, "the difficult part of peacemaker, explaining the difficulties of the white people to the colored & the point of view of the colored people to the white."[1]

The situation had paralyzed the growth of the community to such an extent that it was brought to the attention of 'Abdu'l-Bahá. No doubt hoping the community would work together toward a solution, His response was not immediate. However, when a letter did arrive, it was with seeming reluctance that He offered this advice:

> *I know about everything that is happening in Washington. The sad, somber news is the difference between the white and the colored people. I have written to Mr. Hannen requesting him, if possible, to arrange a special place of meeting for the white people only, and also a special place of meeting for the colored people, and also one for both the white and the colored, so that all may be free. Those who prefer to do so can go to the white meeting. And those who prefer can go to the colored meeting, and those who do not wish to bind themselves either way, they are free, let them go to the meeting of the white and the colored in one place. I can see no better solution to this question.*[2]

This is the letter that Joseph was sent regarding the three meetings:

> *O thou who art firm in the Covenant!*
> *In the matter of white and colored in Washington great difficulties have arisen amongst the believers. According to what is heard they are divided into two parties and this difficulty will become more intense day by day and may end in strife and contention. Strive ye by all means that this difference may not remain and the believers may become united and agreed. At present, it seems it is nearer to wisdom if a meeting is held specially for the white, another meeting specially for the colored and a third meeting both for the white and colored, so that those souls who do not like to associate with the colored race may attend the meeting for the white and those who are out of sympathy with the white may frequent the meeting for the colored and those who are not attached to the colors—white and colored may gather together on a special day or night in one meeting. For the present this question will not be solved save the quiet execution of this plan, otherwise day by day this difference will*

increase. In this manner everyone will be untrammeled and will attend any one of the meetings which is to his liking.

Upon thee be Baha El Abha!
(signed) Abdul-Baha Abbas
21 April 1914
Haifa[3]

Out of obedience, Joseph did his best to follow 'Abdu'l-Bahá's directives. Several letters found among his correspondences, as well as that of Louis Gregory and Agnes Parsons, mention this situation. Further complications and confusion arose as communication between 'Abdu'l-Bahá and the developing communities of the West had essentially been cut off due to the escalation of the war in Europe. The believers desired clarification as to exactly what He intended by suggesting segregated meetings. However, since He couldn't be reached, they could only surmise His reasoning. Some, who were so steeped in the prevalent prejudiced views of society, were so bold as to suggest that this directive supported their opinion that the white and black races should not mingle or marry. Others, who had been clearly instructed by 'Abdu'l-Bahá as early as their first pilgrimages in 1909, were sure the meaning was that if white believers wanted to teach their white friends in separate meetings at first, they could do this; but surely the meetings such as unity feasts, and holy days, should be open to all. The Hannens were clearly in the second camp.

In a letter Pauline wrote to Mrs. Parsons in April of 1914, after making it very clear how much respect she had for Mrs. Parsons—in no little part because of her appointment by 'Abdu'l-Bahá as adviser to the Washington community—she expressed her pleasure with Mrs. Parsons' wish to take no further action until hearing from 'Abdu'l-Bahá. Pauline then shared her true feelings about the proposal for separate meetings:

Now for the next point, whatever we have said or written you regarding our disapproval of Group Meetings, was a very badly written and misunderstood letter. I will acknowledge frankly having expressed myself freely, concerning a Public Baha'i Meeting, or Assembly from which the colored people are excluded. I do not think it in accord with the Divine Teachings. I still maintain that belief, and as strongly as I feel on that point, I would nevertheless, give my whole hearted support if the Assembly through you, desired to try it. Even now, if you decided to support Mrs. A's work, Mr. Hannen and I would work cheerfully for it. Therefore, all personal feelings have no place with us. But that is apart from the question of group meetings. That there is a crying need for the white people (alone) to be taught the Greater Principles of Baha'o'llah by degrees, we have never

> doubted for one instant. As I have written to you before, and do so now, that since you expressed a desire for such groups, I have done my very best to encourage all those who have a talent for that kind of work. . . .[4]

It is clear this was a tricky situation for the Hannens. They held a fierce desire to live according to Bahá'u'lláh's and 'Abdu'l-Bahá's teachings in regard to the oneness of mankind, but were equally compelled to maintain their strong sense of responsibility to uphold the Covenant by doing whatever they understood to be the directions of 'Abdu'l-Bahá, even if such directions seemed to clash with their personal preferences. They loved teaching the Faith to all people, but Pauline at least, could sympathize with Mrs. A's point of view, which was that there were a lot of people who needed to hear the message who were not willing to come to integrated meetings.

Mrs. A confirmed their difference of opinion in a letter to Joseph, dated 24 August 1914, in which she stated:

> Our original difference of opinion arose from your belief that white and colored races should meet together, while I believed in their separation. This difference, which was honestly they should be separate. The only difference remaining is the petty, personal one of whether you should join with us who had already a white meeting at Pythian Temple, or establish an independent white meeting. I wrote you at length, pointing out fully the unwisdom involved in establishing an opposition white meeting, thus, for purely private reasons, causing a split and disharmony among believers and destroying the good reputation of the Washington Assembly. I have urged you to consult with us and cooperate. To my letter, you replied with only a curt acknowledgement and proceeded to establish an opposition white meeting without so much as informing us. It is useless to say that your meeting is not in opposition to us. It was obviously so intended, and is so construed by the believers, some of whom have strayed away from both meetings in order not to "take sides." However the restoration of harmony is easy, and it rests with you. Obey the spirit of Abdul-Baha's command rather than the letter. Follow the threshold of God's unity. Abandon your opposition white meeting and devote your energy and funds to assisting us in upbuilding the regular white Baha'i meeting, now at Pythian Temple.
>
> If you have also opportunity and inclination to assist in the advancement of the colored meeting, I pray that Baha'o'llah will bless your efforts though personally I think the matter better left in the capable hands of Mr. Gregory. As to the mixed meetings, they have been allowed by Abdul-Baha to those who prefer them. I am not one of those, and cannot sanction actively or by implication a course which I firmly believe to be

> to the injury of our race and the destruction of the cause. But we need not discuss that. . . . I feel that my work lies in helping to upbuild the white Baha'i Meeting, and I need and invite the hearty co-operation of all white believers. I hope to see you and Pauline at the next Sunday night meeting.[5]

When Joseph received such letters from Mrs. A, he would send copies to Mrs. Parsons because of her role as adviser to the community, and seek her opinion. Mrs. A did likewise, and poor Mrs. Parsons often found herself in the middle of such debates. Several letters went back and forth between Mrs. Parsons, the Hannens, and Mrs. A in which they each expressed their own opinions about the matter of the "three meetings." During this back-and-forth exchange, a letter was sent from Joseph to 'Abdu'l-Bahá, which explained how he had resolved the issue of the three meetings. The letter, dated 21 July 1914, addresses the situation, but only after mention of some wonderful teaching successes that Joseph hoped would please 'Abdu'l-Bahá. Joseph wrote:

> Thy Tablet about arranging for three kinds of meetings, to meet the present need, was duly received, and the matter of details was at once taken up with Mrs. Parsons. She came to Washington for a conference with the Friends, and as a result, the following have been planned:
>
> For the Assembly (Baha'i) Meeting, attended by all races, Friday nights, at Mrs. deLagnel's Apartment.
>
> For the colored Friends, and also attended by Whites, at the Conservatory of Music, Wednesday nights.
>
> For the Inquirer (White) Sunday afternoons, at 3:30, at Lewis Hall, 1502 Fourteenth Street.
>
> As soon as the demand for a meeting for colored people only manifests itself, this will be planned, through Mr. Gregory. At present there does not appear to be an urgent need, as none of the colored people who will not attend gatherings with the whites, are to be found.
>
> . . . The existence of a Sunday night meeting, at Pythian Temple, was recognized in making these plans; but as this meeting had been started in a spirit of opposition, and its promoters declined to consult, to recognize the function of Mrs. Parsons, or to affiliate in any way, no course seemed open but to establish this Sunday afternoon meeting, in direct compliance with Thy Instructions—to "establish three meetings." For example, Thy Tablet to Mrs. Belmont, telling of the Command to this humble servant, was promulgated before my Instructions were received, thereby showing the unwillingness to confer which has made union in this respect impossible. But as it is, there is just another meeting of teaching, for which we are all happy. Four weekly gatherings, with several group meetings beside,

present the Teachings to the Friends and Inquirers, and the best of all is, that all are well attended, with many strangers present.[6]

These letters point out that there were obviously different perspectives from each side as to who was to blame for the disunity, but the fact that disunity existed was acknowledged by all. This underlining disunity continued in Washington D.C. as the friends suffered without their usual connection to the Center of their Faith. Even Mrs. A left Washington for a while and claimed to "dread the conflict in Washington. If all were in harmony," she wrote in a postcard to Joseph in March of 1916, "we could 'take the city' in 12 months. But alas! The valuable moments are spent by hunting for motes in their brother's eyes."[7] The previous fall, Mrs. Parsons wrote a comprehensive letter to the Washington community, which put the whole situation into perspective. It also expressed some of her own soul searching about her feelings concerning her special position in the community. This is what she wrote in October of 1915:

To the Washington friends:
Dear Servants of Baha'o'llah!
Although I am far away, I am thinking constantly of the affairs of the Cause in Washington.

It is the longing of my heart to assist in the bringing about of Unity amongst you, and I am sure that to this end openness and frankness are necessary. I have tried to see the various problems from all sides. I feel that it is important that I make clear my opinion of my relationship toward you: what I think it means to be a mother in this day. I turn at once to Abdul-Baha for the example. Sometime ago I felt I had reached the place where I could happily do the thing desired by Abdul-Baha if only He would make it clear to me. I wrote Him; "Please tell me—do this; do not do that." No mention of this request of mine was made in my next Tablet; but I received a spiritual answer: "Abdul-Baha is making men, not slaves." In other words, He, like all great spiritual Teachers, utters principles, leaving the creatures the work of deducing laws from them, thus developing, not stifling intelligence. It is usually not until Abdul-Baha is pressed, that He gives a concrete statement for guidance. Now if this be the method of the Great Example, how important it is for the creature, a mere "adviser," to avoid dogmatic statements, simply pointing to the guidance she gets from certain instructions. I deplore the forcing of an opinion by anyone upon another, and feel that only in the case of much contention between the members of an assembly should the adviser utter an emphatic statement.

When Mrs. A wrote me of the need of different meetings, I saw instantly that she was right, and I asked for the matter to be brought before the Committee of Consultation, but when I found that the idea was the cause of great agitation amongst the friends, I urged inaction, until word about it should come from Abdul-Baha. My advice was not followed, and we all know too well the continued inharmony. Abdul-Baha remained silent for a long time, undoubtedly in order that we might work out a solution of the trouble; but finding that the matter continued to disturb the people, He finally answered in no uncertain terms, directing that the different meetings be arranged. If everyone would now be content, much good would result. However, we hear such murmurs as the following: "Although Abdul-Baha allows this, it is well understood what He really wishes." "Although the Pythian Temple Meeting for white people alone is established, it will surely exist but for a short time, when it will be changed into a mixed meeting." In this way the undercurrent of dissatisfaction continues, causing the members of that meeting to feel unsure of their ground. Also, those who are not in sympathy with it are restless, hoping for a change. Dear Friends! I hope you will try to develop a sympathy for every kind of meeting which is for the spread of the Cause, for Abdul-Baha has called such meetings "good."

A Universal Teaching must have a message for all. Those who object to mixed meetings must find a prepared way to receive the message in the manner they are willing to take it. It is for us to provide the means.

Undoubtedly there is an important work to be done by the believers whose special field is the Pythian Temple. They should work spiritually and quietly, making every effort to overcome the prejudices of the inquirers. If this work be done wisely, before the minds of the opposers are fully awakened to the fact that belief in the Oneness of Mankind is spreading among the people, it will have had the necessary time to become so rooted in the hearts that nothing can dislodge it. This belief is a new and tender flower of this Blessed Day, and if we force it into the strong winds of opposition, too soon, its precious growth would be retarded. However, we should know that the ideal Baha'i Meeting is the mixed meeting, and all should unite in giving to it the love and sympathy essential to success.

I approve of trying a Hall again, and think the one of which Mr. Hannen has written me should answer the need of the present time. I advise following the procedure of the Friday meeting, assembling in a group for the study of the Words and the reading of prayers when believers only are present, but changing the plans quickly to meet the requirements of strangers or inquirers when they are there. The success of this new effort will depend upon the degree of severance shown by the members. Only by means of perfect humility and genuine love can the work today be done. I know by my own experience that it is possible to ignore differences and feel united to those not completely of our point of view, basing our love upon the sincerity of others, which in our hearts we are assured of. If differences tempt us to feel estranged from some of the friends, our absolute certainty of their devotion to the Blessed Cause can be a strong uniting power. On this basis I beg the friends to appoint as the Hall Committee Mrs. Coles, Mrs. Haney, and Mr. Gregory, to act for the coming year. If this be done, I urgently request these three friends to accept the work offered. If each desires to be in his true place, and cares not for his way, but instead longs to find the Way, harmony will come—freedom too, for only in the Will of God is freedom found. News has come from Haifa that conditions there are most serious. The Governor has been friendly with Mohammed Ali [arch Covenant-breaker opposed to 'Abdu'l-Bahá], and there is grave danger. With the knowledge before us, can we not make redoubled effort to live the life laid down for God's servants? Knowing that in so doing, we bring to the Blessed Heart of Abdul-Baha the only refreshment which is in our power to offer.

Yours in His Service,
A. S. Parsons[8]

Although placed in the uncomfortable position of being in the middle of this dispute, Mrs. Parsons' desire to be firm in the Covenant, to encourage others in this matter with love and with what she felt to be in the spirit of 'Abdu'l-Bahá's wishes, is clearly evident in her response. Working toward the greater principle of creating unity at all costs was her overriding goal. The Hannens, as well, always put the Master's wishes as their priority. They honored Mrs. Parsons' appointed role as adviser, and therefore considered her guidance and instruction with the utmost respect.

Another person directly involved in this situation was Mrs. Coralie Franklin Cook, a professor at Howard University, and as we've seen in previous chapters, a good friend of the Hannens. She learned of the Bahá'í Faith through them and was very involved in hosting and attending the meetings under discussion. The following letter, written by Mrs. Cook in March 1914 to 'Abdu'l-Bahá (at the request of the Hannens), explained the situation from her perspective as an African American Bahá'í. This article appears in the book *Lights of the Spirit*.

Honored and dearly beloved Teacher:
Only a short time ago, after many months of waiting, I dared to send you a brief letter expressing my love for the Cause and telling you in what way your visit to this Institution had planted a seed, which, already begins to grow and bear fruit.

Writing a letter to you is like no other writing. No sooner do I take up the pen with that intention than I seem somehow, to be ushered into your very Presence. The pen is indeed only a medium and you yourself seem very near.

Perhaps the subject I shall try to write upon is one of such import as to invoke your Presence. However that may be, you will know that I shall write no thoughtless word and shall try to be just and honest in every statement.

It has seemed wise to my good friends Mr. and Mrs. Hannen and Mrs. Haney that I should write you concerning some aspects of the Race Problem in its relation to the Bahá'í Cause here in America. We do not make the mistake of supposing that 'Abdu'l-Bahá does not understand far more about this matter than any believer can possibly show Him, but we do feel it fitting to put on record and into your hands certain facts as expressing the attitude of the colored people themselves concerning race prejudice. Since we are the ones whose progress it impedes and whose footsteps it hounds, surely we must be better prepared to speak than those who view the situation ON THE OUTSIDE.

Race relationship, in the Southern States especially, but more or less thru out the country is in a deplorable condition. In many instances where friendship, mutual sympathy, and good will ought to exist, hostility and venom are manifested by the whites and are met by distrust and dislike on the part of the colored people. To cite the contributing causes which have led up to this direful situation—culminating recently in acts of certain public officials, leading toward segregation and discrimination among the employees of the federal government itself—would be to write a book. Chief among them however, it is safe to say is the popular delusion called "social equality." By some strange phenomenon certain white people think or affect to think, that if a colored person shares in the ordinary privileges which pertain to comfort and convenience, or political or civic right that it means "social equality." That is to say, if permitted to vote, to take part in civic festivities or parades, to ride in the same car, to attend the same public school or place of worship or to be buried in the same grave yard means "social equality." To any but a morbid mind or diseased mind this seems like unbelievable absurdity, which practically carried out, is making the position of the colored people almost unbearable and robbing the American white people of any rightful claims to an exalted position among the nations of men, because they are either active participants in, or silent witnesses of the gross injustice. And yet, as in the days of slavery, when certain heroics rose up against the iniquities of that awful system and said, "These things must not and shall not be," so now the maligned and persecuted black man is not without friends. New Abolitionists, who SEE the nations peril as well as the black man's extremity, have banded together to readjust the situation in ways becoming a Christian nation and a Democratic Government. The Southern Sociological Congress which held its Second Annual Meeting in Atlanta, Ga., last year considered "Six Great Questions," one of which was the Race Problem. It reported that for three days 300 white and 100 black men and women in a spirit of perfect harmony and helpfulness, discussed race relationship and reached a basis of agreement upon co-operative investigation and action which is bound to result in material benefit to both races. Efforts on the part of the hot-headed demagogues to annul the amendments to the National Constitution which conferred citizenship and the franchise upon the black man, have been met by uncompromising opposition from some few members of both houses of Congress who have not yet forgotten the Declaration of Independence nor that message handed down through the ages: "He has made of one blood all nations of men."

No phase of the color question excites so much rancor and misrepresentation as the one of mixed marriage. It is constantly made use of by all classes of whites from the Statesmen to the boot-black and now includes some so-called Bahá'ís to arouse passion and strife and to flatter Saxon vanity. If the whole truth were told, it must be said that many colored people are as strongly opposed to inter-racial marriage as the whites who rant and tear continuously, the difference being that colored people entertain no fear of whole-sale absorption as some whites apparently do. I use the word absorption meaning that in the ratio of 4 to 1 must in time result in the racial identity of the smaller group being lost in that of the larger. Former President Roosevelt has explained in a recent number of The Outlook that this is the accepted mode of race adjustment in Brazil, South America, and is provocative of no race friction whatever, but on the contrary establishes harmony and good will.[9]

As painful as it is to recognize the inequities in the Bahá'í community, the attitude toward race and the fear of "social equality" so prevalent in American society as a whole, couldn't help but exist in the Bahá'í community as well. It took a great deal of courage and strength in the Covenant to overcome what one had been raised to believe. Even when the controversy became so heated that the Hannens were no longer on speaking terms with Mrs. A, Pauline still had sympathy for her position and her sincere desire to see the Faith grow. In a letter to Mrs. Parsons, dated February of 1914, she wrote, "We encouraged Mrs. A to gather her friends, though some of the friends thought we were wrong. But we honestly believed the Confirmations of the Spirit were her assistants. They were always well attended and very interesting people came."[10]

Another letter Pauline wrote mentions that she had weekly meetings with a friend from Howard University during which they had many lengthy and interesting discussions. No doubt these conversations with the Cooks, as well as her close association with the Gregorys, and many other friends of various ethnicities, helped to shape her attitude about race. The following is the conclusion of Mrs. Cook's letter to 'Abdu'l-Bahá, in which she expressed her feelings regarding the position the Bahá'í Faith could, and should, have among people of color in Washington and the country:

> In the light of all these things and many more but time will not here allow is it not evident that the Bahá'í teaching, reiterating the Gospel of the Fatherhood of God and the Brotherhood of man is not only the last hope of the colored people, but must appeal strongly to all persons regardless of race or color who have come to say I am my brother's keeper. To any one of the Bahá'í faith to whom the tempter says "temporize" or let the matter work itself out, I say beware! When was ever a mighty Principle championed by temporizing or delay? I know some must suffer both white and black, but who better able to wear the mantle of suffering than the real Bahá'í? The blessed Báb, Bahá'u'lláh, and the Center of the Covenant, have blazed the path for our feet to tread. Dare we turn back? If anyone has come to realize his duty to the community in which he lives, to the country to which that community is a part, to the world to which that country must contribute its share in the making of the world progress and to God, must he not embrace the Teachings of Bahá'u'lláh as the Greatest instrument put in the hands of man for bringing all the nations of earth under conscious harmony with the Will of God? To open closed doors, to enable mothers to look into the faces of their beloved children and know that they may aspire to serve their day and generation in whatever way their capacity will allow, to remove hate and malice and evil doing, to be no respecter of persons, but to let worth and goodness fix man's status would indeed be the coming of His Kingdom, the doing of His Will, on earth as it is in Heaven. Weary and heart sore, discouraged with the Churches that close their doors to them, the silent pulpits that should thunder forth in trumpet tones against iniquities in the pews, it were strange indeed if the Bahá'í Teachings wakened no response of great hope in the hearts of colored people. If the true believers only stand by the teachings though it requires superhuman courage, and live the life, it is only a question of time when every seeker after truth will be swept into Bahá'í embrace! To falter, to let go one divinely approved Principle would be disastrous! No one could then have faith for Truth is unalterable and cannot change. There are ministers filling hundreds of pulpits today who dare not preach the Truths beating in their breasts for utterance! There are hundreds of hungering souls who never enter the churches because of the hollow mockery they find there. "They ask for bread and are given a stone."

Every noble principle, every lofty ideal, every rule of conduct in the Bahá'í Faith can be defended by passages of our own Bible, the Faith is seeking followers at a time when it would seem as if the Universe itself were challenged to choose between Peace and War, brotherhood and disunion, right and wrong. It is not plain to all that the TEST is crucial and that the times are so momentous that what may seem for the present to put back the Cause of Bahá'í may be in reality the one thing that will put world progress forward immeasurably.

My greetings and my prayer for your blessings,
Coralie F. Cook[11]

Mrs. Cook's measured, thoughtful, and eloquent letter to 'Abdu'l-Bahá is as relevant today as it was one hundred years ago. There can be no doubt that all sincerely longed for a resolution to the disunity in the community.

The following Tablet from 'Abdu'l-Bahá, addressed to Joseph in August of 1914, was published in *Star of the West*:

O thou propagator of the Religion of God!
A few days ago an epistle was written thee. Although I have not any time, yet I immediately give an answer to thy letter:

So that thou mayest know how my heart is attached to thee. Truly I say in the Cause of God thou art sincere. Thou hast no other object save the good pleasure of the Lord and hast consecrated all the time to the Kingdom of God. On this account I have the utmost love for thee.

Praise be to God that the problem of meetings is solved and there is no more cause of dispute. Now the believers must engage their time in teaching the Cause of God, the members of the Bahá'í Assemblies must be infinitely kind towards each other and all their deliberations must be concerning the kingdom of Abha. Promiscuous discussions must be discountenanced, for these things will become the means of luke warmness and the apathy of those who are present. The candles of all the meetings must be the mention of God, the propagation of the Cause of God, the exposition of Divine Proofs and the elucidation of the Principles of His Holiness Bahá'u'lláh. When this condition is obtained, the meeting will become heavenly, celestial, godlike, illumined and the means of the guidance of the erring ones. It will yield most great results.[12]

We are told that racism is America's "most challenging issue." Although progress has been made since these letters were written, within the community and in the country as a whole, it is also very clear that there is still much work to be done.

- 21 -

The Perils and Projects of Pauline

Few people know that Pauline was a breast cancer survivor. To have survived and thrived for more than twenty years after its discovery, during a time without the miracles of modern medicine, is truly astounding. Conflicting accounts from family members have clouded the time-frame of her illness, however, several letters to Joseph during 1917 made mention of Pauline's health and expressed hope for her speedy recovery. This letter from Dr. Zia Bagdadi in May of 1917 offered sound spiritual advice to Joseph. He wrote:

> How is your beloved wife? I humbly supplicate the Holy Threshold of Abha to give her strength and health; to give us all good patience in these days of greatest tests! But as the Beloved said before correspondence and all communications stopped—We must be dignified and patient and face the calamities smilingly. At the time of ease and pleasure the monkey is the happiest of all. The more severe are the trials and ordeals, the more contented we have to be. For all these hardships shall soon pass away and all the faithful believers will rejoice and be thankful.[1]

A letter addressed to Pauline from Louis Gregory, dated 12 March 1917, reads:

> I have been hoping to see you at every meeting but have been constantly disappointed. I miss you very much and hope you will return sometime soon. Mr. Tate, too, who has returned with glowing reports, has inquired about you and no doubt others have felt your absence. I am happy to hear that your illumined sister Miss Fanny Knobloch, as well as yourself, are again well. I hope you will both gladden our assembly with your presence. There is such entire freedom and happiness in talking with you both about the progress of the Cause.[2]

Although letters of good wishes and quick recovery exist, they make no mention of the nature of the illness, until finally, a letter found in Mrs. Parsons' files solves the mystery. The letter was postmarked 5 May 1917, and was sent from South Portland, Maine. It coincides with the many references to her health in 1917, as well as a letter Joseph wrote to a friend mentioning Pauline needing to leave the city very suddenly, with little foreknowledge, for several months. The following letter is in response to a plea from Mrs. Parsons to learn more about the treatment and methods used by Pauline's doctor, because she had a friend who also had cancer. Aside from the procedure mentioned in the letter, we have no way to know if other techniques, such as a mastectomy, were performed at a later date, as no letters were found mentioning further treatment. Pauline's response:

Post dated 5/5/1917
201 Elm St., So. Portland, Maine
Allah'o'Abha!
Dear Mrs. Parsons:
Have just received a letter from Mr. Hannen in which he tells me you would like some information regarding Dr. Messer & his method, for someone in your employ.

First, and of greatest importance is that the patient should come in person, for an examination and explanation from his own lips. He may or may not take the case, but one thing he never guarantees, a cure. He says when any Dr. says that, you had better look out. How can anyone know that he will be alive tomorrow? But one thing is sure & certain, that if the patient can be healed, his method is the one & I believe it with all my heart & soul.

First of all, it is a bloodless operation, therefore the Dr. can see at once if the entire cancer has been removed or not. If not, then he applies his plaster again until the cancer is removed. Then he proceeds to put on another kind of a plaster, and this draws the poison out of the system, while the healing process is going on. He has said a number of times, "I could heal this wound in a hurry, if I wished to, but just see all this poison that is being drawn out. Naturally this would all be absorbed again into the system & break out anew in the same or some other place."

Mine was a very serious case indeed, and had he known how bad it was he would not have taken me. . . . Dear Mrs. Parsons, if you could only hear him explain this method or this one in whom you are interested, you would realize that it is the only sane method.

He has cured many whom the hospitals have pronounced doomed. Yes! Even I know two such cases personally. And in my own case I am convinced the knife would have meant instant death had they removed the entire cancer, or worse than death.

The method is more or less painful according to the temperament of the patient or the seriousness of the case. Personally I suffered agonies from the 20th of February until the Tuesday before the convention. He is still drawing the poison out of the wound but it causes no pain now at all. The fact that I nearly passed out twice was not due to illness, but the heart. The cancer was directly over it. When the cancer came out there was but a layer of skin between the ribs, and the world. Several people could see it throbbing. When the growth was finally removed it weighed a pound & that was only one third of it. The rest having been eaten away by the "black plastic" as we patients call it. Imagine that pressure on the heart. At the same time, another patient having a cancer removed from her breast suffered very little. In fact only gave up two or three days just before it came out. Strange too, hers just stuck to the plaster. It was of course not nearly so large as mine, but oh it is a miracle to see how he gets them out, leaving a clean healthy wound of new skin. I have seen some wonderful cures myself, where a thousand dollars had been spent in hospitals for the knife or x-ray. . . .

Affectionately Yours,
Pauline Hannen[3]

It didn't take Pauline long after her treatment to get back in the thick of things. In a letter to Mrs. Parsons, dated July of 1917, Pauline goes into detail about a project to buy several cemetery plots to be available for the members of the community. In a letter dated 7 July 1917, shortly after her illness, Pauline expressed her joy to be able to go to the cemetery and procure a plot, "There were several of the poor believers present, and they were so happy at the thought that they could contribute their mite. I was appointed to secure the sites, and when I said I did not care to assume the entire responsibility of buying the sites, they voted that what I thought about the locations would surely satisfy the friends."[4]

Pauline's joy in doing this kind of service was expressed in her next letter to Mrs. Parsons (12 July) when she wrote, "It is with a heart overflowing with gratitude to you and all the friends who have so beautifully helped in my hope of years being realized. Namely a few sites for our unprepared and beloved poor. Today I bought the site at Prospect Hill Cemetery, and in a day or two, just as soon as it is a trifle cooler, making the mile and a half walk possible for me, I shall hasten on the wings of love to secure the two sites at Woodlawn. Praise be to God for His Infinite Love and Mercy."[5]

There are several letters over a period of years that describe a Bahá'í community that made every effort to help those who were less financially fortunate. The Master, Whose life was a living example of charity and assistance to those in need, no doubt inspired the community to this form of service. For a while,

Louis Gregory had been in charge of collecting and dispersing funds for the disadvantaged in the community, but when his lengthy teaching trips started taking up more of his time (sometime around January of 1917), he asked Pauline to take over these duties.[6] There are several letters that detail Pauline's service—paying rent, assisting with living expenses, etc. In one such letter to Mrs. Parsons, Pauline expresses that her preference would be to offer an individual the opportunity to do some special work for the Faith, or for Mrs. Parsons or herself, and that she could then pay them rather than just give money.[7] Her correspondence with Mrs. Parsons is full of such details; as the main financial contributor in these efforts, Mrs. Parsons was often informed as to how Pauline and Louis dispersed the funds. It is fascinating to read the details of her plans, and learn how passionate she was about caring for the spiritual development, as well as the physical wellbeing, of those in her community.

In the fall of that same year, Joseph sent a letter to Mrs. Parsons about the teaching work in Washington, describing a series of talks he would soon be giving on the Báb, Bahá'u'lláh, and 'Abdu'l-Bahá. He went on to mention their plans for the upcoming centenary celebration of Bahá'u'lláh's birth at which there would be "special features and a large meeting." At the end of this letter he reported, "Mrs. Hannen is up in New England at this time, visiting several points in the interest of Teaching and the Sunday School work."[8] This was only six months after undergoing strenuous treatment for the removal of a cancerous tumor. What a testament to the power of positive thinking when it comes to healing.

The following event happened before Pauline's illness; however, it serves as an example of the type of activities Pauline loved. Pauline wrote to Mrs. Parsons in January of 1914 to share with her a wonderful teaching experience. It is a delightful demonstration of one of the many ways Pauline found to teach by example as well as by words:

> As one of the least among your children, I should love to tell you of a recent joy that has come to me. Your words to my husband in a recent letter prompted me to do so. You expressed the thought that the Diaries coming so fast must leave Mrs. Hannen very little time for anything else. That is true and yet I have been able to keep up my regular duties, visiting each week the "Little Sisters of the Poor," the Sunday School, visiting some who are ill, helping to arrange some of the meetings for Madame Dreyfus, attending Wed., Friday & Unity Meetings. This is not to blow my own trumpet but to let "Mother" know that I am not neglecting the Lord's Work. But I must acknowledge my lack of energy in raising Temple Funds, because some of the friends consider it wisest to let the friends respond voluntarily and not urge them . . . Now for myself: On Christmas Day Mr. Hannen presented me with a fifty dollar Victrola and some

splendid records. The only pleasure of the world that has any attraction for me is music. I am passionately fond of fine music. We have neither the time nor money to gratify this longing so now through the Bounty of Baha'o'llah in this Day of Wonders, and Sciences we can have this pleasure in a lesser degree.

We all enjoyed this Gift so much on Christmas & our hearts were so full of thanksgiving that one of us exclaimed, "Oh if only we could take this box to some hospital or home and make others happy too, then our joy would be complete." Nothing more was thought of it. My dear son Nategh and my sister were home for the holidays. Time passed swiftly and our regular duties began. My son's stay was very short in order that others might leave New Year's, but he was promised 10 days in January. On the tenth he rushed in and took us all by surprise and we were very happy. After he was home for a few days a thought flashed into his dear head. He caught me in his arms and said, "Mother you find a hospital that will admit us and I [will] see that the Victrola gets there."

At one time I used to visit twice a week the Washington Asylum Hospital. Naturally my heart went out to those poor souls. I know Mrs. Zinkum personally so I phoned and with Mr. Zinkum I completed my arrangements & lo, our prayer was answered. On Friday, at half past 1 p.m. my sister, my son, Mrs. Zinkum and myself began our tour through the various wards. My son attended to the music, my sister mentioned the name of Abdul-Baha in every ward and I did what I could to help make them happy, and they were.

In the one large ward of white women they joined in singing some of the hymns & fairly danced with glee when we played some of the Harry Sanders pieces. In the colored ward (large) we had a most exciting time. An old colored Aunty was aroused from her sleep by one of the comic pieces. She shrieked, "De Debil shoo am loose, where dat debil makin all dat fuss! Yo all better turn to God! I tell ya for the debil is shoo let loose." She went on in this strain for some time and calling all the time upon the Lord to deliver her. (The music was lost of course). The strange part of it was that this old mammy was never known to open her mouth. She was absolutely silent from morning till night. Everyone in the ward was dumbfounded and then consumed with laughter, including the doctors and nurses. I had Carl play the Holy City hoping to calm the old lady. She was quiet for a few moments; her wrinkled old face was beginning to take on a heavenly smile of peace and contentment, and cried out to know where that angel was that was filling the place with heavenly music. Then she began to praise and glorify God. It was touching & although it spoiled the music for some (her voice filling the ward) yet it was worthwhile. She was so enraptured that when I bent over her she began to praise and glorify me, taking (this sinful) me to be an angel direct from Heaven. One colored woman who had been there for a long time (can only use her hands) wanted to know of Mrs. Zinkum, if she thought I would accept the only rag doll she had left, she would love to give it to me to show how happy I made her. She makes them herself whenever she can use her hands. So I have a big rag baby. Now, for the last and by no means least interesting incident. We were taken to the Insane Ward. Rev. Zinkum joined us there for he wished to see what the effect would be upon them.

They were at supper at the time and at the request of the head nurse and Mrs. Zinkum a lively piece was played. After a few moments of breathless silence, save the Victrola, one, then another, and another man left his supper and came to the iron grating, supper forgotten, our presence ignored, while they listened with open mouth and chuckling at Harry Sanders. When the piece was nearly finished one mean looking man came close to Rev. Zinkum, "Why do you play for us such ragtime? (It wasn't) Don't you know that we are all nervous here?" We then played a piece (loud) from William Tell "The Calm." By this time all had left the table and chair after chair was placed for these men, the tables removed, and a few could not be induced to leave the room grating, so lost were they. We then played two familiar hymns. My sister and son and myself hummed a little, then a little louder and louder still as we heard a few timid notes from the men. I had heard "play it again" and asked the men to join us. Oh! Oh! It was the most touching scene. So sweet! So pure as their beautiful voices melted into those of the trinity choir in the Victrola. So solemn, so honest. Rev. Zinkum, himself joining in with heart and soul and Oh the thanks expressed so heartily a thousand times more than repaid us for the trip. We three thank God with all our heart, soul and body for this heavenly joy He granted us. We went to try to cheer them up, but I testify the joy was all ours. Are you not happy with us? It is here they have had such entertainments at the jail and we have the promise of doing so, but it is the first time in the hospital and Insane ward.

At the supper table I tried to work an opening for the message to be given at the jail. They both know the message, so I wouldn't press the matter, but I have every reason to think that Mr. Hannen can finish what I have begun.[9]

Pauline went on to tell Mrs. Parsons about a plan she had to take flowers to the asylum and talk to the people about the Bahá'ís who sent them, always trying to think of ways to give the message.

In another letter to Mrs. Parsons that same year, Pauline describes a teaching experience of a rather different type. She starts out by mentioning she was at a meeting of the Monday Evening Club, and that it was a "most delightful and instructive evening." She continues with this remarkable endeavor:

> What will really please you, I think, is to hear that Mrs. U. . . , paid our Baha'i workers the highest praise, in saying that Mrs. D. . . & her helpers, of which I was one, were the most systematic and successful workers during this rescue work, before the closing up of the "Red Light District." The white people did not follow nor systematize their work. I should like to testify here and now, that Mrs. D . . . is a born worker, among fallen women, I saw her in her element. That the Baha'i spirit was with us, let me tell you of our incident. At Mahogany Hall, a house supported by Senators & Representatives, the white visitors had failed completely. They gave Mrs. D . . . this address to see what she could find out. The woman of the house saw us coming & told us afterwards, "When I saw you women coming I planned to open the door and slam it shut in your faces, because of women who came here yesterday with that holier than thou attitude, but somehow, I felt a different spirit in you women, the moment I opened the door. That is why I let you come in. I know that you women are truly good, and honest and sincere. I will answer all your questions freely and candidly, and will call my girls in that you may talk with them, etc." In a lesser degree was this our reception in all the houses except one.
>
> Dear Mrs. Parsons, I am telling you this because to us it was the manifest power of Baha'o'llah. Mrs. U . . . of course does not know that Mrs. D. . . is a Baha'i, but she too, unconsciously paid tribute to that spirit.
>
> Another reason for telling you of Mrs. D. . .'s wonderful ability is, that as Mother of us all in Washington, I think you should know of certain qualifications we possess in our midst, for some day you may have need of this knowledge. That we are members of the Monday Evening Club, is purely for the purpose of giving the Teachings unlabeled, to as many of these earnest workers as possible.[10]

I haven't found out exactly what the undertakings of the Monday Evening Club were, other than what was described in this letter, but it seems to have been for the purpose of doing what we would now term social work. As one can see from the above samplings of the various activities, Pauline used every means at her disposal to spread the message. She was comfortable with all classes of people, yet humble in her approach. She relied heavily on God to assist her and answered the call to service whenever asked. Both she and Joseph lived up to the beautiful sentiments 'Abdu'l-Bahá wrote to them in January of 1920.

> *O ye two souls of the Kingdom!*
> *Praise be to God day and night ye are confirmed in service and have no other*

motive and desire than the spreading of the Divine Breathings. This is why confirmations from the Kingdom of Abha are reaching ye continually. Your future is very brilliant. So with perfect happiness, joy and with glad tidings live your days and be occupied in service.[11]

\- 22 -

A Dark and Perilous Time

Concurrent with Pauline recovering from her cancer treatment and returning to the teaching field, and D.C. struggling with racial disparities, a crisis was brewing in the heart of the country where the Faith had first taken hold in America. This crisis dealt with another kind of cancerous growth—this one of a spiritual nature. The years during World War I, when the American Bahá'ís were almost completely cut off from communication with 'Abdu'l-Bahá, proved difficult for the young community. Like the Bábís who strayed from the Faith after the Martyrdom of the Báb, and the followers of Moses who turned back to their idol worship when He had gone to the mountain, some American Bahá'ís suffered from lack of good judgment when they lost their connection to the source of guidance. Not only did they struggle with how to handle the issues of racism in their communities, they also grappled with another situation that tested their strength in the Covenant.

In the Chicago community, a few Bahá'ís started their own group called the "Reading Room" against the wishes of the Chicago House of Spirituality. Several letters among the Hannen papers allude to this situation. One of the people involved with the Reading Room was declared a Covenant-breaker by 'Abdu'l-Bahá, and as a result of this person's disobedience, a series of incidents created quite a stir in the community. I came across information in Nathan Rutstein's book about Corinne True that offered some clarity:

> In Chicago, the Bahá'í army's campaign wasn't going well. Ever since 1910 or 1911, undercurrents of disunity had been festering which erupted in 1917–1918. The Master had noted the situation during His visits to Chicago in 1912 and had privately warned both Corinne True and Dr. Bagdadi to be alert to signs of disobedience to the Covenant of Bahá'u'lláh, of which He was the appointed Center. The episode became known as the "Chicago Reading Room Affair," named after the Reading Room which

Luella Kirchner opened in 1913, with the approval of 'Abdu'l-Bahá. The study classes and teaching events held there attracted about a hundred Chicagoans and at first contributed to renewing the vitality of the community, once the hub of Bahá'í activity in America. . . . The extent of the disaffection emanating from the Reading Room became apparent when its members proclaimed it the Chicago Bahá'í Assembly, "as distinct from the House of Spirituality" or Spiritual Assembly, established by the command of 'Abdu'l-Bahá. In addition, loyal and knowledgeable Bahá'ís became aware that ideas . . . very foreign to the teachings of 'Abdu'l-Bahá were being taught in the Reading Room. . . .

In the words of one student of the Reading Room affair, which by then was spreading its negative influence to other Bahá'í communities in America: "The local conflict came to a head in April 1917 at the Boston convention, to which both the House of Spirituality and the Reading Room sent delegates. In the summer the newly elected House of Spirituality determined to expunge the by now rebel Reading Room; and in November, during the Chicago-held Centenary celebrations [12 November 1917] of Bahá'u'lláh's birth, representatives of the national community took up the affair and appointed an investigative committee." On 9 December the committee, whose four members were among the most outstanding Bahá'ís, "reported in favor of the House of Spirituality to a special meeting" of forty-eight believers from nineteen communities. The committee also charged that the Reading Room members "were violators [of the Covenant], creating disunity and spreading false teachings . . ." At the 1918 Convention in Chicago, to which the Reading Room group had been denied representation, the committee's report was unanimously approved, not only by the assembled delegates but by all those attending.[1]

When a person has been named a Covenant-breaker, an offense involving active opposition to (not just disagreement with) the Central and authoritative figures of the Faith, the Bahá'ís are advised not to have any contact with the individual. To make matters even more challenging, during this crisis, communications from 'Abdu'l-Bahá, the only person with the authority to designate a person as a Covenant-breaker, were cut off due to the war. This became a particular problem for the Washington believers in general, and the Hannens in particular, because Leone St. Claire Barnitz was accused of associating with a designated Covenant-breaker. Leone was the sister of Mineola Barnitz, the fiancé of Joseph and Pauline's son Carl. She was also the personal secretary of Agnes Parsons. Leone was not, in fact, a Covenant-breaker, but was only caught up in the controversy because of a past friendship with someone who was declared as one by 'Abdu'l-Bahá. She herself had been an active member of the Faith since her parents became Bahá'ís in 1902, and had served the Faith devotedly in many capacities for all those years. However, when she visited her old friend while on a trip to Chicago, she was accused of guilt by association.

One way this situation affected the Hannens involved their role with National Convention in 1918. Joseph Hannen felt very uncomfortable about attending the convention that year, as did Mrs. Parsons. They knew consultation on the situation in Chicago would be a topic for consideration, and they didn't want to be a part of it. Joseph had been chosen as a delegate, but for various reasons chose not to attend. In a letter written to Mrs. Parsons on 9 April 1918, he asked for her advice:

> I take this opportunity of asking your advice and instructions as to my standing for the appointment as Delegate. My own impulse or feeling is that I would rather not go. For one thing, I feel quite unable to stand even a portion of the expense; but I am not coming to you on that score. Again, I feel disinclination to get into any controversy, and it seems almost inevitable that . . . such a situation arise in Chicago. But again, it may be my duty to participate in what is going on. And if you think so, and that I should be on hand to stand by and with my friends, for the principles for which we have stood, why that would alter the situation, and I should try in some way to respond to the call of duty. But I should regret indeed another trip which would be as futile as that of December 9. But here again: Perhaps it was not futile to have stood with those who withdrew from the gathering of the friends, and particularly since it was my privilege to have stood with you on this occasion.
>
> I hope you will realize, with your splendid intuition and guidance, just how I feel, and where I stand. I know that I have failed to make it clear in the foregoing, but words fail to express one's inmost feelings and convictions upon such an occasion.[2]

Several letters from Mrs. Parsons question if, because of her association with Leone—whom she refers to as, "This staunch little child of God"—she too is suspect.[3] She and Joseph both chose not to attend the convention. In a letter Joseph wrote to Mrs. Parsons after the convention, he reported that Mr. Ober conveyed to him that when delegates from both the House of Spirituality and the Reading Room came to the convention, the Reading Room group was asked to leave and did so without incident. He also explained that she (Mrs. Parsons) was to be considered a "consulting member" of the new Board and she in no sense should feel that she has been "cut off by them." He added, "Indeed, I hope that you will not feel the slightest scintilla of any notion of that kind."[4]

In another letter dated 11 May 1918, Joseph reported to Mr. Remey that Ali Kuli-Khan had spoken to a well-attended meeting on several topics, including loyalty to the government even in times of war, "making it very plain that we were duty bound not to interfere with political questions, but on the other hand to 'support that just government.'" He went on to speak of violation, "making it clear that the original Persian word: 'Nakaz' meant only one who denied the Station of Abdul-Baha, and that the term could not and should not be made to apply to those who might differ from another as to their understanding of a phase of the teachings. In other words, there might be 'Bad Baha'is,' or 'Baha'i students' who made mistakes, but these could not be called 'Nakaz,' and that even as to such people, we should exercise the utmost love and not impute to them wrong motives or criticize them severely." Joseph added his own sentiment, writing, "I hope the Talk may have done much good, and helped to clear the situation."[5]

In April of 1918, Mrs. Parsons wrote a very passionate letter to Mason Remey asking why he hadn't come to her to consult about the situation and the friends he suspected of violation of the Covenant. Although a committee of investigation appointed at the convention had cleared Mrs. Parsons of any wrongdoing, the whole controversy was still a source of great concern.[6] Her letter of 4 June 1918 follows:

> I have your note of May 26th, asking if the acceptance of the findings of the Committee of Investigation by the recent convention have not affected my attitude. No, it has not done so.
>
> When a question arising in the Cause is one regarding such affaires as meetings, etc., it is most right to agree with the majority for the sake of harmony, but when the question touches principle one must be assured of the rightness of one's attitude from the heart as well as from the head. I find no sanction of your position from either of them.
>
> One finds Leona Barnitz, who has not written to Mrs. K for months, cut ruthlessly at a meeting by a Boston member of your group. One finds a loyal Baha'i, Mrs. G, utterly cut off. She has never communicated with Mrs. K. A Miss F—equally sincere—was asked at a recent meeting in Boston to stay away. In your pamphlet called "Protection" you approve the cutting off of one whom you think is merely not your personal friend (page 6). This is truly beyond credence!
>
> The result of such rough handling of the Glorious Cause will be that the great majority of believers finding it impossible to limit the Cause to the bounds you set for it, will leave it, for you are reducing it to the narrowest of sects. No, I do not believe that God approves it. If I should

be alone as far as the creatures are concerned yet, as I think, standing with God, then I am with the majority, since God and one are a majority.

Very faithfully yours,
(signed) Agnes Parsons[7]

During these trying times Mrs. Parsons made every attempt to contact 'Abdu'l-Bahá, seeking His advice on the situation. She contacted Joseph several times for his assistance. At one point when Ali Kuli-Khan, a Bahá'í who was also the Charge d'Affaires of Persia, was out of town temporarily, they devised a plan for Joseph to enlist the State Department to assist them in getting a letter through to 'Abdu'l-Bahá. Mrs. Parsons was adamant the communication remain confidential.[8] This was May of 1918. As late as December of that year, she was still concerned some people might be wary of being seen with her due to the doubts that had been raised. She did say, however, that she never regarded herself as being cut off, but rather, she was more concerned not to make any of the believers feel uncomfortable. Her love of, and obedience to, the Faith was forever an example to the Hannens and other friends in Washington.[9]

With all the turmoil and controversy, and the added stress of not having guidance from the Center of the Faith for an extended period of time, it is truly remarkable how these dear souls, so connected to 'Abdu'l-Bahá, were spiritually guided to make such enlightened decisions. In the midst of it all, Pauline wrote to Mrs. Parsons, giving us another glimpse of her spiritual maturity. On 5 February 1918, she writes:

Now one thing more. I beg of you before accepting any rumors about us, in these days of great testing, that you will ask us about it. I will do the same, for I am not afraid of the truth no matter how it may hurt. You know what I mean don't you? I am grateful to know even the unkind thoughts about me even though they may hurt, because it gives me a chance to correct my faults, which otherwise might never occur to me. If it is false it doesn't hurt.

I love you Mrs. Parsons and am loyal to you, even though we may not see the Chicago matter in the same light. Mothers and daughters can be very devoted even if they do have differences of opinion, can't they?

Mr. Hannen will be glad to come to you, just the word is needed, according to your request last evening.

Believe me to be your loyal little maid-servant.

Humbly serving to the best of my ability.

With sincere love,

Pauline[10]

Coincidently, the following letter from Louis Gregory to his spiritual mother, Pauline, was sent just two days after she wrote her concerns to Mrs. Parsons. In it Louis gave a full explanation to Pauline about the nature of the *Nakazeen,* the name used by the Persian Bahá'ís, for those who turn against the authority of the Center of the Covenant. Especially touching, the prodigal student reached out to his teacher to help her understand the insights he had gleaned since she opened the door to his spiritual education. Portions of the letter follow:

> My dear little Mother:
> Your blessed letter came this morning and made me very happy. I am glad to think that any service of mine may have assisted you to whom I owe so much. I cannot ever forget that it was you who taught me to pray and told me the Greatest Name. It was through this in the Divine Bounty that the Mysteries of God became known to my inmost heart by Spiritual Out-pouring, the vibrations of a Marvelous and Mighty Love. This was the Mercy of the Lord. "He doeth what-so-ever He willeth!"
>
> You may think that I have bad news. No, quite the contrary. There is glorious news! The Boston friends are awake and mindful, Praise be to God!
>
> The violators and their sympathizers were first on the ground and did everything in their power to arouse the prejudice of the assembly against the committee and prevent the people from hearing the report. They filibustered nearly an hour resorting to all sorts of dilatory tactics and obstructive measures . . .
>
> Abdul-Baha "is not one of the creatures." Nor does He make mistakes, as some people here in Boston and a few in Washington believe and teach. This of course is one phase of the Nakaz influence. It is a terrible poison the contagion of which may affect the truest and noblest hearts. The entire Cause in America has felt its effects and some souls who love Abdul-Baha are under its influence and unconsciously are supporters of violation. This is a condition which Abdul-Baha foresaw and told about . . .
>
> You say that love and hate should not dwell in the same heart and I thank you for the suggestion that is only prompted by kindness and love. But I must say in behalf of our noble brother, Zia Bagdadi, that the more I see the subtle and insidious effects of violation, the more I praise and worship him, realizing that he has rendered the Cause of God such service as no other soul has. Like his illustrious father who in the words of Abdul-Baha "silenced their croaking and raving" (referring to the violators) so has Zia stood like a Titan, sword in hand, guarding the children, like this servant and others, who were not mature enough to guard themselves. He has been laughed at by some who profess faith. But when those who laugh awaken they too will acknowledge and praise the heroic services that the

Mighty Soul of Zia is rendering. . . .

Abdul-Baha says that those who violate the Covenant are counted as dead. The dead disintegrate and spread the infection of poison. In an army of a thousand men who are well and one consumptive, the one consumptive can infect the thousand healthy. But the thousand cannot cure the one consumptive.

Not only is association with the Nakazeen dangerous, but the influence of those who knowingly or ignorantly support them is also dangerous. Its effects have been vividly seen during the past weeks. Whatever the stations of those souls may have been who are sympathizing with the violators they lose them when they support the violators. . . .

The assembly has taken action, accepting the findings of the committee and upholding the House of Spirituality. They have drawn up a beautiful letter condemning violation and upholding the House of Spirituality. They have also appointed a committee to take action in weeding out the violators and those who uphold them. Great is the Power of the Covenant! "Can the mosquito of violation with stand the Eagle of the Testament?"

I am grateful for your spiritual discernment and steadfastness under most trying conditions. Those who stand firm may come in for no little abuse, but our Glorious Lord Abdul-Baha, is also a target for the poisonous arrows of the people of darkness.

Yours in humble service,
Louis Gregory[11]

Even Joseph felt very uncomfortable dealing with this situation. He was usually the first one to volunteer his help for any project or challenge, but in the case of dealing with violation of the Covenant, he apologized for not getting involved. He wrote this letter on 13 June 1918 to Louis Gregory, who, at the time, served on the committee to identify and address the violators:

Dearest brother Gregory,
Your good letter of the 9th instant, came duly to hand, and was most welcome. I am always glad to hear from you, and never more so than at this time. It seems veritably that the unrest and antagonism engendered by the present world conflict, are spreading into every relationship of life, and that there is no home so humble, no comradeship so sequestered, no individual so severed, but that the traces are felt. At such a time, a letter of appreciation and fraternal greeting such as yours, is thrice welcome!

As I size up the local situation, I am reminded of a scientific toy which I had when a boy, something along the line of a Loyden jar, or a demonstration of frictional electricity. There were a lot of little balls and other small figures, made of cork and pith. One would rub the glass top of the box in which they were kept, briskly with a cloth, and then the little figures would spring up and adhere to the glass, until there were quite a number of them hanging there. As one after the other would be saturated with electricity, they would drop off. It really seems that I have become satiated with the "Violation" propaganda. I am thoroughly with you and the rest of the Committee, and I admire your good work, of which I approve absolutely. But not having the opportunities that you good people have had, to see the effects and extent of the error, I cannot enthuse over it, and seem to be saturated. Bless you and your work! I wish I might be more enthusiastic over it. But I hope you will not blame me or think I am wavering if I do not go in for it actively.

If I ever permit myself to be proud or satisfied, it is when I think of the little part I was able to play in showing you the Light. In that respect, I feel that when my work here is closed (it will never be finished!) I shall feel that I have not lived in vain, but like a decaying tree, can point to this noble monarch forest which sprang from my spiritual root. So never think I am other than deeply happy in thinking of you and realize that although we may not always agree in the letter, we are always one in spirit.

With Baha'i Love and Greetings, in which Mrs. Hannen joins, and for you and Mrs. Gregory, I am,

Faithfully Yours,
J. H. Hannen[12]

This truly was a dark and perilous time. The cancer of ethnic hatred was spreading throughout the world, erupting in war and bloodshed all over Europe and beyond. And yet there was hope that this would be the war that ended all wars, and that Bahá'u'lláh's teachings of unity and peace would spread throughout the world. Interruption in the ability to communicate directly with 'Abdu'l-Bahá left the new believers seemingly alone and without guidance, however, those who were loyal and attached to the Light overcame the trials of separation and increased their ability to carry on, even while the American community was being severely tested. 'Abdu'l-Bahá often explained to the friends that the tests they encounter are for their own spiritual growth and development, and they should not worry, but rather, be grateful for them. Certainly, the tests that the country, and the Bahá'í community, was going through brought significant strides in the development of both. Although America had to go through another world war, it eventually established the United Nations, and has steadily, through trial and tribulation, inched toward a more united world. The Bahá'í community learned better how to address enemies from within and without, and learned to function when instructions from 'Abdu'l-Bahá were delayed, by always turning to the authoritative texts for guidance. These growing pains were a necessary part of its maturation.

- 23 -

The Divine Plan Revealed

The lack of communication with 'Abdu'l-Bahá between 1916 and 1918 was challenging for the American Bahá'ís, but was just as difficult, if not more so, for 'Abdu'l-Bahá and the friends in the Holy Land. In October of 1918, Joseph received a letter from Ahmad Sohrab, perhaps the first after communications between Haifa and the United States resumed. He wrote:

> Yesterday I was summoned by the Master. Happily I answered the call, and with light heart I turned my back to Haifa and my face toward Acca. . . . I found myself in the presence of the Beloved in Bahjee. [sic] He welcomed me with cheerful words and smiling face and ordered tea to be served to the weary traveler. Later on He said: "Today we have received a number of letters from Port Said. Several of them are addressed in thy name. See when they were written?" I guessed they must be a part of our old letters mailed in the beginning of the war, and after examination I found they bear the dates 1914–1916. Although old, yet they imparted to us the sweet fragrance of the imperishable roses of love. Some of these letters were from you, others from Mrs. Cooper, Miss Irwin, Evelyne Moyne, etc. In the evening we gathered around the Master and a number of the most important letters were translated to Him. He was interested in all the news, and He desired to hear from Mr. Harris, Mr. Hoar, Mr. Wilhelm, Mr. MacNutt, Mrs. True, Mrs. Goodall, Mrs. Parsons, Mr. Remey, yourself and your dear wife. For each one of these friends He had a few words of praise, and wondered what they were engaged in these days and when we will receive their letters. Do they not give us a glimpse of some of the phases of the Cause in America and do they not grant assurance that the friends are all well and busy with the various activities of Truth? Praise be to God that these believers are the embodiments of sincerity, nobleness and truthfulness. It is good to hear that they have engaged the promotion of the Cause of God. It makes me

glad to know that they are zealous and enthusiastic, fervent and hopeful. Tonight I shall pray for them at the Divine Threshold, begging for each and all heavenly Confirmation.[1]

These words remind us of how much the activities of the American Bahá'ís and the events in the Holy Land were bound together spiritually and how much the actions of each affected the other. In time, the controversies that arose began to resolve themselves to some degree, perhaps because of a new focus of attention that had been presented to the friends in the West. A Tablet was received from 'Abdu'l-Bahá in which He encouraged the friends to make a renewed effort in the teaching field. According to Gayle Morrison, "The direction and impetus that He had given their teaching efforts in 1916 helped guide the American Bahá'ís through this difficult time,"[2] when communication was hindered. Due to the communications delay, many of their activities slowed down, but not in the teaching field. Morrison claims that "the immediate response of the Bahá'ís to the part of the Divine Plan that they had received proved that they were worthy of the Master's trust and of the full range of national and international responsibilities that was to become evident when the entire plan was received. Before 'Abdu'l-Bahá wrote the last of the Tablets early in 1917, teachers had been sent into all of the regions of America that He had singled out. At the annual convention that year an attempt was made to set in motion an appropriate teaching program."[3] She continues, "By spring of 1919, when all fourteen Tablets of the Divine Plan (eight written in March and April of 1916, including the five that reached America that year, and six additional tablets composed in February and March 1917) were presented in New York at the annual convention—the 'Convention of the Covenant' as 'Abdu'l-Bahá called it—much had already been done on the home front to prepare the way for the assumption of increased international responsibilities after the war."[4]

These instructions, which became known as the Tablets of the Divine Plan, were destined to be the foundation for many teaching plans to come, which through their unfoldment, resulted in the spread of the Bahá'í Faith to every country in the world. Furthermore, the eventual organization of Regional Councils is based on the original state groupings 'Abdu'l-Bahá chose when addressing the American community. The trials and tests that several of the Bahá'í communities needed to work through during the low period of WWI, seemed to evolve into a new period of victories for the Faith as the Plan began to be implemented. The letters were brought to America by Ahmad Sohrab, a former secretary of 'Abdu'l-Bahá, and were delivered to specified individuals in each of the named regions. In volume VII of *Star of the West,* which covers the year 1916, the regions are listed, naming each of the states and the name of the person who received the Tablet. For the Southern Territory that person was

Joseph Hannen.[5] Five of the first Tablets were published in *Star of the West* in September of 1916. They all emphasized the need of the Friends to teach and spread the message of Bahá'u'lláh.

The friends in Washington, including Joseph and Pauline, had already been involved with several like-minded organizations that led them to meet people whom they thought might be interested in learning about the Bahá'í message. With the new instructions from 'Abdu'l-Bahá, the friends in Washington and elsewhere were willing to accept the challenge of traveling to new places in order to teach the Faith. Louis Gregory was one of the first to respond, and with the support of the Bahá'ís in Washington, such as Mrs. Parsons and the Hannens, he was able to travel to many parts of the South and give the message. During all of his travels he kept in touch with the Hannens, and his letters, which Joseph kept in his files and eventually turned over to the archives, have been a great source of information for historians, such as Gayle Morrison and others. When Louis or other travel teachers needed support with teaching materials, for example, they would write to the Hannens, who in turn would consult with their contacts (usually Mrs. Parsons) for the required resources. By the time the Tablets were presented at National Convention in 1919, a core of travel teachers, experienced in the kind of work that would become essential under the direction of the Tablets of the Divine Plan, had been assembled, and Joseph was already accustomed to the organizational aspects required to maintain such efforts.

According to Morrison:

> In June 1919 *Star of the West* published an outline of this comprehensive plan and a news bulletin on activities in the South, both written by Joseph Hannen. Under the new system—devised with the help of Ahmad Sohrab, a former secretary of 'Abdu'l-Bahá, who brought from the Holy Land the letters that comprised the Divine Plan—regular reports were to be made to and records maintained by a "Central Bureau for the South" in Washington, D.C. The bureau was to serve as a clearinghouse for information vital to the propagation of the Bahá'í Faith in the region, such as the names and addresses of individuals and groups who would be willing to publish articles submitted to them. Moreover, reports by traveling teachers would form the basis of a follow-up system, to assure that places that had been visited would be put on the itineraries of subsequent travelers. Although the staffing of the Central Bureau was not discussed in *Star of the West*, Joseph Hannen was clearly at the heart of the project. During the months ahead, he continued to serve, as he had for so many years, as the leading publicist and administrator of Bahá'í teaching efforts in Southern states.[6]

When the Convention of the Covenant came to be, the Washington Bahá'ís were ready. The following is Joseph's report in *Star of the West,* detailing some of the events of the convention. It offers the reader a glimpse of the feelings expressed and the spirit evoked during that time:

The Convention of 'Abdu'l-Bahá
By Joseph H. Hannen

The convocation of the friends held in New York City, April 26–May 1, 1919, stands out as a unique event in the history of the Baha'i Cause and one which will be forever memorable. When one realizes the lapse of time, weeks and months growing into years, during which communication on the material plane had been interrupted, the absolute joy of receiving the Words of Life, not only in single messages but literally in a volume of general Tablets and advices, explanations and exhortations, will be better understood. The presence at this Convention of our dear brother, Mirza Ahmed Sohrab, who was with Abdul-Baha from 1912 to the end of 1918, when he was sent direct to America, the bearer of precious documents and wonderful, epoch-making instructions, in itself made the occasion historic in the Baha'i annals. Added to that, several cablegrams, received during the progress of the sessions, attested the presence of the Beloved with us, in spirit—a presence which was most manifest to all. "Let this be the Convention of the Covenant"—these words, flashed across the oceans, burned into the hearts of all, and the response was perfect. As day by day the general Tablets were read, and the words given in connection with each presented to us, the plan unfolded before our delighted spiritual eyes and all present were literally swept onward and forward upon the gales of spirituality which proceeded from the Center of spiritual power in the world.

The attendance at this Convention was larger than ever before. The immense banquet hall of the McAlpin Hotel was filled to overflowing at the Feast of Rizwan and hundreds were unable to gain admission. The assembly hall was crowded at each of the sessions of the Congress, nine in number, while the same hall was well filled at the meetings of the Convention.

The fact that while we were gathered, discussing plans for spiritual union and harmony throughout the world, the delegates at Paris, in the Peace Conference, were meeting to establish the new world conditions politically, economically and socially, lent a peculiar power and significance to the gathering of the friends in the metropolis of the new world. Since the last Convention, the thunder of the cannon and the rattle of musketry had been stilled, and the nations of the world, under the terms of the armistice, await the verdict of their representatives, gathered in solemn conclave. Who would have dreamed, ten years ago, when the First Baha'i Temple Unity Convention was held in Chicago, that the events of the world drama, so graphically portrayed by Baha'o'llah and emphasized by Abdul-Baha, would come to such a rapid culmination! It is within the ready recollection of many of us, that the Baha'i teachings were called "ahead of the times" and termed a dream philosophy, perhaps adapted to some future age of the world. And now, how rapidly "the times" have caught up with The Message, so that today men talk the world over in terms of internationalism and world unity, strange to their minds and tongues, but familiar to the Baha'is.

A striking feature of the Feast of Rizwan was the presence and participation of several clergymen and leaders in other broad lines of thought—chiefly those who had been reached and touched by Abdul-Baha when He was in America in 1912. Their words were akin to our teachings, and they—happily privileged to stand upon a higher plane than that of orthodoxy—sensed the need of what the Baha'i teachings offer. The highest notes of jubilation and the strongest messages of hope were given by Baha'i speakers. Truly, the world has had no more significant gathering in its history. And as the Tablets were read which represent the Charter of the New Age, and which outline in no uncertain terms the part America is to play in the spiritualization of the world—there was joy abundant and hope unbounded, to offset all the doubt and uncertainty which the epoch of reconstruction brings to those lacking the spiritual insight and the hope of the age.

Verily, the Convention of the Covenant was and is unique, like the Center of the Covenant, who was with us as surely as the heart of each auditor—unseen, yet filling the body spiritual with the very life-blood of the Spirit,—to be translated into deeds and actions, the effect of which shall never die![7]

Louis Gregory also wrote a very detailed report of the convention proceedings that appeared in *Star of the West.* Included in his report were summaries of speeches by several prominent Bahá'ís, as well as reflections from those who had the bounty to meet 'Abdu'l-Bahá during His trip to America in 1912. Joseph gave a special talk at this convention titled "Religion Must be the Cause of Amity and Friendship." The following poem was written for the occasion. This poem was delivered the same day, 26 April, that Joseph's first grandchild, my father, was born.

THE CALL
by Joseph H. Hannen

O waiting world, Behold! The Master stands,
With healing for thy wounds within His Hands;
For every problem a solution brings—
Glad-tidings herald from the King of Kings!

O weary world! The master brings thee rest,
Freedom for every captive long oppressed.
The Way of Truth again is opened wide,
That all may happily in God abide.

O world perplexed, embittered, sick of strife!
The Master brings a Message of New Life;
The wondrous news that war henceforth shall cease;
The promise of a Thousand Years of Peace!

And O, ye heralds of the Golden Age!
Promise of Prophets, dream of every sage,
The Master calls ye. Rise ye up and go
To spread the news, that all the world may know!

From East to West—from Maine to Golden Gate,
Throughout this land, O hasten! Do not wait!
And to the south land, to old Mexico,
To Central, South America He bids ye go!

O islands of the east and western sea,
Thou too rejoice! The Truth shall come to thee.
A host of heralds from the Lord of Lords,
Thy glad deliverance from bonds affords!

And thou—the Mother-Continent of ours—
So sorely pressed by grisly war's dark powers—
To Europe comes the message of release,
The one assurance of a lasting Peace!

O Eastern land! Vast China and Japan!
Thy pride returneth, as of ancient man!
Thy Great Redeemer standeth at the door,
His heralds hasten—joy forevermore!

O eager world, Thy waited Lord is here!
Fill hearts with hope, abandon every fear.
Forgotten hate, let love reign all-supreme.
And lo accomplished is the Golden Dream!

O ye who know, the Master calleth ye
To rise and serve, that all the world be free!
As millions rose, a few brief moons ago—
To offer life to vanquish threat'ning foe—

So shall ye rally to the Heavenly King,
And life and all to His Cause gladly bring;
Content and happy if it be to die
Or live in exile if but He be nigh.

Count not the cost, ye Army of our God,
Thine is the noblest field man ever trod.
Thy victory is certain as the sun,
Thy flame eternal when the conflict is won!

O Heav'nly world! The Kingdom soon to be,
Where God shall reign o'er all from sea to sea;
Where men of every race shall do His will,
And love of every man each heart shall fill.

O Lordly host, Abdul-Baha commands!
Advance ye, conquer near and distant lands.
"Allah'o'Abha!" is the battle-cry—
Eternal life to those who else must die!

The great new charters of the world are read!
The Word hath spoken—now thy feet must tread,
From north to south, from east to west, the world,
Till far and near His banner is unfurled![8]

After Joseph's address was given, the Tablet to the Southern States was read by him. The prayers that were included in each of the Tablets addressed to the various regions can be found in most Bahá'í prayer books, and are used daily by the friends. The Tablet is omitted here.

During the third session of the convention it was moved, seconded, and voted to name a committee of nineteen individuals "to take into consideration the fourteen points mentioned in the unveiling of *the Divine Plan* and to carry into effect these advises in unity with the Executive Board, . . . In all matters having to do with these fourteen points, the spreading of the Cause, the teaching, etc., action is to be taken by the united consultation of the committee, and sub-committee, named and the Executive Board in consultation."[9] The nineteen members who were nominated and then voted upon were: Mrs. Corinne True, Mrs. Ella Cooper, Wm. H. Randall, Alfred E. Lunt, Dr. Zia Bagdadi, Mrs. May Maxwell, Joseph Hannen, Mrs. Agnes Parsons, Hooper Harris, Harlan Foster Ober, Roy Wilhem, Charles Mason Remey, Dr. Frederick W. D'Evelyn, Louis Gregory, Albert R. Vail, Mrs. Mabel S. Rice-Wray, Mirza Ahmad Sohrab, and Mrs. Mary Hanford.[10]

By the time the next issue of *Star of the West* came out, Joseph was ready with this editorial, sharing some of the teaching activities underway and listing the "fourteen points."

Editorial—The Southern States contributes a General Outline
By Joseph H. Hannen

Careful study of the Tablets to America on Teaching, old and new, develops an increasing sense of the responsibility and opportunity of every Baha'i. It is indeed the trumpet call to action. A new campaign is being waged against ignorance, lack of spirituality, prejudice and sectarianism. Its divine object is unity through love, and the formation of a republic of religions, in which all men shall be brothers, with God the Father of all, and His will shall "be done on earth as it is in heaven."

It is our desire and effort to enlist the co-operation of every friend in the Southern territory, bending a united effort toward the accomplishment of the task set before us. The large delegation which attended the New York Convention from Washington and other points in the Southern field, returned filled with enthusiasm and inspiration, and plans are being made to systematically spread the glad-tidings of the Kingdom. And in this work we have had the benefit of the personal co-operation of Mirza Ahmad Sohrab, who spent much of his time before and shortly after the Convention in Washington, the plans which he outlined, and which are naturally based on a very thorough comprehension of Abdul-Baha's wishes, may be of general interest to the friends everywhere.

The objects to be attained are such as to require the best effort of everyone. There is no one connected with the Cause of God who has not a part in this great plan. With a view of facilitating the general work, and coordinating the efforts of the friends, an outline has been drawn up by Mirza Sohrab, which the Southern section submits to the friends as its contribution to the general outline, and with a constant supplication for guidance and bounty.

The outline is as follows:

1. A Central Bureau to be organized in Washington for the South. Teachers to send the names and addresses of all liberal organizations, clubs and churches who would be willing to have Baha'i lecturers.

2. Teachers traveling to the south send addresses of those to whom they have spoken, to this Bureau and all details of their work.

3. Teachers to send the names and addresses of all liberal organizations, clubs and churches who would be willing to have Baha'i lecturers.

4. Baha'i books to be placed in the libraries of all important centers and teachers to visit the different libraries and see how many books they have and if we can supply them with more.

5. Provision to be made for the publication of literature and books to be widely circulated in the Southern states.

6. Teachers to send the names of one or two large newspapers in each city that would be willing to publish Baha'i articles when sent to them.

7. Monthly reports of the work in the South to be published and circulated in the STAR OF THE WEST and other channels.

8. Monthly articles containing interesting news about the Cause to be sent to important newspapers for publication.

9. Baha'i writers in the South to be encouraged to write Baha'i stories for magazines and press. These stories to be permeated with the transforming power of BAHA'O'LLAH and Abdul-Baha. In this manner we can reach hundreds and thousands that could not be reached otherwise.

10. The follow-up system be developed so that if a teacher has visited a number of towns for a few months past another teacher may follow him up and refresh those talks with those already interested.

11. All the larger towns to be visited and effort be displayed to interesting one or two in each city to open their homes for weekly meetings and study, thus the work may continue without interruption, for unless we try to establish such small centers all public work will bear no fruit—even the birds have nests—thus when someone makes his home the nest of the birds of paradise, people will know where to go and how to get Baha'i teachings.

12. The Central Bureau for the South to keep a card index system of all the friends in this section and send all the vital information regularly to the National Bureau, thus working in unity with that board and receiving inspiration from one another.

13. There should be a school for the training of the youth to be sent out as teachers.

14. A Publicity Bureau to be established.[11]

The article followed with stories from the teaching front:

> Louis G. Gregory and Roy Williams have also been touring the Southern territory and are still in that section. They have visited Richmond, Virginia; Charleston, West Virginia; Huntington, West Virginia, and a number of other points en route. They are sending in lists of those interested, showing splendid results, and are most happy in the work. The following extract from Mr. Gregory's letter describing an incident of their trip to one of the places visited, exhibits the spirit encountered and shows the opportunities to be found: "This morning we visited the Ministerial Union here, which, oddly enough in a Southern community, combines all denominations, save Catholic, and both races. We listened with intense interest to their discussion centering around the summer months. The presiding officer, a Congregational minister, had a clear vision and spoke like a Baha'i! He spoke of the efforts to prevent overlapping in missionary fields, and thought the same thing should apply at home. He believed that a hundred, even fifty years would witness the end of all denominations. Near the close they gave us a brief audience, which made it possible to read the teachings of BAHA'O'LLAH and mention the twelve principles. They, showed keen interest, and the effect was almost electrical upon the advanced thinkers among them. They eagerly took the booklets (Big Ben's) that were offered them, and warmly shook our hands. Next Sunday we are to speak in the church of Dr. H., one who attended the World's Parliament of Religions in 1893. When he agreed to open his pulpit, I asked him if he wanted a "Methodist sermon." "I want your message, whatever it is," he answered, and said he was very happy that liberal and progressive ideals in religion were being advocated.[12]

- 24 -

A Teaching Family

From the time Pauline and Joseph first became Bahá'ís, their passion for teaching the Faith was evident in every piece of correspondence they wrote or address they gave. After the Tablets of the Divine Plan were revealed, their teaching took on an even more earnest tone as they strove to heed their Beloved's wishes. One of the first responses to this new vitality can be found in a letter that C. Mason Remey wrote, which was published in *Star of the West*, Vol. VII. It is an example of the kind of involvement the Bahá'í community, especially in our nation's capital, had in infusing Bahá'í principles into the culture of our country. The country was in the midst of World War I when the Tablets were written. The hope of the nation was that this was to be the war that would end all wars. The Beloved Master was being endangered in His homeland and very little means of communication with Him was available. The desire to spread the message of Peace and International cooperation was widespread. The following opportunity, which Joseph was privileged to participate in, had to be very significant to him on many levels. Note the role he played in this effort toward promoting International Peace at the First Annual Congress of the League to Enforce Peace, a non-Bahá'í group of highly influential people in Washington and later other communities, formed to begin working toward creating an International World Tribunal, an idea which was first envisioned by Bahá'u'lláh half a century earlier, and later developed by 'Abdu'l-Bahá:

The League to Enforce Peace*
Letter from C. Mason Remey

June 1, 1916.
Dear Friends:
On May 26th and 27th we had convening here in Washington the first annual Congress of the League to Enforce Peace. As the Baha'i Movement was represented by delegates to this convention, I am sure it would interest you to know about the matter.

The platform of the League is very much along the lines of universal peace as outlined by Abdu'l Baha in The Mysterious Forces of Civilization. At the invitation of Mr. Wm. H. Short, secretary of the League, Mr. Lunt, president of the Baha'i Temple Unity, appointed a committee of us to represent the Unity at this convention. We sat during the better part of two days listening to speeches by the greatest thinkers and foremost progressivists of this country. The spirit of the sessions was most inspiring. In all of the proceedings we saw the Baha'i spirit manifesting itself for principles of world peace, which were voiced, as far as they went, in accordance with the constructive spiritual teachings of Abdu'l Baha.

Toward the last of the convention the chairman of our committee, Mr. Hannen, was called upon by Mr. Taft, president of the convention, to deliver the greeting of the Baha'is. Mr. Hannen read the following words which had been prepared by our committee:

> The delegates to this assemblage representing the Baha'i Temple Unity are in sincere sympathy with the objects of the League to Enforce Peace.
>
> The Baha'i Movement is for the Oneness of Humanity along religious, economic and social lines.
>
> In the words of BAHA'O'LLAH, the founder of this movement:
>
> "These fruitless strifes, these ruinous wars shall cease, and the Most Great Peace shall come. Let not a man glory in that he loves his country; let him rather glory in that he loves his kind.'"

---

* The League to Enforce Peace was formed in 1915 at a conference at Independence Hall in Philadelphia. It worked for a league of nations, a world court, and mandatory international conciliation. Its president was William Howard Taft; other leaders included Hamilton Holt and Theodore Marburg. When the United States entered WWI, the League adopted a "win-the-war" program. Pacifist groups shunned the LTEP, believing that peace could not be obtained through coercion. However, the League was given credit for influencing President Wilson and others to support the formation of the League of Nations.

This quotation, from the words of BAHA'O'LLAH came as a benediction and a summing up of everything which had gone before. The audience was moved and the applause was not only strong, but sustained for several moments; not a spasmodic outburst of applause such as had greeted some of the speakers, but rather an applause which started and swelled slowly attaining the maximum, and then gradually diminishing.

A banquet followed the proceedings, the last speech of which was made by the President of the United States [Woodrow Wilson], who brought out the following points, which were such as to have brought joy to all of us who are striving to establish the cause of universal peace.

During his remarks, the President said:

> To preserve the peace of the world against political ambition and selfish hostility, in service of a common order, a common justice and a common peace, the United States is ready to join in any association of nations.
>
> Only when the great nations of the world have reached some sort of agreement as to what they hold to be fundamental to their common interest, and as to some feasible method of acting in concert when any nation or group of nations seeks to disturb those fundamental things, can we feel that civilization is at last in a way of justifying its existence and claiming to be finally established. It is clear that nations must in the future be governed by the same high code of honor that we demand of individuals.
>
> The nations of the world have become each other's neighbors; It is to their interest that, they should understand each other. In order that they may understand each other, it is imperative that they should agree to co-operate in a common cause, and that they should so act that the guiding principle of that common cause shall be evenhanded and impartial justice.
>
> We believe in a universal association of the nations to maintain the inviolate security of the highway of the seas for the common and unhindered use of all the nations of the world, and to prevent any war begun either contrary to treaty covenants or without warning and full submission of the causes to the opinion of the world as a virtual guarantee of territorial integrity and political independence.
>
> I came to avow and to give expressions to the confidence I feel that the world is even now upon the eve of a great consummation, when some common force will be brought into existence which shall safeguard right as the first and most fundamental interest of all peoples and all governments, when coercion shall be summoned not to the service of political ambition or selfish hostility, but to the

> service of a common order, a common justice and a common peace. God grant that the dawn of that day of frank dealing and of settled peace, concord and cooperation may be near, at hand.
>
> When we compare these ideas with the great principles of Abdu'l Baha expressed in The Mysterious Forces of Civilization, we can see the marvelous working of the Divine Ordinances in the souls of humanity. May the hope of Abdu'l Baha soon be realized—that America may uphold the standard of Universal Justice among nations.
>
> C. Mason Remey[1]

This incident is just one example of the many ways that the Hannens involved themselves in the teaching field. From the moment she became a Bahá'í in 1902, until her passing in 1939, Pauline Hannen taught the Faith passionately to everyone who showed the slightest glimmer of interest. Every letter she wrote made mention of her teaching opportunities with passion and enthusiasm. Every service she rendered was offered with the hope of an opportunity to spread the message. It was an intense period in Bahá'í history to be able to follow the direct instructions of 'Abdu'l-Bahá. The time was ripe for teaching and spreading the glad-tidings that God's new Messenger had indeed come. Exuberance for giving the message completely consumed the time and energy of those devoted and obedient lovers of 'Abdu'l-Bahá and Bahá'u'lláh who lived in this Heroic Age of the Faith.

In a report to Ahmad Sohrab, Pauline shared details of her first travel-teaching trips and what joy these expeditions brought her:

> In the spring of 1908, with the exception of my trip to Acca, I had the most wonderful time of my life. My sister Miss Knobloch had started an assembly in North Adams, Mass. Through her loving kindness and that of Olive Kretz, a spiritual child of my sister & the leading spirit in North Adams, I was sent for to give more of the Teachings. Those were wonderful days and I realized as never before what the spirit of Baha can do if we let it work through us. From early morning until late at night, I talked of nothing else but the Revelation of Baha'o'llah. Not only in North Adams, but Shelburne Falls, Springfield and other places near there, having the chance for the first & up to the present, the last time, that God allowed me to tell seventy of this Great Day. Some accepted, some were interested and some rejected but the seed was sown. My sister had also had such a wonderful time & having started the Assembly wished me also to have such an experience. God Bless Her and Olive Kretz and all my family for letting me go.[2]

Pauline's experiences teaching in various settings and locations helped her develop the skills of a seasoned teacher, and both she and Joseph became sought-after speakers. Among their correspondences are found frequent praises of their wonderful talks and requests for future speaking engagements.

As early as 1910, Joseph began traveling to Summerduck, Virginia to talk at public meetings. A good friend of the Hannens, Mrs. Viola Duckett, wrote to Pauline with great enthusiasm about one such trip he made. It is one of several letters between them:

> O how I do thank God. I know that it is truly wonderful that the people are so much attracted around here. The Word of God is most penetrating. And what loving assistance God has sent to me, two of His most beautiful and loving servants, is there anything lacking in making this a successful Center. Praise be to God's Holy Name.
>
> O how I love you & your husband. Oh darling, if you could have been here and heard him talk so beautiful [sic] to the people, he gave the message so clearly, that it seems as if no one could help but comprehend the truthfulness of this Great Light. I know how happy it makes you, when dear Brother comes back from here and gives such news, that so many turned out to hear him. I am so glad that it makes him happy. There is no doubt in my mind that Mr. Hannen has made the best possible impression on the people here at Summerduck.[3]

The following correspondence is a response to Lydia Gray, who wrote several letters to Pauline over a period of time. She had a number of difficult questions to which Pauline patiently attempted to give accurate answers, and her response is an example of her deep understanding of the station of 'Abdu'l-Bahá, and the Bahá'í teachings in general.

> Dear Mrs. Gray:
> Your long & by no means tiresome letter received & contrary to my regular method I will start from the end of your letter to answer it, <u>if I can</u>.
>
> <u>No</u>, Abdul-Baha is <u>not</u> <u>Jesus</u>, returned. Abdul-Baha is the servant of Baha & the Servant of the servants of Baha. He is the son of Baha'o'llah; it is to Abdul-Baha all the Baha'i world turns for instructions regarding the mysteries of God & the teachings of His Father Baha'o'llah, & to see the perfect life. He was appointed by Baha'o'llah as the Center of His Covenant to man, and it is for this reason that all the Believers in Baha'o'llah have been commanded by Him to turn to Abdul-Baha. Abdul-Baha is the fulfillment of many prophecies in the Holy Books. Baha'o'llah is the Promised One of the people. He is the return of Christ. He is the Word

made flesh. He is the Lord of the Universe. He is the Messiah of the Jews, Mohammad to the Mohommadans, Zoroaster to the Zoroastrians, etc. Baha'o'llah says: "Verily the Comforter hath come in truth but the children are in manifest error; they know Him not, after He hath come to them with Power, which hath dominated all in the heaven & upon earth, and has come in Great Glory"

"The Spirit of Truth hath come—verily He speaketh not of Himself, from the Presence of the Knowing, the Wise."

"The Father hath come. The possessor of Great Glory."

Baha'o'llah is the Revealer of the Word of God just as Jesus Christ was two thousand years ago, with this one great difference. Jesus Christ (Glory be to Him) declared His Truth to only part of the world, but Baha'o'llah sent His Declaration & challenged every Crown (sic) head & Ruler on this earth. With the exception of the three years when He fled into the mountains to pray & leave the Baha'is to find the Real Manifestation of God, for themselves, He was always before the people, a prisoner and an exile sent from city to city. In spite of the handicap, His Word went forth into the world & made great changes in Nations & people. Jesus the Christ said, "My peace I give unto you, not as the world giveth, etc." Baha'o'llah declared to the whole world, many years before the Nations began to discuss arbitration, He said these words "And the Most Great Peace shall come."

He declared there should be a Universal language & we see the people striving after this, etc. I might go on for quite a while to enumerate the effects of His Words spoken, while yet the third in this . . . Power is still with us. Abdul-Baha is the Perfect Fruit of the Teachings of Baha'o'llah. Yes it is an inspiration to us, who have been so favored as to see with our physical as well as spiritual eyes, His Glory and Majesty. Even those who do not believe in His Divine Mission, testify to His superior knowledge & wisdom & His surpassing love for all humanity, regardless of creed, sect or color.

He has been sent, as are all the manifestations of God to train the souls of men in such wise that the heavenly light may shine universally . . .[4]

Unfortunately the rest of the letter was lost, however, if this letter offers any indication of the manner of talks she gave, it is no wonder people felt Pauline gave the message so clearly and impressively. Additionally, judging from her statements in many such correspondences with numerous people, this kind of teaching by post was part of her daily routine.

Another significant experience for the Hannens, was Joseph's participation in the first International Bahá'í Congress, held as part of the Panama-Pacific International Exposition, 19–25 April 1915, in San Francisco. The National Bahá'í Temple Unity Convention was also held in San Francisco that year, in conjunction with other activities taking place. Nathan Rutstein wrote this about the event:

> 'Abdu'l-Bahá had encouraged the San Francisco Bahá'ís who had arisen to organize "a Congress for universal peace," and another Tablet at that time had called on the believers to "think about going" to the Exposition, describing their central purpose in these words:
>
> > Everyone goes to the Exposition either for amusement or recreation, or in hope of obtaining commercial benefits. But you, who are the believers of God, enter the Exposition with the desire to summon the people to the divine Kingdom . . .
>
> Undoubtedly, the Congress would be a unique opportunity to legitimize the Faith in America, to acquaint some of the leaders of thought with Bahá'u'lláh's teachings, to make influential friends for the Faith. The Congress was considered so important by 'Abdu'l-Bahá that He instructed the American Bahá'ís to hold it even if the Exposition organizers refused to allow religious societies to participate. Rent a nearby hall, He advised. The Master also advised that a cross-section of eloquent speakers be chosen to address the Congress.
>
> Not only were the Bahá'ís allowed to hold their Congress at the Exposition, but its Directorate, in an official reception given to the International Bahá'í Congress, presented a bronze medallion as a symbol of appreciation and recognition of their "universal efforts," whose sole purpose and aim . . . is the unification and solidarity of the people of the world . . .[5]

Rutstein mentions Joseph Hannen as being one of those previously described "eloquent" speakers who participated in the events. Imagine the time and effort that must have gone into making that trip all the way across the country before air travel was available.

Words such as these, directed to Joseph, from 'Abdu'l-Bahá in April of 1914, sustained and inspired the Hannens' passion for teaching:

> *Thy detailed letter was received. Truly it was pure joy, for it contained the particulars of thy trip to Augusta, Georgia. It explained the delivery of an eloquent talk by thee; that thou hast summoned the people to the Kingdom of God and hast spread the Divine Teachings.*
>
> *Consider how every soul who has arisen to serve the Word of God will be confirmed with the heavenly Cohorts. Therefore, be thou happy, because thou art assisted with such service!*[6]

In December of 1916 Pauline wrote to Mrs. Parsons detailing the many activities that were underway. The extent of the Hannens' contribution to the teaching work and their guidance and encouragement reached far beyond the limits of the Washington D.C. community:

> Dear Mrs. Parsons,
> We have been so gloriously busy in serving the Cause that I have not had a minute to do aught else but act promptly as the demands come. You have a wonderful worker in the field in Mrs. Finch. God bless her, she has no desire save to guide souls into the Kingdom, and is tireless. I too have been wonderfully blessed, in Mr. Randall sending me checks to go whenever and wherever I can and the Spirit calls.
>
> I felt just as you and Leona did about going to Springfield, from every standpoint save the urge of the spirit, it would have seemed wisest to wait. But dear Mrs. Parsons, the spirit or urge gave me no rest, day and night, until that glorious Peace Meeting was started. . . .
>
> A lady from Hartford, who attended the Peace Meeting in Springfield, became so enthused over Mr. Randall's talk that she told all her friends about it. Results, a class of 15 or 20 or so wanted one to come and teach them. This I could not do but urged them to invite Mr. Randall and I also wrote him, asking him to go. . . . Another result of that meeting on the 12th was another meeting of 45 Theosophists & friends at the Theosophical Center, Springfield, where my sister was invited to give the Baha'i Message. She spoke for three quarters of an hour and a very keen interest was manifested, many waiting a long time just to shake hands with her. That was Nov. 19th. Now there is a demand for another speaker. I have written Mr. Mills of New York, asking him if he would be willing to go & talk for them. He is so perfectly splendid. . . . Now with the help of God, but I must confess with a heavy heart, the urge is to help the few friends in Baltimore. They want me, and I see trouble ahead. Well I shall soon know if it be guidance. Have partly arranged for a public meeting in January, and have asked Mr. Randall if he will help me there. Have also asked Mr. Cobb if he would be willing to speak to a small number, on Dec. 17th (afternoon) at the home of one of the believers. . . . God has surely blessed Baltimore with the Presence of the Beloved. I am told Abdul-Baha said that they must have a Mashrak-el Azkar if it be only a cellar, a place where all may go. They couldn't even find a cellar where all races could meet. You are so near God up there in the mountains, hallowed by the Feet of the Master, "may my life be a sacrifice to Him," will you not pray that we may be shown the way?
>
> We are having wonderful meetings on Sunday evenings, the spirit is beautiful, and so far as I can judge, all are happy. And by no means always

> the same people present . . . the children's class has increased so that since Nov. 12, ... The attendance the past 3 or 4 Sundays has been 29–27–30 . . . All credit for this success is due to Mrs. Nourse, the vessel used by God for that work. . .
>
> Dear me, I could talk on and on, so much is happening now.[7]

Pauline details various activities including taking flowers to the hospital, coordinating teaching efforts in several states, conducting and organizing children's classes, helping the underprivileged, corresponding on a regular basis with numerous believers and seekers, and accounting for funds used. A busy lady indeed!

Another example of the kind of correspondence Pauline received regularly is this letter from Louis Gregory in which he reports to her about the wonderful teaching opportunities he participated in during his travels throughout the South. He knew letters of this sort always brought great joy to her heart, and whenever Louis found a spare moment to share his joys and trials with his spiritual mother, he would. He writes:

> The message is reaching many souls on both sides of the river. The Portsmouth Star, the daily newspaper of the city has accepted an article from the pen of Roy [Williams] giving the Baha'i teachings concerning the League of Nations. It will appear tomorrow. This paper as well as another daily published in Norfolk and the colored weekly have also accepted for publication brief articles about the Cause and advertising our Sunday Theatre meetings.
>
> Our most wonderful meeting was held in the home of Attorney J. W. Diggs in Norfolk last Wednesday eve. About thirty of his friends, mostly of the professional class, were present. It is glorious to see the Light of God in the faces of those who accept. There was little, if any real opposition. Many questions were asked and answered. Roy Williams, who shows a wonderful grasp of the spirit of the Cause, made a very beautiful address on "the need of an education." It was very simple and sweet and heart appealing. Afterwards they heard the message with the various points of proof. Many of them were ready to accept all that was offered and one of them, a Mr. S . . . although he had never heard the Message before, showed an astonishing ability to answer every question that was asked. He plans to have a meeting at his home next week.
>
> Yesterday we spoke to about 150 school teachers at the Booker T. Washington High School. Before the meeting started two of these teachers who attended a previous meeting, came to us with such expressions of love, radiance and happiness that we knew they had become Baha'is. One said, "I can never again be as I was before that meeting." . . . Quite

a number of them have begun to teach. This sign makes us happy as it is one of the surest ways of attracting the confirmations.

We are hoping, praying, and working to get an assembly started and for this purpose hope to remain until the Feast of NawRuz, celebrating the feast with the new and old believers. We hope they will grow strong enough to withstand the attacks of clergy, and perhaps other reactionary elements. Of course the tests of God are inevitable, but happy are those who remain firm.

Would that it were possible for someone to remain here for a few weeks or months. I wish you or other friends who travel will have them in mind. Even spending an evening with them will be a means of increasing the power of love and attraction in the hearts and aiding firmness in the Covenant.[8]

The letters the Hannens received from Louis Gregory over the years no doubt inspired them to do as much travel teaching as they could fit into their schedules. A 1910 article in *Bahá'í News* listed both Joseph and Pauline as speakers in "a series of informal outdoor meetings . . . given by the Baltimore Assembly during June, July and August."[9]

In another letter to 'Abdu'l-Bahá, dated March of 1914, Joseph wrote regarding an invitation he received to share the message in Augusta, Georgia, some 559 miles away. He traveled for over twenty-four hours to give an address to "a company of interested friends . . . at the home of Mrs. Jackson, and a considerable number received the message."[10] In July of 1914 Joseph wrote to 'Abdu'l-Bahá:

It was our great happiness to visit Philadelphia and the adjoining town of Riverton, New Jersey, on June 19–21. In the former city two meetings were held, one at the residence of Mrs. Revell and her daughters, the house which Thou hast blessed by Thy sojourn, where on Thursday night a goodly company gathered to hear the Message. Thy maid-servant, Pauline, and this servant delivered addresses. Then on Sunday afternoon a public meeting was held at the Theosophical Hall, at which many strangers were present. Pauline had invited numbers who were attending a Convention of the Viavi Company, and this good work of hers brought about a most successful gathering. Then in Riverton, at the hospitable home of Mr. Will K. Bowen, his mother and sister, two inquirers received the Message Saturday night; while on Sunday morning a Colored Sunday School was addressed. . . .[12]

For each of the sample letters I have included, there are hundreds more that space could not allow for. Such was the volume of their activity in the teaching field. 'Abdu'l-Bahá writes:

O ye heralds of the Divine Kingdom!
Verily ye have consecrated your time and your lives to the service of the Kingdom. Day and night, your highest wish is confined to the guidance of people and praise be to God, ye are confirmed and assisted in the promulgation of Divine Teachings. This supreme favor is pregnant with momentous results and this seed which ye have sown in the garden of Reality shall yield an exuberant result.

Every seed shall yield a teeming harvest and every bough shall turn into thriving, fruitful tree.

Reflect ye, how a shrub that has two thousand years ago been planted has grown to be a fruitful tree and is still giving birth to numerous crops.

Communicate with all regions and incite and encourage the souls to be firm and steadfast so that the oneness of the world of humanity may pitch its pavilion upon the apex of the world and denominational, sectarian, racial, patriotic, political and economical prejudices may vanish. The surface of the globe may become one home and all the nations of the world may be protected from the aggression of the devouring wolves.

Convey on my behalf respectful greetings to the honorable mother, and love and fatherly kindness to your beloved children. On their behalf, I supplicate at the Divine Threshold and from every standpoint beg for them unbounded assistance and blessing.

Upon ye be Baha El Abha!
Abdul-Baha Abbas[13]

Translated by Shoghi
March 17, 1919

- 25 -

Joseph the "Correspondent"

The Hannens were certainly involved when it came to service to the Bahá'í Faith, yet it would not be a complete story without including a chapter about the service that Joseph is most noted for—that of correspondent extraordinaire. In this letter, dated October 1919, Joseph is describing his busy schedule:

> When I tell you that I have just received (39) thirty-nine Tablets direct from Abdul-Baha, to be entered in our list and distributed to the recipients, you will see at a glance why I cannot undertake anything else until this most important work is done.
>
> In point of fact, dear Mrs. A . . . , my special work is correspondence. Abdul-Baha has written me to that effect. In proof of this, I am being almost overwhelmed with the quantity of letters to be written. There is correspondence with Messrs. Gregory and Williams, our regular teachers in the field, and with the Board and Teaching Committee, beside a host of other details.[1]

In January of that same year, as correspondence with the Holy Land was becoming more reliable due to the end of the war, Joseph wrote a letter of introduction to Shoghi Effendi—who had recently become 'Abdu'l-Bahá's secretary in the Holy Land—in order to establish a means of direct communication with him. Previously Joseph sent letters to 'Abdu'l-Bahá (from himself as well as believers throughout the eastern and southern parts of the country); when he received replies, he would then forward those replies to the intended recipient(s), which occasionally included forwarding appropriate Tablets to *Star of the West* for publication. The following is an excerpt from Joseph's letter:

> It is my understanding that since the departure from Haifa of my dear friend and brother, Ahmad Sohrab, you are secretary of our Beloved

> Abdul-Baha Abbas. I have great pleasure in greeting you, and in tendering the services of Mrs. Hannen and myself, in any and all ways wherein we can be of any way helpful. It is not likely that you may recall us, but we remember very well indeed meeting you in Haifa and Acca, when we visited there in 1909. Since then, we have watched your career with deep interest. I believe you have written to Mrs. Hannen on some previous occasions. . . .

After inquiring how further communications should be sent, he continues:

> At this time, I beg to place at the disposal of the Master and of yourself, our facilities for receiving and distributing Tablets, sending out copies of Tablets of general interest, diary letters, etc. Mrs. Hannen and I have established a system of attending to these matters, and it is our greatest joy thus to serve the Beloved and the friends. We have two typewriting machines, and both of us can use them. These are at our home. I am a rapid operator, and glad indeed to do this work. Then, we have perhaps the best list of the believers in America and elsewhere, that there is in this country, with the exception of that held by Mr. Remey—and the latter is always at our disposal.[2]

It would seem Joseph's and Shoghi Effendi's letters crossed in the mail because he wrote again in February with this response:

> It was a very great joy to receive your most welcome letter of the 23rd December, which came to hand yesterday. I wrote to you on January 28, showing that our thoughts were attune, and as you will have seen, the substance of your request to be kept advised of the news of the Cause, and of mine that you in turn notify me of important developments over there, was covered in my communication. I shall be most happy to write to you from time to time, as I did to Mirza Ahmad Sohrab, knowing that you will give any items that are of sufficient importance, to the Beloved. Here we are deeply interested in His health, safety and present welfare; also to receive copies of the most important general Tablets and to be kept advised as to developments in the Holy City and Household. We are all rejoiced to know of the new conditions which have come about already, due to the beneficent influence of the British Administration, and that the frightfulness of the old Turkish regime is now but a memory. . . . Here is a letter from your spiritual sister, Pauline, in which she tells more news than I could. Her work is indefatigable, dear Shoghi, and my activities are not to be compared to hers! Supplicate for a special blessing for her, I beg you, and also for my Mother, Mrs. Mary V. Alexander, who, thank God, is still with us, and in fairly good health.

With love, and desiring to be remembered always at the Holy Threshold, I am,

Your devoted brother[3]

The correspondence between Joseph and Shoghi Effendi continued for some time, often mentioning Tablets that would be forthcoming, and always with the expectation that Joseph and Pauline would forward them to the appropriate destinations. Shoghi Effendi writes regularly of 'Abdu'l-Bahá's special love for the Hannens, the "devoted and enkindled soul, Alma Knobloch," and even Joseph's dear mother, Mrs. Alexander.

Another topic that was often discussed in their correspondences was the "diary letters." They were started earlier in 1913 with Ahmad Sohrab and continued for a while with Shoghi Effendi. They consisted of letters sent periodically, telling of the activities of 'Abdu'l-Bahá and developments of the Faith in the Holy Land. When Joseph and Pauline received the "diary letters," they would distribute them to believers all over the country. The following letter to 'Abdu'l-Bahá, dated 22 September 1914, gives an account of the manner in which the diaries were circulated, and the extent of their influence:

> This week the Diary Letters of Mirza Ahmad Sohrab dated July 1, 1914, were sent out, thus marking the close of one year of this work. It may be acceptable to convey something of an outline of the effect of this general correspondence. The maid-servant, Pauline, and I send out the letters regularly. My list comprises: The *Star of the West*, the *Christian Commonwealth*; Mrs. Fannie G. Lesch for Chicago Assembly; Lady Blomfield, Mrs. Henry Fraser, East Rand, Transvaal South Africa, Mr. Wellesley Tudor-Pole, N. R. Vakil, Surat, India, Abbas Ally Butt Cashmiree, Rangoon, Burma, Mr. William H. Hoar, Mohamed Said, Alexandria, Egypt, Miss Annie T. Boylan, New York, and a copy to Mirza Ahmad, beside a copy for our permanent file. Pauline sends to Mrs. Kinney, New York City; Mrs. Parsons; Consul Alexander Schwarz, Stuttgart; Shoghi Effendi Rabbani, for the students at Beirut; Susan I. Moody, Tehran; Rev. Howard Colby Ives; Miss Margareth Döring, Stuttgart; Miss Jessie Revell, Philadelphia; Mr. A. M. Dahl, Pittsburgh; Dr. Pauline Barton-Peeke, Cleveland, O.; Mr. L. G. Gregory; Mrs. Mariam Haney; Miss Juliet Thompson, Mrs. Harriet Latimer, Portland, Oregon; Miss H.A. MacCutchson, Minneapolis, Minn.; and Miss Alma Knobloch, Germany. Until the recent interruption to mails because of the European War the letters were also sent to Vienna and Budapest. Each of those mentioned sends out in turn to others, so that America, Europe and even Asia and Africa are well covered. Many letters have been received commending these Diary Letters; they have been deemed the vital news of the Cause

> in this day. They are reaching out into important circles of influence; as for example it was recently reported by Mrs. Latimer that she supplies the Private Secretary of Mr. William Jennings Bryan, who in turn shares them with his Chief; in another instance Miss Boylan has her letters copied by a believer who is Secretary to Mr. Cortelyou, formerly Private Secretary to President Cleveland and now an important businessman of New York and vicinity; again Miss Juliet Thompson has just written that she has read the letters to the wife of the United States Senator Elkins, of West Virginia, the most influential man in that state, and who is much interested; finally, Mrs. Parsons, writing to Pauline a while ago, says that she finds Mr. Parsons more interested in the letters than anything else that he received. These are but instances of the great good done, and we are happy to be permitted to have some small share in the distribution of these Letters.[4]

News of the teaching work was another theme often filling the pages of correspondence with Shoghi Effendi. The letters described the activities of Louis Gregory and Roy Williams, who were actively teaching throughout the Southern States, as well as Mason Remey, and might also include reports of Josephs own family's teaching efforts. Newspaper clippings that may have mentioned the Faith or other articles of interest were enclosed along with any news pertaining to the Bahá'í activities going on in Washington D.C.[5]

In a letter dated 19 October 1919, Joseph alludes to the special arrangement he organized with the cable company that allowed Shoghi Effendi to send messages to the United States faster and more efficiently:

> I am glad to add this facility to those already available for transacting any matters in connection with which I may be honored with the opportunity of serving at this end of the line. Do not hesitate, dearest Brother, to send me any number of Tablets to deliver, or anything I can do. I am eager indeed for the opportunity to help the Beloved in this small way. My life is devoted to His service and that of His friends, as you know, and it is the same with Pauline."[6]

The sheer volume of Joseph's correspondence, of which he kept meticulous records, is astounding. One can only presume his understanding of the significance of serving at the very beginning of this stupendous Revelation in the Western Hemisphere. Both he and Pauline—and to some extent her sisters, Fanny and Alma—appear to have kept every piece of correspondence they ever wrote or received after they became Bahá'ís; eventually offering them all to the National Archives for posterity. The original letters and Tablets they received from 'Abdu'l-Bahá and Shoghi Effendi were eventually donated to the Bahá'í

World Center to be placed in the International Archives. Joseph had a habit of noting on the top of the correspondences he received, a date indicating when he responded to that letter. In the National Archives alone I estimated 1700 folders containing letters, many from individual believers and the family. Equally impressive are the names of those with whom he and Pauline corresponded. I venture to say there are very few people listed in the Bahá'í history books of that period who did not write to, and or receive, at least one letter from one or more of the Hannens.

Along with the copious amount of personal letters Joseph and Pauline each handled on a regular basis, Joseph was writing articles for *Star of the West*, the monthly national newsletter developed by the Bahá'ís in Chicago, since it began in 1910. Over a hundred of his articles can be found in its publications from 1910–19. He wrote summaries of the teaching work taking place in Washington D.C., as well as articles reporting the activities of National Conventions and Persian American Society Conventions—many of which have been included in previous chapters. In 1919, when the magazine's audience was expanding nationally, the editors wrote this letter to its readers:

> At the Second Baha'i Teaching Convention of the Central States, held in Chicago, May 23rd–25th, 1919, the *Star of the West* offered certain suggestions regarding its development. Among them was, that a representative from every section of the American continent be invited to become a member of its foundation for enlargement. It was deemed advisable by the editors and publishers that nine Baha'is constitute this foundation: Five to be in the Central States at Chicago, because published there—the three constituting the present staff to be augmented by two more—and four to represent the other sections. The following friends were invited by word and telegram to become members of this foundation—subject of course, to the approval of Abdul-Baha and the ratification of their respective sections: Northeastern States, Hooper Harris; Southern States, Joseph Hannen; Central States, Albert Vail, Carl Scheffler; Western States, Helen Goodall; Dominion of Canada, May Maxwell; Editorial Staff, Albert Windust, Gertrude Buikema, Dr. Zia Bagdadi; Honorary Member, Mirza Ahmad Zorab. . . . The convention endorsed the suggestions.[7]

With regard to his work for the Persian-American Educational Society, Joseph wrote in a letter to 'Abdu'l-Bahá, dated 22 September 1914:

> The affairs of the Persian-American Educational Society and the Orient-Occident Unity continue to progress. Numerous letters are constantly written to inquirers at home and abroad—sometimes as many as twelve

> or more in a single evening. Thus the ball of correspondence is kept rolling and the threads of Unity are woven and sent hither and thither, to form the warp and woof of a United Humanity in the days to come, if God willeth![8]

An interesting assignment given to Joseph by 'Abdu'l-Bahá was to be the correspondent with a nationally known magazine called *The Christian Commonwealth.* In 1912 the editor, Mr. Alber Dawson, had written some very favorable articles about the Faith in anticipation of 'Abdu'l-Bahá's visit to America. When 'Abdu'l-Bahá read these articles and then met Mr. Dawson in London, He wrote to Joseph, "It is better that you be the Correspondent of this Journal, and spread it everywhere." He requested Joseph encourage the friends to subscribe to the magazine, which he did. Joseph was also responsible for obtaining 10,000 copies of the magazine and helped distribute them to those interested in receiving it.[9]

Finally, and perhaps most importantly, are the correspondences with his beloved 'Abdu'l-Bahá. An example of the reverent tone of the letters he sent to the Master can be seen in the opening paragraph of a letter sent in May of 1913:

> It is as an inestimable privilege that I address Thee, and first bowing down before Thee and pledging Thee my services in life or death, I declare my firmness in Thee, thanking Thee for the Holy Tablet recently received in which Thou hast called me one of the firm believers. It is my desire ever to so remain.[10]

It was characteristic of Joseph to always stress the unified atmosphere of the gatherings and the spiritual feelings that were imparted. Joseph, with his meticulous records, copious letters, and delightfully descriptive reports, gave us the priceless gift of understanding how this magnificent Faith began its growth and development in America and the world.

- 26 -

Combining Forces: Carl Anthony "Nategh" Hannen and Mineola Barnitz

Carl Anthony Nategh Hannen, the oldest son of Pauline and Joseph Hannen (born 4 May 1895) and Mineola Barnitz (born 2 September 1893) daughter of Leona and Richard Barnitz, grew up in the same Bahá'í community and were very much a part of the first generation of Bahá'ís in America. Carl was seven and Mineola nine when their parents first began to attend Bahá'í classes. From a tender age, they attended Bahá'í Sunday school classes together as well as Bahá'í summer schools at a favorite summer camping spot, Camp Mineola, which Mineola's mother organized. In their teenage years, they both had the great privilege of meeting 'Abdu'l-Bahá when He visited Washington D.C. in 1912. These solid spiritual foundations helped prepare Carl and Mineola for a long life of service to the Bahá'í Faith.

While Joseph and Pauline were working to make peace a reality in the world, Carl joined the Navy at the beginning of World War I. He served as a seaman First Class in the South China Sea. His travels during the war took him to many parts of the Eastern hemisphere. After the war was over, but before Carl finished his tour of duty, Mineola and Carl married on Valentine's Day in 1918. Thus, Mineola spent much of the first months of her marriage separated from Carl while he continued his military service.

In a Tablet dated 18 February 1916, sent to the young couple at the time of their engagement, 'Abdu'l-Bahá wrote these beautiful sentiments:

Tablet to Carl Hannen and Mineola Barnitz.
May their souls be happy!
O ye two heavenly doves!
I have heard that with the utmost joy and fragrances and firmness you intend to live in one lofty nest of the Love of God and similar unto two nightingales

you desire to alight on one branch of the rose-bush; so that in the sweetest melody you may sing together the verses of Oneness.

These susceptibilities and relation which have been born between you are spiritual, physical, luminous and heavenly. I beg of God that this union may become eternal—that is in this material world and in the world of the Almighty.

Upon ye be greeting and praise.
Revealed Feb. 18, 1916
Translated by Ahmad
Haifa, Syria[1]

By all accounts the union of Carl and Mineola was a lasting one and based on many spiritual values. The families, having lived in the same Bahá'í community, shared a lot of history. One letter, which Alma wrote to Fanny in November of 1915, shows her approval of Carl's choice. She wrote:

> Pauline's dear sweet letter has been received, also Paul's letter to you, & the photograph of Nategh & his dear sweet little bride. Nategh loved to speak of the great times he had at Barnitz's & would always have a word of praise for Mineola, so I am not surprised, & most happy that his choice pleases & meets the approval of all his family. Nategh is a most remarkable fine lad with clear judgment & noble aspirations. She will find him a strong good man with every quality to make her happy, & being lovable nature she will win the best qualities & be a suitable helpmate. May God bless them both & guide Nategh safely home again. The photograph is very sweet & pretty & am very thankful for it.[2]

Pauline wrote a most precious letter to Carl and Mineola after their wedding when they were awaiting the birth of their first child. It reveals the influence she had on their lives and the beautiful spirit that pervaded their relationship, and offers sound advice for any young couple expecting to bring a new soul into this world.

> I have wanted a daughter for 23 years, now I have one, ok please don't take sides for or against, just be happy and help God in that wonderful of all mysteries, helping to create an immortal soul. My heart and my prayers will be with you constantly, yours was a spiritual union, the fruit should be very beautiful. I don't mean in form, but character. Much of the character of the babe depends upon your happy spiritual surrounding. For that one reason, above all others I pray that you will have only kind & loving thoughts for all, and steer clear of anyone who suggests any but

loving thoughts. Even if it is me, if I make you unhappy, leave me alone, I will understand.

Carl dear, there is a wonderful bond between us now, and between Papa & I, for the first time I can glimpse how your father must have felt when I was dwelling in heaven with the wonderful mystery of yourself close to my heart. You said once you inherited the faults of both of us. You were mistaken dear, you are good—you have been and always will be tender and thoughtful of the dear child who has given her whole heart & soul in your keeping. You will prove worthy of the trust I know. For your pure desire to make her happy and to be a model for the tiny immortal that may be given in trust, by God, is the foundation of the good that is in both your Father and Mother. The foundation of every happiness is trust; without it life is hell. Win each other's trust—confidence—guard it as the most priceless foundation for a happy home. You will scrap—have misunderstandings, troubles of course—but they will prove bubbles, when you both believe in the word of the other.

Perhaps both of you think this useless, perhaps it is, but I haven't had the real chance to reach your heart, Carl and prepare it for this life of loving sacrifice. So I am taking this chance, as your voyage on the sea of matrimony has just begun now. The precious charge which your little wife will guard with tenderness and love, must be your double charge. Keep her happy & guard her health. During this time of preparation don't think of yourself but the two—the manifested (wife) & the hidden (babe) this training will bring forth those qualities which you admire in father and mother and which you believed you did not possess. Above all never forget the Greatest Name. All this talk holds true whether you become a proud father or not.

Dear daughter, perhaps I have not the right to advise you, but if you will accept it, be careful, spare no pains to keep your health up to the minute, & just as important a matter, is to keep busy and cheerful—and forbid the entrance of any but strong, healthful, happy thoughts. The last will be hardest for you when Carl is away. But for the future happiness of all three, you must keep your mind & time cheerfully occupied. You owe that to Carl, he must leave you & during that time you must live with the little one. No matter what any Dr. may do for you when you need one—DON'T forsake Viavi—it is not medicine it is food. You will be better for it afterwards. Carl get her some cheerful stories to read while you are gone.

Now my dearies I will pay for my preaching by making from time to time the Baby Layette. It will save you quite a penny and give me joy.

Mineola, dear, write me as often as you can & just accept this loving Mother heart for what it is worth.[3]

This letter from Pauline, with so much wisdom imparted, remained in the Hannens' possession for the rest of their lives. And from what I know of my grandparents, was well heeded through the years. Their tenderness and love for each other always showed in everything they did.

Sohayl, their first son, was born in Brooklyn, NY in 1919, the same day that his Grandpa Joseph addressed the Convention of the Covenant. He was originally named Carl Nategh, but when 'Abdu'l-Bahá heard of his birth, He wrote through Ahmad Sohrab to name him Sohayl (the name of one of 'Abdu'l-Bahá's grandsons). He said, "I am hopeful from the Bestowals of the True One that that pearl may be nurtured and developed in the arms of the True One."[4] Little Joseph, Carl and Mineola's second son, soon followed in Washington D.C. in 1920. Unfortunately, he was born after his grandfather and namesake had tragically passed. After Carl left the Navy, the family moved to Milwaukee and then to Shorewood, WI, just outside of Milwaukee, where their daughter Barbara was born in 1925.

When the family lived in Milwaukee and later Shorewood, WI, the area was one big Bahá'í community, encompassing the suburbs. Carl and Mineola served on the Local Spiritual Assembly, along with Beulah (Billy) Barnitz Brown, one of Mineola's sisters. During those years Carl worked as an electrician. The boys, "Soey and Joey," attended school in the area until seventh grade, and spent a great deal of time with Aunt Billy and her husband, Uncle Ralph Brown, and their daughter Marjorie. Marjorie later married Oliver Neddin, and together they became a strong force for the Faith in the town of Mequon, a northern suburb of Milwaukee.

It was also during those years in Milwaukee that Pauline's sister Alma came to live with Carl and family, where she was active in the activities of the Faith in that area. Sister Fanny, as well as Pauline, for a short time, traveled back and forth to South Africa.

During the depression years (1931) Carl, Mineola, and the children moved back to the Washington D.C. area—namely Cabin John Park, MD—for a while, and lived with Grandma (Pauline) Hannen. While there, Carl helped build an addition to the house in order to make room for their family. Pauline shared the home with her sisters, Alma and Fannie, at times, but Fanny was teaching in Miami, and Alma was away traveling on extended teaching trips, giving talks about the Faith. Carl's brother, Paul, lived nearby and was raising a family of his own by then. Paul had three daughters—Nancy, Eleanor, and Priscilla. Paul remained active in the Bahá'í community, however, his wife Eleanor was not a Bahá'í, and so took the children to a Presbyterian Church. "Little Eleanor" as they called their daughter, says that she absolutely loved going on drives with Grandma (Pauline) Hannen, and they would all fight over who got to sit with her. She added that after attending church with her mother, the girls would go to Grandma Hannen's and she would ask what they had learned in church. Then they had their own little Bahá'í Sunday school with Grandma. She always taught them to be good and was always very careful to treat each grandchild equally. When she gave a gift, even ice cream to one, she made sure to send the same in value to each of the others. As this book was being written, Eleanor, who was suffering from cancer at age 83, and has since passed on, told me that when she prayed, she prayed to Pauline because she felt Pauline had a direct line to God. Paul's children, although not Bahá'ís, expressed the highest admiration for their grandmother Pauline (whom they felt was like a "saint") as well as for the other half of the Hannen family who were mostly Bahá'ís. (They never knew Joseph because of his early death.)

Their time in Cabin John Park, MD, allowed the families of Carl and Paul to bond. Sohayl has often said that those times were among the best in his life. He enjoyed spending time with his cousins. Eleanor played the guitar, having been taught to do so by her Uncle Carl, and Soey learned to play the banjo. The whole family loved to sing and started a singing tradition that lasted throughout the years on both sides of the family—even though they ended up living far apart for the rest of their years.

From Maryland, Carl's family moved to Wilmette, IL. Carl had accepted a job as assistant to Mr. Ed Struven. Mr. Struven was in charge of all maintenance at the Bahá'í House of Worship and the surrounding grounds while the building was under construction. Carl served in that position from 1933–42. While there, Carl developed several other hobbies. He took a great interest in teaching Red Cross first aid and safety classes. There are several articles from local newspapers over the years that recount details of Carl Hannen's first aid classes. It seems he had a desire to make sure everyone in the North Shore area was prepared in case of any emergency. This might also explain his dedication to the Boy Scouts of America; he and his boys were also well trained scouts and had a great love for the outdoors, especially fishing and hunting. (The Hannen family archives contains scores of pictures of dead fish and the men and boys who caught them.)

When the Hannens first moved to Wilmette, they lived at 536 Sheridan Road, which now functions as the Ḥaẓíratu'l-Quds (meeting place) of the National Spiritual Assembly of the Bahá'ís of the United States. Originally built by Louis Bourgeois, the architect of the House of Worship, it stands directly across the street from the House of Worship, so that he could look out his window and oversee the construction taking place. For a time, it was the home of Carl and Mineola Hannen's family. While Carl worked at the Temple, Mineola spent time guiding, which involved sharing information about the Faith with visitors to the House of Worship. She often had National Convention delegates staying in her home as well as other visitors who needed lodging.

During those years, when Soey and Joey were teenagers, the Hannens often held parties for the youth in the area. Fanny Knobloch, who spent much of her time travel teaching around the Central States at that time, often stayed in the home as well. She wrote in many of her letters to Alma of the goings on with the family and how busy everyone was attending Bahá'í events, hosting many of them themselves, and guiding or helping at the Temple whenever possible. Often Fanny would speak at public meetings held at the House of Worship, as would Carl occasionally. Even Sohayl gave a talk, although admittedly, public speaking wasn't his thing. He more often could be found out in the lake fishing or helping the friends with their plumbing or other needs, as he later became a plumber by profession.

Little sister Barbara tagged along for many of the activities and also attended school in Wilmette. One of Barbara's best friends was Frances Ogle, who came to visit often. Barbara says she was the only friend whose parents let her cross the busy Sheridan Road by herself. In later years, after WWII, that little friend grew into a sweet and lovely young woman, and in 1946, she and Soey were married. She is my mother, and I've included more about her story in the Epilogue.

In January of 1934, Mineola lost her mother, Leona Barnitz, who had been living in Washington D.C. According to her granddaughter Barbara Hannen Griffin, Leona had been ill and confined to a bed for quite some time before her passing. Mineola received a loving letter from her sister Leone (usually called Lonie), who was also in D.C. working for Mrs. Parsons and making the arrangements for the memorial with help from many of the friends from the area. Shoghi Effendi, who by that time had been appointed Guardian of the Bahá'í Faith, sent the following message to the family:

> Dear Bahá'í Friend,
> Shoghi Effendi wishes me to inform you of the receipt of your letter dated Jan. 6th, and to extend to you and the other members of your family his heartfelt condolences for the great loss you have sustained through the passing away of your devoted mother into the Kingdom of Light. He fully shares the sorrow which her earthly separation from you has undoubtedly brought to your heart. But he is confident that in the next world she has attained that which in this mortal life she has sighed for in vain. The Guardian will fervently pray on her behalf, and will supplicate the Almighty to enable her soul to advance and progress spiritually. May Bahá'u'lláh abundantly reward her for all that she did for the establishment of His Kingdom on earth.
>
> In closing let us assure you of Shoghi Effendi's fervent prayers on behalf of your father, and of his supplications to the Sacred Threshold that he may grow deeper and firmer in his faith. He will also remember Mrs. Parsons, Mrs. Hopkins, Miss Hooper, and our remaining Washington

friends, in his prayers at the Holy Shrines. May the Beloved assist and strengthen them in the path of service to His Faith.

With best and sincere wishes for your brothers and sisters,

Yours in His Service,
(signed) H. Rabbani

(In Shoghi Effendi's own hand)
Dear co-worker: I deeply value the sentiments expressed in your letter and fully share the sorrows which afflict your heart in your earthly separation from your dear mother. The Master will, no doubt, bless her soul, and shower upon her spirit His inestimable favours and bounties. Do not feel discouraged and persevere in your efforts for the spread of our glorious Faith and the consolidation of its nascent institutions. May the Almighty reinforce and sustain you in your continued endeavors.

Your true brother,
(Signed, Shoghi)[5]

When Horace Holley, then Secretary of the National Spiritual Assembly, and his wife Doris took up residence at 536 Sheridan, the Hannen family moved across the street to 112 Linden Ave., a little white house situated next to the parking lot of the House of Worship. The same building later housed the National Bahá'í Center's administrative offices for many years, and stood until 2009 when it was removed to make way for a new Welcome Center. In July of 1939 Fanny wrote a letter to Alma in which she shares the National Spiritual Assembly's plans to move the administration of the Faith from New York to Chicago, and make use of the home Carl and Mineola were living in as the National Bahá'í Center. This of course necessitated another move on their part. Alma in her letter explains that Mineola and Carl had no regrets about the move, but only hoped the NSA would let them stay in the house until the children finished school. This indeed was the case, and the Hannens were so pleased that different family members had the opportunity to visit and stay in their home, nestled in the beautiful shadow of the House of Worship.

Sohayl, who had finished high school by then, worked with his father and Mr. Struven. He occasionally boasted that one of his accomplishments was helping to devise a means of keeping the pigeons from making such a mess in the top of the Temple! He also worked as a night watchman at times, and enjoyed telling stories about what visitors to the Temple thought the purpose of the building was. Theories of everything from sun worship, to keeping alligators or even whales in pits under the steps were shared. The Temple, when the Hannens first moved in across the street, was still under construction and did not yet have the upstairs auditorium or beautiful concrete overlay. As a result, it looked much like a giant mushroom to many who lived in the area, and therefore, had a certain mystique.

Mineola is quoted as saying, "This was, I believe, the happiest period of our lives, being close near the Temple, living on the grounds, helping with guiding the many visitors to the structure, seeing the finishing touches of outer ornamentation and steps go into place was wonderful. Our home was open to all visitors, and for any Bahá'í occasion." Mineola did an amazing job of raising her family on the "North Shore" and putting three children through New Trier High School. She also was called upon to care for the Knobloch sisters off and on through different periods of time, on a very meager income. She had a fantastic capacity for hospitality, and no matter what time, or how bare the cupboard might be, she would always manage something to serve.[6]

When the Hannens moved from 112 Linden, they lived in another house in Wilmette, and then finally, in 1948–49 they built a home in Glenview, IL, a suburb west of Wilmette. They helped establish the Glenview Local Spiritual Assembly, and lived there throughout my childhood. It was in this home my siblings and I spent time at family gatherings and many Bahá'í functions. In 1967, when I graduated from high school, Carl and Mineola sold that house to my parents, Soey and Fran, and moved to Orlando, FL, where they also helped to establish an LSA. They lived there, serving as much as possible, to the end of their days. The communities of Glenview, Illinois and Orlando, Florida greatly benefitted from their tireless services and devotion to the Cause of Bahá'u'lláh.

- 27 -

Joseph Hannen's Tragic Death

After hearing about the myriad ways that Joseph served 'Abdu'l-Bahá and the American Bahá'í community, the monumental tasks he took on with such delight and devotion, the hundreds of believers whose hearts he touched in so many ways, it is hard to imagine how the community withstood the tragedy that was to come. In January of 1920, the Washington Bahá'í community, and indeed the American Bahá'í community, suffered a great and heartbreaking loss. The repercussions his absence caused were monumental. This article from the obituary section of *Star of the West*, Vol. X, presents a thorough account of the terrible event:

> A great calamity has befallen the Washington (D. C.) friends, or to better express it has befallen the Cause in general, through the sudden departure from this world of our good spiritual brother, Joseph Hannen, on January 27th, 1920. We are quite heart-broken over our loss, and we are so shocked and stunned over the abruptness of it all that we scarcely realize that he is no longer with us in this material realm.
>
> In crossing a street he was struck by an auto car which knocked him down and passed over his body. He was hurried in an ambulance to a hospital and later taken to his home. The best possible medical advice was obtained and the friends supplicated and prayed unceasing upon his behalf. He seemed quite unconcerned over his condition, and those who conversed with him could not discern that he realized he was dying. A few minutes after 9 o'clock in the morning of the fifth day after the accident his spirit took flight from this phenomenal world and ascended to the realm of the eternal reality beyond.
>
> Upon the third day after Brother Joseph's departure the friends gathered at the Hannen home for the reading of the burial service. Both colored and white were there. They brought flowers until not only was the

bier hidden from view by these floral offerings, but the chimney piece and various articles of furniture in the room were likewise smothered with blossoms, while the entire house was filled with fragrance thereof. The ceremony was quite simple. It consisted of the reading of a commune followed by the Baha'i burial service with its choral responsive prayers and was concluded by the reading of several selections from the Words of BAHA'O'LLAH and Abdul-Baha upon this subject of the immortality of the soul and of its continuance and perpetuity in the worlds beyond.

At the conclusion of the reading seven of the men Baha'is bore the body from the house. The interment was in the family burial plot in Prospect Hill Cemetery within the city, not very far distant from the Hannen home. Mrs. Knobloch's mortal remains also rest in this plot. At the grave nine utterances from the Hidden Words from the Arabic were read, the friends then chanted in the Persian language in chorus three times the prayer, "The Remover of Difficulties" and a short commune was read, after which the family cast sprays of roses into the open grave and we all returned to our respective homes saddened by this distressing tragedy.

It was during the time of Mirza Abul Fazl's Baha'i ministrations in Washington that Mr. and Mrs. Hannen and the Knobloch family (Mrs. Hannen's mother and sisters) came into the knowledge of the Covenant. Since then up until the very moment when Brother Joseph was stricken he was ever active and serving in the Cause. The last material service which he did for the friends was to go to the post office to get the mail to be forwarded to our traveling Baha'i teachers, Messrs. Gregory, Roy Williams and Mirza Ahmad Sohrab. After the fatal accident the family gave me the letters which he had had upon his person to be forwarded to these friends. Upon examining the envelopes I found them to be stained and bespattered with Brother Joseph's blood, which was a symbolic testimony of his last service to the friends.

During these years of Mr. Hannen's labors he carried many burdens of service to the Cause. He was the standby in the Washington assembly—the one upon whom every one depended. He was always in the meetings and gatherings of the friends, and when anyone wanted anything done quickly and without delay he was the one to whom they turned, knowing that on him they could depend with certainty. Moreover, Brother Joseph was always cheerful and happy in his service, and his firmness in the Covenant was a fortress and protection to all who knew him. He made great sacrifices in the path of Abdul-Baha, the fruits of which many of the friends have already witnessed, while those who knew him are convinced that in time the far-reaching effects of his Baha'i work will become more generally and widely recognized and acknowledged than it is at present.

Joseph Hannen served alike the white and the colored friends. At the request of his family both colored and white united in carrying his remains to the grave. He was ever striving to create unity and good fellowship between the two races.

The friends in all parts of America have telegraphed and written beautiful messages of sympathy and love to the Hannen family. While Mr. Hannen's mother, wife, sons and other relatives are suffering most intensely because of this separation, they are, however, completely resigned to the Will of God and are happy and tranquil in their souls because of God's bounty bestowed upon them and upon their departed loved one in his accepted services to the Center of the Covenant of God.

Charles Mason Remey.[1]

The following is a Tablet of 'Abdu'l-Bahá, revealed to Pauline after the tragic death of her beloved husband. It appeared in *Star of the West,* Vol. XI, No. 5:

To the beloved daughter, Mrs. Hannen, Washington, D.C.—Upon her be Baha'o'llah El-Abha!

He Is God!

O Thou Compassionate Lord!

Thou knowest the magnitude of my sorrow as I engage in this following supplication. The favored servant of the Kingdom, Mr. Hannen, that pure and spotless soul, was the first self-sacrificing person in the path of the Merciful One. At night he was restless and during the day he was untiring. Not a moment did he rest and all his lifetime was consecrated to the service of the Kingdom. In the assemblage of Thy friends he was of Thy favored ones an enkindled torch. In the horizon of guidance he twinkled like a radiant star and in the Abha Paradise he appeared a magnificent palm. He was an illumined soul, merciful, kingly, lordly.

At present that bright candle has been extinguished in the globe of this mortal world that thereby it may shine resplendently in the globe of the Kingdom. That radiant star has set from this world below that it may rise effulgently from the Supreme Horizon.

O Thou Forgiving Lord!

Set up this esteemed soul in Thy glorious Kingdom upon the thrones of everlasting sovereignty and make him a heavenly prince. Help him to soar in the limitless realm and draw him unto the close companionship of heavenly birds in the hidden world. Immerse him in the ocean of Light, and make him the prince over the Realm of Mysteries. Bring him unto the effulgent concourse and help him to attain his object in the realm of Thy presence and the heights of the Supreme Concourse.

Thou art the Forgiver, the Pardoner, and the Compassionate!

O thou daughter of the Kingdom!

This calamity is overwhelming and painful, and undoubtedly its effects are most severe. A thousand times alas, that like unto a star, that glorious personage disappeared from the horizon of the immensity of space. He has arisen from a horizon that knows no setting and has hastened unto a realm that is infinite. He has been detached from this world below and has attained unto Everlasting Life. He has ascended from this gloomy world and hastened to the Center of Light.

Grieve not therefore and be not despondent. Enkindle his lamp and strive that the orchard of his highest wish may abound with fruitful trees. Rest thou assured in the bounties of the Lord of Hosts and endeavor to be confirmed by the favors of the glorious Lord. If he has disappeared from this plane, grieve not, for thou shalt find him in the divine realm. Be not sad at this temporary separation, thou shalt enjoy eternal companionship in the realm above. Be thou therefore patient and forbearing, firm and assured.

Upon thee be Baha-El-Abha!

(Signed) Abdul-Baha Abbas[2]

(Haifa, Palestine, March 19, 1920)

Not only was Joseph missed dearly among the Bahá'í community, but those with whom he worked also appreciated his warm spirit and felt the great loss. A memorial article printed in the Viavi Cause Newsletter, a publication of the company Joseph worked for at the time of his death, reads in part:

JOSEPH H. HANNEN VICTIM OF FATAL ACCIDENT

Manager Correspondence Service Department, Washington Division Eastern Viavi Company, Succumbs to Injuries

An accidental injury; a few days' painful suffering and then the passing of the soul of our associate to its realm in the Great Beyond! That is the record of the last earthly days of Joseph H. Hannen, but to his widow and to his sons; to his intimate Viavi associates and to his numberless friends at Washington and elsewhere, the tragedy of his death will linger so long as the memory of his exemplary life shall endure.

Mr. Hannen was active and prominent in worthy religious, philanthropic and public welfare movements. He was a clear thinker; a ready talker; and an accomplished writer—his literary productions frequently having appeared in American and English publications.

Telegrams of condolence from the Home Office of Viavi at San Francisco; from the Chicago Division and from various Viavi branch houses throughout the country, attested the high esteem in which Mr. Hannen was held by his business associates. The funeral was from his late resi-

> dence; many floral tributes were received and the simple but impressive services of the Baha'i religion were observed as the last mark of respect. Burial was at Prospect Hill Cemetery, Washington, D.C.[3]

Star of the West printed a report detailing the Twelfth Bahá'í Congress-Convention. Joseph Hannen had played a key role in organizing this event since its inception, and it is clear his presence was sorely missed. The article mentioned resolutions to honor his many contributions to the Faith.[4]

The report in *Star of the West* also mentioned the numerous cablegrams and letters Pauline received from the many shocked and grief-stricken friends of her and Joseph. Those 101 letters and thirteen telegrams were part of the package of letters and journals that had remained with the family until long after the passing of those who wrote them. Found in a box in the National Archives, they were not processed and categorized until three years after I submitted my first manuscript. When I was alerted to the contents of that box, which held these precious letters, telegrams, and significant pieces to the puzzle of this book, the timeframe for the editing process became more clear to me. Reading them increased my admiration for Joseph's service tenfold. I was awed to witness the love and affection every writer held for Joseph. The range of places from which they came is remarkable. Many heroes and heroines of the Bahá'í Faith positioned throughout the world, who had received much attention and services from Joseph's work, wrote some of the most touching letters. Ms. Agnes Alexander, who was teaching in Tokyo, Japan, wrote in her letter to Pauline:

> My heart goes to you in great love and I believe that a great and wonderful effect will be produced through the earthly separation from our beloved brother. He is living & rejoicing in His Lord! He has given his life in His Service and it cannot go out, but on and on, and his influence will be felt in all lands, and his "Call" will be heard and immortalized . . . . "His poem ['Call'] has had effect on the hearts in the orient. To a blind friend I read it and then he asked me to read it again . . ."[5]

Friends in the Middle East who had learned of Joseph's devotion and service to the Faith, or perhaps had met him while he was on Pilgrimage, wrote to Pauline as well. One letter came from the Spiritual Committee in Cairo, Egypt, where they held a special memorial service in his honor.[6] Another came from a Bahá'í administrator in a government school in Alexandria, who held a "consecrated meeting especially arranged in his memory, assisted by Shoghi Eff. Rabbani, and Dr. Lutfallah Hakim of England. This meeting was held in Ramleh in the house of one of the new enkindled friends Mr. Joseph Hebeqa."[7] Still others came from friends traveling in France as well as friends of his sister-in-law Alma, who was still serving the Faith in Germany. The most touching to me was a letter from his very close friend Ali Kuli-Khan, who was in Paris at the time:

> I have been thus far unable to write you since the shocking news of Brother Hannen's departure, which stunned me more than any death since my infancy. Truly I could not bring myself to sitting down and writing you. How can I express any grief as the event is far beyond being regretted through a mere word of sympathy. In one word, thousands of workers were represented in the one servant called Brother Joseph. While you lost only a husband, thousands lost a brother & the Cause lost one of its chief supporters in the world.
>
> Your faith is so strong that you will surely resign yourself to the will of the Lord & bear up like a heroine. In a little while, we shall all meet in the world that is eternal. So, let us bear this earthly separation for a while. Needless to say how I loved & admired him & how always he helped me nobly.
>
> Present my sympathy and love to his mother & to all the members of your household. I refuse to believe that he is dead & so I will begin to bear up & pray for him. How can I ever see Washington & not see dear brother Joseph in the flesh. Tears prevent me from expressing the agony of my soul. May the Lord give us all patience!
>
> We are still in Paris. Shoghi Effendi is in Paris for a little change and rest, Mrs. Parsons & party were here & will sail soon from England.
>
> My Baha'i love to you and all the true friends. The family join me in love,
>
> Your brother, Ali Kuli-Khan[8]

Khan's wife Florence wrote a touching letter to Pauline offering her condolences and gratitude for the copy of the Tablet received from 'Abdu'l-Bahá regarding Joseph's passing. She wrote:

> Your beautiful letter to Khan was warmly welcomed. And the wonderful Tablet, whose like I have never read for dear Mr. Hannen, has brought much consolation and pure joy. Callie often speaks of Mr. Hannen with tears in her eyes, and prays for him. But Khan and Marzieh are usually silent because his going has been so genuine a sorrow to us all.
>
> Naturally I cannot even think of Washington without Mr. Hannen! And so I feel a great sympathy for all the friends, as well. Shoghi Effendi had been telling me about this Tablet, and regretting that he had sent his last copy of it away. When it came to us, from you, and thank you a thousand times for it.

> We understand perfectly about being "friend, companion and chum," as well as husband and wife. Khan and I always feel that our friendship for each other is so continuous, that we hardly know at times or think about the marriage part of it. . . . And surely your great love for Mr. Hannen and his for you, and all your united service in the Cause, has crowned you both eternally, with this Immortal Tablet of Confirmation. What more do you want, in reality, dearest Pauline? What more can you have? May the Center of the Covenant sustain you in all your life and work.
>
> May the beautiful Love of Bahá'u'lláh shine upon your Earthly Path in all Glory, as you work on until you meet your beloved husband again, never more to be seemingly separated.[9]

Even a year after Joseph's death, Khan's wife wrote to Pauline that her husband still could not bear to think or speak of Joseph's passing.[10]

As I read through the letters and cablegrams I was struck by how stunned everyone seemed to be. Many questioned why God would take from this plane someone who was such a tireless and effective worker for the Faith. Some even figured that God must need his kind of services on the other side, for why else would this happen. Gertrude Buikema, an editor for *Star of the West,* wrote about her great shock and she wondered how they could spare "such an ardent worker in the Cause." However, after her initial shock she wrote:

> Then, when the great emotion passed, I realized that he had entered the higher realm and I could, in spirit, hear the Master's words, "Well done, thou good and faithful servant!" And I knew that while not with us any longer in body, in spirit he would always be with us. We think of him with the other great souls who had preceded him, doing greater work for the glorious cause than ever before because the limitations have been removed—a member of that "Heavenly Concourse" whom, 'Abdu'l-Bahá said, stand ready to aid all those who arise to serve the Cause.[11]

Many of the friends expressed being sad for Pauline's physical separation from her beloved companion, but offered the encouragement that he would always be there to offer assistance and protection from the next world. Countless letters recalled how Joseph touched their lives in very significant ways with his great love and caring manner, or had assisted them in various situations through his many roles in the Faith. One friend wrote, "It may be that with that wonderful love of his, that blessed quality that always shared, he is indeed consciously opening the doors to us left behind him." The secretary of the Spokane, Washington Assembly wrote, "His wonderful spirit of loving service in the Cause and firmness in the Center of the Covenant is recognized, even by those who may never have come into personal contact with him. The very letters and all communications he sent to Assemblies were the breaths of courtesy and good-will."[12]

Letters came from Bahá'ís, yes, but also neighbors and Viavi colleagues all over the country who admired Joseph's work ethic as well as all the other fine qualities that endeared him to all he met. There are so many wonderful letters from dear friends and spiritual giants—friends like Corinne True, who directed the building of the Temple in Wilmette; John and Louise Bosch, who donated Geyserville School in California; Sarah Farmer, who donated Green Acre School in Maine; Agnes Parsons, affectionately known as the mother of the Washington D.C. community; and the list goes on, all great admirers of Joseph. The heartwarming and spiritually uplifting messages could fill a book to overflowing. It has overwhelmed me trying to pick out just a few of the gems that lie in each one, and I feel incredibly blessed to have had the privilege of reading them. I will just add one more from Joseph's dearest friend, Louis Gregory. Following this letter, I have included the words Gayle Morrison wrote in her biography of Louis. He was in Shreveport, Louisiana when he heard the devastating news:

> My dear Sister in El Abha:
> A letter from Louise, received upon my arrival here this afternoon, brings the sad and shocking news of the passing of your noble husband, my spiritual father and our universally beloved Brother Joseph. Alas! That what seemed wholly incredible should appear to be confirmed by his silence!
>
> My heart is bowed down with grief and my tears have freely flowed to relieve the sorrow of my heart. I can but think and think of his noble life and beautiful service, all given with ceaseless industry, sublime patience and untiring love. He was indeed created in a large mold, large in body, mind and spirit. Himself brave and strong, he was wonderfully compassionate to the weak and suffering. It cannot be conceived that any cry of distress would be unheeded by his tender care and loving sympathy. He was unselfish and generous as few souls ever get to be and could not only forgive, but even forget, the slings and arrows of criticism and opposition. As a loyal Baha'i and firm in the Covenant, his services fit into so many places. He did many things for the Cause of God and its firm ones in the Covenant and did them all well. As I think of the Washington Assembly and our annual conventions, his vacant place makes my tears flow. He shone amongst the brightest and most sincere and was at all times a force for conciliation, unity and peace. He saw humanity as a whole and was free from the limitations of race, color and creed.
>
> What I personally owe to him, you doubtless know, at least in part. It happened that only a few weeks ago a great service which he once ren-

dered me was mentioned and acknowledged in one of our letters. The fact too, that the joint effort and its patience and kindness of himself you were the means of leading this unworthy servant to the Pathway of Light is something that God willing, I shall never forget in time and eternity.

Before praying for the peace and repose of his soul in the Supreme Concourse, I prayed that my own soul might be purified so that I might be worthy to pray for our dear and illumined Brother who through Divine Favor has attained. He is a Martyr to service to the Covenant of God.

My dear spiritual mother, please let your family and all the dear ones know how poignantly I share your grief and always count me,

Your servant in the Covenant,

Louis G. Gregory[13]

In the words of Gayle Morrison, "The Bahá'í teaching effort in the South could ill afford the loss of Joseph Hannen as its champion. Administratively he had been Louis Gregory's counterpart during the early years of Bahá'í expansion in the South. After his death the work continued, but the systematic mobilization of resources by a Central Bureau for the South seems to have died with him."[14]

Mr. Gregory was of course deeply shocked and grief-stricken by the death of his "spiritual parent," but he was equally concerned for Pauline and the rest of the family. He addressed another loving letter of condolence to her. These are his supportive and loving words:

My dear sister in the Covenant,

Although my heart is still sad over the separation, still it is comforting to know that relying on the Supreme Power, which is the Might of the Covenant, you are bearing bravely and even cheerfully the great ordeal that has come to you. Praise be to God, whose strength we are able to bear all trials and difficulties! I hope your strength will day by day increase!

Please convey to dear Mrs. Alexander my most heartfelt sympathy. Tell her that I pray for her to support by Divine Strength the greatest trial that a mother can be called upon to bear. If her noble son occupied so large a place in my life and that of so many others, how wonderfully great must his life have been in the intimate family circle among those who know him best! How brightly did his many virtues shine! What a wonderfully happy companionship is severed! But thank God the separation is only temporary. I know he is infinitely happy and would not for worlds return. But no doubt it is his earnest desire and prayer for the dear loved ones left behind to be comforted.

In thinking, thinking, thinking, as so often I do about him, I have recalled that you once related to me how Abdul-Baha had told him during the pilgrimage, that he would be a martyr in the Cause. He was without

> doubt as much a martyr as those precious souls whose blood dyed the soil of Persia in the early days of the Cause. His labor was ceaseless, his service to the friends of God and all humanity universal in its nature and his forgetfulness of self characteristic of the martyrs. No doubt in being called to the highest station he can even more effectively serve the Cause of God and the loved ones he has left behind. Since He had conferred upon him the honor of martyrdom, and with joy and fragrance drunk up this cup, the effect of his sacrifice will be far-reaching; now and in the years to come the circle of the influence of his life will widen. Pure hearts and severed souls attract the Divine Confirmations.[15]

Pauline lived for another nineteen years after Joseph's passing, continuing to serve the Faith in whatever way she could. Even as her own health began to waver, her spirit of service never waned.

Twelve years after Joseph's passing, The Greatest Holy Leaf passed away in 1932. Fanny Knobloch was serving the Faith mostly in Florida at the time, and often corresponded with Pauline on various subjects. In one letter, she was confused by some of the Bahá'ís reaction to the passing of Bahíyyih Khánum and had written to Pauline for some advice. Fanny couldn't understand why the friends would be sad when such a wonderful spirit had finally been released from this world. After all, her entrance to the spiritual world would have been met with great jubilation on that side of the veil. Why should we be unhappy? Pauline responded to Fanny:

> . . . Another example, I did not mourn and grieve when Joey passed on as most people do, I did not have the power to realize MY LOSS at the time. He is happy, he is going on developing, I would not call him back. Yet as the time goes on I miss him more and more and appreciate his beautiful life and countless services. Abdul-Baha said it was a great calamity yet I did not sense it as such. So it seems to me that in a BIG WAY the passing of great souls releases them from the bonds and fetters of the body and they really can render greater services to all the world, yet at the same time, it is a tremendous loss to those who sense their beauty and love their nearness. The human touch has been removed, the light is still burning brightly but the exquisite beauty of the lamp is gone forever. The manifestations of God have a human as well as a divine station. The WORLD has lost its opportunity of seeing a Perfect Type in human form. The people of the world have sustained a loss of which they are in ignorance, the believers have sustained a loss of which they are in ignorance, some who have sensed to any degree, the purity and beauty of these and other pure souls, will miss the personal and human touch, and can realize to some extent the loss sustained by the ignorant.[16]

- 28 -

South Africa Bound—Fanny Pioneers

Although Joseph's death was a great tragedy for the family, it in no way dampened their enthusiasm for teaching the Cause. The Tablets of The Divine Plan had recently been revealed to the Bahá'í world, and as we have seen in the previous chapters, the Hannens were tirelessly endeavoring to follow the guidance given therein to, "*strive as far as ye are able to send to those parts fluent speakers, who are detached from aught else but God, attracted with the fragrances of God, and sanctified and purified from all desires and temptations.*"[1] The Hannens and Knoblochs were ready and willing to exert all their energies to follow this guidance. Joseph had already given his life in service to this goal. Alma's services in the teaching field in Germany were even mentioned in the Tablets: "*Likewise Miss Knobloch traveled alone to Germany. To what a great extent she became confirmed! Therefore, know ye of a certainty that whosoever arises in this day to diffuse the divine fragrances, the cohorts of the Kingdom of God shall confirm him and the bestowals and the favors of the Blessed Perfection shall encircle him.*"[2] These words must have had an effect on Fanny and later Pauline as they decided to follow in her footsteps and go to South Africa, about which 'Abdu'l-Bahá said, "*. . . in South Africa, a diamond mine is discovered. Although this mine is most valuable, yet after all it is stone. Perchance, God willing, the mine of humanity may be discovered and the brilliant pearls of the kingdom found.*"[3]

Not long after these Tablets were given to America, and seven months after Joseph's passing, Fanny was able to fulfill a dream she'd long held dear. She responded to 'Abdu'l-Bahá's call to bring the message to all corners of the Earth by offering her services as a seasoned public speaker for the Faith in South Africa. Although various accounts of her trip record different dates, her own account states her first of three trips started in July of 1920. An article about her in *The Bahá'í World*, Vol. XI, referring to her second trip reports, "In 1923, Miss Fanny, dauntless and full of hope, went to Capetown, South Africa, to carry the light of Bahá'u'lláh to that country."[4] The Viavi business, for which she had worked for over twenty-six years, also reported in their newsletter about her second trip helping to confirm that date.[5] It was during this second trip that Pauline joined Fanny for much of 1925 to assist her with teaching and to look after her health. After returning to the states for a while so that Fanny could secure more funds and build up her strength, she eventually took a third trip back to South Africa from 1928–30.

The following are excerpts from Fanny's own summary of her teaching successes in southern Africa. It encompasses her three trips but does not give specific dates for each event. Considering her creative style, she may have thought it would make a better story if she put it all together into one narrative. Her full report can be found in *Star of the West.*

Sunny South Africa
By Fanny Knobloch

Whence comes the urge to carry the Glad Tidings twelve thousand miles from home? After weeks of helplessness due to a complete nervous collapse, suddenly an overwhelming desire to go to Johannesburg seized me. Friends tried to dissuade me. Members of the firm reasoned against it—offered me an ocean trip. Not the slightest temptation, was this to me.

After many delays we started on our five weeks' journey from New York to Cape Town, July 22, 1920. Eagerly inquiring fellow-passengers were told of our purpose in visiting South Africa. The stalwart Scotch captain was approached by those interested to know more and an invitation to tea with the captain followed. After giving close attention to the most wonderful story ever told, this rugged, earnest man requested that this story be repeated to the ship's officers and first and second class passengers. He himself arranged for this lecture. Thus through the bounty and assistance of Abdul-Baha, the history and proofs of this great day of God were given, with my heart overflowing with gratitude, to the largest assemblage of that entire journey.

Reading matter was asked for by officers and passengers. Thus soon began the conversation among groups dealing with the Baha'i Teachings. The seeds sown were carried far and wide, into Mozambique, Salaam, Zanzibar, and Lorenco Marques, the Congo and Nairobi. A glorious memory!

Cape Town! Our first port!

With no names or letters of introduction but with a business connection, no time was lost in calling at the office and meeting Mr. and Mrs. Barker, a tall, fine English couple who gave me a warm welcome. The message was listened to with rapt attention. . . . There were many polite inquiries as to my errand in South Africa. To all questions I replied, "No, I am not a tourist. I have a purpose, a goal in view."

"May it be permitted to inquire the purpose?"

Instantly there was absolute stillness in that large drawing room where forty or fifty guests were assembled. My first evening! Can this be the time and place to speak? A moment's wordless appeal to Abdul-Baha, then the first thought put into words: "My visit is for the purpose of sharing with all who are interested in the spiritual uplift of mankind my most precious possession, my faith."

. . . Hearing of a Spanish lady who was interested in comparative religion, we called at her office and soon were lost in the thrilling story of Universal Religion. Suddenly she exclaimed "this is what Miss Busby has been praying for. She is a lady into whose hands a bit of Baha'i literature fell some years ago and she has been praying ever since that God would send someone to South Africa to explain and teach this Faith. Come quickly. We can meet her leaving the post office, for it is almost noon." . . . During those early days on the Cape, Miss Busby became a confirmed believer.

Johannesburg in the Transvaal

Johannesburg, referred to as the New York of South Africa by our British friends, is a large, beautiful and well developed city. At the hotel after breakfast it was a delight to be drawn into conversation by a Hebrew lad who, with his parents and another Hebrew couple, were soon deeply engrossed in discussing the prophethood, although their opinion differed widely from the Baha'i standpoint. In fact, we met several times for an exchange of thought and once in the restful study of Rabbi Senner whose keen intellect responded readily.

Now, to do something in Johannesburg. My wordless supplication for guidance was answered when I was handed a letter from Mrs. Albert Cook of Kuil River in which she asked me to call upon her friend the artist, Beatrice Reid.

Mrs. Reid was tall, slender, dignified, frankly puzzled, by this stranger's early call before nine in the morning. We became so deeply engrossed in the thrilling story of the Cause and the power and majesty of God's Holy Manifestations, that we were amazed to find that two hours had slipped by and here stood the native servant prepared to serve eleven o' clock tea. The next afternoon Mr. and Mrs. Reid entertained a large group of friends to listen to the Message. Telephone calls were made and names and addresses were given me. This made Life truly worthwhile. At the tea were artists, writers and military representatives. The hostess was known as a deep student and her guests were of the same type. What a pleasure to see their eyes brighten when they were told that certain of the prophecies which were taught in childhood referred to Christ, did in truth refer to

Baha'o'llah. Through assistance from on high many exclusive homes in Park Town were opened for me to give the Message.

One of these homes was that of Mr. and Mrs. Kemp. What a joy to know that only the Power of God, reaching us in great waves of blessings through His holy Manifestations made such opportunities possible. House guests, family and invited guests formed the eleven o'clock group; others met at luncheon and departed only in time for the four o'clock tea visitors, and as those left, lo, the dinner guests arrived. Twenty or more came after dinner increasing the number in the spacious drawing room where after dinner coffee was served. The subjects of our talks were the history of the Baha'i Cause and "The root of all knowledge is the knowledge of God." Until two in the morning during those eventful days we talked and answered questions until physically exhausted yet we were trembling with the knowledge that we had experienced a foretaste of heaven.

Lourenco Marques

Lourenco Marques, Portuguese South Africa! At the station I was met by Mr. and Mrs. John Main whom I had met in Johannesburg. They arranged for drawing room talks, the first in the mansion of the Portuguese Governor General, another at the British Club, and others at the Woman's Club, the Sport Club, the Golf Club. Always the Message was listened to with interest, with never an interruption. At the close, although the discussions varied greatly, always the questions regarding the brotherhood of man and universal peace were sure to come. . . .

Martha Root's Visit

A letter from Australia! "China is calling. Can you go?" My reply, "South Africa is calling. We need you."

Our beloved Martha reached Cape Town in December 1924 and was made welcome and happy in the Auleta, Three Anchor Bay, where she became the magnet of attraction among the guests and to the men and women of capacity wherever we went. We had given a series of radio talks and no time was lost in introducing Martha. Arrangements were made for the first broad-cast which Martha had ever done. She was delighted with her success for she had feared that her voice would not carry well.

One hot Sunday afternoon during Christmas week we were entertained by the Chinese Republican Club which was made up of twenty to thirty young Chinese men. Our hosts were dignified and extremely courteous. The only women present besides ourselves were the wife and daughter of the president. Standing at the side of the president, who interpreted, Martha gave a brief but thrilling narrative of her Baha'i services during visits to various parts of China. All listened with rapt attention.

Pauline's Arrival

One hot summer's day when I was back in Cape Town during my second trip to South Africa I received a cable from my sister Pauline in Washington, D.C. saying, "I am coming."

Many months had elapsed since my first arrival in South Africa, and so busy was I with duties in the Cause that I was not aware of the serious condition of my health. Yet the close tie of love caused my sister to sense this condition and she hastened to my side on the first steamer to sail. After five weeks of continuous storms at sea she reached port and landed at sunrise Sunday morning. There were only two passengers. Slowly, the steamer moved into her dock.

Pauline had scarcely landed when she received an invitation to speak in nearby Muizenberg to the Helping Hands, an organization composed of leading women of that picturesque British settlement on the Cape of Good Hope. We met in the historic home known as Hull House. An audience of from forty to fifty greeted the speaker who, through her patient and convincing answers to questions asked at the close of the discourse, won the love and esteem of those present. Many inspiring meetings followed in the home of our hostess and in other houses.

One of the marvelous experiences was the discovering of a brilliant soul, William Fraetes, who was in New York in 1912 and had the blessed privilege of meeting Abdul-Baha, the Servant of God. Abdul-Baha in embracing him called him "My son" and gave him a message for South Africa. During this interview Abdul-Baha had asked him how the British and Afrikander were cooperating and Mr. Fraetes replied, "They are becoming more united." Abdul-Baha told him that only the surface of Africa's wealth in minerals and precious stones had been touched, but that when the people would turn to agriculture and live in unity and harmony, treating the natives justly, South Africa would lead the world in prosperity. He also said that South Africa was the land for youth. Like many gifted souls Mr. and Mrs. Fraetes were poor in this world's goods, yet many hundreds of men and women from all walks in life found their way to their hospitable, though humble home, high up on the mountain side in Muizenberg. On one occasion the government sent Mr. Fraetes on a difficult mission among some wild tribes in the hinterland. Although they have never seen a white brother, yet because of their sensitiveness to the approach of friends or foe, he was received as a friend. In one instance, when Mr. Fraetes, through his interpreter asked an old wrinkled chief, "Do you believe in God," the instant reply was, "We know that there is a Force which seeth all things and knoweth all things." What a definition for the word God, unknown to him! William Fraetes and his dear wife, both believers, were a power for good in the Cape Colony.

Pretoria

Pretoria is the capital of the South African Republic. . . . In this city Mr. and Mrs. Carey generously supported the Cause by opening their home as the center of Baha'i activities. The first South African Baha'i Assembly was organized there. Mr. Carey, a Mason of high standing, brought us in touch with members of that order, as well as with men representing branches of the government. These became, at that time, deeply interested. On one occasion a group of eight of Mr. Carey's friends came to hear more about the Cause. Seated at the long table sipping tea, they listened attentively to the history of the Cause. Questions arose which Mrs. Hannen answered with references from her Bible. One distinguished elderly Mason, who had made notes on his white cuff, turned to our host and voiced the desire of all present: "May we be favored with another hour of study?" As they departed Mrs. Hannen suggested that they bring their Bibles next time.

Again assembled around the table, with no absentees, these inquirers were given exact references in the Bible. As they read these prophecies of the time and place of God's Manifestation, in this Day there were exclamations of surprise. "I have read these verses many times," said one, "and never stopped to think, taking it for granted that they referred to Jesus."

Colonel Cresswell, a Member of Parliament, made it possible for us to address a large audience in Parliament Hall. Among the first to grasp our hand after was a Mrs. Spero, truly a citizen of the world. Having been a personal friend of Mr. and Madam Zamenhof and an Esperanto enthusiast, she expressed her appreciation of the tribute to Dr. Zamenhof, whose love for his fellowmen enabled him to overcome all obstacles in the working out of a universal auxiliary language. He had caught the divine ray sent out by Baha'o'llah. Abdul-Baha declared, "Many people have never heard of Baha'o'llah yet they are doing His Will, because the power of His Word impresses them to do so."

The Orange Tree State

The Orange Tree State is, practically all Afrikander, formerly known as Boers, the Dutch word for farmers. Here lived Mr. and Mrs. Radloff, thirty-six miles from Westbury, the nearest settlement. Mr. Radloff had transformed miles upon miles of veldt or prairie land into productive fields and orchards.

In the Transvaal lies Heidelberg, where we were entertained at the home of Professor Johann Spruyt, an Afrikander, and Mrs. Spruyt of Danish parentage. Almost a year before this during our brief visit in Lower Unkamaas, Natal, Mrs. Spruyt had heard and accepted the great message. Through correspondence she had shared with her parents all she had learned. As a result her father made the trying journey of eight hundred miles to hear the Message direct. He made no interruption until we had finished and then, turning to his wife said, "Mother, we have been Baha'is for several years only we did not know it."

Rhodesia

A three-day trip through the hinterland where there had been no rain for fifteen months brought us to the colorful city of Bulawayo. . . . A lecture was given at the Methodist church, which was filled to capacity and more, with many on the outside leaning against the sills of the open windows. This talk opened the way for giving the Baha'i teachings in a number of homes.

Mrs. MacKeurtain, club woman and welfare worker, introduced herself. Her first words were: "Our Salvation Army meets this afternoon. Will you come and tell them what you have given to me?" We chose to speak on the Golden Rule as given by different Prophets, and this caused surprises and wonder. Could it be that the Golden Rule had been given by others preceding the Savior? The next morning the officer in command of the Rhodesian Salvation Army called on me. He explained that the band had listened to me instead of practicing the previous afternoon. "No," he said, "they are clamoring for more. Will you favor them? I can promise that all the boys will be there—also our younger women." The invitation was accepted. The oneness of true religion was made plain, as well as the signs of the times prophecies which are being fulfilled in our day. As a result the Salvation Army headquarters in other sections of the country were kept informed of my coming and called upon me for instructive talks to their people.

And so scattered throughout this vast country of magnificent distances are many books and many friends of the glorious Cause. . . . In Durban, the principle city of Natal, in Bloemfontein of the Orange Tree State, In Maritzburg, Stellenbosch, Wynberg, St. James, Kalk's Bay, Simon's Town, Caledon Springs, Kimberly,—in all these cities and in others the call of the kingdom has gone forth through various organizations and family groups. Three separate trips were made and in all some six or seven years spent there. But the work is not complete. Sunny Africa is still calling![6]

While Pauline and Fanny traveled throughout South Africa, their sister Alma was in the States living with Pauline's son and daughter-in-law in Milwaukee. They sent several letters to each other sharing how they were feeling about their efforts to spread the Faith in both places. These letters also give a sense of the struggles they endured and the extreme joy they felt at their successes. As an illustration of how Fanny felt about Pauline's teaching abilities, and how much Pauline was contributing to the efforts, below is a portion of a letter Fanny wrote to Alma on 16 April:

> All who have met her, love her. They speak of her as a "winsome little woman," a "gifted woman" and as a most desirable woman to spread the Baha'i Revelation here. It seems so natural to learn when she speaks, not giving a lecture, though I am confident that will be very helpful—but in discussing some phase of the Teachings, she has a marvelous gift of making things well and clearly understood—and seemingly she does it without the slightest effort . . .[7]

After a while the pace of their work may have contributed to some health difficulties. In a letter Pauline wrote to Alma on 16 April 1925, she states:

> Dear Dona [Fanny] is much weaker but just as full of energy and zeal as ever, if not more so. Her heart is not to be counted upon and when she does put forth an extra effort against my will—like running for a car—I am outwardly calm—but inwardly very much alarmed. So whether I teach or not, I can help to keep her that much longer in the Baha'i field of activity. Yesterday she said to me, "How easy, so very easy for me to, if I wished, to end this life—all I need to do is run for a block or two and all would be over."[8]

While Pauline was worrying about Fanny's health, Fanny was writing home about Pauline's breakdowns. She wrote to Alma about an incident where all the believers came to their home and were "grouping themselves close to the bed, the blind Proff seated so that he could hold Pauline's hand as she sat propped up in bed—but most of our young people's class had also come, so we invited them in. That was a room full of happy faces. We read some prayers and Hidden Words. The room was so still the spirit almost overpowering, especially when Agnes (Mrs. Carey) read a prayer and again while Pauline and I chanted—*Is there any remover of difficulties*—Pauline and I felt the presence of Abdul-Baha—all felt the power of the Holy Spirit—many were silently weeping at times and two of the believers felt the power of the Spirit was so great they could hardly stand it."[9] The prayers must have worked, because they continued their travels, although they did move to a more moderate climate and altitude, which helped their health situation.

A letter Pauline wrote to Mineola and Carl in May of 1925 recounts an instance when Fanny's health issues affected their teaching plans, but that the confirmations were there nonetheless. Fanny was recuperating from a bout with the flu so Pauline went to a previously arranged meeting on her own. She writes:

> Because Dona was unable to go out, I had to keep our appointments alone. It has been a wonderful thing for me, because it seems that I speak very well—according to the opinions of the people. A member of Parliament, present at the meeting (private) said to the hostess, "she is a very clever and well-informed speaker & I am grateful to you (Miss Barnes) for giving me this opportunity of hearing Mrs. Hannen." Everyone expressed a desire that Miss Barnes invite them again to hear both Fanny and myself. The questions after the meeting were the greatest joy to me, & it was then the guests seemed to consider me very sharp and intellectual and wondered how I could answer all the questions from such diverse thoughts, and still to satisfy all and leave all happy. To you home folks I want to admit, I came home to Fanny that night just full of thankfulness to Baha'o'llah & Abdul-Baha for the confirmation that was surely mine that evening. Fanny was to have spoken on Universal Peace & Universal Language & I was to say anything—straight from the heart. Both of us were to speak of the Message without reserve. Germans, French, Dutch, So. Africans, Colonials—the hostess the only English & I an American—and all of us harmonious. That was not the first time I had spoken at a meeting, but it was the first time without Fanny & when I handled her subject as well as my own, believe me, I was very happy.[10]

The twelve-page letter is full of teaching stories. Fanny wrote of one particular experience having a significant effect on Pauline:

> Pauline's gift, or shall we say talent, of explaining biblical texts strikes a responsive chord in every group meeting. This alone accounts for the many invitations to speak. Yet during the past three weeks, although we were both expected to club speak, the "Sisters" as we are referred to now, Pauline had to address large and distinguished groups, all strangers to her—all by her lonely, as she puts it, and she did it so well that other invitations were extended before she left the hall.
>
> Doors of opportunity are opening so unexpectedly, and I know they are due to Pauline—whom the big folks of the Washington Assembly considered too much of a child to be called upon to speak. I believe my inability to be with her at these select clubs, representing the "upper crust here" was a blessing in disguise, for Pauline has now proven to herself that she can interest her audience intensely. Thank Heaven for that—she is doing what I could not in a lifetime—yet, our efforts fit together amazingly well.[11]

Toward the end of a year there, Pauline's funds were running very low and Fannie had barely enough to carry her for a year. She wrote,

> By that time Abdul-Baha will guide us still further as He wills, not as we will. Beautiful as is this service of opening their home to us, it is the way she, Mrs. Carey has been sowing the seed, just enough to arouse interest in us, and several invitations are already for Fanny to speak, the Rotary Club, the Theosophists, the Spiritualists and numbers of individuals who wish to meet us. Mrs. Carey tells us, "Now dearies, please remember we are very new to thinking for ourselves, take us as children and lead us on by degrees, won't you?"[12]

She went on to say, "There is only one chance in a thousand of Dona coming back with me to America. If a live wire is really found, one fully informed to carry on the work & her money nearly gone, then & only then will she leave the Cape. Work is almost an impossible thing to find, yet if God wills we may find something to stretch our means a little. This arrangement of quarters by Mr. and Mrs. Carey was without a doubt a God send."[13]

They did manage to stay another year, but alas, in August of 1926, due to health concerns, Pauline and Fanny returned to the States. The following letter from Shoghi Effendi, addressed to both Pauline and Fanny, offers these encouraging words of acknowledgement and direction from the World Center of the Faith. Here I share only the part he wrote in his own hand:

> My dearly beloved—most precious co-workers:
> I was most saddened to learn of your departure from that promising field of service in South Africa, but as the state of your health is primary and vital importance, I'm glad to learn that you have settled for a time in more suitable climes where I trust you will recuperate for your future work in these regions. It is almost impossible to find anyone who can really replace you, and I wish you to urge any of the friends with whom you come in contact and who have the means at their disposal, to visit that country, and pick up the threads which you unfortunately have had to lay down. I also urge you to exert every effort through correspondence to maintain and deepen the interest and the enthusiasm which you have so devotedly aroused in that land. I will pray most fervently for your good health and success.
> Shoghi
> Received in Milwaukee, 23 October 1926[14]

What is truly amazing about Fanny's trips to southern Africa is not only her wonderful teaching successes, which had a great influence on the future teaching of the Faith in that region, but also that she answered the directives of 'Abdu'l-Bahá without concern for her considerable health issues and despite the fears and objections of family and friends. Nothing could dissuade Fanny from returning to the field as soon as she was able. She left the decision in Shoghi Effendi's hands, and as indicated in an article about Fanny published in *The Bahá'í World,* Vol. XI, she returned to Africa once again:

> In 1928, at the age of sixty-eight, she found the courage to return to Africa, where she remained an additional two years. Thus she was able to give fresh impetus to the Faith, encourage the groups already established and awaken many more people to the fact that a New Day had dawned. She worked tirelessly and devotedly, ever having in mind the words of 'Abdu'l-Bahá at their parting in Akka: "If you but knew the value of these days, you would not eat, you would not sleep, you would not walk. You would run and give to all the Glad Tidings!"'[15]

- 29 -

The Sisters Teach to the End

Thy daughters, each of whom has arisen to serve the Kingdom like unto thee and is engaged in the guidance of the souls. In the Assembly of wisdom they are the lighted candles; they sacrifice their lives in the Path of God; they are gardening in thy orchard and irrigating thy rose-garden.[1]

Ye three sisters are, thanks unto God, heavenly farmers and scatter the seeds of the love of God in the lands of the hearts.[2]

This praise—which 'Abdu'l-Bahá conferred upon Pauline, Alma, and Fanny—was the life-giving blood that sustained them and brought them the greatest happiness. Over and over one reads in their letters the great joy they felt when they received a message from their Beloved. These words, true at the time He wrote them, seem to also foreshadow the services they would offer all their days on this earthly plane. When Joseph left this world in such a tragic and sudden manner, Pauline was left to find a way to support herself. The letters from that period often include her concerns of how to make ends meet, which she shared with her beloved sisters. Yet, as difficult as times were, she rarely took on a tone of complaining. Rather she was always trying to reason out a plan that would give her the means to live a modest life but afford her the opportunity to teach the Cause. Her concern for the well-being of her sisters was evident in every letter. In fact, it was usually Pauline who came to the rescue and found the necessary means that would enable her sisters to continue their teaching campaigns, and other services to the Cause. Each letter also made mention of even the slightest success in the teaching work and included any plans for future teaching endeavors—ever the dominant force in their lives.

One of the significant undertakings of the believers in America at that time was the organizing of Race Amity Conventions. Several close friends of Pauline, especially Agnes Parsons and Louis Gregory, were leaders in this effort. If

Pauline hadn't been dealing with Joseph's death and then her trip to Africa, she probably would have been involved in the efforts from the beginning as well. A lengthy article in *The Bahá'í World, 1926–1928*, written by Louis Gregory, provides an excellent account of these conferences and how they developed. Also of note is a letter Louis Gregory wrote to Agnes Parsons discussing the value of these conferences, and whether or not they would yield a positive result, when considering the bleakness of the racial situation in America. He urged Agnes Parsons, who had been given the task of initiating this monumental effort by 'Abdu'l-Bahá, to do so as soon as possible.[3]

According to his later article, the first of these conventions was held in Washington D.C. on 19–21 May 1921.[4] One can only imagine how Joseph would have loved to see and be a part of this blessed event. There were several of these conventions held throughout the United States over the next few years. Christopher Buck's book, *Alain Locke: Faith and Philosophy*, has a chapter dedicated to describing each of the conferences and who participated in them. Pauline is listed as she was on the committee for two years from 1927–29, after returning from Southern Africa.[5] In a letter written in October 1927, Louis says, "I am glad that you have accepted membership on the National Inter-Racial Amity Committee, even tho [sic] you think that you can accept only with certain limitations imposed by your strength. You are a valuable member if you only pray, for your heart is in this great work. I recall with some pleasure that the first and perhaps in many ways the most effective work of this kind was done either by you or members of your family in Washington."[6] Another letter, by Louis to the National and Local Assemblies reporting on the work of the committee, lists as its members Mrs. A. S. Parsons, Dr. Zia Bagdadi, Dr. Alain Locke, Pauline Hannen, and Louis Gregory.[7]

Meanwhile, when Pauline joined Fanny in Africa, Alma made the difficult decision to move back to the United States to be with the family, which consisted of Pauline's two sons, Carl and Paul, and their growing families. Paul's family was still out east in Cabin John Park, MD, not far from Washington D.C., and Carl's family had moved to Milwaukee, Wisconsin by then. In one letter Pauline expressed her great excitement that Alma would have the opportunity to be with Carl's family as they awaited the birth of their third child (Barbara).[8] There are letters from Germany from this same time period that indicate a desire on the part of some of the German Bahá'ís to have Alma return to Germany. However, after much thought and consideration she decided to remain in America with her family, and never did return to Germany.

While Alma resided with her nephew Carl in Milwaukee, she was quick to seek out teaching opportunities in the vicinity. In February 1927, she received invitations to speak in Racine, Wisconsin at a meeting advertised in the local paper,[9] and by the following year she was making plans for an extended teaching trip to Florida. She received this letter from Dr. Walter Guy, a Bahá'í in St. Augustine, Florida and soon-to-be close friend and cohort in the teaching field:

> To Miss Alma Knobloch: Dear Bahá'í Sister,
> Every day we have looked for a letter from you. We welcome you to Florida and pray that your mission will be gloriously successful. To do effective public work we must have an advance date of your arrival here. . . . A big room awaits you, a typewriter and warm welcome and plenty to eat. Come soon. Orlando is not open for you but welcoming arms are out stretched here.[10]

In April that year Alma wrote about the teaching work in St. Augustine, ". . . the oldest city in the United States, Dr. H. B. Guy has been doing splendid work and has introduced the Baha'i Teachings at the Florida Normal Collegian Institute where a class has been established by the teachers for weekly study of the Baha'i Teachings."[11]

This was the first of several trips Alma made to various cities in Florida over the next few decades of her life. The following letter from May Maxwell, no doubt encouraged her to continue her efforts:

> . . . You cannot imagine the happiness your letter brought me, because of what Shoghi Effendi wrote you of the effect of your work upon his heart. Nothing in life produces this happiness which the knowledge of his happiness brings. It is a strange feeling, different from any other experience and you must feel so happy and blessed to know that through your thorough and devoted services you have brought "inexpressible happiness to his heart."
>
> There are those who believe that Shoghi Effendi sometimes writes by way of encouragement to his faithful servants and this is true, but there is a certain way that he writes which is entirely different, a certain outburst of joyous enthusiasm and when I reflect upon the six months I spent with him in Haifa and saw the daily round of his overwhelming work, drudgery, strain and fatigue, I realized the sacred value of those messages of the good news of the progress of the Cause which brought such joy to his heart and such rest to his soul . . .[12]

At another time, May Maxwell, as a member of the National Teaching Committee, wrote to Alma with a request. Louis Gregory was going south to teach, and the committee asked if Alma would go as well and report back with an itinerary of how much it might cost her.[13] Alma must have sought advice from Louis Gregory at that point, inquiring where he felt the greatest needs were and in what way she could be the most effective in her teaching efforts because she received a letter in St. Augustine, Florida, from Louis, then residing in New York, dated 22 March 1928:

> I have your good letter and am glad you are at work in that vast and fertile field sowing the seeds of the Kingdom. I am puzzled somewhat, however, by your insistence upon suggestions from this servant. The people are there, with capacity and waiting the Glad Tidings and you, an experienced teacher, are "Johnny on the Spot!" I think you have read the Divine Plan for the Southern States. I would follow that as near as possible. I think your presence there is a great bounty to that section and I hope you will try especially, seeking day by day "the Most Great Guidance" to increase the number of believers, especially among the whites. This will greatly help both races, as whites when they get the illumination, usually try to share it with the colored. Residence teachers are of great value. I am sure that you will not neglect the colored people who are under such pressures of oppression and trials and who are so grateful and responsive when anyone takes an interest in them and carries to them a message of hope. It is very easy to get an audience with them and nearly all their churches, colleges, schools and other gatherings will give ear. So few of the whites take any interest in them, beyond those they use as servants that whites who go among them and demonstrate a truly friendly spirit are likely to be regarded as super-men. See what reverence they have for Mrs. Kretz and the Guys![14]

Louis sent her another letter in 1928, stating: "May Maxwell is keenly interested in the work of that section and her committee has an appropriation to sustain the general work. It is not as large as it should be, but I am sure that with it she is not likely to forget you."[15]

There were often letters going back and forth between Louis, Alma, Fanny, and Pauline. A pattern of teaching emerged which involved Louis traveling around the Southern States and follow-up teachers returning to speak in the localities Louis had opened to the Faith. Fanny and Alma took on the role of follow-up teachers, giving talks to audiences large and small, on various separate teaching trips. In a report of one teaching trip taken in 1932, Fanny recounts visiting Jacksonville, FL, where she and a friend spoke to a large audience at a gathering arranged by her sister Alma. After leaving Jacksonville and driving 400 miles in the heat, they spoke in Montgomery, Alabama, this time at a State Teachers College for students of color. More than 400 students and teachers attended that talk! They then traveled to Nashville, TN, where they spoke at the Industrial and Agricultural College to over 700 leaders in the field of education—all due to the interest Louis Gregory cultivated. Fanny repeatedly mentions the high esteem countless people she met along the way held for Mr. Gregory. In that same letter Shoghi Effendi thanked her for the lovely photograph she sent to him, and he promised to place it "in the Mansion of Bahá'u'lláh at Bahjí as a token and reminder of your distinguished services to His Cause."[16]

While Alma and Fanny were in Florida, Pauline remained in Washington D.C. Her letters from that time recount the difficulties she faced as a widow, having to rent out rooms in her home to boarders in order to make ends meet. Ultimately, she made the decision to move out of her home in D.C., and move to Cabin John, Maryland near her son Paul and his wife Eleanor. Eleanor's children report that their mother loved Pauline very much, and even considered her to be like a second mother. And although Eleanor continued to raise her three daughters in a Christian Church, the children did attend Bahá'í activities when they were young. Paul and Pauline, along with a few other couples, formed the nucleus of a Bahá'í community in Cabin John.

It was at this time the Bahá'í World suffered a devastating loss. The passing from this earthly plane of Bahíyyih Khánum, the beloved sister of 'Abdu'l-Bahá, and daughter of Bahá'u'lláh, on 15 July 1932. Upon hearing of the great loss, Fanny wrote a letter of sympathy to Shoghi Effendi. His loving response was received:

> (In his hand)
> *Dear and precious co-worker:*
> *I am greatly moved by your touching words and deeply appreciate a message of sympathy coming to me from one whose spirit of service so powerfully reminds me of the Greatest Holy Leaf whose sudden passing we all mourn. I will continue to pray for you from the depths of my heart that your fondest wish in the service of our glorious faith may be fully and speedily realized.*
> *Your true brother,*
> *Shoghi*[17]

After 'Abdu'l-Bahá's passing in 1921, Shoghi Effendi, His grandson, was appointed to be the Guardian of the Bahá'í Faith to which all Bahá'ís should turn for authoritative guidance. All three sisters showed the same love and respect for Shoghi Effendi that they had held for their beloved Master. Their letters reveal a great love and appreciation for him, and his praise, when given, acted as a catalyst, inspiring the sisters to continue their services in any way they could. This touching letter from Pauline to Alma is an example of the joy they felt:

> I am more deeply moved by the Guardian's message through you than I am willing to admit even to myself. It is wonderful, too thrilling, to know

that our beloved Guardian is praying for us. For the first time since last January, I feel the urge to make a real effort to recover sufficiently to do my bit for the Cause now that the "dark days" are so near at hand. Really felt I was serving too, if our financial affairs could be used by two instead of three of us and was content to let things slide. Now it is different, there is something for me to do before God calls me. I really believed my work was over, now I must try to do my part since the Guardian is praying for me. Can't expect you to understand my emotions, my reactions, but promise you I will try to do better. May be able to thank you better and more effectively when we meet."[18]

During the next several years, the United States suffered from the Great Depression. The sisters and the young Hannen families were not unlike the rest of the country, which was full of people struggling to find ways to make a living. Added to that struggle was their intense desire to find ways to teach the Faith. In most cases during those years, both she and Fanny were sustained by Bahá'ís who lived in the communities where they were invited to teach. The National Teaching Committee would often assist with travel expenses, and then individual Bahá'ís in an area would offer room and board in one of their homes in exchange for their help with the teaching efforts. Local Bahá'ís also contributed to the sisters' service by driving them to visit the friends and to give classes and lectures. Other needs were usually met by their sister Pauline, who was still working at the office of *Star of the West,* and was able to send small amounts when needed. Fanny was using the money she had invested or saved while she was working, and while she did her travel teaching she would write Pauline to request she send her some of her own funds as needed.

During the 1930s, Fanny spent much of her time in Miami, sometimes living with her friend Olive (Ollie) Kretze, and sometimes with another friend, Georgie Wiles. She helped build the community to the point where they were able to elect their first Local Spiritual Assembly in 1932. During those years she spent almost every waking hour serving the Faith, making personal connections, teaching classes, giving lectures, often talking about her experiences in South Africa and using them as a springboard to future talks about the Bahá'í Faith. Much of the teaching within the African American community was with her friend Ollie. Fanny was also in Miami when nationally known lecturer and Bahá'í teacher Orcella Rexford conducted a teaching campaign consisting of several classes and lectures, culminating in a talk about the Bahá'í message. When Ms. Rexford had concluded her program, she would arrange for Fanny to address the hundreds who had shown interest in the Faith during her lectures. Those classes were a great joy to Fanny and one of her many successful teaching experiences.

During the summer months, when the heat in Florida was stifling, Fanny spent time in Michigan with Lou and Helen Eggleston. She would visit Bahá'í communities in and around the Central States, assisting with various kinds of teaching campaigns, and even had the opportunity to teach at the first Louhelen Bahá'í summer school session in 1931.

By 1932 Alma had returned to Florida, this time Jacksonville. The National Teaching Committee wrote to her expressing "their deep appreciation of the unique teaching services which [she] rendered the Cause of God during the past year."[19] The committee also inquired how they could best support her efforts. Her response gave a lot of detail and insight into the many varied services she performed during those years. Included below is only a small portion of her response, highlighting several methods she used when teaching the Faith:

> The idea is this: it requires much patience and a good understanding of the Teachings, much love and tact to form a nucleus which is necessary for a starting point, no matter how small in number. When perfect unity exists, it will attract the Divine Spirit and the fragrances of the Abha Kingdom are diffused. This divine spirit attracts kindred spirits (Souls) very different in type and from various paths of life and through this spiritual power spirituality is attained and numbers are increased.
>
> To my mind, classifying the work of the teachers is a dangerous task because conditions and circumstances change, one is apt to become very tired and tried to the utmost, laboring at a given place, become irritated and thereby irritate others. A change is necessary that one may return with new strength and enthusiasm. When visiting Assemblies one receives as much as one gives, it is recreation. The traveling teachers are like the rays of the sun; they refresh and vivify the tender plants. In other words, a teacher who applies him or herself to the different work necessary to build up the Cause, becomes more efficient and a better understanding is obtained, and cooperation the result of real appreciation.[20]

There is a great deal of correspondence between the National Teaching Committee and Alma. From her the committee received detailed reports of all the teaching efforts in Jacksonville, St. Augustine, and various other places in Florida. From the NTC came much praise regarding the exciting work she was doing there. A letter written in 1928 to Pauline from Louis Gregory, who served on the National Spiritual Assembly at that time, states: "The provisions for your sister Alma, so far as the financial part of it goes, is personal with May Maxwell, altho' in accordance with the wishes of Shoghi Effendi, it is paid by her through the National Treasurer. How long it will continue I cannot tell but can only hope and pray for the best." He went on to explain, "Altho' many very worthy people have asked the NSA for funds to travel and teach, it has been found impossible because of limited funds and unusual demands. Those who are informed of the difficulties of the work will certainly help those in the field by their prayers."[21] Given the state of the funds and the precious little financial resources available, one might infer the great appreciation both the National Assembly and Shoghi Effendi held for the services that both Fanny and Alma were rendering the Cause in the teaching field.

The following letter from the National Teaching Committee, written to Alma in February of 1934, was a confirmation and a great boost to her spirits:

> Bahá'í friend: The members of the Teaching Committee were all thrilled and deeply impressed by your good letters of January 19th and 29th, outlining the tremendous services you are rendering in the teaching field. The letter from the Guardian is particularly important, as it outlines a definite line of work for you, and in specific areas. When one is confirmed by direct word from the Guardian that becomes the motivation of our humble efforts. We hope you will keep us informed of your work, and how it progresses, and any suggestions you have to offer that the teaching Committee might do, to aid in the wonderful work going on in Florida. We will wish to use your reports for the Bahá'í News, showing the wave of teaching work going on over the country. Truly it is remarkable, and augurs well for the future.
>
> With Bahá'í Love, Faithfully Yours, Leroy Ioas[22]

While Alma forged on with her teaching trips and activities, poor health and finances were the twin burdens for Pauline in her waning years. During this time she worked for *Star of the West,* where it appears she managed the subscriptions. Often there is mention of her work in "the Office," although it is uncertain whether she meant the Viavi office or *Star of the West.* Repeatedly, Fanny wrote begging her to slow down and rest, worried about Pauline doing too much work for her community and for her family. Pauline, however continued until *Star of the West* ceased publication in 1935.

Pauline's precious correspondence with Louis Gregory expressed some of her troubles during this time, revealing the closeness between them. His membership on the National Spiritual Assembly also helped to strengthen the connection between the NSA and the sisters as they endeavored in the teaching field. Other letters were filled with the wonderful news of the many hungry souls he met and nourished with the teachings of Bahá'u'lláh on his various teaching trips. One example is a letter he wrote of his trip through the South with Willard McKay, a white Bahá'í. In this letter, he began by thanking Pauline for her prayers—feeling they were a help in making for a successful trip. His letters most certainly gave great joy to Pauline in her late years. This one was written in 1931:

We were inseparable, traveling, eating and living and serving together, sometimes sleeping in the same room and even the same bed, the meetings making a deep impression phenomenally as well as spiritually. Our being together in the south seemed to be accepted in the south without a single incident to mar complete harmony. Bus drivers, policemen, bell boys, restaurant keepers were always courteous as well as college presidents and professors and other people of rank. In Atlanta, a clergyman requested that a Baha'i study class be started in his church, which will be done. During our stay of three days at Tuskegee, seven meetings were addressed and the Principal gave his regular Sunday evening time to talk to an audience of 1800. The son and daughter-in-law of the late Booker Washington announced their allegiance to the Cause and Prof. George W. Carver, the great scientist, says that Baha'i is the only way to unite humanity. His is the embodiment of science and spirituality.

We are protected from all dangers in what seemed a most extraordinary way. Doing what our beloved Guardian wanted seems in itself the greatest protection. Is not this the law? [23]

A letter dated July 1933, written on behalf of Shoghi Effendi, congratulating the community of Cabin John Park, Maryland for forming their first Local Spiritual Assembly, must have brought with it a great deal of joy and sense of accomplishment. This kind of news was always received with great enthusiasm by the Guardian, which in turn greatly pleased the sisters.

(In his own hand)
Dear co-workers: I was so pleased and gratified to hear from you—the news you gave me filled my heart with thankfulness and joy. May the Almighty protect and sustain you, guide you in your activities and enable you to render the Faith notable and memorable service. Your true Brother, Shoghi[24]

Pauline had also become intensely interested in the Temple Fund. Perhaps because her son Carl was working at the Temple, and the family was volunteering their service in numerous ways, she had a greater understanding of the monetary assistance needed to complete the project. In one letter, she admits to Alma that Fanny would think she was daffy for the Temple fund, considering the financial needs of the family. She wrote to Alma in 1933:

Mr. Earley said that all but 30 pieces of the dome are done. . . . In fact he says that the whole thing has been accomplished to this point passing reason, reason would have said and did say, IMPOSSIBLE! IT CAN'T BE DONE. It is an utter impossibility and represents superhuman activity. He said it was the most remarkable thing how everybody from the

> smallest workman on the place to the skilled laborers became more and more obsessed with the beauty and the spirit of the thing to such a degree that time meant nothing. They labored night and day and almost sweat blood to carry out the desire of the Guardian. Earley is a Catholic, as you know, and still is, but declares that the power that went with the word of Shoghi Effendi and the spirit of the architect have almost made the impossible a possibility.[25]

Pauline, now in her early sixties, wrote to Fanny in the winter of 1934. From this letter we learn she is working at the *Bahá'í Magazine* office in D.C., but commuting to the city as she is living in a cabin in the countryside of Cabin John Park. She shares her feelings about a rather new approach to teaching that Paul had suggested: "having, say once a month, an open meeting, social in a way, to get people to come in & have an exchange of ideas, they may hear enough of the Bahá'í Teachings. On some of the phases expressed, that perhaps would incline them to consider further, etc." With the Faith spreading beyond the bigger cities, the Bahá'ís were looking for interesting ways to share the message with as many people as possible. The world had gone through a terrible war, and perhaps the times were changing and the topic of religion was becoming less enticing. This type of meeting Paul Hannen was suggesting became a more common method of teaching for many years.

She also mentions the passing of Mrs. Agnes Parsons. She was struck by an automobile and died several days later from complications caused by the accident. No doubt her sudden passing was felt by the whole family, not only because of their close personal relationship, but also given the important role she played in the D.C. community and the Bahá'í community at large.

The financial situation in the United States during the 1930s was precarious at best, and for the Bahá'í community, there were many discussions and consultations regarding how to sustain the teachers in the field who were in need of monetary assistance. There were those who longed to spend every minute teaching the Faith and who were very good at it; Alma and Fanny being among them. If the funds were available, they would have offered this service full-time for the rest of their lives. Alas, that was not possible, and eventually the National Teaching Committee had to make the difficult decision to use their limited resources for other kinds of projects; foremost among them being the completion of the House of Worship in Wilmette and the development of Bahá'í schools. The below letter from the National Teaching Committee to Alma reflects these hard realities. It reads:

> Dear Bahá'í sister: It was a real inspiration to the entire Convention, to hear from you and your good sister, those inspiring details of the Teaching work you have been engaged in for so long a time. Your work in

> Florida has surely been confirmed by the Master and I am sure will yield fruit . . . I presume you heard the reports of the National treasurer at the Convention, which indicates we are about $11,000 in debt now, and must raise $60,000 within the next ten months, if we are to fulfill our obligation. . . . therefore we are not in a position to assist those like your good self who should be raising the Call . . . I have always found that under such situations, the Master guides us in the pathway of true service for that particular time. I am sure He will guide you! . . .
> With deep Bahá'í love, I am Leroy Ioas[26]

Although this news may have been disappointing on one level, it certainly did not stop the sisters from continuing to teach wherever and whenever they were asked. If a community requested assistance from the sisters, that community would also find them accommodation and help with their immediate needs. Because so many of the letters written between the sisters are undated, it is difficult to discern exactly when they traveled to the locations mentioned in the letters. For the purposes of this book it is sufficient to say that every opportunity to teach was taken when at all possible. It would take another whole book to include all of the letters and details that sang the sisters' praises.

- 30 -

The Final Goodbyes

In 1936, or thereabouts, as Alma left Cabin John, Pauline's letters were filled with the struggles of caring for Fanny and other local Bahá'í friends, as well as her newest grandchild Priscilla. A letter written in 1936 hinted at Pauline's awareness that her teaching days might be coming to an end and that poor health was becoming more of an obstacle for her. In a letter to Alma, Pauline writes rather nostalgically: "Alma dear I stood just outside the bus and saw the top of your head, and once when you placed your smaller articles on the rack, but you never looked out even when the bus left. Had you forgotten me so quickly? No! Because you have written several times. Such a busy life compared to Cabin John or any other place for that matter. Thank God! For that is the Real Life, Teaching."[1]

Pauline, although the youngest of the three sisters, was succumbing at a more rapid pace to the difficulties of aging. She was now sixty-four years old, a breast cancer survivor, and a diabetic. By 1938, Pauline moved to Wilmette to live with Carl and Mineola as she needed more care and assistance, which Mineola was willing and able to give. At times Fanny stayed with them as well. Every letter she wrote to Alma, who was tirelessly serving the Faith in Florida, shares how each family member was passing the time, how Pauline was in need of care, and how she herself longed to be out teaching. In one such letter to Alma, Fanny says:

> All of our Mother's Tablets instruct us to be Happy—I know You are, Pauline is most of the time—so Fanny must catch up, or at least try to catch up with them—a feeling of unrest has seized me, as of a change in my life—possibly it is merely due to feeling "not wanted" in active service of the Cause—home duties, the constant attendance on Pauline, house bound as it were—have created a yearning to do more than that—however what ever may come it will be right—for my earnest supplication for

> us Sisters is Thy Will be done, O Lord. As guides in the Temple, one feels the unrest due to world conditions.[2]

The letters of their later years discuss their numerous activities. Fanny details the committee meetings Carl and Mineola were involved with, and all the activities the young people, (my father, aunt, and uncle) participated in. Often Carl or Fanny gave talks at the Temple. Other letters told of study classes they attended, emphasizing that these classes were the best way to teach because of the bonds of friendship they created. There is not room to include all the many activities they took part in, but suffice it to say, the three sisters, to the very end of their earthly lives, had no thought but that of service to their Lord.

However, in addition to the many victories they won, there was also hardship. One letter details an episode when Pauline suffered from a stroke while another recounts her cataract surgery at a time when it took weeks of keeping one's eyes covered before knowing if the surgery was successful.[3] No doubt it was a trying time for everyone in the family. Several letters mention that the constant care Pauline required was causing great strain on everyone, and describe how the family set up a double bed for her use so that someone could sleep near her in the event she needed help during the night. Concern for the hardship that their presence posed for Carl and Mineola weighed heavily on Fanny, and she shared feelings of her guilt over eating food that could have been given to the growing boys. The letters are filled with praise for Carl, Mineola, and their children for all the effort and loving care they gave to their dearly loved grandmother during those difficult years. She somewhat apologetically mentions, "Pauline may rally and live on—struggle on indefinitely, and she may be set free—to join and share the extraordinary glorious Station of Joseph—don't think me hard hearted Alma—but I hope Abdul-Baha will free her pure spirit."[4] Each of the letters from this period mention how Mineola, Carl, and the boys carried the burden and joy of caring for each of the sisters as they moved toward their final journeys.

As they struggled, each opportunity to teach the Faith was admired and praised by the others in letters that passed between them. They are full of news of the continuous services each was rendering. This letter Pauline wrote to Alma conveys her feelings so well:

> Dearest and dearly beloved Alma,
>
> Another and seemingly confirmed year has passed and unquestionably a very blessed year in which you have been enabled to serve your Lord. May you be granted the privilege of being one of those who will be carried through the terrible days of God and be among those to be the servants of Baha'o'llah when the New World order is to be established. The Guardian gives very great importance to those souls who come through triumphantly.

> Oh Alma if anyone has that courage, you have. God's Will be done and we are content. You have always been a wonderful spiritual power in my estimation. I thank God from the bottom of my heart that I was born into such a family of spiritual dynamos, all of them and to be chosen by such a powerful servant of Abdul-Baha as Joseph.
>
> Alma, I do pray that you may reach the very highest attainment possible for humans. And believe me when I say that I am your humble servant and affectionate Schnuddle.[5]

Even though Pauline was weak and very ill, she had good days and bad. On one of those good days she suddenly decided she was up to the long trip back to Cabin John—her home—to live near her son Paul and his family. She also longed to spend some of her remaining time with the newest granddaughter Priscilla who was just a few years old. By that time, she also felt Carl and Mineola needed a break from the constant care she required.

Once in Cabin John, she seemed to improve for a short time, and several letters detail her activities. But finally, on 4 October 1939, Pauline's earthy life came to a close. She passed away peacefully while she slept. As Louis Gregory wrote in her memorial for *Bahá'í World:*

> . . . although sudden, not so tragic, as that of her distinguished husband many years ago. The grief of those who loved her, at this inevitable separation, is in a measure assuaged by thoughts of the joyous reunion of these two souls, in the realm of Light, "Under the shadow of the Favor of their Lord." In a Tablet written them jointly by Abdul-Baha just a short time previous to the accident which deprived Brother Joseph of mortal life, He said to them, prophetically, "Your future is very brilliant."[6]

As we now know from the letters that make mention of her discomfort during the last several years of her life, it is not unusual that her friends perhaps did not know how close the end was for her. Louis also shared in the memorial that, though she was in pain for several years, she did not complain. His words are a fitting tribute to her life, "How healing to the sick; how consoling to the distressed; how enlightening to the children and to those of mature years; how harmonizing an influence; how self-sacrificing; how ceaselessly active!"[7] The National Assembly in their condolences to the family spoke of "the great loss sustained by the Cause in the passing of Mrs. Pauline A. Hannen."[8] Finally, this message from Haifa dated 5 November 1939 on behalf of Shoghi Effendi, must have brought some measure of joy to the family at this sad time:

> Dear Miss Knobloch,
>
> Your kind & moving message to the Guardian dated Oct. 14th had reached

him, & he feels indeed unutterably grieved to know of the sad news of the passing away of your dearly beloved sister, Mrs. Pauline Hannen. He cannot but profoundly deplore her departure at such a time when the teaching force in America has just come to sustain such a grievous blow as the passing of our beloved Martha Root. This is truly an added loss to the Cause in America and will keenly be felt by all the friends, particularly those teachers who by virtue of their close collaboration with dear Mrs. Hannen had come to profoundly admire her teaching qualities, her devotion & other self-consecration to the Faith. The teaching services she has so indefatigable [sic] rendered in the Southern States constitutes, in particular such record of high achievement as cannot but evoke feelings of deepest admiration in all hearts & spur her dear co-workers in these regions to follow up with fuller determination & vigour than ever the great teaching task to which she has so nobly consecrated her entire life & energies.

The Guardian feels moved to convey to you, to your dear sister Fanny as well as the Hannens' two sons Carl & Paul, the brotherly sympathy in your most sad bereavement. He too will pray to God that He may richly bless the soul of your departed sister & also bestow abiding comfort upon your grief stricken hearts.

Renewing to you again his very warm and affectionate greetings.

Yours in His Service, H. Rabbani

[added in his own hand]

Dear and valued Co-worker:

My heart overflows with deep and loving sympathy in the severe loss you have suffered, the Cause your sister served so lovingly suffered too by her passing, but her reward in the world beyond is immense and undoubted. The memory of her past services will never perish. The spirit that so powerfully impelled her to serve so long and so devotedly will continue to inspire those who will labour after her to follow her example & to extend the work she so zealously performed. I will specially and fervently pray for her departed soul.

Your true and grateful brother, Shoghi[9]

Pauline's body was laid to rest in Prospect Hills Cemetery in Washington D.C. alongside her beloved mother Amalie Knobloch and husband Joseph, just a short distance from the home in which she lived when she first heard of the Bahá'í Faith thirty-seven years earlier.

After Pauline's death, Alma moved back to Cabin John and continued Pauline's work. In her will, Pauline left all of her possessions, including the home in Cabin John, to her sisters; a sign of her concern for their welfare after her absence. Alma wrote of her return and her feelings about Pauline's passing;

> Pauline's passing is like a dream; [I] feel as though she will return from a trip and must have everything ready for her. Leona did her part beautifully—pure silk that folded richly and she looked handsome. Everyone spoke of the spiritual services and how beautiful everything was conducted. The flowers were beautiful . . . Pauline's things are all just where they were—I feel as though on a visit—still live out of my satchels—have one drawer. This is a strange world. Fondest love and best wishes to one and all. Please return love and greetings to Mrs. and Mr. Haggard and all the dear friends especially Mrs. True. Lovingly, Aunt Alma[10]

The family received letters from all the many friends the sisters had made on their extensive teaching trips. For the next few years Alma remained an active part of the Cabin John Assembly. Even as late as November of 1943 she wrote a letter to the National Teaching Committee detailing the activities in Cabin John and the surrounding area. No doubt she was a dynamic part of those activities right up to the end.

On 22 December 1943, Alma joined her beloved sister Pauline in the Abhá Kingdom. There are many letters of condolence from all parts of the world, extolling the wonderful qualities and services of dear Alma. A letter from Horace Holly, Secretary of the National Assembly, expressed the grief that was felt throughout the country at her passing.[11] Daisy Moore, a believer from South Carolina, wrote of Alma joining the ranks of several other dear souls in the Abhá Kingdom and how they would join forces to help the teaching work of those left on this plane.[12] A letter from the Augusta, Georgia LSA recalled the services and contributions Alma made to the growth of their community. Another touching letter came from George Latimer, addressed to Fanny, reminding her of the time they spent together in Dublin, New Hampshire, with 'Abdu'l-Bahá. He wrote:

> It was a grievous shock to me to see the notice in the last Bahá'í News of the passing of our beloved Miss Alma and I want to express to you my heartfelt sympathy at this loss of one of our great pioneer teachers.
>
> How often do I recall the happy hours we spent together in Germany and I feel that the Master linked our families together, first in Dublin, New Hampshire and later in Haifa, when He spoke so lovingly of her work in Stuttgart. I read from my note-book many times and often tell friends how the Master compared her physical stature to the greatness of her spiritual being.
>
> It is strange, the mysteries of the spirit world, but it seems that always when a new era in the progress of the Faith opens up, a number of the old faithful souls are called. I lost my father very suddenly in September, and although he was in his 85th year and due for her [sic] eternal reward, yet

he was actively serving as Secretary of our Assembly. Then dear mother Revell was called and now Miss Alma. I am sure that their noble spirits will reinforce from the Supreme Concourse in the active days that lie just ahead during this eventful centennial year.

Rest assured in her eternal bounties and know that we will offer up our prayers for her.

With loving thoughts and prayers for you, the last of three faithful sisters, I am,

Sincerely yours,

George Latimer[13]

Alma's body was buried alongside that of her sister in the family plot in Prospect Hills Cemetery, Washington D.C.

Around the same time as Alma's passing, Fanny fell and broke her neck and was moved to the Evanston Hospital, very near to the House of Worship. When she was released from the hospital Fanny made her home once again in Wilmette with Carl's family. As the end of her life on this plane drew nearer and nearer, Fanny began to have more difficulty with her eyesight in addition to other infirmities that come with aging. In November of 1940, she received this loving letter from Rúhíyyih Khánum, the wife of Shoghi Effendi, and the daughter of her dear friend May Maxwell. She wrote:

Dearest Fanny Knobloch,

Mother always had the greatest love and admiration for you and so often spoke of you to me. I am sure souls like you & mother & other "old timers" who have given every moment of their time to the service of the Cause will be together eternally!

It is for the younger ones to try to show the same spirit of dedication to the Beloved so that we too may be with you all.

I am very sorry to hear that your eyes are failing. But as long as you have a tongue you will be teaching! & You know the Teachings already so well that I am sure you don't need to read very much. Of course the beloved Guardian is always sending some new thoughts to America. But you have loads of people to save your eyes by reading to you.

I am so glad you wrote to me dear friend, & I shall offer my humble prayers for you when I go to the Holy Shrines.

Lovingly in His Path,

Rúhíyyih[14]

Finally, the point came when Fanny needed more care. The boys, having joined the Navy, had left to serve their tour of duty during World War II. My father Sohayl recalls it was a very difficult time for the whole family during the war years. When the war ended and the boys returned—Joseph with a wife and daughter, and Sohayl soon to marry and move out on his own—it became clear that the level of care Fanny needed as she approached her final years was beyond the abilities of Carl and Mineola to manage on their own. Her desire to join her sisters and other loved ones in the spirit world was evident as she often cried out in anguish for God to release her from this mortal life. The family made the difficult decision to move Fanny to a nursing home, not far from the new home Carl had built in Glenview, IL. She spent the remaining years of her life there.

Viola Ioas Tuttle wrote a wonderful tribute to Fanny for the memoriam section of the *Bahá'í World*. I will use her words to recount Fanny's last days in this physical world:

> When I visited her at the nursing home on her eighty-ninth birthday, she said, among other things, "if you thanked God on your knees every remaining hour of your life, you could never thank Him enough for having allowed you to live at this time." And again, "Now when the pain in my back becomes severe, I say it is only for a little while, and then I shall leave this body and see our Lord face to face. So will you and all your family, and all these early believers. It is wonderful, isn't it?"
>
> She held my hand tightly, and did not know that I was writing down with my right hand what she said, for her sight was almost gone.
>
> Her release came on December 9, 1949. A little less than ninety years old at the time of her passing, she was the first born of the three illustrious Knobloch sisters, Fanny, Alma and Pauline; and the last to pass away.
>
> Funeral services were held in Washington, D.C. Her body was interred beside her sisters, as well as Pauline's husband, Joseph Hannen, and their beloved mother Amalie Knobloch. It was upon the death of her mother . . . that 'Abdu'l-Bahá had written, "Happy are those who visit the luminous resting place, and through thy commemoration receive and acquire spiritual powers."[15]

On 14 December 1949, a cablegram was received through Horace Holly from Shoghi Effendi. It read, "GRIEVE PASSING BELOVED, DISTINGUISHED, EXEMPLARY PIONEER FAITH, FANNY KNOBLOCH. MEMORY HER NOTABLE SERVICES IMPERISHABLE, HER REWARD ABHA KINGDOM BOUNTIFUL, ASSURED EVERLASTING."[16] I will end this journey with these wonderfully precious words of our beloved Guardian Shoghi Effendi, written in 1929—which, though addressed to Alma—make mention of her dearly loved sisters, Fanny and Pauline, as well. It is a beautiful tribute to their glorious lives of service.

> *My dear and precious co-worker:*
> *Your past and present services are imprinted on my heart, and I cherish the strongest hope for still greater services in the days to come. The name of your-*

self and your two dear sisters will ever live in the annals of the Cause and you have all three proved yourselves worthy servants of a gracious and loving master. I will continue to pray for you all from the very depths of my heart.
Shoghi[17]

In January of that same year, 1949, I was born. My father Sohayl married Frances Ogle in 1946, whom he had known since childhood as his little sister Barbara's best friend. After their marriage, she soon became a Bahá'í and then gave birth to my brother James Carl Hannen in 1948, me in 1949, Linda Marie (Hawkins) in 1950, William Robert, "Bob," in 1952, and in 1960 Peter Joseph, all of whom are Bahá'ís, actively engaged in their communities. Although my parents have passed on to the Abhá Kingdom since I embarked upon this project, at the time of this writing they have sixteen grandchildren, many of whom are Bahá'ís, and fourteen great-grandchildren, with more on the way. They were both very happy at the end of their lives, and expressed their joy at knowing someone was writing about the Hannens' and Knoblochs' and Barnitzes' contributions to the Faith of Bahá'u'lláh. I shall be forever grateful to have descended from a family of "spiritual dynamos," as Pauline sometimes called her sisters, mother, and husband, and to have these giants of service to emulate to the best of my humble ability. I am also very grateful to my grandparents Carl and Mineola, my parents Sohayl and Frances, and my Aunt Barbara and Uncle Joe, for setting such fine examples for all of us for generations to come.

I add these two additions at the end as a tribute to the foundation of love found in this wonderful family.

Joseph's poem:
Mrs. Pauline Hannen
(Heart promptu Poem)
I do not speak imagined praise
In superstition's stilted phrase;
But from the heart into the look
And read a letter of the living Book.

You're sweet and gentle, meek and mild,
Possessed of the spirit of a child—
The spirit which into Heaven takes,
The spirit which a Heaven makes.

On this self-smitten earth you stand,
Extending e're the helping hand
To kith and kindred, friends and foe,
Doing the Deeds that love doth show.

Your queenly qualities I'll not compute,
Selecting, though, your sweetest attribute.
I call you "Lamp of Love,
That smiles as a star above.

Fixed in the firmament on high,
Lifted to lofty station by
The might of meekness, O Bahá'í True!
This testimony I bear of you.
J. H. Hannen[18]

Fanny to Pauline:

Allaho Abha Jan. 27, 1922

My priceless little Motherly Sister,

How little you realize your wonderful inspiring ability!

But for your loving persistent effort, neither Joey, Mamma, Mother, Alma, Mr. Gregory or I would have entered the Cause of God.

It was your heart afire with the love of service that sent Alma out into the vineyard of the Lord. It was you and you alone who enkindled and fanned into a blaze the wee small ability within me into a service which enriched me with the love and commendation of our Lord.

Pauline, if there were any way in which I could prove this—gladly, I'd give my life, gladly do more than that—go out and teach, go anywhere—and take my chances at earning my living, no matter how good or how meager it might be—I am ready because of my unshakable confidence in you, to stake my all—and follow your directions. At this particular time there is such a crying need of money among us, I need various articles of clothing, all easy enough for some Bahá'ís, but we can only get these necessities little by little and precious heart of my heart, how can I justify myself to Dona, in accepting your all?

Yes, some pretty deep thinking has been and is being done—the uncertainty is within myself. I suffered so much because of my delay in getting passage. Now I see how blessed was that delay. I was with you dear during the greatest blow received in your life time—and I thank God for having made that possible. . . .

With my heart's deepest love and affection.

Devotedly, Your Dona[19]

Epilogue

In the days when the Faith was very young in America, it was not always an easy choice to become a Bahá'í because it meant you were different than most of your peers. My family had the benefit of growing up near the House of Worship and the National Center of the Faith in America. That meant there were a number of other Bahá'ís in the greater Chicago area who became our peers and friends. My siblings and I had a Bahá'í Sunday school to attend, youth conferences to go to, and during our sensitive teenage years, a youth group to be involved with. We spent almost every Sunday at the House of Worship with our Bahá'í friends.

My father, Sohayl, recalls growing up in Wilmette in the 1930s as some of his most difficult years. There were very few Bahá'ís his age, although growing up near the Temple did mean that there were some other Bahá'í youth. They were active in their circle of Bahá'í friends, and even tried their hand at giving Bahá'í talks when encouraged. He and his brother Joe also attended Louhelen Bahá'í school several summers (then known as Davison Bahá'í summer school) in Davison, Michigan, and made lasting friendships there. Being close to the Temple and other Bahá'í youth no doubt helped him through those years.

In 1949 Carl and Mineola moved to Glenview, IL—just a fifteen-minute drive from the Temple. My brother Jim and I were already part of the family when we moved in with them. My sister Linda was born there. We moved into our own co-op apartment in nearby Skokie in 1952, where my brother Bob (William Robert) was born. We attended feasts and all manner of events and activities at my grandparents' home. That home is full of memories for me.

Around 1957, Sohayl's growing family moved to the first single home of their own in Northfield Township. It was in this home that my youngest brother Peter was born in 1960. While we lived and were active in the small Bahá'í community of Northfield Township, my grandparents continued their Bahá'í activities in Glenview, and their home was always a center of activity for that community.

In 1967 Carl and Mineola left Glenview to spend the rest of their lives in the warmer climate of Florida. They had been living in the same home they built in 1949. They sold the house to my parents, and our family moved in before I left for college. Thus, the house remained a Bahá'í house, where Soey and Fran Hannen continued to live out their days holding countless Bahá'í functions.

When Carl and Mineola moved to Orlando, they again helped form, and serve on, the first Local Spiritual Assembly. They were very engaged in the Bahá'í community there for as long as they were physically able.

Carl and Mineola celebrated their fiftieth wedding anniversary in 1968 in Orlando. It was the only time my whole family went together to see them in Florida. Many Bahá'ís from the area attended the event to honor this special union. Certainly 'Abdu'l-Bahá's prediction had been true, that this union would last for eternity. They were loving to each other to the end.

When Carl passed away in 1972, their daughter Barbara and granddaughter Susan, who had also been living in Orlando since 1968, moved in with Mineola to help care for her. Their daughter Barb is quoted in his memorial as saying that her father's great happiness was in deepening the knowledge of the believers: "This was Dad's life. He was always so proud when those to whom he had spoken and helped with understanding the Teachings would then become active pioneers in other communities."[1] A memorial article in Volume XV of *The Bahá'í World,* begins with this message from the National Spiritual Assembly of the United States:

> THE MEMBERS OF THE NATIONAL SPIRITUAL ASSEMBLY ARE GRIEVED TO LEARN OF THE PASSING OF CARL. HIS LONG AND MANY SERVICES TO BAHÁ'U'LLÁH WILL LONG BE REMEMBERED BY HIS NUMEROUS GRATEFUL FELLOW BAHÁ'ÍS AROUND THE WORLD. WE ASSURE YOU OF OUR PRAYERS FOR PROGRESS OF HIS SOUL IN ABHA KINGDOM AND FOR COMFORT TO YOU AND YOUR FAMILY IN YOUR GREAT SORROW. HAVE CABLED WORLD CENTER FOR PRAYERS AT HOLY SHRINES.
>
> *National Spiritual Assembly of the Bahá'ís of the United States*

The article ends with a message from the Universal House of Justice, which honors Carl with this statement:

> GRIEVED LEARN PASSING CARL HANNEN HIS STEADFAST DEVOTION CAUSE SINCE DAYS MASTER LONG PERIOD DEDICATED SERVICE HOUSE WORSHIP WARMLY REMEMBERED CONVEY FAMILY ASSURANCE PRAYERS PROGRESS HIS SOUL ABHA KINGDOM.[2]

The last years of Mineola's life were spent in a nursing home. She passed to the Abhá Kingdom on 17 November 1993 at the age of 102, and was interred next to Carl in the Highland Memory Gardens Cemetery in Orlando, Florida.

They are among the last of a generation so personally touched by the physical and spiritual presence of 'Abdu'l-Bahá in their midst. They dedicated every aspect of their lives in service to Him and the Cause of His Father, Bahá'u'lláh.

In the year 2000, my husband Bruce and I were living in Rockford, Illinois, when we decided to take a trip to Washington D.C. As soon as my family heard that I was planning this trip, I suddenly got calls from family members telling me I must visit the gravesite of Pauline, Joseph, and all the Knobloch family. Apparently, the family had wanted to put a grave marker on the grave for some time, but the opportunity to attend to the matter had not yet presented itself.

I agreed to make an appointment with the caretaker and I promised to visit the gravesite when I arrived in Washington. We learned from the caretaker there that over the years, the site became a victim of neglect and abuse. He took on, as a labor of love, a gradual cleanup and restoration of the cemetery to a respectable state. However, money was not available to completely restore all the headstones.

He showed us the spots where Joseph, Pauline, and several Knoblochs were buried. It was disappointing that no physical marker indicated who lay below us, only grass. While we were preparing for our trip, the Washington Bahá'ís told us there was a Tablet revealed for Amalie that they had decided to read at her grave when planning outreach activities in their neighborhood. However, when the friends did try to go to the site, they had difficulty finding the correct spot. I felt strongly that this situation needed to be remedied. The following letter from Mr. Walter R. Wootten of Raleigh, North Carolina, written 6 November 1972, to Carl Hannen was found among the Hannen family papers, and illustrates the issue quite well.

> Dear Mr. Hannen,
> I thought I would write you and let you know that carloads of Bahá'ís from North Carolina have been making pilgrimages to the luminous resting place of your kingly and noble father, Joseph Hannen, and the illustrious Knobloch sisters and their saintly mother, Amalie, at Prospect Hill Cemetery, Washington D.C. We attribute the success of our teaching endeavors to the "spiritual powers" promised whoever visits their "luminous resting place." Moreover, we are quite puzzled and saddened by the fact that the most lordly spiritual nobility of the Southern States are bereft of a fitting grave marker, marking their resting place.
>
> It may take some time, however, yet those of us who are laboring to rear the administrative institutions of our Holy Faith here in the South have not, and will not forget the tireless labors of your father and the Knobloch family at home and abroad, and wish to place a temporary grave marker at their resting place as a preliminary to a more fitting one

in the fullness of time to be a turning point of pilgrimage in the Atlantic Seaboard similar to Thornton Chase's grave site in Los Angeles.

Our loving prayers and best wishes to you, Carl, and to your dear wife, Mineola.

Alláh-u-Abhá
Walter R. Wootten[3]

The rough draft of a response was found in the same envelope, which thanked the Raleigh Bahá'ís for their thoughts and let them know that Carl had passed away the previous year. Mineola had been entertaining such thoughts about the headstone as well and would contact people to see what could be done. However, no further steps had been taken as Mineola was aging and unable to follow up on the matter. Therefore, as no one had yet taken on the job, my family's urgency about visiting the site was understandable.

During the following year, I contacted all the relatives I could find, including several who were not Bahá'ís, but were understanding of the significance of their ancestors' relationship to Bahá'í history. Many of them were willing to make contributions to purchase a headstone to mark the grave—nothing grandiose, but rather an upright headstone naming all the souls who were laid to rest in the group of adjoining graves. The names of the Knoblochs were engraved on one side and the Hannens were on the other. The names included two babies, and other family members as well, who were laid to rest in the same group of graves.

In the summer of 2001, with the help of the Washington D.C. Local Spiritual Assembly, we organized a family reunion and dedication ceremony at the gravesite. In attendance, along with many Washington friends, were four grandchildren of Joseph and Pauline, nine great-grandchildren, four great-great-grandchildren, as well as several spouses. The Assembly hosted a lunch and a wonderful reception for the family and friends at the Bahá'í center. The occasion was an especially happy one for many of us because the younger generation, including myself, had never met most of our relatives who lived scattered across the country. It was a truly moving reunion for all.

In 2010, my mother, Fran Hannen at the age of eighty-five, passed on to the Abhá Kingdom. My father, Sohayl, died the following year (2011) in the home he helped to build. My uncle Joe passed a few years later in February of 2014 in Ocala, Florida. Paul's daughters, Nancy McCullough and Eleanor Raley, also passed away while I was working on this book, and Barbara Griffin passed in November of 2016, leaving Priscilla Kleinman as the last living grandchild of Pauline and Joseph.

It is my great hope and desire that in reading about these spiritual dynamos, their descendants will become as inspired as I have while writing this book.

Endnotes

Abbreviations found in endnotes:

HKFP—Hannen Knobloch Family Papers
NBA—National Bahá'í Archives in Wilmette, IL
HKC—Hannen Knobloch Collection
BAWDC—Bahá'í Archives of Washington D.C.
TABC—Translations of Tablets of 'Abdu'l-Bahá Collection, at the National Bahá'í Archives

All of the Tablets to family members can also be found in the Hannen family archives, originals of which were sent to the World Center during the time of Shoghi Effendi.

Chapter 1—Setting the Stage

1. Hushidar Motlagh, Ed., *I Shall Come Again*, p. 201.
2. Peter Smith, *A Concise Encyclopedia of the Bahá'í Faith,* pp. 22–23.
3. Robert H. Stockman, *The Bahá'í Faith in America: Early Expansion, 1900–1912,* Vol. 2, pp. 80–87.
4. Abu'l-Faḍl was greatly blessed to have 'Abdu'l-Bahá name one of the doors of the Shrine of the Báb in his honor. In addition, he was immensely honored to have the title Apostle of Bahá'u'lláh bestowed on him by Shoghi Effendi.
5. Robert H. Stockman, *The Bahá'í Faith in America: Early Expansion, 1900–1912,* Vol. 2, p. 80.
6. Anita Chapman, "History of Washington, D.C. Bahá'í Community 2005–2008," http://dcbahai.org. This is a website for the History of the Washington, D.C. Bahá'í Community.
7. Robert H. Stockman, *The Bahá'í Faith in America: Early Expansion, 1900–1912,* Vol. 2, pp. 135–37.

Chapter 2—A Family Awakens

1. A photograph was found among the personal items of Barbara Griffin (Mineola Barnitz Hannen's daughter) and the handwriting was identified by her as that of Mineola Hannen. Ms. Griffin also shared that Mineola always referred to her own mother as "Mamma." On the other side is a photograph of a Sunday school class where she identifies a "Grandma Phelps." There are references to the Frank Phelps family as early Bahá'ís in Washington D.C., but they are not related to the Hannens or Barnitzes. From the Hannen Family Archives.
2. 'Abdu'l-Bahá, *Tablets of 'Abdu'l-Bahá Abbas* Vol. 1, letter to Mrs. Leona Barnitz, p. 180. The copies used of *Tablets of 'Abdu'l-Bahá Abbas* are early copies included in the Hannen Family Archives at Judy Moe's home, which have handwritten names of recipients of each copy next to each Tablet.
3. Barbara Griffin, conversations with author over several years. (Barbara is the granddaughter of Pauline and Joseph Hannen, and Richard and Leona Barnitz, and daughter of Carl and Mineola Hannen. She lived in Ocala, FL, and passed away in November 2016.)
4. Marzieh Gail, *Summon up Remembrance,* pp. 180–82.
5. Joseph Hannen, letter to Ahmad Sohrab, 29 May 1909, Ahmad Sohrab Papers, NBA.
6. Pauline Hannen, letter to Ahmad Sohrab, May 1909, Ahmad Sohrab Papers, NBA.
7. Robert H. Stockman, *The Bahá'í Faith in America: Early Expansion, 1900–1912,* Vol. 2, p. 137.
8. Fanny Knobloch with assistance of Georgie Brown Wiles. "Fanny Alvine Stories," chapters 3–4, unpublished manuscript edited by Judy Moe. HKFP, NBA.
9. Website for German-American Heritage Society of Greater Washington, D.C. "German-American Tour of Washington, D.C."
10. Hannen Family Archives—Kept in Judy Hannen Moe's home, Rockford, IL, at time of publication. Records from Prospect Hills Cemetery, Washington D.C., were used as well as family records passed down to author.
11. Fanny Knobloch with assistance of Georgie Brown Wiles, "Fanny Alvine Stories," chapters 3–4, unpublished manuscript edited by Judy Moe, HKFP, NBA.
12. Records from Prospect Hills Cemetery show a gravesite for a baby, Gladys Hannen, buried in the family plot. Barbara Hannen Griffin also confirmed that Carl had a baby sister who died.
13. This information was given to the author by Lex Musta, a Bahá'í historian who lives in Washington, D.C. and has studied the Bahá'í history of that area for several years.

14. Pauline Hannen, personal recollections, "Adult Classes," HKC, BAWDC.
15. Alma Knobloch, personal recollections, "How I Became a Bahá'í," HKC, BAWDC.
16. Ibid., "Experiences with 'Abdu'l-Bahá," HKFP, NBA and HKC, BAWDC.
17. 'Abdu'l-Bahá, *Tablets of 'Abdu'l-Bahá Vol. II*, letter to Alma Knobloch, pp. 243–44.
18. Joseph Hannen to Ahmad Sohrab, 29 May 1909, NBA.
19. Alma Knobloch, personal recollections, starts "Pastor Mentzel . . ." HKC, BAWDC.
20. Fanny Knobloch, untitled manuscript of memoirs, "Chapter I," HKFP, NBA. The quote in this section about Manifestations is the authorized version in the 2014 edition of *Some Answered Questions*. Her paper quoted page 115 of the earlier version.
21. Marjory Brown (Neddin). This unpublished manuscript, which is the story of her Grandfather Richard Barnitz's life, was written sometime during her school years, and can be found in the Hannen Family Archives.
22. Pauline Hannen, letter to Ahmad Sohrab, May 1909, "Becoming a Bahá'í," NBA.
23. Alma Knobloch, personal recollections, "An experience in the early part of my life," HKC, BAWDC.

Chapter 3—Joseph's Early Story

1. This information originated from several letters of various relatives of Joseph's mother and father, handed down to family members. They are currently in the Hannen Family Archives.
2. Frank Hannen, letter to Ella Anthony, 22 May 1881, HKFP, NBA
3. Ibid., letter to Mr. and Mrs. Jos Anthony (Mary's mother and father), 7 May 1882, HKFP, NBA.
4. Eleanor Hannen Rally—granddaughter of Pauline and Joseph Hannen—personal recollections obtained by phone call from author (2009). She died later that same year.
5. Joseph Hannen, unpublished manuscript titled "Diary," (only entry), HKFP, NBA.
6. Ibid., letter to Max, 7 December 1891, HKFP, NBA.
7. Ibid., letter to Pauline Hannen, 9 August 1894, HKFP, NBA.
8. Ibid.
9. Joseph Hannen, letter to Pauline Hannen, 7 August 1897, HKFP, NBA.
10. *The Viavi Cause*, p. 5. From a page of a newsletter that was found in the Hannen Family Archives with an obituary of Joseph Hannen.
11. "The virtual Dime museum: The Viavi Treatment." Accessed at http://www.thevirtualdimemuseum.com/2008/05/viavi-treatment.html

Chapter 4—Guidance Pours Forth

1. The National Bahá'í Archives currently has thirty-two file boxes of correspondence by Joseph and Pauline Hannen, Fanny and Alma Knobloch, and various other family members. The Washington, D.C. Bahá'í Archives has eight file boxes of letters and notes, etc.
2. Robert H. Stockman, *The Bahá'í Faith in America: Early Expansion, 1900–1912,* Vol. 2, p. 78.
3. 'Abdu'l-Bahá, Tablet to Pauline Hannen, 29 May 1903, TABC, NBA.
4. Sandra Hutchison, *'Abdu'l-Bahá in America: Agnes Parsons' Diary,* (foreword), p. viii.
5. Robert H. Stockman, *The Bahá'í Faith in America: Early Expansion, 1900–1912,* Vol. 2, p. 220.
6. According to Peter Smith's *A Concise Encyclopedia of the Bahá'í Faith,* "Ahmad Sohrab and Julie Chanler established the New History Society in New York City to propagate the Bahá'í teachings. When he refused to place this venture under the control of the local Bahá'í Assembly a confrontation with the National Spiritual Assembly ensued, and Sohrab and Chanler were excommunicated (1930), [the correct terminology would be that they were declared Covenant-breakers]." For several years previous to this, Sohrab performed many services for the Faith and was a close friend of the Hannens.
7. Robert H. Stockman, *The Bahá'í Faith in America: Early Expansion, 1900–1912,* Vol. 2, p. 220.
8. 'Abdu'l-Bahá, Tablet to Joseph Hannen, 29 January, 1906, TABC, NBA.
9. Ibid., Tablet to Mrs. [Amalie] Knobloch and Fanny Knobloch, 27 March 1906, TABC, NBA.
10. Ibid., Tablet to Joseph Hannen, 27 March 1906, TABC, NBA.
11. Ibid., Tablet to Mrs. Amalie Knobloch, 25 July 1906, TABC, NBA.
12. Ibid., Tablet to Master Paul and Master Carl Hannen, 9 December 1906, TABC, NBA. This Tablet can also be found in *O God, My God . . . Bahá'í Prayers and Tablets for Children and Youth,* revised edition (Bahá'í Publishing Trust, 1984), number 35.
13. Ibid., Tablet to Mrs. Leona Barnitz, *Tablets of 'Abdu'l-Bahá Vol. 1,* pp. 179–80.
14. Ibid., Tablet to Beulah Barnitz, *Tablets of 'Abdu'l-Bahá, Vol. 1,* p. 181
15. Ibid., Tablet to Mineola Barnitz, *Tablets of 'Abdu'l-Bahá, Vol. 1,* p. 180.
16. Robert H. Stockman, *The Bahá'í Faith in America: Early Expansion, 1900–1912,* Vol. 2, pp. 233–34.

Chapter 5—The Real Work Begins

1. 'Abdu'l-Bahá, Tablet to Washington Believers through Laura Barney, 7 December 1904. Copied by Alma Knobloch, and currently held in Bahá'í

Archives of Washington, D.C. According to the Research Department at the Bahá'í World Center, a portion of this Tablet is from a Tablet written to Charles Mason Remey, and the original may not be available. Selections that could not be authenticated have not been included.

2. Robert H. Stockman, *The Bahá'í Faith in America: Early Expansion, 1900–1912, Vol. 2*, p. 223.
3. Ibid., p. 224.
4. C. Mason Remey, "Obituary Joseph H. Hannen," *Star of the West*, Vol. X, No. 19, p. 345.
5. "Who's who in Viavi?" *The Viavi World*, Vol. III, January 1913.
6. Robert H. Stockman, *The Bahá'í Faith in America: Early Expansion, 1900–1912, Vol. 2*, p. 222.
7. 'Abdu'l-Bahá, quoted in Ibid.
8. Ibid., pp. 222–23.
9. Ibid., p. 224.
10. Leone St. Claire Barnitz, memoir listing Bahá'í experiences, found in Barnitz papers in Hannen Family Archives.
11. 'Abdu'l-Bahá, to those who attended Camp Mineola during the 1905 summer session, 26 March 1906, HKC, BAWDC.
12. Robert H. Stockman, *The Bahá'í Faith in America: Early Expansion, 1900–1912,* Vol. 2, p. 281.
13. Ibid.
14. Ibid., p. 283.
15. Ibid., p. 326.
16. Pauline Hannen, letter to Alma Knobloch, 29 August 1906, HKFP, NBA.
17. Ibid., letter to Ahmad Sohrab, May 1909, NBA.

Chapter 6—Accepting the "Most Challenging Issue"

1. Pauline Hannen, personal recollections (about teaching "among colored people"), p. 1, HKC, BAWDC, HKFP, and NBA. The story is also found in a briefer version in Robert H. Stockman, *The Bahá'í Faith in America: Early Expansion, 1900–1912, Vol. 2*, p. 225.
2. Bahá'u'lláh, The Hidden Words, Arabic, no. 68.
3. Pauline Hannen, personal recollections.
4. Ibid. Mrs. York was not the first Bahá'í of African descent; that distinction belonged to Robert Turner, the butler of Mrs. Phoebe Apperson Hearst, widow of Senator George Hearst. Robert had become a Bahá'í in 1898, even traveling with Phoebe and several other early Bahá'ís to 'Akká to meet 'Abdu'l-Bahá. There is a record of other Bahá'ís of African descent in Alabama, but that community of Bahá'ís was not sustained for one reason or another. Pauline and Joseph's outreach has been recognized by several histori-

ans as the first sustained and successful effort to teach in the African-American community. See Gayle Morrison, *To Move the World*, p. 4, note.

5. Ibid., personal recollections.
6. Ibid.
7. Robert H. Stockman, *The Bahá'í Faith in America: Early Expansion, 1900–1912,* Vol. 2, p. 225.
8. Pauline Hannen, personal recollections.
9. Robert H. Stockman, *The Bahá'í Faith in America: Early Expansion, 1900–1912,* Vol. 2, p. 226.
10. OZ Whitehead, *Some Bahá'ís to Remember,* p. 76.
11. Pauline Hannen, Personal Recollections, p. 6. This Tablet from 'Abdu'l-Bahá to Pocahontas Pope can also be found in *The Compilation of Compilations,* vol. 2 (Bahá'í Publications Australia, 1991), no. 2101. This updated translation was used.
12. Gwendolyn Etter-Lewis, "Race, Gender, and Difference," *Lights of the Spirit,* p. 71.
13. Ibid., p. 72.
14. Ibid., p. 72.
15. Christopher Buck, *Alain Locke: Faith and Philosophy,* p. 78.

Chapter 7—A Radiant Pupil (Louis Gregory)

1. Louis Gregory, "Some Recollections of the Early Days of the Bahá'í Faith in Washington, D.C.," Louis Gregory Papers, pp. 1–2. BAWDC. Written 7 December 1937 at Tuskegee Institute, Alabama.
2. Pauline Hannen, personal recollections ("teaching among colored people"), pp. 3–4, HKFP, NBA.
3. Louis Gregory, letter to Joseph Hannen, 23 July 1909, HKFP, NBA. This is also quoted in Morrison, p. 6.
4. Ibid., "Some Recollections of the Early Days of the Bahá'í Faith in Washington, D.C.," pp. 4–5.
5. Gayle Morrison, *To Move the World*, pp. 32–33. The Bethel Literary and Historical Society was founded on 9 November 1881 in Bethel Hall, part of the Union Bethel Church. Its founder, Bishop Payne, intended this to be a forum in which "maturity of thought, breadth of comprehension, sound scholarship, lofty patriotism and exalted philanthropy could find a cordial welcome, and where the widest reasonable latitude could be given to the expression of thought." [Information provided by Lex Musta]
6. Joseph Hannen, in *Bahá'í News,* Vol. I, no. 3, p. 18.
7. Robert H. Stockman, *The Bahá'í Faith in America: Early Expansion, 1900–1912, Vol. 2,* pp. 343–44.

8. Christopher Buck, *Alain Locke: Faith & Philosophy*, p. 38. See pp. 38–40 for an account of teaching among the black community in D.C. and the Hannens' contributions.
9. Louis Gregory, letter to Pauline Hannen, 10 February 1911, HKFP, NBA.
10. Gayle Morrison, *To Move the World*, p. 35.
11. Ibid. p. 36.
12. Ibid.
13. Joseph Hannen, "News from the Occident, Washington, D.C.," *Star of the West.* Vol. II, no. 3, p. 9.
14. Pauline Hannen, personal recollections (about "teaching among colored people"), p. 5, HKFP, NBA. The Tablet from 'Abdu'l-Bahá to Louis Gregory referred to in this manuscript, dated 1909, can also be found in *The Power of Unity: Beyond Prejudice and Racism*, p. 66 (Bahá'í Publishing Trust, 1986). This updated authorized translation was used here.
15. Louis Gregory, letter to Pauline Hannen, 19 September 1912, HKFP, NBA.
16. Ibid.
17. Ibid., 30 September 1912, HKFP, NBA.
18. Joseph Hannen, letter to Louis Gregory, 10 December 1919, Louis Gregory Papers, NBA, quoted in Morrison, p. 315.
19. Gayle Morrison, *To Move the World*, p. 32.
20. 'Abdu'l-Bahá, Tablet to Pauline Hannen, 5 May 1910, TABC, NBA.

Chapter 8—Alma Knobloch Answers the Call

1. Alma Knobloch, personal memoirs, "Experiences with 'Abdu'l-Bahá," HKC, BAWDC.
2. Ibid., "A Call to Germany," *Bahá'í World*, vol. 7, pp. 732–45.
3. Rosa Schwartz, "Alma Knobloch in Memoriam," *Bahá'í World*, vol. 9, p. 642. (The picture that is labeled Alma Knobloch in this memoriam is actually a photo of Pauline Hannen).
4. Wikipedia, "History of Bahá'í Faith in Germany," "Alma Knobloch."
5. Robert Weinberg, *Lady Blomfield: Her Life and Times*, p. 101.
6. Susan Pfaff-Grossmann, *Hermann Grossmann, Hand of the Cause of God: A life for the Faith*, p. 14.
7. Gayle Morrison, *To Move the World*, p. 47.
8. Rosa Schwartz, Alma Knobloch in Memoriam, *Bahá'í World*, vol. 9, p. 642.
9. There are many letters from Alma to Fanny and Pauline during 1915, which tell of Alma's activities during the war years. They can be found in the BAWDC.
10. Charles Mason Remey, 22 August 1914, letter to American Bahá'ís, in *Star of the West*, Vol. 5, pp. 185–86.

11. Alma Knobloch, letter to Fanny Knobloch and Pauline Hannen, 9 April 1915, HKC, BAWDC.
12. Wikipedia, "History of Bahá'í Faith in Germany."
13. 'Abdu'l-Bahá, *Tablets of the Divine Plan*, no. 7.8–9.

Chapter 9—Loss of a Matriarch

1. 'Abdu'l-Bahá, Tablet to Amalie Knobloch, 24 February 1910, TABC, NBA.
2. Pauline Hannen, letter to Alma Knobloch, undated, HKFP, NBA. Written after Amalie's passing and delivered to Alma personally. Another shorter version appeared in an early Bahá'í Bulletin published by the Bahá'í Publishing Society in New York. (Vol. 1, October 1908.)
3. 'Abdu'l-Bahá, Tablet to the friends and maidservants . . . who were assembled . . . at the memorial of Amalie Knobloch; through Lua and Mírzá Ahmad, 14 October 1909.
4. Joseph Hannen, in *Bahá'í News*, Vol. 1, no.2, pp. 12–13.
5. 'Abdu'l-Bahá, Visiting Tablet for Mrs. Amalie Knobloch, 24 February 1910, translated 29 March 1910, TABC, NBA.

Chapter 10—Fanny and Alma Meet the Master: Pilgrimage Accounts

1. Alma Knobloch, "Experiences with 'Abdu'l-Bahá," HKC, BAWDC.
2. Fanny Knobloch, personal memoirs; this is found in chapter 2, "Our Journey Starts," of an unpublished manuscript, HKC, BAWDC.
3. Viola Ioas Tuttle, "Fanny Knobloch in Memoriam," *The Bahá'í World*, vol. 11, pp. 474–75.

Chapter 11—Pauline and Joseph Meet 'Abdu'l-Bahá: Pilgrimage Accounts

Note: This chapter is largely made up of excerpts from letters Joseph and Pauline Hannen wrote home to their family while on pilgrimage to Haifa in the spring of 1909. He wrote to his mother and she wrote to Fanny and the children. Sometimes Pauline added notes to Joseph's mother at the end of his letters. Their expectation seems to have been that the recipients would share the letters with each other. The original letters are found at the National Bahá'í Archives.

1. Joseph Hannen, letter to his mother (Mrs. Alexander), 7 February 1909, HKFP, NBA.
2. Pauline Hannen, letter to Fanny Knobloch and children, 7 February 1909, HKFP, NBA.
3. Ibid.
4. Joseph Hannen, letter to his mother (Mrs. Alexander), 7 February 1909, HKFP, NBA.
5. Ibid.
6. Pauline Hannen, letter to loved ones, 16 February 1909, HKFP, NBA.

7. Ibid., letter to Grandmother, Carl and Paul, 4 March1909, Cairo, Egypt, HKFP, NBA.
8. Joseph Hannen, p. 19 in notebook, HKFP, NBA.
9. Pauline Hannen, letter to family, 4 March 1909.
10. Ibid., letter to Beloved Ones, 12 March 1909, typed manuscript in HKFP, NBA.
11. Joseph Hannen, letter to his mother, 22 February 1909, HKFP, NBA.
12. Pauline Hannen, undated manuscript written after her return from pilgrimage, HKFP, NBA.
13. Ibid., undated manuscript entitled "Kindness," HKFP, NBA.
14. Ibid., letter to Beloved Ones, Stuttgart, Germany, 29 March1909, HKFP, NBA.
15. Joseph Hannen, letter to his mother, Cairo, Egypt, 5 March1909, HKFP, NBA.
16. Pauline Hannen, undated letter while in Germany. Found in notebook, p. 36, HKFP, NBA.
17. Joseph Hannen, report to Ahmad Sohrab, 29 May 1909, p.11, NBA.
18. 'Abdu'l-Bahá, Tablet to Joseph Hannen, Through Mirza Moneer Zain, (No date given on letter), Starts, "Thy letter dated July 12th, 1909, was received," TABC, NBA.

Chapter 12—The Persian-American Connections

1. Robert H. Stockman, *The Bahá'í Faith: Early Expansion, 1900–1912,* Vol. 2, pp. 354–55.
2. 'Abdu'l-Bahá, in *Bahá'í News,* Vol. I, no. 4, pp. 8–9.
3. Joseph Hannen, "The Persian American Educational Society," *Star of the West,* Vol. I, no. 5, pp. 2–8, written 10 May 1910.
4. Ibid., "Corresponding Secretary, Persian American Educational Society," *Bahá'í News,* Vol. I, no. 17, pp. 18–19.
5. Ibid., "Persian American Educational Society," *Star of the West,* Vol. II, no. 7, 8, pp. 3–7.
6. Ibid.
7. Maḥmúd-i-Zarqání, *Maḥmúd's Diary,* p. 49.
8. Joseph Hannen, "Persian American Educational Society," *Star of the West,* Vol. VII, no. 1, 1916, pp. 4–5. Also found in BAWDC.
9. Ibid., p. 6.
10. Lissan-i-Hozooz, letter to Joseph Hannen, 12 September 1911, HKFP, NBA.
11. William Irvine, Head Master, The Mercersburg Academy, letter to Joseph Hannen, 21 March 1912, HKFP, NBA.
12. Joseph Hannen, letter to William Hoar, 17 August 1914, HKFP, NBA. (There are many pieces of correspondence between Mr. Hoar and Joseph Hannen relating to the P.A.E.S. on various topics of concern. This was just one minor issue.)

13. William Hoar, letter to Joseph Hannen, 29 July 1914, HKFP, NBA.
14. Marzieh Gail, *Arches of the Years,* p. 145.
15. 'Abdu'l-Bahá, Tablet to Joseph Hannen, 26 April 1919, TABC, NBA; *Star of the West,* Vol. 10, p. 94.
16. Joseph Hannen, letter to Shoghi Effendi, 7 July 1919, HKFP, NBA.
17. Shoghi Effendi, letter to Joseph Hannen, 15 October 1919, HKFP, NBA.

Chapter 13—'Abdu'l-Bahá Comes to America

1. 'Abdu'l-Bahá, "Tablet to the American Friends from 'Abdu'l-Bahá, 28 April 1911," in *Star of the West,* Vol. II no. 4, pp. 6–7.
2. Allen Ward, *239 Days,* p. 11.
3. Shoghi Effendi, *The World Order of Bahá'u'lláh,* p. 85.
4. Allen Ward, *239 Days,* pp. 8–9.
5. Pauline Hannen, letters to Alma Knobloch mostly written May 10, 13, and June 11 of 1912, found in the Bahá'í Archives in Washington D.C. This selection is on pages 29–35 in the notebook. For the rest of the chapter I will indicate selections from this notebook with page numbers.
6. Ibid., letter to Alma Knobloch, Hannen Family Archives.
7. Robert H. Stockman, *'Abdu'l-Bahá in America,* p. 90.
8. Agnes Parsons, *'Abdu'l-Bahá in America: Agnes Parsons' Diary,* p. 44.
9. Joseph Hannen, "'Abdu'l-Bahá in America," *Star of the West,* Vol. III, pp. 6–8.
10. Pauline Hannen, notebook, pp. 35–37, BAWDC.
11. Fanny Knobloch, letter to Alma Knobloch, 5 May 1912, HKC, BAWDC.
12. Pauline Hannen, notebook, pp. 37–39 then skips to page 1, BAWDC.
13. Fanny Knobloch, 4 May 1912.
14. Pauline Hannen, notebook, p. 2.
15. Joseph Hannen, "'Abdu'l-Bahá in America," *Star of the West,* Vol. III.
16. Ibid.
17. Pauline Hannen, "Personal Recollections," pp. 7–8, HKC, BAWDC.
18. Ibid., notebook, pp. 5–7, BAWDC.
19. Ibid., pp. 7–8.
20. Ibid., pp. 9–10.
21. Fanny Knobloch, 5 May 1912.
22. Pauline Hannen, "Personal Recollections," pp. 11–12.
23. Ibid., notebook, pp. 12–13, BAWDC.
24. Ibid., memoirs about Marion Anderson.
25. Ibid, added note by Alma.
26. Joseph Hannen, "'Abdu'l-Bahá in America," *Star of the West,* Vol. III.
27. Pauline Hannen, notebook, pp. 13–15, BAWDC.
28. Ibid., pp. 9–10, BAWDC.
29. Joseph Hannen, "'Abdu'l-Bahá in America," *Star of the West,* Vol. III.
30. Fanny Knobloch, 5 May 1912.

Chapter 14—Chicago

1. Joseph Hannen, "The Public Meetings of the Fourth Annual Convention of Bahá'í Temple Unity," *Star of the West,* Vol. III, no. 4, pp. 3–5.
2. Bruce Whitmore, *The Dawning Place,* p. 263.
3. Pauline Hannen, letter to Alma Knobloch, undated page titled "Chicago," 1912, HKC, BAWDC.
4. Ibid., recollections, pages labeled "Chicago continued" pp. 7–15, HKFP, NBA.
5. Maḥmúd-i-Zarqání, *Maḥmúd's Diary,* p. 71
6. Pauline Hannen, "'Abdu'l-Bahá in Chicago," p. 1, HKFP, NBA.
7. Maḥmúd-i-Zarqání, *Maḥmúd's Diary,* p. 70.
8. Pauline Hannen, "'Abdu'l-Bahá in Chicago: Temptation," p. 2, HKFP, NBA.
9. Ibid., p. 9.
10. Ibid., "'Abdu'l-Bahá in Chicago: Chicago, My Hearing," pp. 3–4, HKFP, NBA.

Chapter 15—Pittsburg and Philadelphia

1. Pauline Hannen, letter to Fanny Knobloch, 11 June 1912, notebook, pp. 24–27, HKC, BAWDC.
2. Carl Hannen, letter to Pauline Hannen, 7 May 1912, HKFP, NBA.
3. Ibid., 12 May 1912, HKFP, NBA.
4. Allen Ward, *239 Days,* p. 64.
5. Pauline Hannen, letter to Alma Knobloch, May 1912. Portions of this account are in notebook, pp. 22–24, HKFP, BAWDC.
6. Ibid., 11 June 1912, also in notebook, pp. 44–48, HKC, BAWDC.

Chapter 16—Special Visit in Dublin, NH

1. Allen Ward, *239 Days,* pp. 117–18.
2. Joseph Hannen, "With 'Abdu'l-Bahá in Dublin, New Hampshire," *Star of the West,* Vol. III, no. 11, pp. 3–4.
3. Pauline Hannen, letter to Alma Knobloch; Pauline's accounts of Dublin visit, written 5 August 1912, HKFP, NBA.
4. Joseph Hannen, "With 'Abdu'l-Bahá in Dublin, New Hampshire," *Star of the West,* Vol. III, no. 11, pp. 5–6.
5. Pauline Hannen, letter to Alma Knobloch; Pauline's accounts of Dublin visit, written 5 August 1912, HKFP, NBA.

Chapter 17—Final DC Visit

1. Pauline Hannen, letter to Alma Knobloch, 14 November 1912, HKFP, NBA.
2. Ibid., letter to Beloved Ones, 15 November 1912, HKFP, NBA.

3. Ibid., 16 November 1912, HKFP, NBA.
4. Ibid., 18 November 1912, HKFP, NBA.
5. Allen Ward, *239 Days,* pp. 180–83, (this includes the 9 November 1912 talk given at the Hannen home also found in *Promulgation of Universal Peace.*)
6. Pauline Hannen, letter to Beloved Ones, 19 November 1912, HKFP, NBA.
7. Ibid., letter to Beloved Ones, 27 November 1912, HKFP, NBA.
8. Allen Ward, *239 Days,* pp. 207–09.
9. 'Abdu'l-Bahá, Tablet to Joseph Hannen, from Paris, 11 June 1913, TABC, NBA.

Chapter 18—Fanny & Alma in Paris

1. Alma Knobloch, "Paris, Feb 12, 1913," HKFP, NBA.
2. Fanny Knobloch, personal memoirs, HKC, BAWDC.
3. Ibid., "Fanny's first morning in Paris, May 21, 1913," HKC, BAWDC.
4. Alma Knobloch, "Paris 1913," personal memoirs, HKC, BAWDC.

Chapter 19—Mother of Bahá'í Children's Classes

1. Pauline Hannen, letter to Joseph Hannen, May 1917, (Hotel Worthy, Springfield, MA), HKFP, NBA.
2. Marzieh Gail, *Summon Up Remembrance,* p. 181.
3. Pauline Hannen, letter to Ahmad Sohrab, May 1909, "Becoming Bahá'í," HKFP, NBA.
4. Ibid., "Account about teaching 'colored people,'" pp. 8–13, HKFP, NBA.
5. 'Abdu'l-Bahá, Tablet to Pauline Hannen, 28 July 1913, TABC, NBA. This Tablet can also be found in *Selections from the Writings of 'Abdu'l-Bahá,* no. 124 (Bahá'í Publishing, 2010). This authorized translation is used here.
6. Pauline Hannen, letter to Mrs. E. Grace Foster of Chicago, 20 January 1920, HKFP, NBA.
7. Ibid., letter to Agnes Parsons, 19 September 1917, HKFP, NBA.
8. Ahmad Sohrab, letter to Joseph & Pauline Hannen, Ramleh, Egypt, 19 August 1913, HKFP, NBA.
9. 'Abdu'l-Bahá, Tablet to Pauline Hannen, 5 July 1910, TABC, NBA.

Chapter 20—Disunity Issues

1. Gayle Morrison, *To Move the World,* p. 73.
2. Ibid., pp. 75–76.
3. 'Abdu'l-Bahá, Tablet to Joseph Hannen, 21 April 1914, TABC, NBA.
4. Pauline Hannen, letter to Agnes Parsons, April 1914, Agnes Parsons Correspondence, NBA.
5. Aseyeh Allen, letter to Joseph Hannen, 24 August 1914, HKFP, NBA
6. Joseph Hannen, letter to 'Abdu'l-Bahá, 21 July 1914, HKFP, NBA.

7. Aseyeh Allen, letter to Joseph Hannen, postmarked 17 March 1916, HKFP, NBA.
8. Agnes Parsons, letter to Washington, D.C. Bahá'í Community, 13 October 1915, HKFP, NBA.
9. Coralie Cook, letter to 'Abdu'l-Bahá, 2 March 1914, in *Lights of the Spirit*, pp. 237–39. For complete letter see pp. 237–43.
10. Pauline Hannen, letter to Agnes Parsons, February 1914, Agnes Parsons Papers, NBA.
11. Coralie Cook, letter to 'Abdu'l-Bahá, 2 March 1914, in *Lights of the Spirit*, pp. 242–43.
12. 'Abdu'l-Bahá, Tablet to Joseph Hannen, 6 August 1914, TABC, NBA; also published in *Star of the West*, Vol. 5, p. 138.

Chapter 21—The Perils and Projects of Pauline

1. Zia Bagdadi, letter to Joseph Hannen, 19 May 1917, HKFP, NBA.
2. Louis Gregory, letter to Pauline Hannen, 12 March 1917, HKFP, NBA.
3. Pauline Hannen, to Agnes Parsons, postmarked 5 May 1917, Agnes Parsons Papers, NBA.
4. Ibid., letter to Agnes Parsons, 7 July 1917.
5. Ibid., 12 July 1917.
6. Ibid., about Louis Gregory, October 10, 1916, Agnes Parsons Papers, NBA.
7. Ibid.
8. Joseph Hannen, letter to Agnes Parsons, 18 October 1917, Agnes Parsons Papers, NBA.
9. Pauline Hannen, letter to Agnes Parsons, 28 January 1914, Agnes Parsons Papers, NBA.
10. Ibid., 14 February 1914.
11. 'Abdu'l-Bahá, Tablet to Joseph and Pauline Hannen, 23 January 1920, TABC, NBA.

Chapter 22—A Dark and Perilous Time

1. Nathan Rutstein, *Corrine True: Faithful Handmaid of 'Abdu'l-Bahá*, pp. 128–30.
2. Joseph Hannen, letter to Agnes Parsons, 9 April 1918, Agnes Parsons Papers, NBA.
3. Agnes Parsons, letter to Joseph Hannen, 5 May 1918, HKFP, NBA
4. Joseph Hannen, letter to Agnes Parsons, 11 May 1918, Agnes Parsons Papers, NBA.
5. Ibid.
6. Agnes Parsons, letter to Mason Remey, 28 April 1918, copy to Joseph Hannen, HKFP, NBA.
7. Ibid, 4 June 1918.

8. Joseph Hannen, letter to Agnes Parsons, 15 May 1918, Agnes Parsons Papers, NBA.
9. Agnes Parsons, letter to Joseph Hannen, 4 December 1918, HKFP, NBA.
10. Pauline Hannen, letter to Agnes Parsons, 5 February 1918, Agnes Parsons Papers, NBA.
11. Louis Gregory, letter, to Pauline Hannen, 7 February 1918, HKC, BAWDC.
12. Joseph Hannen, letter to Louis Gregory, 13 June 1918, HKFP, BAWDC.

Chapter 23—The Divine Plan Revealed

1. Ahmad Sohrab, letter to Joseph Hannen, Haifa, Syria, 14 October 1918, HKC, BAWDC.
2. Gayle Morrison, *To Move the World*, p. 96.
3. Ibid.
4. Ibid., p. 97.
5. Editors of *Star of the West,* "Teaching Campaign—A Suggestion," *Star of the West,* Vol. VII. pp. 112–13.
6. Gayle Morrison, *To Move the World*, p. 101.
7. Joseph Hannen, "The Convention of 'Abdu'l-Bahá," *Star of the West,* Vol. X, pp. 54–56.
8. Ibid., "The Call," written for the 1919 National Convention, *Star of the West,* Vol. X, pp. 50–53.
9. Alfred Lunt, "Third Session," *Star of the West,* Vol. X, no. 3, p. 332.
10. Ibid, p. 334.
11. Joseph Hannen, "The Southern States Contributes a General Outline," *Star of the West,* Vol. X, no. 5, pp. 88–89.
12. Ibid.

Chapter 24—A Teaching Family

1. C. Mason Remey, "The League to Enforce Peace," 1 June 1916, *Star of the West,* Vol. VII, pp. 47–48.
2. Pauline Hannen, letter to Ahmad Sohrab, 1909, HKFP, NBA.
3. Viola Duckett, Summerdale, VA, letter to Pauline Hannen, 1910, HKFP, NBA.
4. Pauline Hannen, letter to Lydia Gray, (no date), HKFP, NBA.
5. Nathan Rustein, *Corinne True: Faithful Handmaiden of 'Abdu'l-Bahá*, pp. 121–23.
6. 'Abdu'l-Bahá, Tablet to Joseph Hannen, 18 April 1914, TABC, NBA.
7. Pauline Hannen, letter to Agnes Parsons, 9 December 1916, Agnes Parsons Papers, NBA.
8. Louis Gregory, letter to Pauline Hannen, 15 March 1919, HKFP, NBA.
9. "Baltimore," *Bahá'í News,* Vol. I, no. 6, p. 12.

10. Joseph Hannen, letter to 'Abdu'l-Bahá, 24 March 1914, HKFP, NBA.
11. Ibid., 21 July 1914.
12. Ibid., letter to Shoghi Effendi, 29 June 1919, HKFP, NBA.
13. 'Abdu'l-Bahá, Tablet to Joseph and Pauline Hannen, 17 March 1919, TABC, NBA.

Chapter 25—Joseph the "Correspondent"

1. Joseph Hannen, letter to Aseyeh Allen, 23 October 1919, HKFP, NBA.
2. Ibid., letter to Shoghi Effendi, 28 January 1919, HKFP, NBA.
3. Ibid., 9 February 1919.
4. Ibid., letter to 'Abdu'l-Bahá, 22 September 1914, HKFP, NBA.
5. Ibid., letter to Shoghi Effendi, 17 April 1919, HKFP, NBA.
6. Ibid., 19 October 1919.
7. Editors, *Star of the West,* Vol. X, no. 7, pp. 128–29.
8. Joseph Hannen, letter to 'Abdu'l-Bahá, 22 September 1914, HKFP, NBA.
9. "The Christian Commonwealth," *Star of the West,* Vol. III, no. 12, p. 8.
10. Joseph Hannen, letter to 'Abdu'l-Bahá, 15 May 1913, HKFP, NBA.

Chapter 26—Combining Forces: Carl Anthony "Nategh" Hannen and Mineola Barnitz

1. 'Abdu'l-Bahá, Tablet to Carl and Mineola Hannen, 18 February 1916, TABC, NBA.
2. Alma Knobloch, letter to Fanny Knobloch, 8 November 1915, HKC, BAWDC.
3. Pauline Hannen, letter to Carl and Mineola Hannen, (no date), "Not until now did I know where to reach you, . . ." HKFP.
4. 'Abdu'l-Bahá, to Ahmad Sohrab, 28 October 1919, forwarded to Joseph Hannen.
5. Shoghi Effendi, letter to Leone Barnitz and family, 25 January 1934, HKFP, NBA.
6. Much of the information in this chapter, including this quote of Mineola, comes from a memorial written for Mineola's funeral by Bea Buckley (Somerhalder) and then confirmed by family members and the writer's firsthand knowledge, Hannen Family Archives.

Chapter 27—Joseph Hannen's Tragic Death

1. Charles Mason Remey, Joseph Hannen Memoriam, *Star of the West,* Vol. X, pp. 345–46.
2. 'Abdu'l-Bahá, Tablet to Pauline Hannen, 19 March 1920, TABC, NBA; (also published in *Star of the West,* Vol. XI, no. 5).
3. Viavi Newsletter; a clipping from this newsletter was among the Hannen Family papers.

4. Alfred Lunt, "Report of the Twelfth Annual Mashrekol-Azkar Convention, held in New York City," *Star of the West*, Vol. XI, p. 194.
5. Agnes Alexander, letter to Pauline Hannen from Tokyo, Japan, 18 March 1920, HKFP, NBA.
6. Spiritual Committee Bahá'ís of Cairo, Egypt, 8 April 1920, HKFP, NBA.
7. Mohamed Said Adhany, letter to Mrs. Hannen, 17 May 1920, HKFP, NBA.
8. Ali Kuli-Khan, letter to Pauline Hannen, 12 April 1920, HKFP, NBA.
9. Ronhameh Florence Khanum, letter to Pauline Hannen, 8 June 1920, HKFP, NBA.
10. Ibid., 15 January 1921.
11. Gertrude Buikema, letter to Pauline Hannen, 15 February 1920, HKFP, NBA.
12. Mabel King, Secretary of Spokane Spiritual Assembly, letter to Pauline Hannen, 11 February 1920, HKFP, NBA.
13. Louis Gregory, letter to Pauline Hannen, 5 February 1920, HKFP, NBA.
14. Gayle Morrison, *To Move the World*, p. 112.
15. Louis Gregory, letter to Pauline Hannen, 18 February 1920, HKFP, NBA.
16. Pauline Hannen, letter to Fanny Knobloch, 27 July 1932, HKFP, NBA.

Chapter 28—South Africa Bound: Fanny Pioneers

1. 'Abdu'l-Bahá, *Tablets of the Divine Plan,* no. 6.6.
2. Ibid., no. 7.8.
3. Ibid., no. 7.14.
4. Viola Ioas Tuttle, "Fanny Knobloch in Memoriam," *Bahá'í World,* Vol. XI, p. 475.
5. James Sharp, "From One Good Cause to Another," article in Viavi Newsletter.
6. Fanny Knobloch, "Sunny South Africa," unpublished manuscript, HKFP, NBA.
7. Ibid., letter to Alma Knobloch, l6 April 1925, HKFP, NBA.
8. Pauline Hannen, letter to Alma Knobloch, 16 April 1925, HKFP, NBA.
9. Fanny Knobloch, letter to Alma Knobloch, no date, HKFP, NBA.
10. Pauline Hannen, letter to Mineola and Carl Hannen, 18 May 1925, HKC, BAWDC.
11. Fanny Knobloch, letter to Alma Knobloch, 1 June 1925, HKFP, NBA.
12. Pauline Hannen, letter to Alma Knobloch, 19 July 1925, HKC, BAWDC.
13. Ibid.
14. Shoghi Effendi, letter on his behalf to Fanny Knobloch and Pauline Hannen, 12 September 1926, HKC, BAWDC.
15. Viola Ioas Tuttle, "Fanny Knobloch in Memoriam," *The Bahá'í World*, Vol. XI, p. 475.

Chapter 29—The Sisters Teach to the End

1. 'Abdu'l-Bahá, Visiting Tablet revealed for Amalie Knobloch, 24 February 1910, HKC, BAWDC.
2. Ibid., Tablet to Alma Knobloch, 29 April 1921, copied in a notebook, HKC, BAWDC. This was translated by Aziz Ullah Khan S. Bahadur.
3. Louis Gregory, letter to Agnes Parsons, 16 December 1920, Agnes Parsons Papers, NBA.
4. Ibid., "Inter-Racial Amity," *The Bahá'í World*, Vol. II, 1926–28, p. 281.
5. Christopher Buck, *Alain Locke: Faith and Philosophy*, p. 73.
6. Louis Gregory, letter to Pauline Hannen, 26 October 1927, HKC, BAWDC.
7. Ibid., Ex. Sec. The National Inter-Racial Amity Committee, letter to National and Local Spiritual Assemblies, 12 December 1927, copy in HKFP, NBA.
8. Pauline Hannen, letter to Alma Knobloch, 1 July 1925, HKFP, NBA.
9. Andrew Nelson, Racine Bahá'í Assembly, letter to Alma Knobloch, 24 February 1927, HKFP, NBA.
10. Walter Guy, letter to Alma Knobloch, 18 February 1928, HKFP, NBA.
11. Alma Knobloch, letter, 11 April 1928, HKC, BAWDC.
12. May Maxwell, letter to Alma Knobloch, 27 June 1928, HKC, BAWDC.
13. Ibid., letter from National Teaching Committee to Alma Knobloch, date unknown, HKC, BAWDC.
14. Louis Gregory, letter to Alma Knobloch, 22 March 1928, HKC, BAWDC.
15. Ibid., letter to Alma Knobloch, 7 July 1928, HKFP, NBA.
16. Fanny Knobloch, "Bahá'í Teaching Trip," HKC, BAWDC.
17. Shoghi Effendi, letter on his behalf to Alma Knobloch, 21 January 1932, HKFP, NBA.
18. Pauline Hannen, letter to Alma Knobloch, 15 November 1936, HKFP, NBA.
19. Randall Brown, NTC, letter to Alma Knobloch, 1932, HKFP, NBA.
20. Alma Knobloch, letter to Mrs. Randall Brown, NTC, 29 June 1932, HKFP, NBA.
21. Louis Gregory, letter to Pauline Hannen, 1 February 1928, HKFP, NBA.
22. Leroy Ioas, NTC, letter to Alma Knobloch, 4 February 1934, HKC, BAWDC.
23. Louis Gregory, letter to Pauline Hannen, 18 December 1931, HKC, BAWDC.
24. Shoghi Effendi, letter on his behalf of to Bahá'í Spiritual Assembly of Cabin John Park, Maryland, Care of Mrs. Margaret Patzer, Secretary, 25 July 1933, HKFP, NBA.
25. Pauline Hannen, letter to Alma Knobloch, 20 November 1933, HKFP, NBA.
26. Leroy Ioas, letter to Alma Knobloch, 9 June 1934, HKC, BAWDC.

Chapter 30—The Final Days

1. Pauline Hannen, letter to Alma Knobloch, 30 June 1937, HKFP, NBA.
2. Fanny Knobloch, letter to Alma Knobloch, Labor Day, circa 1938, HKFP, NBA.
3. Ibid., circa 1938, HKFP, NBA.
4. Ibid.
5. Pauline Hannen, letter to Alma Knobloch, 2 September 1938, HKFP, NBA.
6. Louis Gregory, "Pauline Knobloch Hannen in Memoriam," *Bahá'í World*, Vol. VIII, p. 661.
7. Ibid.
8. National Spiritual Assembly, letter to Local Spiritual Assembly of Cabin John, MD, 7 November 1939, HKC, BAWDC.
9. Shoghi Effendi, letter on his behalf to Alma Knobloch, 5 November 1939, HKC, BAWDC.
10. Alma Knobloch, letter to Fanny Knobloch, 22 March 1928, HKC, BAWDC.
11. Horace Holly, to Bahá'í Friends, quoted in a letter to Carl Hannen from Herbert Patzer of Cabin John, MD LSA, 26 January 1944.
12. Daisy Moore, letter to Mineola Hannen, 24 January 1944, HKC, BAWDC.
13. George Latimer, letter to Fanny Knobloch, 9 February 1944, HKFP, NBA.
14. Ruhiyyíh Khanum, letter to Fanny Knobloch, 5 November 1940, Hannen Family Archives.
15. Viola Ioas Tuttle, "Fanny Knobloch in Memoriam," *Bahá'í World*, Vol. XI, p. 476.
16. Shoghi Effendi, 14 December 1949, quoted in Washington D.C. Newsletter, January 1950, Hannen Family Archives.
17. Ibid., letter to Alma Knobloch, 23 February 1929, HKFP, NBA.
18. Joseph Hannen, "Heart Promptu Poem," to Mrs. Pauline Hannen, Hannen Family Archives.
19. Fanny Knobloch, letter to Pauline Hannen, 27 January 1922, HKFP, NBA.

Epilogue

1. Barbara Griffin, interview with author.
2. Gertrude Henning, "Carl A. Hannen in Memoriam," *The Bahá'í World*, Vol. XV, pp. 510–11.
3. Mr. Walter R. Wootten of Raleigh, North Carolina, letter to Carl Hannen, 6 November 1972, Hannen Family Archives.

Bibliography

Many Tablets of 'Abdu'l-Bahá—written to Amalie Knobloch, Alma Knobloch, Fanny Knobloch, Pauline Hannen, Joseph Hannen, Carl Hannen, Minneola Barnitz (Hannen), Buehla Barnitz (Brown), and Leona Barnitz from 1903–1920—are included in this book. The originals are held at the Bahá'í World Center Archives in Haifa, Israel, but copies can be found in the Translations of Tablets of 'Abdu'l-Bahá Collection and in other collections at the Bahá'í National Archives in Wilmette, IL or in the Hannen Knobloch Collection at the Bahá'í Archives of Washington D.C. and the Hannen Family Archives in the home of the author. Many can also be found in various volumes of *Star of the West*. All available details concerning the dates and recipients of the Tablets are included in the endnotes along with information regarding the archives in which copies were accessed.

This book also contains a high volume of letters, reports, and manuscripts written by Pauline and Joseph Hannen, Fanny and Alma Knobloch, and many other early Bahá'ís. The original papers can be found in either the Bahá'í Archives of Washington D.C. (BAWDC), the Hannen Knobloch Collection (HKC), the National Bahá'í Archives in Wilmette, IL (NBA), or the Hannen Knobloch Family Papers (HKFP). The location of each is indicated in the endnotes.

Works of Bahá'u'lláh

The Hidden Words. Translated by Shoghi Effendi. Wilmette, IL: Bahá'í Publishing, 2002.

Works of 'Abdu'l-Bahá

Paris Talks: Addresses Given By 'Abdu'l-Bahá in Paris in 1911. 12th ed. London: Bahá'í Publishing, 2011.

Promulgation of Universal Peace: Talks Delivered by 'Abdu'l-Bahá during His Visit to the United States and Canada in 1912. Compiled by Howard MacNutt. 2d ed. Wilmette, IL: Bahá'í Publishing, 2012.

Selections from the Writings of 'Abdu'l-Bahá. Compiled by the Research Department of the Universal House of Justice. Translated by a Committee at the Bahá'í World Center and Marzieh Gail. Wilmette, IL: Bahá'í Publishing, 2010.

Some Answered Questions. Translated by a committee of the Universal House of Justice. Pocket-size ed. Wilmette, IL: Bahá'í Publishing Trust, 2014.

Tablets of Abdul-Baha Abbas. 3 vols. New York: Bahai Publishing Society, 1909–16.

Tablets of the Divine Plan. 1st pocket-sized ed. Wilmette, IL: Bahá'í Publishing Trust, 1993.

Works of Shoghi Effendi

God Passes By. New ed. Wilmette, IL: Bahá'í Publishing Trust, 1974.

The World Order of Bahá'u'lláh: Selected Letters. 1st pocket-size ed. Wilmette, IL: Bahá'í Publishing Trust, 1991.

Other Works

Bahá'í World: An International Record. Vols. II, VII, IX, XI. Compiled by the National Spiritual Assembly of the Bahá'ís of the United States and Canada. Wilmette, IL: Bahá'í Publishing Committee, 1952.

Buck, Christopher. *Alain Locke: Faith & Philosophy.* Los Angeles: Kalimat Press, L.A. 2005.

Chapman, Anita. "History of Washington, D.C. Bahá'í Community 2005–2008." http://dcbahai.org.

Etter-Lewis, Gwendolyn and Richard Thomas (eds). *Lights of the Spirit: Historical Portraits of Black Bahá'ís in North America 1898–2000.* Wilmette IL: Bahá'í Publishing, 2006.

Gail, Marzieh. *Arches of the Years.* Oxford: George Ronald, 1991.

———. *Summon up Remembrance.* Oxford: George Ronald, 1987.

Hutchison, Sandra. *'Abdu'l-Bahá in America: Agnes Parsons Diary.* Los Angeles: Kalimat Press, 1996.

Maḥmúd-i-Zarqání, *Maḥmúd's Diary.* Oxford: George Ronald, 1998.

Morrison, Gayle. *To Move The World: Louis G. Gregory and the Advancement of Racial Unity in America.* Wilmette, IL: Bahá'í Publishing Trust, 1982.

Motlagh, Hushidar, Ed.D. *I shall Come Again.* Mt. Pleasant, MI: Global Perspective, 1992.

Musta, Lex. Personal interviews with author. 2009–2012.

Pfaff-Grossman, Susan. *Hermann Grossman, Hand of the Cause of God: A Life for the Faith.* Oxford; George Ronald, 2009.

Rally, Eleanor Hannen. Personal interview with author. 2009.

Rutstein, Nathan. *Corinne True: Faithful Handmaid of 'Abdu'l-Bahá.* Oxford: George Ronald, 1987.

Sharp, James. "From One Good Cause to Another," *The Viavi World*. Clipping in Hannen Family Archive.

Smith, Peter. *A Concise Encyclopedia of the Bahá'í Faith*. Oxford: One World: 2002.

Star of the West. Multiple volumes cited.

Stockman, Robert H. *The Bahá'í Faith in America: Early Expansion, 1900–1912*, Vol 2. Oxford, George Ronald: 1995.

———. *'Abdu'l-Bahá in America*. Wilmette, IL: Bahá'í Publishing, 2012.

The Viavi World. "Who's Who in Viavi?" Vol. III, January 1913; Obituary Joseph Hannen, 1920. Clipping in Hannen Family Archives

Ward, Allen. *239 Days: 'Abdu'l-Bahá's Journey in America*. Wilmette, IL: Bahá'í Publishing Trust, 1979.

Weinberg, Robert. *Lady Blomfield: Her Life and Times*. Oxford: George Ronald, 2012.

Whitehead, OZ. *Some Bahá'ís to Remember*. Oxford: George Ronald, 1976.

Whitmore, Bruce. *The Dawning Place: The Building of a Temple, the Forging of a Global Religious Community*. Wilmette, IL: Bahá'í Publishing, 2015.

Index

Knobloch sisters: Alma, Pauline, Fannie

Pauline and Joseph Hannen and Fannie Knobloch

Pauline Hannen in wedding dress

Alma Knobloch

Fannie Knobloch

Pauline Knobloch in 1891

Joseph Hannen in 1891

Alma Knobloch with early Bahá'ís in the Washington D.C. area, circa 1905

Paul and Carl Hannen with grandmother Amalie Knobloch around 1906

Mary V. Anthony Hannen Alexander, Joseph's mother

Naw-Rúz celebration at the Hannen home in 1906

Carl and Mineola Barnitz Hannen
soon after marriage in 1918

Joseph Hannen

Alma Knobloch in Germany

Secretary Joseph at his desk

Pauline Hannen

Painting of Pauline and Joseph Hannen
done by Washington D.C. artist Mr. Daniel Allen